T0280065

H.L. MENCKEN

AN ACIDIC ANTHOLOGY

CHRIS EDWARDS

EDITOR

SEE SHARP PRESS ◆ TUCSON, ARIZONA

info@seesharppress.com
www.seesharppress.com

Edwards, Chris.
    H.L. Mencken / Chris Edwards ; Tucson, Ariz. : See Sharp Press, 2024
    Includes bibliographical references and index.
    333 p. ; 23 cm.
    ISBN 978-1-947071-50-6

    I. Edwards, Chris. II. Title.

818

CONTENTS

INTRODUCTION

In Memoriam H.L.M.

On a thickly muggy and stiflingly hot summer day in 1925, a man arose to speak at the end of what had developed into the trial of the century. Forget the Lindbergh kidnapping trial, the Manson murder trial, or even the O.J. media trial. The real trial of the 20th century was the Scopes "monkey trial" in a courtroom in Dayton, Tennessee. The trial was not, as most observers believed, whether high school science teacher John T. Scopes had lectured his students on Charles Darwin's theory of evolution (he had). It was, in effect, humanity's soul that was on trial. "The soul is immortal and religion deals with the soul; the logical effect of the evolutionary hypothesis is to undermine religion and thus affect the soul," pronounced William Jennings Bryan in an epigrammatically poignant statement.

The trial was initially instigated as a publicity stunt dreamed up by the newly-formed American Civil Liberties Union (ACLU), in collaboration with the city leaders of the economically struggling Tennessee town of Dayton. On one side of the dock was the most famous defense attorney of his era, Clarence Darrow. On the other was the century's preeminent orator and defender-of-the-faith, three-time presidential candidate William Jennings Bryan. Covering the trial for the *Baltimore Sun* was an unapologetically acerbic reporter named H. L. Mencken, who meted out such barbs as this:

> If the Anti-Evolutionists in Tennessee were aware of the existence of any other religions than their own, they might realize that it is the very genius of religion itself to evolve from primary forms to higher forms. The author of the anti-evolution bill is obviously nearer in mental development to the nomads of early biblical times than he is to the intelligence of the young man who is under trial.

Most people think that Scopes and science scored a knockout victory in Tennessee. Reading Mencken would certainly lead to this conclusion. Of Bryan he gibed:

> Once he had one leg in the White House and the nation trembled under his roars. Now he is a tinpot pope in the Coca-Cola belt and a brother to the forlorn pastors who belabor half-wits in galvanized iron tabernacles behind the railroad yards…It is a tragedy, indeed, to begin life as a hero and to end it as a buffoon.

In fact, this was no victory for science or evolution, and it may surprise readers to learn that Scopes' guilty verdict was overturned on a minor technicality involving the levying of a fine over $50 by a judge instead of a jury. Out of embarrassment by the bad publicity the state was receiving, the Tennessee state legislators used this technical misstep to prevent the case from reaching the State Supreme Court. Who can blame them after reading comments like this about the trial from Mencken:

> Let no one mistake it for comedy, farcical though it may be in all its details. It serves notice on the country that Neanderthal man is organizing in these forlorn backwaters of the land, led by a fanatic, rid of sense and devoid of conscience. Tennessee, challenging him too timorously and too late, now sees its courts converted into camp meetings and its Bill of Rights made a mock of by its sworn officers of the law.

H. L. Mencken's acidic barbs against William Jennings Bryan and the people supporting his anti-Darwinian campaign are just a sampling of the man's prodigious output over half a century of commentary on a wide range of topics, including America, politics, quacks and hoaxes (my favorite), culture, journalism (his chosen profession), literature, sex and morality, and religion (my other favorite), expertly curated in this volume by Chris Edwards (with an introduction that matches Mencken's style sentence for sentence!). In this context, I especially enjoyed Mencken's obituary for Bryan, "In Memoriam W.J.B." (which I hadn't seen before), starting with his description of Bryan's appeal to the people of Dayton:

> Making his progress up and down the Main street of little Dayton, surrounded by gaping primates from the upland valleys of the Cumberland Range, his coat laid aside, his bare arms and hairy chest shining damply, his bald head sprinkled with dust—so accoutred and on display he was obviously happy. He liked getting up early in the morning to the tune of cocks crowing on the

dunghill. He liked the heavy, greasy victuals of the farmhouse kitchen. He liked the country sounds and country smells. I believe that this liking was sincere—perhaps the only sincere thing in the man. His nose showed no uneasiness when a hillman in faded overalls and hickory shirt accosted him on the street, and besought him for light upon some mystery of Holy Writ. The simian gabble of the cross-roads was not gabble to him, but wisdom of the occult and superior sort.

As the adroit editor of this fine volume notes in the introduction to this obit, "Insincere eulogies make for the worst form of literature, so thankfully Mencken saw no reason to let Bryan's death remake his opinion of the man's life." What an understatement!

He was, in fact, a charlatan, a mountebank, a zany without shame or dignity. His career brought him into contact with the first men of his time; he preferred the company of rustic ignoramuses. It was hard to believe, watching him at Dayton, that he had traveled, that he had been a high officer of state. He seemed only a poor clod like those around him, deluded by a childish theology, full of an almost pathological hatred of all learning, all human dignity, all beauty, all fine and noble things. He was a peasant come home to the barnyard. Imagine a gentleman, and you have imagined everything that he was not. What animated him from end to end of his grotesque career was simply ambition—the ambition of a common man to get his hand upon the collar of his superiors, or, failing that, to get his thumb into their eyes. He was born with a roaring voice, and it had the trick of inflaming half-wits. His whole career was devoted to raising those half-wits against their betters, that he himself might shine. His last battle will be grossly misunderstood if it is thought of as a mere exercise in fanaticism—that is, if Bryan the Fundamentalist Pope is mistaken for one of the bucolic Fundamentalists.

And Mencken is just getting warmed up—don't get him started on religion…or politics and politicians…or sex prudes…or his fellow journalists…and you won't be able to stop reading! There is no one like him, save possibly the late Christopher Hitchens. Having known Hitch and shared a few whiskeys with the man as he opined on the buffoons and half-wits of his time, I can only imagine what an experience it must have been to share a bar tab with the inimitable H. L. Mencken. Next best thing: pour a glass of your favorite poison, kick back in an easy chair, and open this book to any page and start reading…

Ask a professional critic to write about himself and you simply ask him to do what he does every day in the practise of his art and mystery. There is, indeed, no criticism that is not a confidence, and there is no confidence that is not self-revelation. When I denounce a book with mocking and contumely, and fall upon the poor author in the brutal, Asiatic manner of a drunken longshoreman, a Ku Kluxer, or a midshipman at Annapolis, I am only saying, in the trade cant, that the fellow disgusts me—that his ideas and his manner are somehow obnoxious to me, as those of a Methodist, a golf player, or a clog dancer are obnoxious to me—in brief, that I hold myself to be a great deal better than he is and am eager to say so.

—Michael Shermer (editor of *Skeptic* magazine and author of *Why People Believe Weird Things: Pseudoscience, Superstition, and Other Confusions of Our Times*, and *Conspiracy: Why the Rational Believe the Irrational*)

PREFACE

Let's start with a stupid question, typical of those asked about American historical figures: "What would H.L. Mencken think of American life if he were resurrected today?"

The answer: He would think the same damn thing he thought a century ago, because evangelical dimwits, political carnival barkers, and sociopathic social reformers are still applying their trades and selling snake oil.

Mencken understood early on that he was a literary stylist more than a philosopher; his sentences flow with a Beethoven-like cadence often punctuated with low humor. He's the only English-language writer who could write about high literature and philosophy without sounding pretentious, and who insults everybody but somehow makes everyone feel better about themselves.

He's just fun to read, and that became the guiding principle for choosing the pieces for this anthology. Here, we've selected what we consider his most entertaining writings, but with an eye toward those that are still relevant. Mencken writes to entertain, but while readers eagerly turn the pages they get a gradual education in skepticism.

H.L Mencken lived from 1880 to 1956, an impressive lifespan for a man who kept exercise at bay with brandy and cigars, and who probably never got his heart rate above that produced by punching typewriter keys. Mencken lived in an era when a fat man could be a hero; the public encountered him not through his image or his ability to converse on a talk show, but only through his writing. Modern authors must be witty in person, relatable on talk shows, and often pleasant to look at. Mencken could just write well and be done with it, and he did it constantly; it was through the constant and rapid practice of his trade that he developed his skills to a rare degree.

His day-in-day-out writing routine resulted in great consistency. His writing flows with just the right amount of clever word-choice so that the reader never feels that Mencken is being pretentious; rather, he makes you feel as if you are a colleague of a highly intelligent man. His enemy was stupidity, not power, and he had targets galore: idiocy manifests itself just about everywhere.

It's easy to use sarcasm effectively when the subject is a person or institution in power, and at least one commentator thinks that FDR's New Deal ruined Mencken's writing well before 1948 when a stroke ruined his cognitive powers. Why? Because the New Deal benefited common people, and in attacking it Mencken was effectively punching down. Mencken did not consider himself a man of the people—he was a man *above* the people. It's no accident that he did his best writing in the 1920s when big business was in the saddle. And it's no accident that a majority of the newspaper and magazine pieces in this anthology stem from that decade.

Mencken also wrote autobiographical books about specific phases of his life: *Happy Days* (1940), *Newspaper Days* (1941), and *Heathen Days* (1943), and there are two heavy modern biographies of Mencken: *The Skeptic: A Life of HL Mencken* (2003), by Terry Teachout, and *Mencken: The American Iconoclast, the Life and Times of the Bad Boy of Baltimore* (2005), by Marion Elizabeth Rogers. Both are admirable and neither preaches about Mencken's excesses or prejudices. It's probably best that these biographers had a go at Mencken two decades ago, before literary critics saw it as their mission to cleanse the western canon of racism and misogyny. Mencken would not survive a "woke" pummeling of his life or a feminist re-reading of his written works, but more about that as this anthology goes on. These biographies are mentioned, and recommended, only so that readers will know that this anthology concerns Mencken's *writing*; his life story has already been well covered, and we need not revisit it here.

Just take a moment to think of the times that Mencken lived through! Born in 1880, Mencken was fifteen when Frederick Douglass, who had been enslaved in Maryland, died. Just a year after Mencken's birth, President James Garfield, shot by a nut case in 1881, died (quite literally) at the hands of his quack surgeons. The doctors did not believe in washing their hands, as they hadn't accepted the germ theory of disease, so, they poked their fingers into Garfield's bullet wound, thus causing infection. In that same year, 1881, Czar Alexander II in Russia died from one of the modern world's first successful terrorist attacks. Twenty years later, President William McKinley was assassinated by another nut job.

At that time, Russia, the Ottoman Empire, and the Austro-Hungarian Empire all existed as actual monarchies; this was the case until Mencken was well into his thirties, and he would have been pushing forty when the Spanish Flu came and went, after killing at least 50 million people. This was just about the time that the first flappers started jiggling to jazz tunes, and only slightly after modern populist politics began its rise with William Jennings Bryan. This was the era of Mencken's best writing, before the Great Depression and before the sedentary life of a smoking, drinking, over-eating writer caused blockages in his blood vessels; it was an era where all the old authorities in public life seemed not just discredited, but incompetent, leaning towards evil.

In the 1920s, America gloried in religious revivalism, jazz music, wordy literature, picture shows, and idiot politicians. Male social clubs, ranging from the Elks to the Ku Klux Klan (the Klan had a separate female division) proliferated. It was a time when the suffragettes did not know what to crusade *for* now that women had a federally guaranteed right to vote, and didn't know what to crusade *against* now that alcohol had been banned. Mencken's very best material comes from the exact middle of the decade (1925), when he covered the Scopes trial in Tennessee. Forty-five-year-old Mencken was in his writerly prime, and given this opportunity to display his atheism and his acerbic wit he delivered some of the best American journalism ever produced. Mencken knew that, while the case was ostensibly about the teaching of evolution in a single high school, American "buncombe," of which Creationism is only one strand, was really on trial. (Two of Mencken's best pieces on the Scopes trial, "In Memoriam W.J.B." and "The Hills of Zion," are included in this anthology.)

After reading a huge amount of Mencken's work, I've realized that there is a kind of genius in recognizing the boundaries of one's own talents, and Mencken possessed it. A great reader of novels, he wrote literary criticism but no literature. Mencken wrote like an intellectual and not a pseudo-intellectual, which means that he confined his writing to subjects that he was interested in and understood.

One suspects this partially explains why he never wrote much about the Spanish Flu, which killed over 600,000 people in the U.S. alone. (Fear of the heavy hand of the Wilson Administration was likely an even more important reason.)

Even so, Mencken did make bad predictions about political primaries and elections that no one cared about even at the time, and he rants on for too long about the effects of Anglo-Saxon blood on American culture, but even these writings still entertain.

In this era of 24-hour-a-day media bombardment, it's almost possible to consider Mencken's time as a halcyon era. Yes, it was poxed with misogyny, racism, polio, religious fanatics, and world wars, but it was also possible to talk with friends about a good new book, and literate people didn't have to listen to anyone discuss the merits of NFL draft picks.

A preface that begins with a stupid question should end with a stupid statement (stupid if only because it's obvious), and here it is: It's a good thing that Mencken is not around. He could not have functioned in this modern world where most people refuse to read anything longer than a social media post, where only powerful white men are considered acceptable targets for comedy, and where any "oppressed" group must be sainted. In Mencken's time, the Ku Kluxers, Anti-Saloon League, American Legion, Rotary Clubbers, and fundamentalist zealots claimed a purity and piety that put them beyond reproach, above their inferiors (that is, everyone else)—now, just about everyone has staked out the same claim to moral superiority. America in Mencken's time was just as stupid and corrupt as it is now, only then intelligent people could have a few laughs at its expense.

The best reason to dive into Mencken now is the same as it was then— because it's hugely amusing to read his dark takedowns of the myriad grotesqueries in this menagerie of a nation.

—Chris Edwards

FOREWORD

I've known Chris Edwards for nearly two decades, and have been consistently impressed with the amount of work he produces, its variety, and its quality. Over the past 15 years he's written two books on skepticism, *Disbelief 101: A Young Person's Guide to Atheism* (as S.C. Hitchock) and *Spiritual Snake Oil: Fads and Fallacies in Pop Culture*, several professional books on education, and a sci-fi/fantasy novella, *The Strongman's Tale*. He's also a regular contributor to *Skeptic* magazine, and is currently working on two more books, a biography of Elvis Presley and a novel about corruption in professional boxing—and all the while raising a family and enduring the horrors of the American educational system as a history instructor.

All this made him the ideal person to compile and edit this new collection of H.L. Mencken's writings. Chris's interests are as wide ranging as Mencken's, many of his attitudes (especially regarding religion and other forms of quackery) are very similar to Mencken's, and his writing style is similarly entertaining and pungent. It would have been hard to find a man better suited to the job of selecting the best writings of America's most famous skeptic.

* * *

A century ago H.L. Mencken wrote, "The American people, taking one with another, constitute the most timorous, sniveling, poltroonish, ignominious mob of serfs and goose-steppers ever gathered under one flag in Christendom since the end of the Middle Ages."

Not much has changed since then—at least as regards national character.

Things are just as dark in other areas. The most salient is probably the dismal state of the education system, from which flow many other evils. As in Mencken's day, critical thinking courses are almost nonexistent in the schools, and science courses usually consist of learning facts, not in understanding *how* those facts were established—through use of the scientific method, which in itself is a good introduction to critical thinking.

The dearth of critical thinking skills is largely responsible for both the rampant anti-intellectualism in this country and the millions of cognitively impaired Americans who fall prey to conspiracy theories, misinformation and disinformation, and absurd religious and political beliefs. Almost worse, these delusional dolts resent those who inform them of facts they don't want to hear, and are perversely proud of their willful ignorance.

This isn't the result of stupidity. Back in the 1920s Mencken stated:

> The school statistics show that the average member of the American Legion can read and write after a fashion, and is able to multiply eight by seven after four trials, but they tell us nothing about his actual intelligence. The returns of the Army itself, indeed, indicate that he is stupid almost beyond belief—that there is at least an even chance that he is a moron.

Astoundingly, since then the average IQ has *risen* by about 30 points. But, immersed as we are in a sea of idiocy, that's hard to believe. As George Carlin put it, "Think about how stupid the average person is, and [then] realize half of them are stupider than that."

Still, facts are facts, and Americans today are more intelligent than they were in Mencken's day. So, the problem isn't that they lack intelligence, it's that they don't know how to use it; they don't know how to think critically, and aren't even aware that they don't know how. To put a bright red cherry atop this *merde* sundae, the less informed people are the more informed they *think* they are, and the more certain they are that they're right.

To make matters even worse, millions upon millions, probably a majority, of Americans have been subjected to childhood religious indoctrination—and are now subjecting their own children to it. Part of that indoctrination, in a huge number of cases, consists of the drilled-in belief that doubt and questioning are bad, sinful, that they come from the devil.

The results of such religious indoctrination, compounded by lack of critical thinking skills, are horrendous. Tens of millions still deny the overwhelming scientific consensus that the Earth is heating up due to the burning of fossil fuels. They deny the reality that fossil fuel use is to blame for rising temperatures, which in turn cause ever-increasing disasters: droughts, heatwaves, floods, wild fires, sea level rise, plummeting wildlife populations, and myriad other awful things.

Tens of millions also buy into other nonsensical, anti-scientific crap, such as anti-vaccination claims. They accept the entirely unsupported anti-vax assertions of snake oil salesmen such as Andrew Wakefield and Robert F. Kennedy, Jr., don't get their own kids vaccinated, and fight vaccination mandates in the schools—often in abusive, sometimes violent, ways. The end result is that outbreaks of entirely preventable, once almost completely suppressed diseases, such as measles, have reappeared, and are increasing. One suspects that polio will be next; scattered cases have already surfaced.

The gullible who buy into anti-scientific conspiracy theories also tend to buy into political conspiracy theories, the most lurid being the morbidly delusional Qanon and Pizzagate "theories" (in reality, wild conjectures)— "theories" so sick and crazy they'd have beggared the imaginations of John Wayne Gacy or Jeffrey Dahmer. Distracted by such idiocy, conspiracy nut jobs not only do nothing to help solve the very real, very serious problems facing us all, they become obstacles to dealing with those problems.

Perhaps even worse, these same wack jobs tend to join theofascist cults worshiping grotesque would-be dictators, who they see as means to an end: imposing their perverted excuse for morality upon the rest of us, and in the process destroying what passes for democracy in this country. Not incidentally, many of these foaming-at-the-mouth authoritarians are in favor of murderous violence, and some resort to it—the victims usually being Jews, blacks, hispanics, and gay people.

In Mencken's day there were mass fascist movements (KKK, American Legion, Silver Shirts, the Bund) and dozens of lynchings annually. Today, an entire political party has become a fascist personality cult, and we have *daily* mass shootings.

Another aspect of this dismal situation is that the news media, overall, is almost as bad now as it was in Mencken's day. At the time Mencken wrote, the most important part of the media was the daily newspaper, which was almost entirely driven by the profit motive. The result was timorousness; in order to maintain profits, newspapers did virtually nothing to challenge the rich and powerful. The most outstanding example of that was the newspapers' abject acquiescence to, and in some cases promotion of, the lies and propaganda that led to America's entry into World War I, and the accompanying near-total suppression of anti-war dissent and free speech.

Just as telling, the newspapers refused to touch America's third rail: religion. In the early 1920s Mencken noted:

> The astounding program of this organization [KKK] was discussed in the newspapers for months on end, and a committee of Congress sat in solemn state to investigate it, and yet not a single newspaper or Congressman, so far as I am aware, so much as mentioned the most patent and important fact about it, to wit, that the Ku Klux Klan was, to all intents and purposes, the secular arm of the Methodist Church . . .

Today, things seem every bit as bad. The corporate media served as propagandists for George W. Bush and Dick Cheney in the run-up to their war of aggression against Iraq, with virtually no visible dissent. "Progressive" MSNBC even fired the host of its most popular program, Phil Donohue, because he opposed the invasion.

Following 9/11, virtually all of the media slavishly repeated (or, at least, failed to question) the Bush-Cheney Administration's assertion that Saddam Hussein was in league with Al Qaeda, even though that assertion was on-its-face absurd: Saddam was a secularist, and Al Qaeda was (and is) composed of religious fanatics who considered Saddam a very bad Muslim. To make matters worse, the Bush Administration also claimed that Saddam had stockpiled chemical weapons of mass destruction (WMDs), was further developing both chemical and biological weapons, and was actively pursuing a nuclear weapons program.

The topper was that *all* of the evidence linking Saddam to Al Qaeda, nukes, and other WMDs was fabricated—and the media, with very few exceptions, reported Bush and company's lies as fact, without question or investigation. This was near-exact repetition of the disgraceful behavior of the newspapers prior to and during World War I.

The reticence of the media in its coverage of religion is also nearly as bad now as it was in Mencken's day. While writing the preface to *24 Reasons to Abandon Christianity*, I noticed, and mentioned, an excellent example of such timidity in an unexpected place:

> Even . . . those who know better often stay silent rather than utter a word about the 800-pound simian on the sofa. . . . The "Ideas" section of the BBC News site [featured] four short videos, "Prejudice Unpacked," a mini-series of sorts. The videos dealt with misogyny, racism, homophobia, and anti-semitism, and they all bore near-identical titles, such as "Why are people anti-Semitic?" and "Why are people sexist?" A subtitle asks, "Why do people hold prejudices—like racism, homophobia and sexism?" and then adds, "We explore some of the root causes."

> *None* of the videos contain a single word about Christianity, one of the root causes of the evils these videos profess to analyze (especially anti-semitism which, since the writing of the gospels, is almost entirely due to Christianity). This type of deliberate blindness—less charitably, gutlessness—is routine in the media and in everyday life. It's an all-too-common form of cowardice . . .

But it gets worse.

Today, the media is even more dismal in some ways than in Mencken's time. The most popular "news" network is a roiling open sewer spouting feculent geysers of hate, aggrieved self-pity, racist dog whistles, and terror-inducing misinformation and disinformation; this "news" network is so dishonest that it paid a $787.5 million settlement to a single victim in 2023 over some of its defamatory lies.

The owners of the social media cesspit are nearly as bad. They rake in billions by prodding dimwits into diving head first, jaws agape, into their putrid pool of hate, fear, lies, and conspiracy theories.

Still, things aren't completely black. There have been notable improvements in American life since Mencken was excoriating the "booboisie." The first that comes to mind is the significant increase in the average lifespan due to scientific and technological advances, especially the introduction of vaccines to prevent or ameliorate horrible diseases such as measles, polio, shingles, Covid, HPV, influenza—the list goes on.

Another is that Americans have been gradually freeing themselves from the perverted morality imposed on them by sadistic Puritans. When Mencken wrote, divorce was difficult to obtain, abortion was flat out illegal as was contraception, and even providing information about abortion and contraception was a criminal offense. Today, even though our hard-won rights are under renewed attack, things are better.

None of this would have surprised Mencken except, perhaps, the increased freedom from restrictive morality, which would have delighted him.

So, please sit back, read on, and enjoy Mencken's wit and sarcasm—and marvel at how much of what he wrote a century ago is still relevant.

—Charles Bufe (author of *24 Reasons to Abandon Christianity: Why Christianity's Perverted Morality Leads to Misery and Death*, *Alcoholics Anonymous: Cult or Cure?*, and *The American Heretic's Dictionary*)

Publisher's Note

Mencken's writings contain a number of oddities, including unusual capitalization (e.g., "Federal government"), unusual spellings (e.g., "practise," used multiple times as both noun and verb), and sometimes both (e.g., "Postoffice"). His punctuation is also unusual in some ways, especially in his use of colons and semicolons, which he tends to use interchangeably—sometimes he uses them correctly, sometimes he doesn't—and to a lesser extent his use of commas, which he generally uses correctly, but occasionally inserts them where they're inappropriate and at times omits them where they're clearly called for.

There's also the matter of archaicisms, the most common being "to-day"; it went out of style in the 1930s, but was still the preferred usage when Mencken wrote the pieces in this anthology. As well, Mencken occasionally uses archaic punctuation, such as em dashes preceding commas (—,); that and similar usages were common when Mencken wrote, but look decidedly odd today.

We've retained all of Mencken's unusual usages, but did correct a very few spellings which were clearly typos. In the few places where we were in doubt, we retained the spellings in the original sources.

Then there's the matter of italicization (or lack of it) in book and magazine titles. The sources we drew upon for this anthology were inconsistent, sometimes putting titles in quotation marks, other times italicizing them, and occasionally leaving them in Roman (normal) type without quotation marks. For the sake of uniformity, we've put all such titles in italics, in keeping with modern usage.

Finally, Mencken had the annoying habit of including uncommon, untranslated foreign words and phrases in his writing. Most are in German, some in French and Latin, a few in Italian, and even, in at least one instance, Arabic (rendered in the Roman alphabet). To save readers time and aggravation, we've translated all foreign-language terms and phrases, bar the most common, and have inserted the English equivalents [in brackets] following the terms in question.

1

AMERICA

ON BEING AN AMERICAN

[*If you read enough Mencken, you'll eventually come to the conclusion that he wasn't kidding when he excoriated this country. His writing is often at its most effective when he's serious, though sarcastic. An example: "It is, for example, one of my firmest and most sacred beliefs, reached after an inquiry extending over a score of years and supported by incessant prayer and meditation, that the government of the United States, in both its legislative arm and its executive arm, is ignorant, incompetent, corrupt, and disgusting—and from this judgment I except no more than twenty living lawmakers and no more than twenty executioners of their laws."*

As I write these words in 2022, Americans are coming to terms with the mass slaughter of elementary school students by a lone gunman. (I am confident, knowing this country, that something similar will be the case no matter when you read this.) The cops, heroes all, called for reinforcements, then stood outside and busied themselves with donut consumption while the gunman executed 19 children and two teachers inside a fourth-grade classroom. America's politicians, when confronted with all of this, offered thoughts and prayers, and probably fortified their own offices with bulletproof glass. Meanwhile, several state legislators called special sessions to ban transgender students from playing girls sports and to piously declare that teenaged victims of rape should be forced to carry to term the unexpected little blessings from God in their uteri. One can only imagine what Mencken would have said about all this.]

1

Apparently there are those who begin to find it disagreeable—nay, impossible. Their anguish fills the Liberal weeklies, and every ship that puts out from New York carries a groaning cargo of them, bound for Paris, London, Munich, Rome and way points—anywhere to escape the great curses and atrocities that make life intolerable for them at home. Let me say at once that I find little to cavil at in their basic complaints. In more than one direction, indeed, I probably go a great deal further than even the Young

Intellectuals. It is, for example, one of my firmest and most sacred beliefs, reached after an inquiry extending over a score of years and supported by incessant prayer and meditation, that the government of the United States, in both its legislative arm and its executive arm, is ignorant, incompetent, corrupt, and disgusting—and from this judgment I except no more than twenty living lawmakers and no more than twenty executioners of their laws. It is a belief no less piously cherished that the administration of justice in the Republic is stupid, dishonest, and against all reason and equity— and from this judgment I except no more than thirty judges, including two upon the bench of the Supreme Court of the United States. It is another that the foreign policy of the United States—its habitual manner of dealing with other nations, whether friend or foe—is hypocritical, disingenuous, knavish, and dishonorable—and from this judgment I consent to no exceptions whatsoever, either recent or long past. And it is my fourth (and to avoid too depressing a bill, final) conviction that the American people, taking one with another, constitute the most timorous, sniveling, poltroonish, ignominious mob of serfs and goose-steppers ever gathered under one flag in Christendom since the end of the Middle Ages, and that they grow more timorous, more sniveling, more poltroonish, more ignominious every day.

So far I go with the Fugitive Young Intellectuals—and into the Bad Lands beyond. Such, in brief, are the cardinal articles of my political faith, held passionately since my admission to citizenship and now growing stronger and stronger as I gradually disintegrate into my component carbon, oxygen, hydrogen, phosphorus, calcium, sodium, nitrogen and iron. This is what I believe and preach, *in nomine Domini*, Amen. Yet I remain on the dock, wrapped in the flag, when the Young Intellectuals set sail. Yet here I stand, unshaken and undespairing, a loyal and devoted Americano, even a chauvinist, paying taxes without complaint, obeying all laws that are physiologically obeyable, accepting all the searching duties and responsibilities of citizenship unprotestingly, investing the sparse usufructs of my miserable toil in the obligations of the nation, avoiding all commerce with men sworn to overthrow the government, contributing my mite toward the glory of the national arts and sciences, enriching and embellishing the native language, spurning all lures (and even all invitations) to get out and stay out—here am I, a bachelor of easy means, forty-two years old, unhampered by debts or issue, able to go wherever I please and to stay as long as I please—here am I, contentedly and even smugly basking beneath the Stars and Stripes, a better citizen, I daresay, and certainly a less murmurous and exigent one, than thousands who put the Hon. Warren Gamaliel Harding beside Friedrich Barbararossa and Charlemagne, and hold the Supreme Court to be directly inspired by the Holy Spirit, and belong ardently to every Rotary Club, Ku Klux Klan and Anti-Saloon League, and choke with emotion when the band plays "The Star Spangled Banner," and believe with the faith of little children that one of Our Boys, taken at random, could dispose in a fair fight of ten Englishmen, twenty Germans, thirty Frogs, forty Wops, fifty Japs, or a hundred Bolsheviki.

Well, then, why am I still here? Why am I so complacent (perhaps even to the point of offensiveness), so free from bile, so little fretting and indignant, so curiously happy? Why did I answer only with a few academic "Hear, Hears" when Henry James, Ezra Pound, Harold Stearns and the emigrés of Greenwich Village issued their successive calls to the corn-fed *intelligentsia* to flee the shambles, escape to fairer lands, throw off the curse forever? The answer, of course, is to be sought in the nature of happiness, which tempts to metaphysics. But let me keep upon the ground. To me, at least (and I can only follow my own nose) happiness presents itself in an aspect that is tripartite. To be happy (reducing the thing to its elementals) I must be: a. Well-fed, at ease from sordid cares, at ease in Zion. b. Full of a comfortable feeling of superiority to the masses of my fellow-men. c. Delicately and unceasingly amused according to my taste.

It is my contention that, if this definition be accepted, there is no country on the face of the earth wherein a man roughly constituted as I am—a man of my general weaknesses, vanities, appetites, prejudices, and aversions—can be so happy, or even one-half so happy, as he can be in these free and independent states. Going further, I lay down the proposition that it is a sheer physical impossibility for such a man to live in These States and not be happy—that it is as impossible to him as it would be to a schoolboy to weep over the burning down of his school-house. If he says that he isn't happy here, then he either lies or is insane. Here the business of getting a living, particularly since the war brought the loot of all Europe to the national strong-box, is enormously easier than it is in any other Christian land—so easy, in fact, that an educated and forehanded man who fails at it must actually make deliberate efforts to that end. Here the general average of intelligence, of knowledge, of competence, of integrity, of self-respect, of honor is so low that any man who knows his trade, does not fear ghosts, has read fifty good books, and practices the decencies stands out as brilliantly as a wart on a bald head, and is thrown willy-nilly into a meager and exclusive aristocracy. And here, more than anywhere else that I know of or have heard of, the daily panorama of human existence, or private and communal folly—the unending procession of governmental extortions and chicaneries, of commercial brigandages and throat-slittings, of theological buffooneries, of aesthetic ribaldries, of legal swindles and harlotries, of miscellaneous rogueries, villainies, imbecilities, grotesqueries, and extravagances—is so inordinately gross and preposterous, so perfectly brought up to the highest conceivable amperage, so steadily enriched with an almost fabulous daring and originality, that only the man who was born with a petrified diaphragm can fail to laugh himself to sleep every night, and to awake every morning with all the eager, unflagging expectation of a Sunday-school superintendent touring the Paris peep-shows.

A certain sough of rhetoric may be here. Perhaps I yield to words as a chautauqua lecturer yields to them, belaboring and fermenting the hinds with his Message from the New Jerusalem. But fundamentally I am quite as sincere as he is. For example, in the matter of attaining to ease in Zion, of getting a fair share of the national swag, now piled so mountainously high. It seems to me, sunk in my Egyptian night, that the man who fails to do this in the United States to-day is a man who is somehow stupid—maybe not on the surface, but certainly deep down. Either he is one who cripples himself unduly, say by setting up a family before he can care for it, or by making a bad bargain for the sale of his wares, or by concerning himself too much about the affairs of other men; or he is one who endeavors fatuously to sell something that no normal American wants. Whenever I hear a professor of philosophy complain that his wife has eloped with some moving-picture actor or bootlegger, who can at least feed and clothe her, my natural empathy for the man is greatly corrupted by contempt for his lack of sense. Would it be regarded as sane and laudable for a man to travel the Soudan [Sudan] trying to sell fountain-pens, or Greenland offering to teach double-entry bookkeeping or counterpoint? Coming closer, would the judicious pity or laugh at a man who opened a shop for the sale of incunabula in Little Rock, Ark., or who demanded a living in McKeesport, Pa., on the ground that he could read Sumerian? In precisely the same way it seems to me to be nonsensical for a man to offer generally some commodity that only a few rare and dubious Americans want, and then weep and beat his breast because he is not patronized. One seeking to make a living in a country must pay due regards to the needs and tastes of that country. Here in the United States we have no jobs for grand dukes, and none for *Wirkliche Geheimraten* [king's advisors], and none for palace eunuchs, and none for masters of the buck-hounds, and none (any more) for brewery *Todsaufer* [misspelling, probably taste testers]—and very few for oboe-players, metaphysicians, astrophysicists, assyriologists, water-colorists, stylites and epic poets. There was a time when the *Todsaufer* served a public need and got an adequate reward, but it is no more. There may come a time when the composer of string quartettes is paid as much as a railway conductor, but it is not yet. Then why practice such trades—that is, as trades? The man of independent means may venture into them prudently; when he does so, he is seldom molested; it may even be argued that he performs a public service by adopting them. But the man who has a living to make is simply silly if he goes into them; he is like a soldier going over the top with a coffin strapped to his back. Let him abandon such puerile vanities, and take to the uplift instead, as, indeed, thousands of other victims of the industrial system have already done. Let him bear in mind that, whatever its neglect of the humanities and their monks, the Republic has never got half enough bond salesmen, quack doctors, ward leaders, phrenologists, Methodist evangelists, circus clowns, magicians, soldiers, farmers, popular song writers, moonshine distillers, forgers of gin labels, mine guards, detectives, spies, snoopers, and *agents provocateurs*. The rules are set by Omnipotence; the discreet man observes them. Observing them, he is safe beneath the starry bed-tick, in fair weather or foul. The *boobus Americanus* is a bird that knows no closed season—and if he won't come down to Texas oil stock, or one-night cancer cures, or building lots in Swamphurst, he will always come down to Inspiration and Optimism, whether political, theological, pedagogical, literary, or economic.

The doctrine that it is *infra digitatem* [out of reach] for an educated man to take a hand in the snaring of this goose is one in which I see nothing convincing. It is a doctrine chiefly voiced, I believe, by those who have tried the business and failed. They take refuge behind the childish notion that there is something honorable about poverty *per se*—the Greenwich Village complex. This is nonsense. Poverty may be an unescapable misfortune, but that no more makes it honorable than a cocked eye is made honorable by the same cause. Do I advocate, then, the ceaseless, senseless hogging of money? I do not. All I advocate—and praise as virtuous—is the hogging of enough to provide security and ease. Despite all the romantic superstitions to the contrary, the artist cannot do his best work when he is oppressed by unsatisfied wants. Nor can the philosopher. Nor can the man of science. The best and clearest thinking of the world is done and the finest art is produced, not by men who are hungry, ragged and harassed, but by men who are well-fed, warm and easy to mind. It is the artist's first duty to his art to achieve that tranquility for himself. Shakespeare tried to achieve it; so did Beethoven, Wagner, Brahms, Ibsen and Balzac. Goethe, Schopenhauer, Schumann and Mendelssohn were born to it. Joseph Conrad, Richard Strauss and Anatole France have got it for themselves in our own day. In the older countries where competence is far more general competition is thus more sharp, the thing is often cruelly difficult, and sometimes almost impossible. But in the United States it is absurdly easy, given ordinary luck. Any man with a superior air, the intelligence of a stockbroker, and the resolution of a hat-check girl—in brief, any man who believes in himself enough, and with sufficient cause, to be called a journeyman—can cadge enough money, in this glorious commonwealth of morons, to make life soft for him.

And if a lining for the purse is thus facilely obtainable, given a reasonable prudence and resourcefulness, then balm for the ego is just as unlaboriously got, given ordinary dignity and decency. Simply to exist, indeed, on the plane of a civilized man is to attain, in the Republic, to a distinction that should be enough for all save the most vain; it is even likely to be too much, as the frequent challenges of the Ku Klux Klan, the American Legion, the Anti-Saloon League, and other such vigilance committees of the majority testify. Here is a country in which all political thought and activity are concentrated upon the scramble for jobs—in which the normal politician, whether he be a President or a village road supervisor, is willing to renounce any principle, however precious to him, and to adopt any lunacy, however offensive to him, in order to keep his place at the trough. Go into politics, then, without seeking or wanting office, and at once you are as conspicuous as a red-haired blackamoor—in fact, a great deal more conspicuous, for red-haired blackamoors have been seen, but who has ever seen or heard of an American politician, Democrat or Republican, Socialist or Liberal, Whig or Tory, who did not itch for a job? Again, here is a country in which it is an axiom that a business man shall be a member of the Chamber of Commerce, an admirer of Charles M. Schwab, a reader of the *Saturday Evening Post*, a golfer—in brief, a vegetable. Spend your hours of escape from *Geschäft* [your profession] reading Remy du Gourmont or practicing the violoncello, and the local Sunday newspaper will infallibly find you and hymn you as a marvel—nay, your banker will summon you to discuss your notes, and your rivals will spread the report (probably truthful) that you were pro-German during the war. Yet again, here is a land in which women rule and men are slaves. Train your women to get your slippers for you, and your ill fame will match Galileo's or Darwin's. Once more, here is the Paradise of the back-slappers, of democrats, of mixers, of go-getters. Maintain ordinary reserve, and you will arrest instant attention—and have your hand kissed by the multitudes who, despite democracy, have all the inferior man's unquenchable desire to grovel and admire.

Nowhere else in the world is superiority more easily attained. The chief business of the nation, as a nation, is the setting up of heroes, mainly bogus. It admired the literary style of the late Woodrow; it respects the theological passion of Bryan; it venerates J. Pierpoint Morgan; it takes Congress seriously; it would be unutterably shocked by the proposition (with proof) that a majority of its judges are ignoramuses, and that a respectable minority of them are scoundrels. The manufacture of artificial *Durchlauchten* [nobility titles], *k.k. hoheiten* [royal titles] and even gods goes on feverishly and incessantly; the will to worship never flags. Ten iron-molders meet in the back-room of a near-beer saloon, organize a lodge of the Noble and Mystic Order of American Rosicrucians, and elect a wheelwright Supreme Worthy Whimwham; a month later they send a notice to the local newspaper that they have been greatly honored by an official visit from that Whimwham, and that they plan to give him a jeweled fob for his watch-chain. The chief national heroes—Lincoln, Lee, and so on—cannot remain mere men. The mysticism of the medieval peasantry gets into the communal view of them, and they begin to sprout haloes and wings. As I say, no intrinsic merit—at least, none commensurate with the mob estimate—is needed to come to such august dignities. Everything American is a bit amateurish and childish, even the national gods. The most conspicuous and respected American in nearly every field of endeavor, saving only the purely commercial (I exclude even the financial) is a man who would attract little attention in any other country. The leading American critic of literature, after twenty years of diligent exposition of his ideas, has yet to make it clear what he is in favor of, and why. The queen of the *haut monde* [high society], in almost every American city, is a woman who regards Lord Reading as an aristocrat and her superior, and whose grandfather slept in his underclothes. The leading American musical director, if he went to Leipzig, would be put to polishing trombones and copying drum parts. The chief living American military man—the national heir to Frederick, Marlborough, Wellington, Washington and Prince Eugene—is a member of the Elks, and proud of it. The leading American philosopher (now dead, with no successor known to the average pedagogue) spent a lifetime erecting an epistemological defense for the national aesthetic maxim: "I don't know nothing about music, but I know what I like." The most eminent statesman the United States has produced since Lincoln [Theodore Roosevelt] was fooled by Arthur James

Balfour, and miscalculated his public support by more that 5,000,000 votes. And the current Chief Magistrate of the nation [Warren G. Harding]—its defiant substitute for czar and kaiser—is a small-town printer who, when he wishes to enjoy himself in the Executive Mansion, invites in a homeopathic doctor, a Seventh Day Adventist evangelist, and couple of moving-picture actresses.

2

All of which may be boiled down to this: that the United States is essentially a commonwealth of third-rate men—that distinction is easy here because the general level of culture, of information, of taste and judgment, of ordinary competence is so low. No sane man, employing an American plumber to repair a leaky drain, would expect him to do it at the first trial, and in precisely the same way no sane man, observing an American Secretary of State in negotiation with Englishmen and Japs, would expect him to come off better than second best. Third-rate men, of course, exist in all countries, but it is only here that they are in full control of the state, and with it of all the national standards. The land was peopled, not by the hardy adventurers of legend, but simply by incompetents who could not get on at home, and the lavishness of nature they found here, the vast ease with which they could get livings, confirmed and augmented their native incompetence. No American colonist, even in the worst days of the Indian wars, ever had to face such hardships as ground down the peasants of Central Europe during the Hundred Years War, not even such hardships as oppressed the English lower classes during the century before the Reform Bill of 1832. In most of the colonies, indeed, he seldom saw any Indians at all: the one thing that made life difficult for him was his congenital dunder-headedness. The winning of the West, so rhetorically celebrated in American romance, cost the lives of fewer men than the single battle of Tannenenberg , and the victory was much easier and surer. The immigrants who have come in since those early days have been, if anything, of even lower grade than their forerunners. The old notion that the United States is peopled by the offspring of brave, idealistic and liberty loving minorities, who revolted against injustice, bigotry and mediaevalism at home—this notion is fast succumbing to the alarmed study that has been given of late to the immigration of recent years. The truth is that the majority of non-Anglo-Saxon immigrants since the Revolution, like the majority of Anglo-

Saxon immigrants before the Revolution, have been, not the superior men of their native lands, but the botched and unfit: Irishmen starving to death in Ireland, Germans unable to weather the *Sturm und Drang* [turmoil] of the post-Napoleonic reorganization, Italians weed-grown on exhausted soil, Scandinavians run to all bone and no brain, Jews too incompetent to swindle even the barbarous peasants of Russia, Poland and Roumania. Here and there among the immigrants, of course, there may be a bravo, or even a superman—e.g., the ancestors of Volstead, Ponzi, Jack Dempsey, Schwab, Daugherty, Debs, Pershing—but the average newcomer is, and always has been simply a poor fish.

Nor is there much soundness in the common assumption, so beloved of professional idealists and wind-machines, that the people of America constitute "the youngest of the great peoples." The phrase turns up endlessly; the average newspaper editorial writer would be hamstrung if the Postoffice suddenly interdicted it, as it interdicted "the right to rebel" during the war. What gives it a certain specious plausibility is the fact that the American Republic, compared to a few other existing governments, is relatively young. But the American Republic is not necessarily identical with the American people; they might overturn it to-morrow and set up a monarchy, and still remain the same people. The truth is that, as a distinct nation, they go back fully three hundred years, and that even their government is older than that of most other nations, e.g., France, Italy, Germany, Russia. Moreover, it is absurd to say that there is anything properly describable as youthfulness in the American outlook. It is not that of young men, but that of old men. All the characteristics of senescence are in it: a great distrust of ideas, an habitual timorousness, a harsh fidelity to a few fixed beliefs, a touch of mysticism. The average American is a prude and a Methodist under his skin, and the fact is never more evident than when he is trying to disprove it. His views are not those of a healthy boy, but those of an ancient paralytic escaped from the *Greisenheim* [old people's home]. If you would penetrate to the causes thereof, simply go down to Ellis Island and look at the next shipload of immigrants. You will not find the spring of youth in their step; you will find the shuffling of exhausted men. From such exhausted men the American stock has sprung. It was easier for them to survive here than it was where they came from, but that ease, though it made them feel stronger, did not actually strengthen them. It left them what they were when they came: weary peasants, eager only for the comfortable security of a pig in a sty. Out of that eagerness has issued many of the noblest manifestations of American *Kultur*: the national hatred of war, the pervasive suspicion of the aims and intents of all other nations, the short way with heretics and disturbers of the peace, the unshakable belief in devils, the implacable hostility to every novel idea and point of view.

All these ways of thinking are the marks of the peasant—more, of the peasant long ground into mud of his wallow, and determined to stay there—the peasant who has definitely renounced any lewd desire he may have ever had to gape at the stars. The habits of mind of this dull, sempiternal *fellah* [peasant laborer]—the oldest man in Christendom—are, with a few modifications, the habits of mind of the American people. The peasant has a great practical cunning, but he is unable to see any further than the next farm. He likes money and knows how to amass property, but his cultural development is but little above that of the domestic animals. He is intensely and cocksurely moral, but his morality and his self-interest are crudely identical. He is emotional and easy to scare, but his imagination cannot grasp an abstraction. He is a violent nationalist and patriot, but he admires rogues in office and always beats the tax-collector if he can. He has immovable opinions about all the great affairs of state, but nine-tenths of them are imbecilities. He is violently jealous of what he conceives to be his rights, but brutally disrespectul of the other fellow's. He is religious, but his religion is wholly devoid of beauty and dignity. This man, whether city or country bred, is the normal Americano—the 100 per cent Methodist, Odd Fellow, Ku Kluxer, and Know Nothing. He exists in all countries, but here alone he rules—here alone his anthropoid fears and rages are accepted gravely as logical ideas, and dissent from them is punished as a sort of public offense. Around every one of his principal delusions—of the sacredness of democracy, of the feasibility of sumptuary law, of the incurable sinfulness of all other peoples, of the menace of ideas, of the corruption lying in all the arts—there is thrown a barrier of taboos, and woe to the anarchist who seeks to break it down!

The multiplication of such taboos is obviously not characteristic of a culture that is moving from a lower plane to a higher—that is, of a culture still in the full glow of its youth. It is a sign, rather, of a culture that is slippiing downhill—one that is reverting to the most primitive standards and ways of thought. The taboo, indeed, is the trade-mark of the savage, and wherever it exists it is a relentless and effective enemy of civilized enlightenment. The savage is the most meticulously moral of men; there is scarcely an act of his daily life that is not conditioned by unyielding prohibitions and obligations, most of them logically unintelligible. The mob-man, a savage set amid civilization, cherishes a code of the same draconian kind. He believes firmly that right and wrong are immovable things—that they have an actual and unchangeable existence, and that any challenge of them, by word or act, is a crime against society. And with the concept of wrongness, of course, he always confuses the concept of mere differentness—to him the two are indistinguishable. Anything strange is to be combatted; it is of the Devil. The mob-man cannot grasp ideas in their native nakedness. They must be dramatized and personalized for him, and provided with either white wings or forked tails. All discussion of them, to interest him, must take the form of a pursuit and scotching of demons. He cannot think of a heresy without thinking of a heretic to be caught, condemned and burned.

The Fathers of the Republic, I am convinced, had a great deal more prevision than even their most romantic worshipers give them credit for. They not only sought to create a governmental machine that would be safe from attack without; they also sought to create one that would be safe from attack within. They invented very ingenious devices for holding the mob in check, for protecting the national polity against its transient and illogical rages, for securing the determination of all the larger matters of state to a concealed but none the less real aristocracy. Nothing could have been further from the intent of Washington, Hamilton and even Jefferson than that the official doctrines of the nation, in the year 1922, should be identical with the nonsense heard in the chautauqua, from the evangelical pulpit, and on the stump. But Jackson and his merry men broke through the barbed wires that were so carefully strung, and ever since 1825 *vox populi* has been the true voice of the nation. To-day there is no longer any question of statesmanship, in any real sense, in our politics. The only way to success in American public life is flattering and kowtowing to the mob. A candidate for office, even the highest, must either adopt its current manias *en bloc*, or convince it hypocritically that he has done so, while cherishing reservations *in petto* [in private]. The result is that only two sorts of men stand any chance whatever of getting into actual control of affairs—first, glorified mob-men who genuinely believe what the mob believes, and secondly, shrewd fellows who are willing to make any sacrifice of conviction and self-respect in order to hold their jobs. One finds perfect examples of the first class in Jackson and Bryan. One finds hundreds of specimens of the second among the politicians who got themselves so affectingly converted to Prohibition, and who voted and blubbered for it with flasks in their pockets. Even on the highest planes our politics seems to be incurable mountebankish. The same Senators who raised such raucous alarms against the League of Nations voted for the Disarmament Treaty—a far more obvious surrender to English hegemony. And the same Senators who who pleaded for the League on the ground that that its failure would break the heart of the world were eloquently against the treaty. The few men who maintained a consistent course in both cases, voting either for or against both League and treaty, were denounced by the newspapers as deliberate marplots, and found their constituents rising against them. To such an extent had the public become accustomed to buncombe that simple honesty was incomprehensible to it, and hence abhorrent!

As I have pointed out in a previous work, this dominance of mob ways of thinking, this pollution of the whole intellectual life of the country by the prejudices and emotions of the rabble, goes unchallenged because the old landed aristocracy of the colonial era has been engulfed and almost obliterated by the rise of the industrial system, and no new aristocracy has arisen to take its place, and discharge its highly necessary functions. An upper class, of course, exists, and of late it has tended to increase its power, but it is culturally almost indistinguishable from the mob: it lacks absolutely anything even remotely resembling an aristocratic point of view. One searches in vain for any sign of the true Junker [German nobility] spirit in the Vanderbilts, Astors, Morgans, Garys and other such earls and dukes of the plutocracy; their culture, like their aspiration, remains that of the pawnshops. One searches in vain, too for the aloof air of the don in the official *intelligentsia* of the American universities; they are timorous and orthodox, and constitute a reptile *Congregatio de Propaganda Fide* [Congregation for the Propagation of the Faith, a Catholic missionary organization] to match Bismarck's *Reptilienpresse* [reptile press]. Everywhere else on earth, despite the rise of democracy, an organized minority of aristocrats survives from a more spacious day, and if its personnel has degenerated and its legal powers have decayed it has at least maintained some vestige of its old independence of spirit, and jealously guarded its old right to be heard without risk of penalty. Even in England, where the peerage has been debauched to the level of a political baptismal found for Jewish money-lenders and Wesleyan soap-boilers, there is sanctuary for the old order in the two ancient universities, and a lingering respect for it in the peasantry. But in the United States it was paralyzed by Jackson and got its death blow from Grant, and since then no successor to it has been evolved. Thus there is no organized force to oppose the irrational vagaries of the mob. The legislative and executive arms of the government yield to them without resistance; the judicial arm has begun to yield almost as supinely, particularly when they take the form of witch-hunts; outside the official circle there is no opposition that is even dependably articulate. The worst excesses go almost without challenge. Discussion, when it is heard at all, is feeble and superficial, and girt about by the taboos that I have mentioned. The clatter about the so-called Ku Klux Klan, two or three years ago, was typical. The astounding program of this organization was discussed in the newspapers for months on end, and a committee of Congress sat in solemn state to investigate it, and yet not a single newspaper or Congressman, so far as I am aware, so much as mentioned the most patent and important fact about it, to wit, that the Ku Klux Klan was, to all intents and purposes, the secular arm of the Methodist Church, and that its methods were no more than physical projections of the familiar extravaganzas of the Anti-Saloon League. The intimate relations between church and Klan, amounting almost to identity, must have been plain to every intelligent American, and yet the taboo upon the realistic consideration of ecclesiastical matters was sufficient to make every public soothsayer disregard it completely.

I often wonder, indeed, if there would be any intellectual life at all in the United States if it were not for the steady importation in bulk of ideas from abroad, and particularly, in late years, from England. What would become of the average American scholar if he could not borrow wholesale from English scholars? How could an inquisitive youth get beneath the surface of our politics if it were not for such anatomists as Bryce? Who would show our statesmen the dotted lines for their signatures if there were no Balfours and Lloyd-Geprges? How could our young professors formulate aesthetic judgments, especially in the field of letters, if it were not for such gifted English mentors as Robertson Nicoll, Squire and Chatton-Brock? By what process, finally, would the true style of a visiting card be determined, and the *hoefflich* [expectant] manner of eating artichokes, if there were no reports from Mayfair? On certain levels this naive subservience must needs irritate every self-respecting American, and even dismay him. When he recalls the amazing feats of the English war propagandists between 1914 and 1917—and their even more amazing confessions of method since—he is apt to ask himself quite gravely if he belongs to a free nation or to a crown colony. The thing was done openly, shamelessly, contemptuously, cynically, and yet it was a gigantic success. The office of the American Secretary of State, from the end of Bryan's grotesque incumbency to the end of the Wilson administration, was little more than an antechamber of the British Foreign Office. Dr. Wilson himself, in the conduct of his policy, differed only from such colonial premiers as Hughes and Smuts. Even after the United States got into the war it was more swagger for a Young American blood to wear the British uniform than the American uniform. No American ever seriously questions an Englishman or Englishwoman of official or even merely fashionable position at home. Lord Birkenhead was accepted as a gentleman everywhere in the United States; Mrs. Asquith's unbelievable imbecilities were heard with hushed fascination; even Lady Astor, an Americn married to an expatriate German-American turned English viscount, was greeted with solemn effusiveness. During the latter part of 1917, when New York swarmed with British military missions, I observed in *Town Topics* a polite protest against a very significant habit of certain of their gallant members: that of going to dances wearing spurs, and so macerating the frocks and heels of the fawning fair. The protest, it appears, was not voiced by the hosts and hostesses of these singular officers: they would have welcomed their guests in trench boots. It was left to a dubious weekly, and it was made very gingerly.

The spectacle, as I say, has a way of irking the American touched by nationalistic weakness. Ever since the day of Lowell—even since the day of Cooper and Irving—there have been denunciations of it. But however unpleasant it may be, there is no denying that a chain of logical causes lies behind it, and that they are not to be disposed of by objecting to them. The average American of Anglo-Saxon majority, in truth, is simply a second-rate Englishman, and so it is no wonder that he is spontaneously servile, despite all his democratic denial of superiorities, to what he conceives to be first-rate Englishmen. He corresponds, roughly, to an English Nonconformist of the better-fed variety, and he shows all the familiar characters of the breed. He is truculent and cocksure, and yet he knows how to take off his hat when a bishop of the Establishment passes. He is hot against the dukes, and yet the notice of a concrete duke is a singing in his heart. It seems to me that this inferior Anglo-Saxon is losing his old dominance in the United States—that is, biologically. But he will keep his cultural primacy for a long, long while, in spite of the overwhelming inrush of men of other races, if only because those newcomers are even more clearly inferior than he is. Nine-tenths of the Italians, for example, who have come to these shores in late years have brought no more of the essential culture of Italy with them than so many horned cattle would have brought. If they become civilized at all, settling here, it is the civilization of the Anglo-Saxon majority that they acquire, which is to say the civilization of the English second table. So with the Germans, the Scandinavians, and even the Jews and Irish. The Germans, taking one with another, are on the cultural level of greengrocers. I have come into contact with a great many of them since 1914, some of them of considerable wealth and even of fashionable pretensions. In the whole lot I can think of but a score or two who could name off-hand the principal works of Thomas Mann, Otto Julius Bierbaum, Ludwig Thoma or Hugo von Hofmannsthal. They know much more about Mutt and Jeff than they know about Goethe. The Scandinavians are even worse. The majority of them are mere clods, and they are sucked into the Knights of Pythias, the chautauqua and the Methodist Church almost as soon as they land; it is by no means a mere accident that the national Prohibition Enforcement Act bears the name of a man theoretically of the blood of Gustavus Vasa, Svend of the Forked Beard, and Eric the Red. The Irish in the United States are scarcely touched by the revival of Irish culture, despite their melodramatic concern with Irish politics. During the war they supplied diligent and dependable agents to the Anglo-Saxon White Terror, and at all times they are very susceptible to political and social bribery. As for the Jews, they change their names to Burton, Thompson, and Cecil in order to qualify as true Americans, and when they are accepted and rewarded in the national coin they renounce Moses altogether and get themselves baptized in St. Bartholomew's Church.

Whenever ideas enter the United States from without they come by way of England. What the London *Times* says to-day, about Ukrainian politics, the revolt in India, a change of ministry in Italy, the character of the King of Norway, the oil situation in Mesopotamia, will be said week after next by the *Times* of New York, and a month or two later by all the other American newspapers. The extent of this control of American opinion by English news mongers is but little appreciated in the United States even by professional journalists. Fully four-fifths of all the foreign news that comes to the American newspapers comes through London, and most of the rest is supplied either by Englishmen or by Jews (often American-born) who maintain close relations with the English. During the years 1914–1917 so many English agents got into Germany in the guise of American correspondents—sometimes with the full knowledge of their Anglomaniac American employers—that the Germans, just before the United States entered the war, were considering barring American correspondents from their country altogether. I was in Copenhagen and Basel in 1917, and found both towns—each an important source of war news—full of Jews representing American journals as a side-line to more delicate and confidential work for the English department of press propaganda. Even to-day a very considerable proportion of the American correspondents in Europe are strongly under English influences, and in the Far East the proportion is probably still larger. But these men seldom handle really important news. All that is handled from London, and by trustworthy Britons. Such of it as is not cabled directly to the American newspapers and press associations is later clipped from English newspapers, and printed as bogus letters or cablegrams.

The American papers accept such very dubious stuff, not chiefly because they are hopelessly stupid or Anglomaniac, but because they find it impossible to engage competent American correspondents. If the native journalists who discuss our domestic politics avoid the fundamentals timorously, then those who venture to discuss foreign politics are scarcely aware of the fundamentals at all. We have simply developed no class of experts in such matters. No man comparable, say to Dr. Dillon, Wickham Steed, Count zu Reventlow or Wilfrid Seawen Blunt exists in the United States. When, in the Summer of 1920, the editors of the Baltimore *Sun* undertook plans to cover the approaching Disarmament Conference at Washington in a comprehensive and intelligent manner, they were forced, willy-nilly, into employing Englishmen to do the work. Such men as Brailsford and Bywater, writing from London, three thousand miles away, were actually better able to interpret the work of the conference than American correspondents on the spot, few of whom were capable of anything beyond the most trivial gossip. During the whole period of the conference not a professional Washington correspondent—the flower of American political journalism—wrote a single article upon the proceedings that got further than their surface aspects. Before the end of the sessions this enforced dependence upon English opinion had an unexpected and significant result. Facing the English and the Japs in an unyielding alliance, the French turned to the American delegation for assistance. The issue specifically before the conference was one on which American self-interest was obviously identical with the French self-interest. Nevertheless, the English had such firm grip upon the machinery of news distribution that they were able, in less than a week, to turn American public opinion against the French, and even to set up an active Francophobia. No American, not even any of the American delegates, was able to cope with their propaganda. They not only dominated the conference and pushed through a set of treaties that were extravagantly favorable to England; they even established the doctrine that all opposition to those treaties was immoral!

When Continental ideas, whether in politics, in metaphysics or in the fine arts, penetrate to the United States they nearly always travel by way of England. Emerson did not read Goethe; he read Carlyle. The American people, from the end of 1914 to the end of 1918, did not read first-handed statements of the German case; they read English interpretations of those statements. In London is the clearing house and transformer station. There the latest notions from the mainland are sifted out, carefully diluted with English water, and put into packages for the Yankee trade. The English not only get a chance to ameliorate or embellish; they also determine very largely what ideas Americans are to hear at all. Whatever fails to interest them, or is in any way obnoxious to them, is not likely to cross the ocean. This explains why it is that most literate Americans are so densely ignorant of many Continentals who have been celebrated at home for years, for example, Huysmans, Hartleben, Vaihinger, Morezhkovsky, Keyserling, Snoilsky, Mauthner, Altenberg, Heidenstam, Alfred Kerr. It also explains why they so grossly overestimate various third-raters, laughed at at home, for example Brieux. These fellows simply happen to interest the English *intelligentsia*, and are thus palmed off upon the gaping colonists of Yankeedom. In the case of Brieux the hocus-pocus was achieved by one man, George Bernard Shaw, a Scotch blue-nose disguised as an Irish patriot and English soothsayer. Shaw, at bottom, has the ideas of a Presbyterian elder, and so the moral frenzy of Brieux enchanted him. Whereupon he retired to his chamber, wrote a flaming Brieuxiad for the American trade, and founded the late vogue of the French Dr. Sylvanus Stall on this side of the ocean.

This wholesale import and export business in Continental fancies is of no little benefit, of course, to the generality of Americans. If it did not exist they would probably never hear of many of the salient Continentals at all, for the obvious incompetence of most of the native and resident introducers of intellectual ambassadors makes them suspicious even of those who, like Boyd and Nathan, are thoroughly competent. To this day there is no American translation of the plays of Ibsen; we use the William Archer Scotch-English translations, most of them atrociously bad, but still better than nothing. So with the works of Nietzsche, Anatole France, Georg Brandes, Turgeniev, Dostoyevsky, Tolstoi, and other moderns after their kind. I can think of but one important exception: the work of Gerhart Hauptmann, came into English by and under the supervision of Ludwig Lewisohn. But even here Lewisohn used a number of English translations of single plays: the English were still ahead of him, though they stopped half way. He is, in any case, a very extraordinary American, and the Department of Justice kept an eye on him during the war. The average American professor is far too dull a fellow to undertake so difficult an enterprise. Even when he sports a German Ph.D. one usually finds on examination that all he knows about modern German literature is that a *Mass* of Hofbrau [amount of beer in a regulation-sized mug] in Munich used to cost 27 *Pfennig* downstairs and 32 *Pfennig* upstairs. The German universities were formerly very tolerant of foreigners. Many an American, in preparation for professing at Harvard, spent a couple of years roaming from one to the other of them without picking up enough German to read the *Berliner Tageblatt* [*Berlin Daily News*]. Such frauds swarm in all our lesser universities, and many of them, during the war, became eminent authorities upon the crimes of Nietzsche and the errors of Treitschke.

3

In rainy weather, when any old wounds ache and the four humors do battle in my spleen, I often find myself speculating sourly as to the future of the Republic. Native opinion, of course, is to the effect that it will be secure and glorious; the superstition that progress must always be upward and onward will not down; in virulence and popularity it matches the superstition that money can accomplish anything. But this view is not shared by most reflective foreigners, as any one may find out by looking into such a book as Ferdinant Kurnberger's *Der Amerikamude*, Sholom Asch's *America*, Ernst von Wolzogen's *Ein Dichter in Dollaria*, W.L. George's *Hail, Columbia!*, Annalise Schmidt's *Der Amerikanische Mensch* or Sienkiewicz's *After Bread*, or by hearkening unto the confidences, if obtainable, of such returned immigrants as Georges Clemenceau, Knut Hamstsun, George Santayana, Clemens von Pirquet, John Masefield and Maxim Gorky, and, via the ouija board, Antonin Dvorak, Frank Wedekind and Edwin Klebs. The America Republic, as nations go, has led a safe and easy life, with no serious enemies to menace it, either within or without, and no grim struggle with want. Getting a living here has always been easier than anywhere else in Christendom; getting a secure foothold has been possible to whole classes of men who would have remained submerged in Europe, as the character of our plutocracy, and no less of our *intelligentsia* so brilliantly shows. The American people have never had to face such titanic assaults as those suffered by the people of Holland, Poland and half a dozen other little countries; they have not lived with a ring of powerful and unconscionable enemies about them, as the Germans have lived since the Middle Ages; they have not thrown their strength into far-flung and exhausting colonial enterprises, like the English. All their foreign wars have been fought with foes either too weak to resist them or too heavily engaged elsewhee to make more than a half-hearted attempt. The combats with Mexico and Spain were not wars; they were simply lynchings. Even the Civil War, compared to the larger European conflicts since the invention of gunpowder, was trivial in its character and transient in its effects. The population of the United States, when it began, was about 31,000,000—say 10 per cent under the population of France in 1914. But after four years of struggle, the number of men killed in action or dead of wounds, in the two armies, came to but 200,000—probably little more than a sixth of the total losses of France between 1914 and 1918. Nor was there any very extensive destruction of property. In all save a small area in the North there was none at all, and even in the South only a few towns of any importance were destroyed. The average Northerner passed through the four years scarcely aware, save by report, that war was going on. In the South the breath of Mars blew more hotly, but even there large numbers of men escaped service, and the general hardship everywhere fell a great deal short of the hardships suffered by the Belgians, the French of the North, the Germans of East Prussia, and the Serbians and Rumanians in the World War. The agonies of the South have been much exaggerated in popular romance; they were probably more severe during Reconstruction, when they were chiefly psychical, than they were during the actual war. Certainly General Robert E. Lee was in a favorable position to estimate the military achievement of the Confederacy. Well, Lee was of the opinion that his army was very badly supported by the civil population, and that its final disaster was largely due to that ineffective support.

Coming down to the time of the World War, one finds precious few signs that the American people, facing an antagonist of equal strength and with both hands free, could be relied upon to give a creditable account of themselves. The American share in that great struggle, in fact, was marked by poltroonery almost as conspicuously as it was marked by knavery. Let us consider briefly what the nation did. For a few months it viewed the struggle idly and unintelligently, as a yokel might stare at a sword-swallower at a county fair. Then, seeing a chance to profit, it undertook with sudden alacrity the ghoulish office of *Kriegslieferant* [war supplier]. One of the contestants being debarred, by chance of war, from buying, it devoted its whole energies, for two years, to purveying to the other. Meanwhile, it made every effort to aid its customer by lending him the cloak of its neutrality—that is, by demanding all the privileges of a neutral and yet carrying on a stupendous wholesale effort to promote the war. On the official side, this neutrality was fraudulent from the start, as the revelations of Mr. Tumulty have since demonstrated; popularly it became more and more fraudulent as the debts of the customer contestant piled up, and it became more and more apparent—a fact diligently made know by his partisans—that they would be worthless if he failed to win. Then, in the end, covert aid was transformed into overt aid. And under what conditions? In brief, there stood a nation of 65,000,000 people, which without effective allies, had just closed two and a half years of homeric conflict by completely defeating an enemy state of 135,000,000 and two lesser ones of more than 10,000,000 together, and now stood at bay before a combination of at least 140,000,000. Upon this battle-scarred and war-weary foe the Republic of 100,000,000 freemen now flung itself, so lifting the odds to 4 to 1. And after a year and a half more of struggle it emerged triumphant—a knightly victory surely?

There is no need to rehearse the astounding and unprecedented swinishness that accompanied this glorious business—the colossal waste of public money, the savage persecution of all opponents and critics of the war, the open bribery of labor, the half-insane reviling of the enemy, the manufacture of false news, the knavish robbery of enemy civilians, the incessant spy hunts, the floating of public loans by a process of blackmail, the degradation of the Red Cross to partisan uses, the complete abandonment of all decency, decorum and self-respect. The facts must be remembered with shame by every civilized American; lest they be forgotten by the generations of the future. I am even now engaged with collaborators upon an exhaustive record of them, in twenty volumes folio. More important to the present purpose are two things that are apt to be overlooked, the first of which is the capital fact that the war was "sold" to the American people, as the phrase has it, not by appealing to their courage, but by appealing to their cowardice—in brief, by adopting the assumption that they were not warlike at all, and certainly not gallant and chivalrous, but merely craven and fearful. The first selling point of the proponents of American participation was the contention that the Germans, with gigantic wars still raging on both fronts, were preparing to invade the United States, burn down all the towns, murder all the men, and carry off all the women—that their victory would bring staggering and irresistible reprisals for the American violation of the duties of a neutral. The second selling point was that the entrance of the United States would end the war almost instantly—that the Germans would be so overwhelmingly outnumbered, in men and guns, that it would be impossible for them to make any effective defense—above all, that it would be impossible for them to inflict any serious damage upon their new foes. Neither argument, it must be plain, showed the slightest belief in the warlike skill and courage of the American people. Both were grounded upon the frank theory that the only way to make the mob fight was to scare it half to death, and then show it a way to fight without risk, to stab a helpless antagonist in the back. And both were mellowed and reinforced by the hint that such a noble assault, beside being safe, would also be extremely profitable—that it would convert very dubious debts into very good debts, and dispose forever of a diligent and dangerous competitor for trade, especially in Latin America. All the idealist nonsense emitted by Dr. Wilson and company was simply icing on the cake. Most of it was abandoned as soon as the bullets began to fly, and the rest consisted simply of meaningless words—the idiotic babbling of a Presbyterian evangelist turned prophet and seer.

The other thing that needs to be remembered is the permanent effect of so dishonest and cowardly a business upon the national character, already far too much inclined toward easy ventures and long odds. Somewhere in his diaries Wilfrid Seawen Blunt speaks of the marked debasement that showed itself in the English spirit after the brutal robbery and assassination of the South African Republics. The heroes that the mob followed after Mafeking [Boer War battle] Day were far inferior to the heroes that it followed in the days before the war. The English gentleman began to disappear from public life, and in his place appeared a rabble-rousing bounder obviously almost identical with the American professional politician—the Lloyd-George, Chamberlain, F.E. Smith, Isaacs-Reading, Churchill, Bottomley, Northcliffe type. Worse, old ideals went with old heroes. Personal freedom and strict legality, says Blunt, vanished from the English tables of the law, and there was a shift of the social and political center of gravity to a lower plane. Precisely the same effect is now visible in the United States. The overwhelming majority of conscripts went into the army unwillingly, and once there they were debauched by the twin forces of the official propaganda that I have mentioned and a harsh, unintelligent discipline. The first made them almost incapable of soldierly thought and conduct; the second converted them into cringing goose-steppers. The consequences display themselves in the amazing activities of the American Legion, and in the rise of such correlative organizations as the Ku Klux Klan. It is impossible to fit any reasonable concept of the soldierly into the familiar proceedings of the Legion. Its members conduct themselves like a gang of Methodist vice-crusaders on the loose, or a Southern lynching party. They are forever discovering preposterous burglars under the national bed, and they advance to the attack, not gallantly and at fair odds, but cravenly and in overwhelming force. Some of their enterprises, to be set forth at length in the record I have mentioned, have been of almost unbelievable baseness—the mobbing of harmless Socialists, the prohibition of concerts by musicians of enemy nationality, the mutilation of cows designed for shipment abroad to feed starving children, the roughing of women, service as strike-breakers, the persecution of helpless foreigners, regardless of nationality.

During the last few months of the war, when stories of the tyrannical ill-usage of conscripts began to filter back to the United States, it was predicted that they would demand the punishment of the guilty when they got home, and that if it was not promptly forthcoming they would take it into their own hands. It was predicted, too, that they would array themselves against the excesses of Palmer, Burleson and company, and insist upon a restoration of that democratic freedom for which they had theoretically fought. But they actually did none of these things. So far as I know, not a single martinet of a lieutenant or captain has been manhandled by his late victims; the most they have done has been to appeal to Congress for revenge and damages. Nor have they thrown their influence against the mediaeval despotism which grew up at home during the war; on the contrary, they have supported it actively, and if it has lessened since 1919 the change has been wrought without their aid and in spite of their opposition. In sum, they show all the stigmata of inferior men whose natural inferiority has been made worse by oppression. Their chief organization is dominated by shrewed ex-officers who operate it to their own ends—politicians in search of jobs, Chamber of Commerce witch-hunters, and other such vermin. It seems to be wholly devoid of patriotism, courage, or sense. Nothing quite resembling it existed in the country before the war, not even in the South. There is nothing like it anywhere else on earth. It is a typical product of two years of heroic effort to arouse and capitalize the worst instincts of the mob, and it symbolizes very dramatically the ill effects of that effort upon the general American character.

Would men as degraded in gallantry and honor, so completely purged of the military virtues, so submerged in baseness of spirit—would such pitiful caricatures of soldiers offer the necessary resistance to a public enemy who was equal, or perhaps superior in men and resouces, and who came on with confidence, daring and resolution—say England supported by Germany as *Kriegslieferant* [war supplier] and with her inevitable swarms of continental allies, or Japan with the Asiatic hordes behind her? Against the best opinion of the chataugquas, of Congress and of the patriotic press I presume to doubt it. It seems to me quite certain, indeed, that an American army fairly representing the American people, if it ever meets another army of anything remotely resembling like strength, will be defeated, and that defeat will be indistinguishable from rout. I believe that, at any odds less than two to one, even the exhausted German army of 1918 would have defeated it, and in this view, I think, I am joined by many men whose military judgment is far better than mine—particularly by many French officers. The changes in the American character since the Civil War, due partly to the wearing out of the old Anglo-Saxon stock, inferior to begin with, and partly to the infusion of the worst elements of other stocks, have surely not made for the fostering of military virtues. The old cool head is gone, and the old dogged way with difficulties. The typical American of to-day has lost all the love of liberty that his forefathers had, and all their distrust of emotion, and pride in self-reliance. He is led no longer by Davy Crockets; he is led by cheer leaders, press agents, word-mongers, up-lifters. I do not believe that such a faint-hearted and inflammatory fellow, shoved into a war demanding every resource of courage, ingenuity and pertinacity, would give a good account of himself. He is fit for lynching-bees and heretic-hunts, but he is not fit for tight corners and desperate odds.

Nevertheless, his docility and pusillanimity may be overestimated, and sometimes I think that they are overestimated by his present masters. They assume that there is absolutely no limit to his capacity for being put upon and knocked about—that he will submit to any invasion of his freedom and dignity, however outrageous, so long as it is depicted in melodious terms. He permitted the late war to be "sold" to him by the methods of the grind-shop auctioneer. He submitted to conscription without any of the resistance shown by his brother democrats of Canada and Australia. He got no further than academic protests against the brutal usage he had to face in the army. He came home and found Prohibition foisted on him, and contented himself with a few feeble objurgations. He is a pliant slave of capitalism, and ever ready to help it put down fellow-slaves who venture to revolt. But this very weakness, this very credulity and poverty of spirit, on some easily conceivable to-morrow, may convert him into a rebel of a peculiarly insane kind, and so beset the Republic from within with difficulties quite as formidable as those which threaten to afflict it from without. What Mr. James N. Wood calls the corsair of democracy—that is, the professional mob-master, the merchant of delusions, the pumper-up of popular fears and rages—is still content to work for capitalism, and capitalism knows how to reward him to his taste. He is the eloquent statesman, the patriotic editor, the fount of inspiration, the prancing milch-cow of optimism. He becomes public leader, Governor, Senator, President. He is Billy Sunday, Cyrus K. Curtis, Dr. Frank Crane, Charles E. Hughes, Taft, Wilson, Cal Coolidge, General Wood, Harding. His, perhaps, is the best of trades under democracy—but it has its temptations! Let us try to picture a master corsair, thoroughly adept at pulling the mob nose, who suddenly bethought himself of that Pepin the Short who found himself mayor of the palace and made himself King of the Franks. There were lightnings along that horizon in the days of Roosevelt; there were thunder growls when Bryan emerged from the Nebraska steppes. On some great day of fate, as yet unrevealed by the gods, such a professor of the central democratic science may throw off his employers and set up a business for himself. When that day comes there will be plenty of excuse of black type on the front pages of the newspapers.

I incline to think that military disaster will give him his inspiration and his opportunity—that he will take the form, so dear to democracies, of a man on horseback. The chances are bad to-day simply because the mob is relatively comfortable—because capitalism has been able to give it relative ease and plenty of food in return for docility. Genuine poverty is very rare in the United States, and actual hardship is almost unknown. There are times when the proletariat is short of phonograph records, silk shirts and movie tickets, but there are very few times when it is short of nourishment. Even during the most severe business depression, with hundreds of thousands out of work, most of these apparent sufferers, if they are willing, are able to get livings outside their trades. The cities may be choked with idle men, but the country is nearly always short of labor. And if all other resources fail, there are always public agencies to feed the hungry: capitalism is careful to keep them from despair. No American knows what it means to live as millions of Europeans lived during the war and have lived, in some places, since: with the loaves of the baker reduced to half size and no meat at all in their meatshop. But the time may come and it may not be far off. A national military disaster would disorganize all industry in the United States, already sufficiently wasteful and chaotic, and introduce the American people, for the first time in their history, to genuine want—and capital would be unable to relieve them. The day of such disaster will bring the savior foreordained. The slaves will follow him, their eyes fixed ecstatically upon the newest New Jerusalem. Men bred to respond automatically to shibboleths will respond to this worst and most insane one. Bolshevism, said General Foch, is a disease of defeated nations.

But do not misunderstand me: I predict no revolution in the grand manner, no melodramatic collapse of capitalism, no repetition of what has gone on in Russia. The American proletarian is not brave and romantic enough for that; to do him simple justice, he is not silly enough. Capitalism, in the long run, will win in the United States, if only for the reason that every American hopes to be a capitalist before he dies. Its roots go down to the deepest, darkest levels of the national soil; in all its characters, and particularly in its antipathy to the dreams of man, it is thoroughly American. To-day it seems to be immovably secure, given continued peace and plenty, and not all the demagogues in the land, consecrating themselves desperately to the one holy purpose, could shake it. Only a cataclysm will ever do that. But is a cataclysm conceivable? Isn't the United States the richest nation ever heard of in history, and isn't it a fact that modern wars are won by money? It is not a fact. Wars are won to-day, as in Napoleon's day, by the largest battalions, and largest battalions, in the next great struggle, may not be on the side of the Republic. The usurious profits it wrung from the last war are as tempting as negotiable securities hung on the wash-line, as pre-Prohibition Scotch stored in open cellars. Its knavish ways with friends and foes alike have left it only foes. It is plunging ill-equipped into a competition for a living in the world that will be to the death. And the late Disarament Conference left it almost ham-strung. Before the conference it had the Pacific in its grip, and with the Pacific in its grip it might have parlayed for a fair half of the Atlantic. But when the Japs and the English had finished their operations upon the Feather Duster, Popinjay Lodge, Master-Mind Root, Vacuum Underwood, young Teddy Roosevelt and the rest of the so-willing dupes there was apparent a baleful change. The Republic is extremely insecure to-day on both fronts, and it will be more insecure to-morrow. And it has no friends.

However, as I say, I do not fear for capitalism. It will weather the storm, and no doubt it will be the stronger for it afterward. The inferior man hates it, but there is too much envy mixed with his hatred, in the land of the theoretically free, for him to want to destroy it utterly, or even to wound it incurably. He struggles against it now, but always wistfully, always with a sneaking respect. On the day of Armageddon he may attempt a more violent onslaught. But in the long run he will be beaten. In the long run the corsairs will sell him out, and hand him over to his enemy. Perhaps—who knows?—the combat may raise that enemy to genuine strength and dignity. Out of it may come the superman.

4

All the while I have been forgetting the third of my reasons for remaining so faithful a citizen of the Federation, despite all the lascivious inducements from expatriates to follow them beyond the seas, and all the surly suggestions from patriots that I succumb. It is the reason which grows out of my mediaeval but unashamed taste for the bizarre and indelicate, my congenital weakness for comedy of the grosser varieties. The United States, to my eye, is incomparably the greatest show on earth. It is a show which avoids diligently all the kinds of clowning which tire me most quickly—for example, royal ceremonials, the tedious hocus-pocus of *haut politique* [high poltics], the taking of politics seriously—and lays chief stress upon the kinds which delight me unceasingly—for example, the ribald combats of demagogues, the exquisitely ingenious operations of master rogues, the pursuit of witches and heretics, the desperate struggles of inferior men to claw their way into Heaven. We have clowns in constant practice among us who are as far above the clowns of any great state as a Jack Dempsey is above a paralytic—and not a few dozen or score of them, but whole droves and herds. Human enterprises which, in all other Christian countries, are resigned despairingly to an incurable dullness—things that seem devoid of exhilirating amusement by their very nature—are here lifted to such vast heights of buffoonery that contemplating them strains the midriff almost to breaking. I cite an example: the worship of God. Everywhere else on earth it is carried on in a solemn and dispiritng manner; in England, of course, the bishops are obscene, but the average man seldom gets a fair chance to laugh at them and enjoy them. Now come home. Here we not only have bishops who are enormously more obscene than even the most gifted of the English bishops; we have also a huge force of lesser specialists in ecclesiastical mountebankery—tin-horn Loyolas, Savonarolas and Xaviers of a hundred fantastic rites, each performing untiringly and each full of a grotesque and illimitable whimsicality. Every American town, however small, has one of its own: a holy clerk with so fine a talent for introducing the arts of jazz into the salvation of the damned that his performance takes on all the gaudiness of a four-ring circus, and the bald announcement that he will raid Hell on such and such a night is enough to empty all the town blind-pigs and bordellos and pack his sanctuary to the doors. And to aid him and inspire him there are traveling experts to whom he stands in the relation

of a wart to the Matterhorn—stupendous masters of theological imbecility, contrivers of doctrines utterly preposterous, heirs to the Joseph Smith,
Mother Eddy and John Alexander Dowie tradition—Bryan, Sunday, and
their like. These are the eminences of the American Sacred College. I delight in them. Their proceedings make me a happier American.

Turn now to politics. Consider, for example a campaign for the Presidency. Would it be possible to imagine anything more uproariously idiotic—a deafening, nerve-wracking battle to the death between Tweedle-
dum and Tweedledee, Harlequin and Sganarell, Gobbo and Dr. Cook—the
unspeakable, with fearful snorts, gradually swallowing the inconceivable?
I defy any one to match it elsewhere on this earth. In other lands, at
worst, there are at least intelligible issues, coherent ideas, salient personalities. Somebody says something, and somebody replies. But what did
Harding say in 1920, and what did Cox reply? Who was Harding, anyhow,
and who was Cox? Here, having perfected democracy, we lift the whole
combat to symbolism, to transcendentalism, to metaphysics. Here we had
a pair of palpably tin cannon with blank cartridges charged with talcum
powder, and so let fly. Here one may howl over the show without any uneasy reminder that it is serious, and that some one may be hurt. I hold that
this elevation of politics to the plane of undiluted comedy is peculiarly
American, that nowhere else on this disreputable ball has the art of the
sham-battle been developed to such fineness. Two experiences are in point.
During the Harding-Cox combat of bladders an article of mine, dealing
with some of its more melodramatic phases, was translated into German
and reprinted by a Berlin paper. At the head of it the editor was careful to
insert a preface explaining to his readers, but recently delivered to democracy, that such contests were not taken seriously by intelligent Americans,
and warning them solemnly against getting into sweats over politics. At
about the same time I had dinner with an Englishman. From cocktails to
bromo seltzer he bewailed the political lassitude of the English populace—
its growing indifference to the whole partisan harlequinade. Here were two
typical foreign attitudes: the Germans were in danger of making politics
too harsh and implacable, and the English were in danger of forgetting
politics altogether. Both attitudes, it must be plain, make for bad shows.
Observing a German campaign, one is uncomfortably harassed and stirred
up; observing an English campaign (at least in times of peace), one falls
asleep. In the United States, the thing is done better. Here politics is purged
of all menace, all sinister quality, all genuine significance, and stuffed with
such gorgeous humors, such inordinate farce that one comes to the end of

a campaign with one's ribs loose, and ready for *King Lear,* or a hanging, or a course of medical journals.

But feeling better for the laugh, *Ridi si sapis* [laugh, if you are wise], said Martial. Mirth is necessary to wisdom, to comfort, above all, to happiness. Well, here is the land of mirth, as Germany is the land of metaphysics and France is the land of fornication. Here the buffoonery never stops. What could be more delightful than the endless struggle of the Puritan to make the joy of the minority unlawful and impossible? The effort is itself a greater joy to one standing on the side-lines than any or all of the carnal joys that it combats. Always, when I contemplate an uplifter at his hopeless business, I recall a scene in an old-time burlesque show, witnessed for hire, in my days as a drama critic. A chorus girl executed a fall upon the stage, and Rudolph Krausemeyer, the Swiss comedian, rushed to her aid. As he stooped painfully to succor her, Irving Rabinovitz, the Zionist comedian, fetched him a fearful clout across the cofferdam with a slap-stick. So the uplifter, the soul-saver, the Americanizer, striving to make the Republic fit for the Y.M.C.A. secretaries. He is the eternal American ever moved by the best of intentions, ever running *a la* Krausemeyer to the rescue of virtue, and ever getting his pantaloons fanned by the Devil. I am naturally sinful, and such spectacles caress me. If the slap-stick were a sash-weight the show would be cruel, and I'd probably complain to the *Polizei.* As it is, I know that the uplifter is not really hurt, but simply shocked. The blow, in fact, does him good, for it helps to get him into Heaven, as exegetes prove from Matthew v, 11: ["Blessed are you when people insult you, persecute you and falsely say all kinds of evil against you because of me."] and so on. As for me, it makes me a more contented man, and hence a better citizen. One man prefers the Republic because it pays better wages than Bulgaria. Another because it has laws to keep him sober and his daughter chaste. Another because the Woolworth Building is higher than the cathedral at Chartres. Another because, living here, he can read the New York *Evening Journal.* Another because there is a warrant out for him somewhere else. Me, I like it because it amuses me to my taste. I never get tired of the show. It is worth every cent it costs.

That cost, it seems to me is very moderate. Taxes in the United States are not actually high. I figure, for example, that my private share of the expense of maintaining the Hon. Mr. Harding in the White House this year will work out to less that 80 cents. Try to think of better sport for the money: in New York it has been estimated that it costs $8 to get comfortably tight, and $17.50, on an average, to pinch a girl's arm. The United States Senate will cost me perhaps $11 for the year, but against that expense set the subscription price of the *Congressional Record*, about $15, which, as a journalist, I receive for nothing. For $4 less than nothing I am thus entertained as Solomon never was by his hooch dancers. Col. George Brinton McClellan Harvey costs me but 25 cents a year; I get Nicholas Murray Butler free. Finally, there is young Teddy Roosevelt, the naval expert. Teddy costs me, as I work it out, about 11 cents a year, or less than a cent a month. More, he entertains me doubly for the money, first as naval expert, and secondly as a walking *attentat* [attempt] on democracy, a devastating proof that there is nothing, after all, in that superstition. We Americans subscribe to the doctrine of human equality—and the Rooseveltii reduce it to an absurdity as brilliantly as the sons of Veit Bach. Where is your equal opportunity now? Here in this Eden of clowns, with the highest rewards of clowning theoretically open to every poor boy—here in the very citadel of democracy we found and cherish a clown *dynasty*!

(*Prejudices, Third Series*)

THE SAHARA OF THE BOZART

[*Southerners often seem perversely proud of being dumbass "just plain folks" (or at least enjoy playing the part). The reason for this could well be that the Yankees who control(led) the popular media have tended to define the South through stereotypes. And there are only two ways to respond to a stereotype: one is to reject it, and the other is to "own it" by exemplifying and exaggerating it. Many Southerners have chosen the latter.*

Mencken mocks them mercilessly here, beginning with the title: "Bozart" is Mencken's rendering of how a Southerner would pronounce "Beaux Arts."

Taking Southern stupidity as a given, Mencken details how he previously tried to explain that doltishness and its accompanying brutality: "Another time," he writes, "I published a short discourse on lynching, arguing that the sport was popular in the south because the backward culture of the region denied the populace more seemly recreations. Among such recreations I mentioned those afforded by brass bands, symphony orchestras, boxing matches, amateur athletic contests, shoot-the-chutes, roof gardens, horse races, and so on."

As was usually the case, Mencken was right. One of the last recorded lynchings was of teenaged Emmitt Till, in Mississippi in 1955. In 1961 Mississippi State was integrated, and shortly after began recruiting black football players. Black men could hardly be lynched then! Their feet were more entertaining when gaining yards on the field than when twitching while hanging from trees.]

"Alas, for the South! Her books have grown fewer—She never
was much given to literature."

In the lamented J. Gordon Coogler, author of these elegaic lines, there was the insight of a true poet. He was the last bard of Dixie, at least in the legitimate line. Down there a poet is now almost as rare as an oboe-player, a dry-point etcher or a metaphysician. It is, indeed, amazing to contemplate so vast a vacuity. One thinks of the interstellar spaces, of the colossal reaches of the now mythical ether. Nearly the whole of Europe could be lost in that stupendous region of fat farms, shoddy cities and paralyzed cerebrums: one could throw in France, Germany and Italy, and still have room for the British Isles. And yet, for all its size, all its wealth and all the "progress" it babbles of, it is almost as sterile, artistically, intellectually, culturally, as the Sahara Desert. There are single acres in Europe that house more first-rate men than all the states south of the Potomac; there are probably single square miles in America. If the whole of the late Confederacy were to be engulfed by a tidal wave tomorrow, the effect upon the civilized minority of men in the world would be but little greater than that of a flood on the Yang-tse-kiang. It would be impossible in all history to match so complete a drying up of a civilization.

I say a civilization because that is what, in the old days, the South had, despite the Baptist and Methodist barbarism that reigns down there now. More, it was a civilization of manifold excellences—perhaps the best that the Western Hemisphere has ever seen—undoubtedly the best that Those States have ever seen. Down in the middle of the last century, and even beyond, the main hatchery of ideas on this side of the water was across the Potomac bridges. The New England shopkeepers and theologians never really developed a civilization; all they ever developed was a government. They were, at their best, tawdry and tacky fellows, oafish in manner and devoid of imagination; one searches the books in vain for mention of a salient Yankee gentleman; as well look for a Welsh gentleman. But in the south there were men of delicate fancy, urbane instinct and aristocratic manner—in brief, superior men—in brief, gentry. To politics, their chief diversion, they brought active and original minds. It was there that nearly all the political theories we still cherish and suffer under came to birth. It was there that the crude dogmatism of New England was refined and humanized. It was there, above all, that some attention was given to the art of living—that life got beyond and above the state of a mere infliction and became an exhilarating experience. A certain noble spaciousness was in the ancient southern scheme of things. The Ur-Confederate had leisure. He liked to toy with ideas. He was hospitable and tolerant. He had the vague thing that we call culture.

But consider the condition of his late empire today. The picture gives one the creeps. It is as if the Civil War stamped out every last bearer of the torch, and left only a mob of peasants on the field. One thinks of Asia Minor, resigned to Armenians, Greeks and wild swine, of Poland abandoned to the Poles. In all that gargantuan paradise of the fourth-rate there is not a single picture gallery worth going into, or a single orchestra capable of playing the nine symphonies of Beethoven, or a single opera-house, or a single theater devoted to decent plays, or a single public monument (built since the war) that is worth looking at, or a single workshop devoted to the making of beautiful things. Once you have counted Robert Loveman (an Ohioan by birth) and John McClure (an Oklahoman) you will not find a single southern poet above the rank of a neighborhood rhymemaster. Once you have counted James Branch Cabell (a lingering survivor of the *ancien régime*) you will not find a single southern prose writer who can actually write. And once you have—but when you come to critics, musical composers, printers, sculptors, architects and the like, you have to give it up, for there is not even a bad one between the Potomac mud-flats and the Gulf. Nor an historian. Nor a sociologist. Nor a scientist. In all these fields, the south is an awe-inspiring blank—a brother to Portugal, Serbia and Estonia.

Consider, for example, the present estate and dignity of Virginia—in the great days indubitably the premier American state, the mother of Presidents and statesmen, the home of the first American university worthy of the name, the *arbiter elegantiarum* [judge of taste] of the western world. Well, observe Virginia to-day. It is years since a first-rate man, save only Cabell, has come out of it; it is years since an idea has come out of it. The old aristocracy went down the red gullet of war; the poor white trash are now in the saddle. Politics in Virginia are cheap, ignorant, parochial, idiotic; there is scarcely a man in office above the rank of a professional job-seeker; the political doctrine that prevails is made up of hand-me-downs from the bumpkinry of the Middle West—Byranism, Prohibition, vice crusading, all that sort of filthy claptrap; the administration of the law is turned over to professors of Puritanism and espionage; a Washington or a Jefferson, dumped there by some act of God, would be denounced as a scoundrel and jailed overnight. Elegance, *esprit*, Culture? Virginia has no art, no literature, no philosophy, no mind or aspiration of her own. Her education has sunk to the Baptist seminary level; not a single contribution to human knowledge has come out of her colleges in twenty-five years; she spends less than half upon her common schools, *per capita*, than any northern state spends. In brief, an intellectual Gobi or Lapland. Urbanity, *politesse*, chivalry? Go to! It was in Virginia that they invented the device of searching for contraband whisky in women's underwear.... There remains, at the top, a ghost of the old aristocracy, a bit wistful and infinitely charming. But it has lost all its old leadership to fabulous monsters from the lower depths; it is submerged in an industrial plutocracy that is ignorant and ignominious. The mind of the state, as it is revealed to the nation, is pathetically naive and inconsequential. It no longer reacts with energy and elasticity to great problems. It has fallen to the bombastic trivialities of the camp-meeting and chautauqua. Its foremost exponent—if so flabby a thing may be said to be foremost—is a statesman whose name [Woodrow Wilson] is synonymous with empty words, broken pledges and false pretenses. One could no more imagine a Lee or a Washington in the Virginia of to-day than one could imagine a Huxley in Nicaragua. I chose the Old Dominion, not because I disdain it, but precisely because I esteem it. It is, by long odds, the most civilized of the southern states, now as always. It has sent a host of creditable sons northward; the stream kept running into our own times. Virginians, even the worst of them, show the effects of a great tradition. They hold themselves above other southerners, and with sound pretension. If one turns to such a commonwealth as Georgia the picture becomes far darker. There the liberated lower order of whites have borrowed the worst commercial bounderism of the Yankee and superimposed it upon a culture that, at bottom, is but little removed from savagery. Georgia is at once the home of the cotton-mill sweater and of the most noisy and vapid sort of chamber of commerce, of the Methodist parson turned Savonarola and of the lynching bee. A self-respecting European, going there to live, would not only find intellectual stimulation utterly lacking; he would actually feel a certain insecurity, as if the scene were the Balkans or the China Coast. The Leo Frank affair [antisemitic lynching] was no isolated phenomenon. It fitted into its frame very snugly. It was a natural expression of Georgian notions of truth and justice. There is a state with more than half the area of Italy and more population than either Denmark or Norway, and yet in thirty years it has not produced a single idea. Once upon a time a Georgian printed a couple of books that attracted notice, but immediately it turned out that he [Joel Chandler Harris, "author" of the Uncle Remus stories] was little more than an amanuensis for the local blacks—that his works were really the products, not of white Georgia, but of black Georgia. Writing afterward as a white man, he swiftly subsided into the fifth rank. And he is not only the glory of the literature of Georgia; he is, almost literally, the whole of the literature of Georgia—nay of the entire art of Georgia.

Virginia is the best of the south to-day, and Georgia is perhaps the worst. The one is simply senile; the other is crass, gross, vulgar and obnoxious. Between lies a vast plain of mediocrity, stupidity, lethargy, almost of dead silence. In the north, of course, there is also grossness, crassness, vulgarity. The north, in its way, is also stupid and obnoxious. But nowhere in the north is there such complete sterility, so depressing a lack of all civilized gesture and aspiration. One would find it difficult to unearth a second-rate-city between the Ohio and the Pacific that isn't struggling to establish an orchestra, or setting up a little theatre, or going in for an art gallery, or making some other effort to get into touch with civilization. These efforts often fail, and sometimes they succeed rather absurdly, but under them there is at least an impulse that deserves respect, and that is the impulse to seek beauty and to experiment with ideas, and so to give the life of every day a certain dignity and purpose. You will find no such impulse in the south. There are no committees down there cadging subscriptions for orchestras; if a string quartet is ever heard there, the news of it has never come out; an opera troupe, when it roves the land, is a nine days wonder. The little theater movement has swept the whole country, enormously augmenting the public interest in sound plays, giving new dramatists their chance, forcing reforms upon the commercial theater. Everywhere else the wave rolls high—but along the line of the Potomac it breaks upon a rockbound shore. There is no little theater beyond. There is no gallery of pictures. No artist ever gives exhibitions. No one talks of such things. No one seems to be interested in such things.

As for the cause of this unanimous torpor and doltishness, this curious and almost pathological estrangement from everything that makes for a civilized culture, I have hinted at it already, and now state it again. The south has simply been drained of all its best blood. The vast blood-letting of the Civil War half exterminated and wholly paralyzed the old aristocracy, and so left the land to the harsh mercies of the poor white trash, now its masters. The war, of course, was not a complete massacre. It spared a decent number of first-rate southerners—perhaps even some of the best. Moreover, other countries, notably France and Germany, have survived far more staggering butcheries, and even showed marked progress thereafter. But the war not only cost a great many valuable lives; it also brought bankruptcy, demoralization and despair in its train—and so the majority of the first-rate southerners that were left, broken in spirit and unable to live under the new dispensation, cleared out. A few went to South America, to Egypt, to the Far East. More came north. A southerner of good blood almost always does well in the north. He finds, even in the big cities, surroundings fit for a man of condition. His peculiar qualities have a high social value, and are esteemed. He is welcomed by the codfish aristocracy as one palpably superior. But in the south he throws up his hands. It is impossible for him to stoop to the common level. He cannot brawl in politics with the grandsons of his grandfather's tenants. He is unable to share their fierce jealousy of the emerging black—the cornerstone of all their public thinking. He is anesthetic to their theological and political enthusiasms. He finds himself an alien at their feasts of soul. And so he withdraws into his tower, and is heard of no more. Cabell is almost a perfect example. His eyes, for years, were turned toward the past; he became a professor of the grotesque genealogizing that decaying aristocracies affect; it was only by a sort of accident that he discovered himself to be an artist. The south is unaware of the fact to this day; it regards Woodrow Wilson and Col. John Temple Graves as much finer stylists, and Frank L. Stanton as an infinitely greater poet. If it has heard, which I doubt, that Cabell has been hoofed by the Comstocks, it unquestionably views that assault as a deserved rebuke to a fellow who indulges a lewd passion for fancy writing, and is a covert enemy to the Only True Christianity.

What is needed down there, before the vexatious public problems of the region may be intelligently approached, is a survey of the population by competent ethnologists and anthropologists. The immigrants of the north have been studied at great length, and any one who is interested may now apply to the Bureau of Ethnology for elaborate data as to their racial strains, their stature and cranial indices, their relative capacity for education, and the changes that they undergo under American *Kultur*. But the older stocks of the south, and particularly the emancipated and dominant poor white trash, have never been investigated scientifically, and most of the current generalizations about them are probably wrong. For example, the generalization that they are purely Anglo-Saxon in blood. This I doubt very seriously. The chief strain down there, I believe, is Celtic rather than Saxon, particularly in the hill country. French blood, too, shows itself here and there, and so does Spanish, and so does German. The last named entered from the southward, by way of the limestone belt just east of the Alleghenies. Again, it is very likely that in some parts of the south a good many of the plebeian whites have more than a trace of negro blood. Interbreeding under concubinage produced some very light half-breeds at an early day, and no doubt appreciable numbers of them went over into the white race by the simple process of changing their abode. Not long ago I read a curious article by an intelligent negro, in which he stated that it is easy to pass as white in the south on account of the fact that large numbers of southerners accepted as white have distinctly negroid features. Thus it becomes a delicate and dangerous matter for a train conductor or a hotel-keeper to challenge a suspect. But the Celtic strain is far more obvious than any of these others. It not only makes itself visible in physical stigmata—e.g., leanness and dark coloring—but also in mental traits. For example, the religious thought of the south is almost precisely identical with the religious thought of Wales. There is the same naive belief in an anthropomorphic Creator but little removed, in manner and desire, from an evangelical bishop; there is the same submission to an ignorant and impudent sacerdotal tyranny, and there is the same sharp contrast between doctrinal orthodoxy and private ethics. Read Caradoc Evans' ironical picture of the Welsh Wesleyans in *My Neighbors*, and you will be instantly reminded of the Georgia and Carolina Methodists. The most booming sort of piety, in the south, is not incompatible with the theory that lynching is a benign institution. Two generations ago it was not incompatible with an ardent belief in slavery.

It is highly probable that some of the worst blood of western Europe flows in the veins of the southern poor whites, now poor no longer. The original strains, according to every honest historian, were extremely corrupt. Philip Alexander Bruce (a Virginian of the old gentry) says in his *Industrial History of Virginia in the Seventeenth Century* that the first native-born generation was largely illegitimate. "One of the most common offenses against morality committed in the lower ranks of life in Virginia during the seventeenth century," he says, "was bastardy." The mothers of these bastards, he continues, were chiefly indentured servants, and "had belonged to the lowest class in their native country." Fanny Kemble Butler, writing of the Georgia poor whites of a century later, described them as "the most degraded race of human beings claiming an Anglo-Saxon origin that can be found on the face of the earth—filthy, lazy, ignorant, brutal, proud, penniless savages." The Sunday-school and the chautauqua, of course, have appreciably mellowed the descendants of these "savages," and their economic progress and rise to political power have done perhaps even more, but the marks of their origin are still unpleasantly plentiful. Every now and then they produce a political leader who puts their secret notions of the true, the good and the beautiful into plain words, to the amazement and scandal of the rest of the country. That amazement is turned into downright incredulity when news comes that his platform got him into high office, and that he is trying to execute it.

In the great days of the south the line between the gentry and the poor whites was very sharply drawn. There was absolutely no intermarriage. So far as I know there is not a single instance in history of southerner of the upper class marrying one of the bondswomen described by Mr. Bruce. In other societies characterized by class distinctions of that sort it is common for the lower class to be improved by extra-legal crosses. That is to say, the men of the upper class take women of the lower class as mistresses, and out of such unions spring the extraordinary plebeians who rise sharply from the common level, and so propagate the delusion that all other plebeians would do the same thing if they had the chance—in brief, the delusion that class distinctions are merely economic and conventional, and not congenital and genuine. But in the south the men of the upper classes sought their mistresses among the blacks, and after a few generations there was so much white blood in the black women that they were considerably more attractive than the unhealthy and bedraggled women of the poor whites. A southerner of good family once told me in all seriousness that he had reached his majority before it ever occurred to him that a white woman might make quite as agreeable a mistress as the octaroons of his jejune fancy. If the thing has changed of late, it is not the fault of the southern white man, but of the southern mulatto women. The sightly yellow girls of the region, with improving economic opportunities, have gained self-respect, and so they are no longer as willing to enter into concubinage as the grand-dames were.

As a result of this preference of the southern gentry for mulatto mistresses there was created a series of mixed strains containing the best white blood of the south, and perhaps of the whole country. As another result the poor whites went unfertilized from above, and so missed the improvement that so constantly shows itself in the peasant stocks of other countries. It is a commonplace that nearly all negroes who rise above the general are of mixed blood, usually with the white predominating. I know a great many negroes, and it would be hard for me to think of an exception. What is too often forgotten is that this white blood is not the blood of the poor whites but that of the old gentry. The mulatto girls of the early days despised the poor whites as creatures distinctly inferior to negroes, and it was thus almost unheard of for such a girl to enter into relations with a man of that submerged class. This aversion was based upon a sound instinct. The southern mulatto of today is proof of it. Like all other half-breeds he is an unhappy man, with disquieting tendencies toward anti-social habits of thought, but he is intrinsically a better animal than the pure-blooded descendant of the old poor whites, and he not infrequently demonstrates it. It is not by accident that the negroes are making faster progress, economically and culturally, than the masses of the whites. It is not by accident that the only visible aesthetic activity in the south is wholly in their hands. No southern composer has ever written music so good as that of half a dozen white-black composers who might be named. Even in politics, the negro reveals a curious superiority. Despite the fact that the race question has been the main political concern of the southern whites for two generations, to the practical exclusion of everything else, they have contributed nothing to its discussion that has impressed the rest of the world so deeply and so favorably as three or four books by southern negroes.

Entering upon such themes, of course, one must resign one's self to a vast misunderstanding and abuse. The south has not only lost its old capacity for producing ideas, it has also taken on the worst intolerance of ignorance and stupidity. Its prevailing mental attitude for several decades past has been that of its own hedge ecclesiastics. All who dissent from its orthodox doctrines are scoundrels. All who presume to discuss its ways realistically are damned. I have had, in my day, several experiences in point. Once, after I had published an article on some phase of the eternal race question, a leading southern newspaper replied by printing a column of denunciation of my father, then dead nearly twenty years—a philippic placarding him as an ignorant foreigner of dubious origin, inhabiting "the Baltimore ghetto" and speaking a dialect recalling that of Weber & Fields—two thousand words of incandescent nonsense, utterly false and beside the point, but exactly meeting the latter-day southern notion of effective controversy. Another time, I published a short discourse on lynching, arguing that the sport was popular in the south because the backward culture of the region denied the populace more seemly recreations. Among such recreations I mentioned those afforded by brass bands, symphony orchestras, boxing matches, amateur athletic contests, shoot-the-chutes, roof gardens, horse races, and so on. In reply another great southern journal denounced me as a man "of wineshop temperament, brass-jewelry tastes and pornographic predilections." In other words, brass bands, in the south, are classed with brass jewelry, and both are snares of the devil? To advocate setting up symphony orchestras is pornography! Alas, when the touchy southerner attempts a greater urbanity, the result is often even worse. Some time ago a colleague of mine printed an article deploring the arrested cultural development of Georgia. In reply he received a number of protests from patriotic Georgians, and all of them solemnly listed the glories of the state. I indulge in a few specimens:

"Who has not heard of Asa G. Chandler, whose name is synonymous with Coca-Cola, a Georgia product?"

"The first Sunday-school in the world was opened in Savannah."

"Who does not recall with pleasure the writings of . . . Frank L. Stanton, Georgia's brilliant poet?"

"Georgia was the first state to organize a Boys' Corn Club in the South— Newton County, 1904."

"The first to suggest a common United Daughters of the Confederacy badge was Mrs. Raymes, of Georgia."

"The first to suggest a state historian of the United Daughters of the Confederacy was Mrs. C. Helen Plane (Macon convention, 1896)."

"The first to suggest putting to music Heber's 'From Greenland's Icy Mountains' was Mrs. F.R. Goulding of Savannah."

And so on, and so on. These proud boasts came, remember, not from obscure private persons, but from "Leading Georgians"—in one case, the state historian. Curious sidelights upon the ex-Confederate mind! Another comes from a stray copy of a negro paper. It describes an ordinance lately passed by the city council of Douglas, Ga., forbidding any trousers presser, on penalty of forfeiting a $300 bond, to engage in "pressing for both white and colored." This in a town, says the negro paper, where practically all of the white inhabitants have "their food prepared by colored hands," and "the clothes which they wear right next to their skins washed in houses where negroes live"—houses in which the clothes "remain for as long as a week at a time." But if you marvel at the absurdity, keep it dark! A casual word, and the united press of the south will be upon your trail, denouncing you bitterly as a scoundrelly Yankee, a Bolshevik Jew, an agent of the Wilhelmstrasse. . . .

Obviously, it is impossible for intelligence to flourish in such an atmosphere. Free inquiry is blocked by the idiotic certainties of ignorant men. The arts, save in the lower reaches of the gospel hymn, the phonograph and the chautauqua harangue, are all held in suspicion. The tone of public opinion is set by an upstart class but lately emerged from industrial slavery into commercial enterprise—the class of "hustling" business men, of "live wires," of commercial club luminaries, of "drive" managers, of forward-lookers and right-thinkers—in brief, of third-rate southerners inoculated with all the worst traits of the yankee sharper. One observes the curious ef-

fects of an old tradition of truculence upon a population now merely push-
ful and impudent, of an old tradition of chivalry upon a population now
quite without imagination. The old repose is gone. The old romanticism is
gone. The philistinism of the new type of town-boomer southerner is not
only indifferent to the ideals of the old south; it is positively antagonistic to
them. That philistinism regards human life, not as an agreeable adventure,
but as a mere trial of rectitude and efficiency. It is overwhelmingly utilitar-
ian and moral. It is inconceivably hollow and obnoxious. What remains of
the ancient tradition is simply a certain charming civility in private intercourse—often broken down, alas, by the hot rages of Puritanism, but still
generally visible. The southerner, at his worst, is never quite the surly cad
that the Yankee is. His sensitiveness may betray him into occasional bad
manners, but in the main he is a pleasant fellow—hospitable, polite, good-
humored, even jovial. . . . But a bit absurd. . . . A bit pathetic.

(*Prejudices, Second Series*)

THE AMERICAN TRADITION

[*While it never repudiated violence, the Ku Klux Klan of the 1920s should not be confused with the terrorist organizations of the Reconstruction and Civil Rights eras. The 1920s Klan was more of an expensive social club for white Protestants, especially in the South and Midwest. From 1920 to 1925, under the leadership of the Texan D.C. Stephenson, the Indiana Klan grew to the point where about one out of every three white males were members. In 1923, in Kokomo, Indiana after a three-day rally over the Fourth of July weekend that drew about 100,000 attendees (and where a fortune was made selling Klan merchandise), Stephenson took the title of Grand Dragon.*

In the following year, the Klan's pick, Edward L. Jackson, won the gubernatorial election. Not long after, Stephenson, apparently believing himself above the law, snagged a pretty young secretary, Madge Oberholtzer, and took her on a train trip to Chicago. Stephenson, a sadist, enjoyed biting off large chunks of flesh while raping his victims, and his kidnapped secretary became one of those victims. She tried to kill herself and, rather than get her medical help, Stephenson and his thugs rushed her back to her parents. The young woman lived a few days, just long enough to give a testimony, and then died. Stephenson was convicted of rape and murder in 1925, and his life sentence essentially ended the Klan's Midwest power.

The way in which the Klan dissolved in Indiana says something about the organization in the 1920s. Members considered themselves a moral force, and although they used intimidation as a common tactic, no murders and almost no violent acts can be directly attributed to the Klan of the 1920s. (There were however, over 300 lynchings in that decade in the U.S., and Klan members undoubtedly participated in a large number of those horrific murders.)

Klan members in the 1920s were white Protestants who feared Catholicism most, but also considered integration and immigration serious threats. This Klan is still present in the form of the Republican Party, only the Protestants and Catholics in it now cooperate in attempts to impose state control over every American woman's body.

Mencken's essay, "The American Tradition," provides a healthy antidote to this type of toxic, authoritarian "Americanism." Time permitting, it should be read aloud in classrooms every morning following the Pledge of Allegiance.]

1

Ever since Dr. William Crary Brownell, de l'Académie Américaine, published his little volume, *Standards*, in 1917, a vast hullabaloo has been going on among the native white, Protestant *Gelehrte* [scholars] of the Republic, particularly in the great open spaces of the South and Middle West, in favor what they call the American tradition in letters. Perhaps I libel Brownell, a worthy if somewhat gummy man, by hinting that he started this whooping; it may be that its actual generator was George Creel, the Rev. Dr. Newell Dwight Hillis, the Hon. James M. Beck, the Hon. A. Mitchell Palmer or some other such master-mind of that patriotic and intelligent era. Whatever its parentage, it was at least born in the holiest of wedlock, and to the applause of all right-thinking men; and if I now presume to pull its ear I surely hope that no one will suspect that I thereby question its legitimacy. It is, in fact, absolutely and irrefragably from snout to *os calcis* [heel], not only in outward seeming and demeanor, but also in inner essence, and anyone who flouts it also flouts everything that is most sacred in the spirit of Americanism. To that business I herewith address myself briefly.

What, then, is the spirit of Americanism? I precipitate it conveniently into the doctrine that the way to ascertain the truth about anything, whether in the realms of exact knowledge, in the purple zone of the fine arts or in the empyrean regions of metaphysics, is to take a vote upon it, and that the way to propagate that truth, once it has been ascertained and proclaimed by lawful authority, is with a club. This doctrine, it seems to me, explains almost everything that is indubitably American, and particularly everything American that is most puzzling to men of older and less inspired cultures, from American politics to American learning, and from the lush and unprecedented American code of morals to the amazing and almost fabulous American code of honor. At one end it explains the archetypical buffooneries of the Ku Klux Klan, the American Legion, the Anti-Saloon League, the Department of Justice and all other such great engines of cultural propaganda, and at the other end it explains the amusing theory that the limits of the nation's aesthetic adventures are to be fixed by a vague and self-appointed camorra of rustic Ph.D.'s, and that any artist, indigenous or imported, who dares to pass them is not only a sinner against the beautiful but also a traitor to the flag, and that he ought, shall and must be throttled by the secular arm. Patriotism thus gathers in aesthetics and gives it suck, as it has already given suck to ethics. There are artists who are criminal and must be put down, as anarchists and polygamists are put down. The fancies of the poet in his velvet coat, the vast soarings and grapplings of the metaphysician in his damp cell, the writhings of the logician chained to his rock, become either right or wrong, and whatever is right in them is American and whatever is wrong is not American.

How far this last notion goes under the Constitution is best shown, not in the relatively pianissimo pronunciamentoes of such suave and cautious dons as Brownell, who are themselves often sadly polluted by foreign ideas, despite their heroic struggle to remember Valley Forge and San Juan Hill, but in the far more frank and passionate bulls of their followers in the seminaries of the cow States, where every male of *Homo sapiens* has copious *vibrisse* [hair] on his chest and Nordic blue eyes in his head, and is a red-blooded, go-getting, up-and-coming he-man. I introduce at once a perfect specimen, Doughty of Texas—a savant but little known in the diabetic East, but for long a favorite expert in comparative morals in the university at Austin—not a professor, alas, for he lacks the Ph.D., but *amicus curiae* [friend of the court] to the other professors, as befits his trade of jurisconsult, and a frequent author of critical papers. Doughty has passion but he also has diligence: a combination not too common. Unlike the lean and slippered Beers of Yale, who once boasted that he had read none of the books he was denouncing, Doughty is at pains to look into even the most subversive, as a dutiful *Censor Librorum* looks into even *Science and Health* and the works of Dr. Marie C. Stopes. Some time ago, determined to get at and expose the worst, he plowed magnificently through a whole library—through all the new poetry from Carl Sandberg to *The Spoon River Anthology*, and all the new novels from Dreiser to Waldo Frank, and all the vast mass of immoral criticism accompanying them, from that in the *Dial* and the *Nation* to that in the *Little Review, S4N* and the *Chicago Literary Times.* "For many months now," he reported, when he emerged at last, "there has passed before me the whole ghastly array. . . . I have read the 'books'; the 'fiction' and the 'verse'; the 'drama,' the 'articles' and the 'essays'; the 'sketches' and the 'criticisms,' and whatever else is squeaked and gibbered by these unburied and not-to-be-handled dead. . . . It is this unnamable by-product of congenital deficiency, perverted dissipation and adulterated narcotics . . . which I refer to as 'modern [American] literature.'"

And what is the Texas Taine's verdict upon modern American literature? The verdict, in brief, of all other right-thinking, forward-looking he-men, North, East, South, West—the verdict of every American who truly loves the flag, and knows congenitally what is right and what is wrong. He

not only finds that it is, in itself, nothing but "swept-up rottenness and garbage—the dilute sewage of the sordid mental slums of New York and Chicago"; he also finds that the ladies and gentlemen who comprise it are no
more than "a horde of chancre-laden rats," they constitute a "devil's crew of
perverted drug-addicts," that they are engaged unanimously upon a "flabby and feeble assault . . . upon that ancient decency that for unnumbered
generations of the white Northern races of mankind, at least, has grown
and strengthened as a seed cast upon kindly soil," and, finally, that "no one
of the 'writers' of this unhappy array was in the service of the United States
in the Great War"—in brief, that the whole movement is no more than a
foul conspiracy to tear down the flag, uproot the Republic and exterminate
the Nordic Blond, and that, in consequence, it is the duty of every American who is a member "of a white Nordic race, save the Teutonic," to come
sliding down the pole, grab the tarpot and go galloping to the alarm. So
concluding and stating in rich Texas phrases, the Doughty proceeds to read
specifically a typical book by one of these immigrant foes to "the heritage
of American and English men." . . . The one he chooses is "Jurgen," by James
Branch Cabell, of Virginia!

2

This long-horned policeman of letters, I admit, is more exuberant than
most. There are no soothing elms on the campus at Austin; instead there
is only the cindered plaza de toros of the Ku Klux Klan. Patriotism, down
there, runs wilder than elsewhere. Men have large hands and loud voices.
The sight of the flag makes their blood leap and boil; when it is affronted
they cannot control themselves. Nevertheless, the doctrine thus stated in
harsh terms by the dreadful Doughty, is, in its essence, precisely the doctrine of his more urbane colleagues—of Brownell de l' Académie Américaine, of Branders Matthews de l' Académie Américaine, of Sherman de
Académie Américaine, of Erskine de l'Institut Nacional, of Boynton of
old Beers, of all the rest. It is a doctrine, as I have said, that is thoroughly
American—as American, indeed, as Prohibition, correspondence schools,
the Knights of Pythias or chewing gum. But by the same token it is a doctrine that has no more fundamental sense or dignity than the politics of a
Coolidge or the theology of a Billy Sunday. It is the product of men who,
drilled beyond their capacity for taking in ideas and harrowed from infancy by harsh and unyielding concepts of duty, have borrowed the patriotic

philosophy of suburban pastors and country schoolmarms, and now seek to apply it to the consideration of phenomena that are essentially beyond their comprehension, as honor is beyond the comprehension of a politician. It is rural Fundamentalism in the black gown and disarming whiskers of *Wissenschaft* [mathematical science]; its inevitable fruit is what Ernest Boyd has aptly called Ku Klux Kriticism.

The simple truth, of course, is that the standards and traditions these sublimated Prohibition enforcement officers argue for so eloquently have no actual existence in the first-line literature of the American people—that what they demand is not a lofty fidelity of a genuine ideal, but only an artificial and absurd subservience to notions that were regarded with contempt by every American of the civilized minority even when they prevailed. In other words, what they argue for is not a tradition that would take in Poe, Hawthorne, Emerson, Whitman and Mark Twain, but a tradition that would pass over all these men to enhance Cooper, Bryant, Donald G. Mitchell, N.P. Willis, J.G. Holland, Charles Dudley Warner, Mrs. Sigourney and the Sweet Singer of Michigan. Even Longellow, I daresay, must be left out, for didn't he drink of green and terrible waters in Paris as a youth and didn't Poe accuse him of stealing from the Spanish and the German? Certainly even Longfellow, to go back to Doughty's interdict, "simmered in the devil's cauldron of Central Europe" and was "spewed out of Italy and France." Could Bryant himself qualify? Didn't he trifle with strange tongues and admire enemy aliens? And what of Lowell? His Dante studies surely had a sinister smack; one can't imagine a Texas Grand Goblin approving them. Bayard Taylor I refrain from mentioning at all. His translation of *Faust* came to a just judgment at last when it was hurled from the shelves of every American university patronized by the issue of 100 per cent Americans. Its incineration on a hundred far-flung campuses, indeed, was the second great patriotic event of the *annus mirabilis* [miracle year] which saw the launching of Brownell's *Standards* and the entrance of the Ku Klux Klan into literary criticism.

How little the patriot-pedagogues know of the veriest elements of American literary history was shown very amusingly some time ago when one of them, a specialist in the Emerson tradition, got himself into a lather denouncing some Greenwich Village Brandes for arguing that beauty was independent of morals and its own sufficient justification—only to be confronted by the disconcerting fact that Emerson himself had argued the same thing. Can it be that even pedagogues are unaware that Emerson came to fame by advocating a general deliverance from the stupid and flabby tradition his name is now evoked to support, that his whole system of ideas was an unqualified protest against hampering traditions of every sort, that if he were alive today he would not be with the professors but unalterably against them? And Emerson was surely not alone. Go through the list of genuinely first-rate men: Poe, Hawthorne, Whitman, Mark Twain. One and all they stood outside the so-called tradition of their time; one and all they remained outside the tradition that pedants try so vainly to impose upon a literature in active being today. Poe's poems and tales not only seemed strange to the respectable dolts of his time; they seemed downright horrible. His criticism, which tells us even more about him, was still worse: it impinged upon such dull fellows as Griswold exactly as *Jennie Gerhardt* impinged upon the appalled tutors in the alfalfa colleges. And what of Hawthorne? Hawthorne's onslaught upon the Puritan ethic was the most formidable and effective ever delivered, save only Emerson's. And Whitman? Whitman so staggered the professors that it is only within the last few years that they have begun to teach him at all; those who flourished in 1870 avoided all mention of him as carefully as their successors today avoid mention of Dreiser or Cabell. And Mark Twain? I put a professor on the stand, to wit, my Christian friend, Phelps of Yale. Go to Phelps' "Essays on Modern Novelists," and you will find a long and humorous account of the efforts of unintelligent pedagogues to read Mark out of the national letters altogether—and go to Van Wyck Brooks' *The Ordeal of Mark Twain* and you will discover what great damage that imbecility did to the man himself. Phelps printed his book in 1910. It was the first book by a doctor of beautiful letters to admit categorically that Mark was an artist at all! All the other professors, even in 1910, were still teaching that Washington Irving was a great humorist and Mark a mere clown, just as they are teaching now that the criticism of Howells and Lowell was superior to the criticism of Huneker, and Henry van Dyke is a great artist and Cabell a bad one.

Historically, there is thus nothing but folly and ignorance in all the current prattle about a restoration of ancient American tradition. The ancient American tradition, in so far as it was vital and productive and civilized, was obviously a tradition of individualism and revolt, not of herd-morality and conformity. If one argues otherwise, one must inevitably argue that the great men of the Golden Age were not Emerson, Hawthorne, Poe and Whitman, but Cooper, Irving, Longfellow and Whittier. This nonsense, no doubt, is actually argued in the prairie seminaries; it even has its prophets, perhaps, in back-waters of the East; certainly one finds little in controversion of it in the prevailing text-books. But it remains nonsense all the same.

The fact that it has been accepted for years explains the three great disgraces of American letters: the long neglect of Whitman, Melville and Mark Twain. And the fact that it is now challenged actively—that practically all young Americans of any appreciable intelligence now rebel against it—that the most significant sign of the times, in many ways, is the open revolt of the new generation against the teaching of their elders—this fact explains the new vigor that has got into American literature, and its consequent running amok. That running amok, to be sure, is leading to excesses—but so did the running amok of Whitman lead to excesses; so did the timorous running amok of Mark Twain. In order to get the rest of *Leaves of Grass* we must somehow manage to survive *A Woman Waits for Me*; in order to get *Huckleberry Finn* we must swallow the buffooneries of *The Innocents Abroad*. In brief, we must be willing to pay a price for freedom, for no price that is ever asked for it is half the cost of doing without it.

3

It so happens that many of the men and women who have sought to exercise this freedom in our time have been of stocks other than the so-called Anglo-Saxon, either wholly or in part—that they have represented the newer stocks which threaten, not only in the fine arts but in practically all departments of human activity, including even business, to oust the Anglo-Saxon from his old hegemony. The fact, in a day of increasing racial consciousness, has greatly colored the whole controversy and made it extraordinarily bitter. The doctrine gradually set up between 1914 and 1917, and given the full force of law in the latter year, that a citizen of German blood, or suspected of German blood, stood on a plane inferior to that occupied by a citizen of British blood, and had a less valid claim to the equal protection of the Constitution and the laws—this doctrine was extended, in the post-war years of terror, to all Americans not specifically Anglo-Saxon. How seriously it has been taken in the more remote parts of the Republic is well displayed by the strophes that I have quoted from good Doughty—a gentleman who seems quite as content to take his anthropology from Madison Grant and Gertrude Atherton as he is to take his manners from the cattle-herders of his native steppes. Even more ludicrous attempts to set up Ku Klux criteria in letters might be dredged from the writings of more urbane, and, in theory, more intelligent and civilized critics—for example, Brander Matthews. The rancorous animosity that has pursued such men as Dreiser is certainly not wholly aesthetic, or moral; it is, to a very large extent, racial. The man is obviously not an Anglo-Saxon; ergo, there is something sinister about him, and he must be put down. The more solid becomes his position as a man of letters, the more offensive he becomes to the colonial mind. His crime, indeed, is that he has made headway—that a new American tradition, differing radically from the old one that pedagogues preach, tends to grow up round him—that in European eyes, and even in English eyes, he becomes more typical of America than any of the literary Knights of Pythias who are pitted against him. It thus becomes a matter of self-preservation to dispose of him, and when it turns out to be difficult to do so by logical means then there is a quick and easy recourse to evangelistic means.

The effects of this holy war, alas, have differed greatly from those intended. Far from alarming and stampeding the non-Anglo-Saxons upon whom it has been waged, it has actually forced them, despite their differences into a certain common action, and so made them far more formidable that they were when it began. And far from establishing any superiority in the Anglo-Saxon, it has only spread the suspicion that, for all his pretensions, he must be a very inferior fellow at bottom, else he would not be so eager to call in the mob to help him in a purely literary feud. As one who has stood on the battlements for years, and smelt the powder of every salvo, I can only report that I have come to believe in this inferiority thoroughly, and that it seems to me to be most obvious in those who most vociferously uphold the so-called American tradition. They are, in the main, extremely stupid men, and their onslaughts are seldom supported by any formidable weight of metal. What they ask the rest of us to do, in brief, is simply to come down voluntarily and irrationally to their own cultural level—the level of a class that easily dominated the country when it was a series of frontier settlements, but that has gradually lost leadership as civilization has crept in. The rest of us naturally refuse, they thereupon try to make acquiescence a patriotic matter, and to alarm the refractory with all sorts of fantastic penalties. But it must be obvious that they fail far more often than they succeed—and their failure is a melancholy proof of their intrinsic inferiority. The current of thought in the United States, at least among the relatively civilized minority, is not actually toward the abject colonialism that they advocate; it is against that colonialism. We are further from sweetness and light today than we ever were before, and we are further from cultural slavery to the harassed and care-worn Motherland. With overwhelming numbers on their side, and every form of external authority, and all the prevailing shibboleths, the spokesmen of Anglo-Saxon domination come to grief every time they tackle the minority within the minority, and at no time do they come to grief more dramatically than when they prepare for battle, in the traditional Anglo-Saxon manner, by first tying their opponents' hands.

When I speak of Anglo-Saxons, of course, I speak inexactly and in the common phrase. Even within the bounds of that phrase the American of the prevailing stock is Anglo-Saxon only partially, for there is probably just as much Celtic blood in his veins as Germanic, and his norm is to be found, not South of the Tyne and west of the Severn, but on the bleak Scotch hills. Among the first English colonists there were unquestionably many men of purely Teutonic stock from the East and South of England, and their influence is yet visible in many characteristic American folkways, in certain traditional American ideas—some of them now surviving only in national hypocrisies—, and, above all, in the fundamental peculiarities of the American dialect of English. But their Teutonic blood was early diluted by Celtic strains from Scotland, from the north of Ireland and from the West of England, and today those Americans who are regarded as being most thoroughly Anglo-Saxons—for example, the mountaineers of the Appalachian slopes from Vermont to Georgia—are obviously far more Celtic than Teutonic, not only physically but also mentally. They are leaner and taller than the true English, and far more given to moral obsessions and religious fanaticism. A Methodist revival is not an English phenomenon; it is Scotch. So, fundamentally, is Prohibition. So is the American tendency, marked by every foreign student of our history, to turn all political combats into moral crusades. The English themselves, of course, have been greatly polluted by Scotch, Irish and Welsh blood during the past three centuries, and for years past their government has been largely in the hands of Celts, but though this fact, by making them more like Americans, has tended to conceal the difference that I am discussing, it has certainly not sufficed to obliterate it altogether. Such a man as Lloyd George, in all his ways of thinking, is almost precisely like an American—but the English notion of humor remains different from the American notion, and so does the English view of personal liberty, and on the same level of primary ideas there are many other obvious differences.

But though I am thus convinced that the American Anglo-Saxon wears a false label, and grossly libels both of the great races from which he claims descent, I can imagine no good coming of trying to change it. Let him call himself whatever he pleases. Whatever he calls himself, it must be plain that the term he uses designates a genuinely distinct and differentiated race—that he is separated definitely, in character and habits of thought, from the men of all other recognizable strains—that he represents, among the peoples of the earth, almost a special species, and that he runs true to type. There is, indeed, very little tendency to variation in him—that is, in the mass. The traits that he developed when the first mixture of races took place in colonial days are the traits that he still shows; despite the vast changes in his material environment, he is almost precisely the same, in the way he thinks and acts, as his forefathers were. Some of the other great races of men, during the past two centuries, have changed very notice-ably—for example, think of the complete dying out of adventurousness in the Spaniards and its sudden appearance in the Germans—but the Ameri-can Anglo-Saxon has stuck to his hereditary guns. Moreover, he tends to show much less variation than other races between man and man. It is an axiom that, when five Russians or Germans meet, there are four parties in conflict, but it is equally an axiom that, among a hundred Americans, at least ninety-five will be found to hold exactly the same views upon all sub-jects that they can grasp at all, and may be trusted to react exactly alike to all ordinary stimuli. No other race, save it be the Chinese, is so thoroughly solid, or so firmly unresponsive to ideas from without.

4

The good qualities of this so-called Anglo-Saxon are many, and I am certainly not disposed to question them, but I here pass them over without apology, for he devotes practically the whole of his literature and fully a half of his oral discourse to celebrating them himself, and so there is no danger that they will ever be disregarded. No other known man, indeed, is so violently the blowhard, save it be his English kinsman; even the French-man, by comparison, is relatively modest and reticent. In this fact lies the first cause of the ridiculous figure he commonly cuts in the eyes of other people: he brags and blusters so incessantly that, if he actually had the com-bined virtues of Socrates, the Cid and the Twelve Apostles, he would still go beyond the facts, and so appear a mere Bombastes Furioso. This habit, I believe, is fundamentally English, but it has been exaggerated in the Amer-icano by his larger admixture of Celtic blood. In late years in America it has taken on an almost pathological character, and is to be explained, per-haps, only in terms of the Freudian necromancy. Braggadocio, in the 100 per cent American—"we won the war," "it is our duty to lead the world," "the land of the free and the home of the brave," the "Americanization" movement, and so on—is probably no more than a protective mechanism erected to conceal an inescapable sense of inferiority.

That this inferiority is real must be obvious to any impartial observer. Whenever the Anglo-Saxon, whether of the English or of the American variety, comes into sharp conflict with men of other stocks, he tends to be worsted, or, at best, to be forced back upon extraneous and irrelevant aids to assist him in the struggle. Here in the United States his defeat is so palpable that it has filled him with vast alarms, and reduced him to seeking succor in grotesque and extravagant devices. In the fine arts, in the sciences and even in the more complex sorts of business the children of the later immigrants are running away from the descendants of the early settlers. To call the roll of Americans eminent in almost any field of human endeavor beyond that of mere dull money-grubbing is to call a list of strange and often outlandish names; even the panel of Congress presents a startling example. Of the Americans who have come into notice during the past fifty years as poets, as novelists, as critics, as painters, as sculptors and in the minor arts, less than half bear Anglo-Saxon names, and in this minority there are few of pure Anglo-Saxon blood. So in the sciences. So in the higher reaches of engineering and technology. So in philosophy and its branches. So even in industry and agriculture. In those areas where the competition between the new and the old blood-streams is most sharp and clear-cut, say in New York, in seaboard New England and in the farming States of the upper Middle West, the defeat of the Anglo-Saxon is overwhelming and unmistakable. Once his predominance everywhere was actual and undisputed; today, even where he remains heavily superior numerically, it is largely sentimental and illusory.

The descendants of the later immigrants tend generally to move upward; the descendants of the first settlers, I believe, tend plainly to move downward, mentally, spiritually and even physically. Civilization is at its lowest mark in the United States precisely in those areas where the Anglo-Saxon still presumes to rule. He runs the whole South—and in the whole South there are not as many first-rate men as in many a single city of the mongrel North. Wherever he is still firmly in the saddle, there Ku Kluxery flourishes, and Fundamentalism, and lynching, and Prohibition, and all the other stupid and anti-social crimes of inferior men. It is not in the big cities, with their mixed population, that the death-rate is highest, and politics most corrupt, and religion nearest to voodooism, and every decent human aspiration suspect; it is in the areas that the recent immigrations have not penetrated, where "the purest Anglo-Saxon blood in the world" still flows. I could pile up evidences, but they are not necessary. The fact is too plain to be challenged. One testimony will be sufficient: it comes from two inquirers who made an exhaustive survey of a region in Southeastern Ohio, where "the people are more purely American than in the rest of the State":

> Here gross superstition exercises strong control over the thought and action of a large proportion of the people. Syphilitic and other venereal diseases are common and increasing over whole counties, while in some communities nearly every family is afflicted with inherited or infectious disease. Many cases of incest are know; inbreeding is rife. Imbeciles, feeble-minded, and delinquents are numerous, politics is corrupt, and selling of votes is common, petty crimes abound, the schools have been badly managed and poorly attended. Cases of rape, assault, and robbery are of almost weekly occurrence within five minutes walk of the corporation limits of the county seats, while in another county political control is held by a self-confessed criminal. Alcoholic intemperance is excessive. Gross immorality and its evil results are by no means confined to the hill districts, but are extreme also in town.

As I say, the American of the old stock is not unaware of this steady, and, of late, somewhat rapid degeneration—this gradual loss of his old mastery in the land his ancestors wrung from the Indian and the wild cat. He senses it, indeed, very painfully, and as if in despair of arresting it in fact, makes desperate efforts to dispose of it by denial and concealment. These efforts often take grotesque and extravagant forms. Laws are passed to hobble and cage the citizen of newer stocks in a hundred fantastic ways. It is made difficult and socially dangerous for him to teach his children the speech of his fathers, or to maintain the cultural attitudes that he has inherited from them. Every divergence from the norm of the low-caste Anglo-Saxon is treated as an *attentat* against the commonwealth, and punished with eager ferocity. On the level of the country Ku Kluxers the thing goes to the length of downright assault; a man in Arkansas or Mississippi who ventured to speak a foreign language, or to concern himself with such of the fine arts as country Methodists cannot comprehend, or to let it be known that he was a member of the Roman Catholic Church would run some risk of being tarred and feathered by his neighbors, or of having his house burned down over his head. Worse, there is scarcely less pressure in the higher reaches of the intellect. The demand for a restoration of what is called American tradition in letters is nothing more or less, at bottom, than a demand for a supine and nonsensical conformity—a demand that every American, regardless of his racial character and his natural way of thinking, force all his thoughts into the low-caste Anglo-Saxon mold. It is bound to fail of effect, of course, and in that very fact lies the best of imaginable proofs of the mental poverty of those who voice it. It is not brought forward in an effort at persuasion; it is issued as an order, raucously and absurdly—and every time it is flouted the Anglo-Saxon slips another inch down the hill. He cannot prevail in fair competition, and, for all his bellicose flourishes, he cannot prevail by force and intimidation. There remains for him the role of martyr, and in this he already begins to display himself affectingly. The music of Americans, we are told gravely, is barred out of our concert halls and opera houses because their managers and conductors are all accursed foreigners. American painters and sculptors have to struggle against a dense tide of immigrants. American criticism has become so anti-American that poets and novelists of the old stock are on a sort of blacklist, and cannot get justice. Only in the colleges does the Anglo-Saxon intellectual hold his own, and even there he is now menaced by swarms of Jews, and must devise means of putting them down or perish with his brothers of the fine arts.

5

It so happens that I am myself an Anglo-Saxon—one of far purer blood, indeed, than any of the half-bleached Celts who pass under the name in the United States and England. I am Angle and I am Saxon, and I am very little else, and that little is all safely white, Nordic, Protestant and blond. Thus I feel free, without risk of venturing into bad taste, to regard frankly the *soi-disant* [so-called] Anglo-Saxon of this incomparable Republic and his rather less dubious cousin of the Motherland. How do the two appear to me, after a quarter of century spent largely in accumulating their disfavor? What are the characters that I discern most clearly in the so-called Anglo-Saxon type of man? I may answer at once that two stick out above all others. One is his curious and apparently incurable incompetence—his congenital inability to do any difficult thing easily and well, whether it be isolating a bacillus or writing a sonata. The other is his astounding susceptibility to fears and alarms—in short, his hereditary cowardice.

To accuse so enterprising and successful a race of cowardice, of course, is to risk immediate derision; nevertheless, I believe that a fair-minded examination of its history will bear me out. Nine-tenths of the great feats of derring-do that its sucklings are taught to venerate in school—that is, its feats as a race, not the isolated exploits of its extraordinary individuals, most of them at least partly of other stocks—have been wholly lacking in even the most elementary gallantry. Consider, for example, the events attending the extension of the two great empires, English and American. Did either movement evoke any genuine courage and resolution? The answer is palpably no. Both empires were built up primarily by swindling and butchering unarmed savages, and after that by robbing weak and friendless nations: Mexico, Spain, the Boer republics. Neither produced a hero above the average run of those in the movies; neither exposed the folks at home to the slightest danger of reprisal. The battles of Omdurman and Manila Bay were typical of these great swarmings of the Anglo-Saxon—the first a bald massacre, and the second a combat at odds of at least fifty to one. They produced highly typical Anglo-Saxon heroes—Kitchener, an Irishman, and Dewey, largely French. Almost always, indeed, mercenaries have done the Anglo-Saxon's fighting for him—a high testimony to his common sense, but scarcely flattering, I fear, to the truculence he boasts of. The British empire was won mainly by Irishmen, Scotchmen and native allies, and the American empire, at least in large part, by Frenchmen and Spaniards. Moreover, neither great enterprise cost any appreciable mount of blood; neither presented grave and dreadful risks; neither exposed the conqueror to the slightest danger of being made the conquered. The British won most of their vast dominions without having to stand up in a single battle against a civilized and formidable foe, and the Americanos won their continent at the expense of a few dozen puerile skirmishes with savages. All the Indian wars in American history, from the days of John Smith to those of Custer, did not bring down as many men as the single battle of Tannenberg. The total cost of conquering the whole area from Plymouth Rock to the Golden Gate and from Lake George to the Everglades, including even the cost of driving out the French, Dutch, English and Spaniards, was less that the cost of defending Verdun.

So far as I can make out there is no record in history of any Anglo-Saxon nation entering upon any great war without allies, nor upon any war at all when there the slightest danger of getting beaten, or even of suffering serious damage. The French have done it, the Dutch have done it, the Germans have done it, the Japs have done it, and even such inferior nations as the Danes, the Spaniards, the Boers and the Greeks have done it, but never the English or Americans. Can you imagine the English taking such a chance as the Germans took in 1914, or as the Turks took in 1922, or as the French prepare to take today? Can you imagine the United States resolutely facing a war in which the odds against it were as huge as they were against Spain in 1898? It seems to me that the facts of history are wholly against any such fancy. The Anglo-Saxon always tries to take a gang with him when he goes to war, and even when he has it behind him he is very uneasy and prone to fall into panic at the first threat of genuine danger. Here I put an unimpeachably Anglo-Saxon witness on the stand, to wit, Dr. Charles W. Eliot, of Harvard. I find him saying, in an article quoted with approbation by the Congressional Record, that during the Revolutionary War the colonists now hymned so eloquently in the school-books "fell into a condition of despondency from which nothing but the steadfastness of Washington and the Continental army and the aid from France saved them," and that "when the War of 1812 brought grave losses a considerable portion of the population experienced a moral collapse, from which they were rescued only the exertions of a few thoroughly patriotic statesmen and the exploits of three or four American frigates on the seas"—to say nothing of an enterprising Corsican gentleman, Bonaparte by name. In both these wars the Americans had enormous and obvious advantages, in terrain, in allies and in men; nevertheless, they fought, in the main, very badly, and from the first shot to the last a majority of them stood in favor of making peace on almost any terms. The Mexican and Spanish Wars I pass over as perhaps too obscenely ungallant to be discussed at all; of the former, General U.S. Grant, who fought in it, said that it was "the most unjust war ever waged by a stronger against a weaker nation." Who remembers that, during the Spanish War, the whole Atlantic Coast trembled in fear of the Spaniards' feeble fleet—that all New England had hysterics every time a strange coal-barge was sighted on the sky-line, that the safe-deposit boxes of Boston were emptied and their contents transferred to Worcester, and that the Navy had to organize a patrol to save the coast towns from depopulation? Perhaps those Reds, atheists and pro-Germans remember it who also remember that during the World War the entire country went wild with fear of an enemy who, without the aid of divine intervention, obviously could not strike it a blow at all—and that the great moral victory was gained at last with the assistance of twenty-one allies and at odds of eight to one.

But the American Civil War remains? Does it, indeed? The almost unanimous opinion of the North, in 1862, was that it would be over after a few small battles; the first soldiers were actually enlisted for but three months. When, later on, it turned unexpectedly into a severe struggle, recruits had to be driven to the front by force, and the only Northerners remaining in favor of going on were Abraham Lincoln, a few ambitious generals and the profiteers. I turn to Dr. Eliot again. "In the closing year of one war," he says, "large portions of the Democratic Party in the North and of the Republican party advocated surrender to the Confederacy, so down-hearted were they." Down-hearted at odds of two to one! The South was plainly more gallant, but even the gallantry of the South was largely illusory. The Confederate leaders, when the war began, adopted at once the traditional Anglo-Saxon device of seeking allies. They tried and expected to get the aid of England, and they actually came very near succeeding. When hopes in that direction began to fade (i.e., when England concluded that tackling the North would be dangerous), the common people of the Confederacy, the progenitors of the chivalric Ku Kluxers of today, threw up the sponge, and so the catastrophe, when it came at last, was mainly internal. The South failed to bring the quaking North to a standstill because, to borrow a phrase that Dr. Eliot uses in another connection, it "experienced a moral collapse of unprecedented depth and duration." The folks at home failed to support the troops in the field, and the troops in the field began to desert. Even so early as Shiloh, indeed, many Confederate regiments were already refusing to fight.

This reluctance for desperate chances and hard odds, so obvious in the military record of the English-speaking nations, is also conspicuous in times of peace. What a man of another and superior stock almost always notices, living among so-called Anglo-Saxons, is (a) their incapacity for prevailing in fair rivalry, either in trade, in the fine arts or in what is called learning—in brief, their general incompetence, and (b) their invariable effort to make up for this incapacity by putting some inequitable burden upon their rivals, usually by force. The Frenchman, I believe, is the worst of chauvinists, but once he admits a foreigner to his country he at least treats that foreigner fairly, and does not try to penalize him absurdly for his mere foreignness. The Anglo-Saxon American is always trying to do it; his history is a history of recurrent outbreaks of blind rage against peoples who have begun to worst him; hence Know Nothingism, Ku Kluxery, American Legionism, and all the rest of it. Such movements would be inconceivable in an efficient and genuinely self-confident people, wholly assured of their superiority, as a Frenchman is of his or a German of his, and they would be equally inconceivable in a truly gallant and courageous people, disdaining unfair advantages and overwhelming odds. Theoretically launched against some inferiority in the non-Anglo-Saxon man, either as patriot, as democrat or as Christian, they are actually launched at his general superiority, his greater fitness to survive in the national environment. The effort is always to penalize him for winning in fair fight, to handicap him in such a manner that he will sink to the general level of the Anglo-Saxon population, and, if possible, even below it. Such devices, of course, never have the countenance of the Anglo-Saxon minority that is authentically superior, and hence self-confident and tolerant. Of that minority I do not speak here. It is serene in peace as it is brave in war. But in the United States, at least, it is pathetically small, and it tends steadily to grow smaller and feebler. The communal laws and the communal mores are made by the folk, and they offer all the proof that is necessary, not only of its general inferiority, but also of its alarmed awareness of that inferiority. The normal American of the "pure-blooded" majority goes to rest every night with an uneasy feeling that there is a burglar under the bed, and he gets up every morning with a sickening fear that his underwear has been stolen.

6

It is difficult, I submit to admire such a people unreservedly, despite the good qualities that I have passed over. They lack the ease and tolerance, the fine adventurousness and love of hazard which go with a sense of firm security—in other words, with a sense of genuine superiority. The Anglo-Saxon of the good herd is, in many important respects, the least civilized of men and the least capable of true civilization. His political ideas are crude and shallow. He is almost totally devoid of aesthetic feeling; he does not even make folk-lore or walk in the woods. The most elementary facts about the visible universe alarm him, and incite him to put them down. Educate him, make a professor of him, teach him how to express his soul, and he still remains palpably third-rate. He fears ideas almost more cravenly than he fears men. His blood, I believe, is running thin; perhaps it was not much to boast of at the start; in order that he may exercise any functions above those of a trader, a pedagogue or a mob orator, it needs the stimulus of other and less exhausted strains. Poe, Whitman, Mark Twain— these were typical products of such crosses. The fact that they increase is the best hope of the intellect in America. They shake the old race out of its spiritual lethargy, and introduce it to disquiet and experiment. They make for a free play of ideas. In opposing the project, whether in politics, in letters or in the ages-long struggle toward the truth, the prophets of Anglo-

Saxon purity and tradition only make themselves ridiculous. Under the absurd *Kultur* that they advocate Aggasiz would have been deported and Whitman would have been hanged, and the most eminent literati flourishing in the Republic today would be Edgar Guest and Dr. Frank Chase.

The success of these so-called Anglo-Saxons in the world, I am convinced, has been due, not so much to their merits but to their defects—and especially to their high capacity for being alarmed and their aversion to what may be called romance—in other words, to their harshly practical minds, their disdain of intellectual enterprise, their dull common sense. They have saved their hides and their money while better sportsmen were taking chances. But the bitter must go with the sweet. Such qualities belong to *Lumbricus terrestris* [the earthworm] rather than to *Homo sapiens*. They may be valuable, but they are not pretty. Today, at the height of his triumph in the world, the Anglo-Saxon somehow looks shabby—England trembling before one-legged and bankrupt France, the United States engaged in a grotesque pogrom against the wop, the coon, the kike, the papist, the Jap, the what-not—worse, engaged in an even more grotesque effort to put down ideas as well as men—to repeal learning by statute, regiment the arts by lynch-law, and give the puerile ethical and theological notions of lonely farmers and corner grocers the force and dignity of constitutional axioms. As I stand on the side-lines, observing the show, I find it very hard to admire. But, save when ethyl alcohol in dilute aqueous solution has dulled my native pity, I find it even harder to laugh.

(*Prejudices, Fourth Series*)

FROM THE MEMOIRS OF A SUBJECT OF THE UNITED STATES

[*Americans are simple people who like cheap stuff and dislike complicated thoughts. The Constitution, far from being a god-ordained document brought down from the mount by Washington, Adams, Jefferson, Madison, and Franklin, actually reads like a cobbled-together agglomeration of 18th-century British philosophy and governmental ordinances, with a knee bent to the slave states. We just can't, as Americans, bring ourselves to recognize this because that would incur upon us the power to chuck the whole thing and start over with a government that might make more sense. But, as Mencken notes in this essay, Americans just aren't smart enough to connect their problems with governmental functions and philosophy. Consider this passage regarding Prohibition:*

"Even the popular discontent with Prohibition is not a discontent with its sneaking and knavishness—its wholesale turning loose of licensed blacklegs and blackmailers, its appalling degradation of the judiciary, its corruption of Congress, its disingenuous invasion of the Bill of Rights. What is complained of is simply the fact that Scotch is dubious and costs too much."

Similarly, when told of an oil spill that blackens the shores of the Pacific, or of the murderous activities of princes and pashas in oil-rich regions who subject their citizens to codified Islamic terror, or given information that burning fossil fuels will in time barbeque those living in South Asia and millions upon millions of the rest of us, Americans only complain about high gas prices. Even free peoples, as Mencken indicates, become subjects when they are too stupid to be anything else.]

---

1. Government by Bounder

Of government, at least in democratic states, it may be said briefly that it is an agency engaged wholesale, and as a matter of solemn duty, in the performance of acts which all self-respecting individuals refrain from as a matter of common decency. The American newspapers supply examples every day, chiefly issuing out of the Federal tribunals, judicial and administrative. The whole process of the Federal law, indeed, becomes a process of bounderism. Its catchpolls are not policemen, in any rational and ordinary sense, but simply sneaks and scoundrels with their eyes glued eternally in knot-holes. Imagine a man of ordinary decency discovering his son reading an account of the proceedings against the once celebrated Lady Cathcart, now happily forgotten? Would his exposition of the case take the form of patriotic hallelujahs, or would he caution the boy that such things are not done by gentlemen? No wonder the teaching of patriotism in the Republic is being handed over to virgin schoolma'ams, who know of honor only as an anatomical matter! The business becomes too difficult for men who must face their fellow-men daily, and therewith the ancient prejudices of the race. Those prejudices, for unnumbered countries, have run against the man who mouths the frailties of a fair one in the market-place. But the commission of Uncle Sam, it appears, repeals that obligation of elemental honor, as it repeals every other. One sworn to uphold the Constitution becomes straightaway a licentiate in swinishness, with a mandate to examine the female guests of the nation publicly, and to denounce all who are not *virgo intacta*. This mandate covers not only the lowly ruffians told of to guard the ports, but also magnificoes of ministerial rank. The Cabinet of a great Christian nation meets behind locked doors to perform a business which, if done by an honest Elk, would bring his board of governors together to kick him out.

If such obscenities were rare one might set them down to moral profit and loss, and so try to forget them. But they happen every day. If a Cathcart case is not on the front pages, then a Whitney case or Kollontai case is there. And day in and day out the newspapers are filled with the revolting muckeries of Prohibition agents, and their attendant district attorneys and judges. The whole trend of American legislation, and with it of jurisprudence, seems to be toward such ideas of dignity and decency as prevail in remote and forlorn country villages, among the human debris of Prohibition. A court of justice, once a place where the state intervened to curb the savagery of the strong, is now an arena of savagery both cruel and cynical. The notion seems to be that any device or deceit or brutality is fair, so long as it helps to fill the jails. The government, through its authorized agents, sets itself deliberately to lure men into so-called crime, and then punishes them mercilessly for succumbing. Is there such a thing as a *contrat social*? Then certainly it is getting heavy blows in the Federal Union. For if it is not based upon the expectation that one citizen will treat another with common decency, it is based upon nothing more than a shadow—and that expectation is fast becoming vain among us. The natural confidence that every man should have in his fellows—that they will not hit below the belt, that they will not abuse his natural trust, that he may rely upon them, in a given situation, to act according to the principles of fair-play prevailing immemorially among civilized men—this confidence, when it touches American officialdom, has no longer any basis in fact. The government, under the Volstead Act, is a spy and a snitcher, just as, under the Immigration Act, it is a brute and a blackguard, and under the Alien Property Act, a common thief.

Obviously, such things cannot go on without having profound effects upon the general American character. A government, though it may be worse than the average man it governs, is still made up of just such average men. If, by some process of legal decay, it is set to disgusting acts, then the consequence must be that, in the long run, they will become less disgusting. How the business has worked in other lands has been displayed with much snuffling by specialists in Americanism; unfortunately, they seem to show no interest in the phenomena when it is repeated at home. I have spoken of the father with a son ripe for instruction in the traditional decencies. Unfecund myself, I can only imagine the difficulties, but it must be obvious that they are serious. How, indeed, is he to interpret such an inescapable transaction as the Cathcart uproar? Is it his duty to tell his son that gentlemen set their dogs upon loose women? Or is it his duty to say that the United States is not a gentleman—nay, not even a decent thug?

Such doings, it seems to me, flow quite naturally out of the democratic theory. It holds, *imprimis* [first of all], that cads make just as good governors as civilized and self-respecting men, and it holds, *secundo*, that the notions of propriety and decency held by the mob are good enough for the state, and ought, in fact, to have the force of law. Thus it becomes increasingly difficult to be a good American, as the thing is officially defined, and remain what all the other peoples of the world regard as a good citizen—

that is, one who views the acts and ideas of his fellows with a tolerant and charitable eye, and wishes them to be free and happy. The whole tendency of American Law, in this day, is to put down happiness wherever it is encountered, and the *mores* of the land march with the law. The doctrine seems to be that it is the highest duty of the citizen to police his fellows. What they naturally want to do is precisely what they must be kept from doing. To this business a large and increasing class of professional snouters and smellers addresses itself. How many noses it can muster, God only knows, but the number must be immensely large. In the single State of Ohio, with the Anti-Saloon League in the saddle, there are certainly at least five thousand, and every prowling village deacon and petty urban blackmailer is free to join the force as a volunteer. And in more civilized regions, where public opinion, even in the mob, runs against such putridities, the Federal government supplies the scoundrels.

This antagonism between democratic Puritanism and common decency is inherent in the nature of the two things, and leads to conflicts in all so-called "free" countries, but it is only in the United States that it has reached the stage of open and continuous war, with Puritanism sweeping the field and common decency in flight. Thus life in the Republic grows increasingly uncomfortable to men of the more urbane and seemly sort, and, despite the great material prosperity of the country, the general stock of happiness probably diminishes steadily. For the thing that makes us enjoy the society of our fellows is not admiration of their inner virtues but delight in their outward manners. It is not enough that they are headed for heaven, and will sit upon the right hand of God through all eternity; it is also necessary that they be polite, generous, and, above all, trustworthy. We must have confidence in them in order to get any pleasure out of associating with them. We must be sure that they will not do unto us as we should refuse, even for cash in hand, to do unto them. It is the tragedy of the Puritan that he can never inspire this confidence in his fellow-men. He is by nature a pedant in ethics, and hence he is by nature a mucker. With the best of intentions he cannot rid himself of the belief that it is his duty to save us from our follies—i.e., from all the non-puritanical acts and whimsies that make life charming. His duty to let us be happy takes second, third or fourth place. A Puritan cannot be tolerant—and with tolerance goes magnanimity. The late Dr. Woodrow Wilson was a typical Puritan—of the better sort, perhaps, for he at least toyed with the ambition to appear as a gentleman, but nevertheless a true Puritan. Magnanimity was simply beyond him. Confronted, on his death-bed, with the case of poor old Debs, all his instincts compelled him to keep Debs in jail. I daresay that, as a purely logical matter, he saw clearly that the old fellow ought to be turned loose; certainly he must have known that Washington would not have hesitated, or Lincoln. But Calvinism triumphed as his intellectual faculties decayed. In the full bloom of health, with a plug hat on his head, he aped the gentry of his wistful adoration very cleverly, but lying in bed, stripped like Thackeray's Louis XIV, he reverted to his congenital Puritanism, which is to say, bounderism.

Of such sort are the grand seigneurs of the nation—the custodians of its dignity and honor. They speak for it to the world. They set the tone of the national life at home. Is there any widespread murmuring against them? I wish I could report that there was, but I see no sign of it. Instead, there seems to be only a resigned sort of feeling that nothing can be done about it—that the swinishness of government lies in the very nature of things, and so cannot be changed. Even the popular discontent with Prohibition is not a discontent with its sneaking and knavishness—in wholesale turning loose of licensed blacklegs and blackmailers, its appalling degradation of the judiciary, its corruption of Congress, its disingenuous invasion of the Bill of Rights. What is complained of is simply the fact that Scotch is dubious and costs too much. As bootlegging grows more efficient, I suppose even that complaint will sink to a whisper, perhaps in the form of a snigger. Of any forthright grappling with the underlying indecency there is little show. It would be difficult, in most American communities, to get signers for even the most academic protest against it. The American, played upon for years by a stream of jackass legislation, takes refuge in frank skulking. He first dodges the laws, and then he dodges the duty of protesting against them. His life becomes a process of sneaking through back-alleys, watching over one shoulder for the cop and over the other for his neighbor. Thus a-tremble (and with a weather eye open for Bolsheviks, atheists and loose women), he serves the high oath that government of the people, by the people, and for the people shall not perish from the earth.

2. Constructive Proposal

A mood of constructive criticism being upon me, I propose forthwith that the method of choosing legislators now prevailing in the United States be abandoned and that the method used in choosing juries being substituted. That is to say, I propose that the men who make our laws be chosen by chance and against their will, instead of by fraud and against the will of all the rest of us, as now. But isn't the jury system itself imperfect? Isn't it occasionally disgraced by gross abuse and scandal? Then so is the system of justice devised and ordained by the Lord God Himself. Didn't He assume that the Noachian Deluge would be a lasting lesson to sinful humanity— that it would put an end to all manner of crime and wickedness, and convert mankind into a race of Methodists? And wasn't Noah himself, its chief beneficiary, lying drunk, naked and uproarious within a year after the ark landed on Ararat? All I argue for the jury system, invented by man, is that it is immeasurably better than the scheme invented by God. It has its failures and its absurdities, its abuses and its corruptions, but taking one day with another it manifestly works. It is not the fault of juries that so many murderers go unwhipped of justice, and it is not the fault of juries that so many honest men are harassed by preposterous laws. The juries find the gunmen guilty: it is the judges higher up who deliver them from the noose, and turn them loose to resume their butcheries. It is from judges again, and not from juries, that Volsteadian padlocks issue, and all the other devices for making a mock of the Bill of Rights. Are juries occasionally sentimental? Then let us not forget that it was their sentimentality, in the Eighteenth Century, that gradually forced a measure of decency and justice into the English Criminal Law. It was a jury that blocked the effort of the Department of Justice to railroad Senator Wheeler to prison on false charges. It was another jury that detected and baffled the same Department's perjurers in the O'Leary case, during the late war. And it was yet another jury that delivered the eminent Fatty Arbuckle from what was, perhaps, the most disingenuous and outrageous persecution ever witnessed in a civilized land.

Would any American Legislature, or Congress itself, have resisted the vast pressure of the bureaucracy in these cases? To ask the question is to answer it. The dominant character of every legislative body ever heard of, at least in this great free Republic, is precisely its susceptibility to such pressure. It not only leaps when the bureaucracy cracks the whip; it also leaps to the whip-cracking of scores of extra-legal (and often, indeed, *il*legal) agencies. The Anti-Saloon League, despite its frequent disasters, is still so powerful everywhere that four legislators out of five obey it almost instinctively. When it is flouted, as has happened in a few States under an adverse pressure yet more powerful, the thing is marvelled at as a sort of miracle. The bureaucracy itself is seldom flouted at all. When it is in a moral mood, and heaving with altruistic sobs, the thing simply never happens. It is argued the Congress has nevertheless defied it, and Dr. Coolidge with it? Then the argument comes from persons whose studies of Washington pathology have been very superficial. At least nine-tenths of the idiocies advocated by Dr. Coolidge and his highly dubious friends have been swallowed by both Houses with no more than a few reflex gags. Even the celebrated Warren appointment was defeated in the Senate by only a few votes—and the few votes were delivered, as connoisseurs will recall, by a process indistinguishable from an act of God. It is my contention that a jury of plain men, issuing unwilling from their plumbing-shops and grocery-stores and eager to get back to work, would have rejected Warren without leaving their box, and that the same jury, confronted by such things as the World Court imbecility, would dispose of them just as quickly.

Why were the learned Senators so much less intelligent and so much less resolute? For a plain reason: Fully two-thirds of them were not thinking of Warren as they voted; they were thinking of their jobs. The problem before them was not whether elevating the preposterous Warren was a reasonable and laudable measure, likely to benefit and glorify the United States, but whether voting for Warren would augment or diminish their chance of reelection. In other words, they were not free agents, and in consequence not honest men. They had sought their jobs on their bellies, and they were eager to keep them, even at the cost of groveling on their bellies again. Say the worst you can say against a box of twelve jurymen, and you can never say that. Not one among them sought his job. Not one among them wants to keep it. The business before them presents itself as a public duty to be done, not as an opportunity for private advantage. They are eager only to get it done decently, and go home.

So my proposal is that our Legislatures be chosen as our juries are now chosen—that the names of all the men eligible in each assembly district be put into a hat (or, if no hat can be found that is large enough, into a bathtub), and tat a blind moron, preferably of tender years, be delegated to draw out one. Let the constituted catchpolls then proceed swiftly to this man's house, and take him before he can get away. Let him be brought into court forthwith, and put under a stupendous bond to serve as elected, and if he cannot furnish the bond, let him be kept until the appointed day in the nearest jail.

The advantages that this system would offer are so vast and so obvious that I hesitate to venture into the banality of rehearsing them. It would, in the first place, save the commonwealth the present excessive cost of elections, and make political campaigns unnecessary. It would, in the second place, get rid of all the heart-burnings that now flow out of every contest at the polls, and block the reprisals and charges of fraud that now issue from the heart-burnings. It would, in the third place, fill all the State Legislatures with men of a peculiar and unprecedented cast of mind—men actually convinced that public service is a public burden, and not merely a private snap. And it would in the fourth and most important place, completely dispose of the present degrading knee-bending and trading in votes, for nine-tenths of the legislators, having got into office unwillingly, would be eager only to finish their duties and go home, and even those who acquired a taste for the life would be unable to do anything to increase the probability, even by one chance in a million, of their reelection.

The disadvantages of the plan are very few, and most of them, I believe, yield readily to analysis. Do I hear argument that a miscellaneous gang of tin-roofers, delicatessen dealers and retired bookkeepers, chosen by hazard, would lack the vast knowledge of public affairs needed by makers of laws? Then I can only answer (a) that no such knowledge is actually necessary and (b) that few, if any, of the existing legislators possess it. The great majority of public problems, indeed, are quite simple, and any man who may be trusted to grasp their elements in ten days who may be—and is—trusted to unravel the obfuscations of two gangs of lawyers in the same time. In this department the so-called expertness of the so-called experts is largely imaginary. The masters of the tariff who sit at Washington know little about the fundamental philosophy of protection, and care less; the subject, if discussed on the floor, would send the whole House flying to the Capitol bootleggers. The knowledge that these frauds are full of is simply knowledge of how many votes an extra ten cents on aluminum dishpans may be counted on producing, and how much the National Association of Brass Cuspidor Manufacturers deserves to be given for its campaign contribution of $10,000. Such is the science of the tariff as it is practiced by the professors who now flourish. It is my contention that a House of malt-and-hop dealers, garage mechanics and trolley conductors, brought in by the common hangman, would deal with the question with quite as much knowledge, and with a great deal more honesty. It might make mistakes, but it would not, at least be pledged to them in advance. Some of its members might sell out, but there would remain, at worst, a workable minority of honest men.

The tariff, in any case, is no longer an issue. Neither are most of the other great politico-economical puzzles that harassed the statesmen of an elder day. They have all been solved; the two great parties agree upon them, with a few wild fellows dissenting. But as economics and finance go out, morals come in. The legislation of to-day is chiefly made up of quack cure-alls, invented by fanatics and supported by the bureaucracy. Well, I ask you what sort of Legislature is the more likely to swallow these cure-alls: one made up of professionals eager to hold their jobs, or one made up of amateurs eager only to get rid of their jobs?

My scheme would have the original merit, if it had no other, of barring the professionals from the game. They would lose their present enormous advantages as a class, and so their class would tend to disappear. Would that be a disservice to the state? Certainly not. On the contrary, it would be a service of the first magnitude, for the worst curse of democracy as suffer under it today, is that it makes public office a monopoly of a palpably inferior and ignoble group of men. They have to abase themselves in order to hold it. The fact reflects itself in their general character, which is obviously low. They are men congenitally capable of ignoble acts, else they would not have got into public life at all. There are, of course, exceptions to that rule among them, but how many? What I contend is simply that the number of such exceptions is bound to be smaller in the class of professional job-seekers than it is in any other class, or in the population in general. What I contend, second, is that choosing legislators from that population, by chance, would reduce immensely the proportion of such crawling, slimy men in the halls of legislation, and that the effects would be instantly visible in a great improvement in the justice and reasonableness of the laws.

Are juries ignorant? Then they are still intelligent enough to be entrusted with your life and mine. Are they venal? Then they are still honest enough to take our fortunes into their hands. Such is the fundamental law of the Germanic peoples, and it has worked for nearly a thousand years. I have launched my proposal that it be extended upward and onward, and the mood of constructive criticism passes from me. My plan belongs to any reformer who cares to lift it.

3. The Nature of Government

What ails the world mainly, at least in the political sense, is that its governments are too strong. It has been a recurrent pest since the dawn of civilization. Government is always depicted, in the orthodox texts, as the creation of the people governed; the theory is that they created it in order to secure their own safety and promote their daily business. But no Professor Oppenheimer was needed to demonstrate that it is really something imposed from without, or, at events, the heir and assign of something imposed from without. Its interests and those of the people it governs are the same only occasionally, and then usually accidentally. True enough, it must sometimes throw them bones, and even whole beefsteaks, lest they grow desperate and attempt to destroy it, but such concessions are always made grudgingly, and withdrawn very promptly the moment it looks safe.

The history of the United States would make all this plain enough, if that history were studied realistically. Consider, for example, the matter of liberty. The American people profess to esteem liberty very highly—so highly, in fact, that their common talk about it seems somewhat lyrical and excessive to the people of most other nations. They seem to believe that there is more of it on tap in the Republic than anywhere else on earth—that the Republic was actually founded for the sole purpose of giving it to them. Yet it must be obvious that their hold upon it is always precarious, and that their government tries to take it away from them whenever possible—not completely, perhaps, but always substantially. That government resisted their demand for it at the very start, and yielded only after a very severe struggle. The Bill of Rights was not in the original Constitution: it got in only as amendments. Ever since then, at every opportunity, the government has tried to weaken it. Here parties and personalities count for very little. The most successful raids upon the Bill of Rights so far recorded were made by Abraham Lincoln, a Republican and the spokesman (in theory) of the inferior man, and by Woodrow Wilson, a Democrat and the agent of what passes, in the United States, for an aristocracy.

The men who constitute the government always try to make it appear, of course, that they carry on their activities in a patriotic and altruistic way— in brief, that they are full of public spirit. But that pretension deceives no one, not even *Homo boobiens*. The average man, whatever his errors otherwise, at least sees clearly that the government is something lying outside him and outside the generality of his fellow men—that it is a separate, independent and often hostile power, only partly under his control, and capable, on occasion, of doing him great harm. In his romantic moments, he may think of it as a benevolent father or even as a sort of *jinn* or god, but he never thinks of it as part of himself. In times of trouble he looks to it to perform miracles for his benefit; at other times he sees it as an enemy with which he must do constant battle. Is it a fact of no significance that robbing the government is everywhere regarded as a crime of less magnitude that robbing an individual, or even a corporation? In the United States today it is punished only when it is complicated by some secondary, and, in the public judgment, worse offense—for example, depriving crippled war veterans of their lawful relief. Otherwise, it carries a smaller penalty and infinitely less odium than acts that are intrinsically trivial—for example, spitting on the sidewalk or marrying two wives. None of the thieves who robbed the government at Hog Island during the war has ever gone to jail. The airship contractors, though they made off with nearly a billion dollars, are still all at large. So are all the camp contractors. More, the man who broke up the feeble and abortive effort to punish those scoundrels—who denounced that effort as, in some mysterious way, an *attentat* against public morality—that man is now first in succession to the presidency of the Republic. His indignation plainly had public sentiment behind it. He was and is an accomplished professor of the mind of man under democracy.

Other politicians, less gifted in that science, often take the other side, and come to grief. They assume absurdly that the public conscience is opposed to robbing the government, and try to climb into popularity and high office by pursuing the gay fellows who do it. The attempt almost always fails. The great masses of the plain people, true enough, enjoy the chase, as they enjoy, indeed, *any* chase. The damning evidence, as it unrolls, delights them; they devour every accusation, however ill supported. But it usually turns out in the end that they do not care to eat the game. The minute the evidence is all in they lose interest; there is no demand from them for the jailing of the accused. On the contrary, they sympathize with the accused, and show it actively when the time comes to supply conscripts for the trial jury. Perhaps the safest men in the whole United States to-day are the gentlemen who have been indicted for robbing the government. Every such indictment is a sort of policy of insurance against going to jail.

What lies behind all this, I believe, is a deep sense of the fundamental antagonism between the government and the people it governs. It is apprehended, not as a committee of citizens chosen to carry on the communal business of the whole population, but as a separate and autonomous corporation, mainly devoted to exploiting the population for the benefit of its own members. Robbing it is thus an act almost devoid of infamy—an exploit rather resembling those of Robin Hood and the eminent pirates of tradition. When a private citizen is robbed a worthy man is deprived of the fruits of his industry and thrift; when the government is robbed the worst that happens is that certain rogues and loafers have less money to play with than they had before. The notion that they have earned that money is never entertained; to most men it would seem extremely ludicrous. They are simply rascals who, by accident of law, have a somewhat dubious right to a share in the earnings of their fellowmen. When that share is diminished by private enterprise the business is, on the whole, far more laudable than not.

The average man, when he pays taxes, certainly does not believe he is making a prudent and productive investment of his money; on the contrary, he feels that he is being muleted [charged] in an excessive amount for services that, in the main, are useless to him, and that, in substantial part, are downright inimical to him. He may be convinced that a police force, say, is necessary for the protection of his life and property, and that an army and navy safeguard him from being reduced to slavery by some vague foreign kaiser, but even so he views these things as extravagantly expensive—he sees in even the most essential of them an agency for making it easier for the exploiters constituting the government to rob him. The policeman, in fact, is his symbol for a thief. The army and navy, as he sees them, are blankets for mere display, ostentation and waste—of his hard-earned money. The rest of the government is purely predatory and useless; he believes that he gets no more benefit from its vast and costly operations than he gets from the money he lends to his wife's brother. It is a power that stands over him constantly, ever alert for new chances to squeeze him. If it could do so safely it would strip him to the hide. If it leaves him anything at all, it is simply prudentially, as a farmer leaves a hen some of her eggs.

Thus he see nothing wrong, in the sense that robbing a neighbor is wrong to him, in turning the tables upon it whenever the opportunity offers. When he steals anything from it he is only recovering his own, with fair interest and decent profit. Two gangs thus stand confronted: on the one hand the gang of drones and exploiters constituting the government, and on the other hand the body of prehensile and enterprising citizens. The latter is certainly not made up exclusively, as the liberals and other such romantics seem to think, of bankers, railroad stockholders, great industrialists and other such magnificoes. There is plenty of room in it for more lowly men, if only they have the courage to horn in. During the late war all the union men of the nation, by pooling their strength and so dispersing the risk, made a magnificent and successful effort to get their share: they stole almost as much, in all probability as the dollar-a-year men. And when the war was over the soldiers, deprived of their chance while the going was good, demanded it belatedly. The chief argument for the bonus was not that the veterans of the war had leaped gallantly to the defense of democracy, for at least two-thirds of them, as everyone knows, tried their best to evade service. The chief argument was that they were forced into the army against their will and in violation of their private interests—that they didn't get their fair chance at the loot. They did not demand the punishment of those who looted while they served; they only demanded a rectification of the injustice which kept them honest themselves.

The difference between the two gangs—of professionals and of amateurs—is that the former has law on its side, and so enjoys an unfair advantage. Worse, it makes the very laws it profits by. Yet worse, it controls all the agencies which execute them, including the courts. The other gang is almost unarmored. The government is always able, when it happens to be so disposed, to single out a few of its ring-leaders and clap them into jail. Such proceedings, of course, are unpopular, but they are nevertheless possible. But the government gang is well-nigh immune to punishment. Its worst extortions, even when they are baldly for private profit, carry no certain penalties under our laws. Since the first days of the Republic less than a dozen of its members have been impeached, and only a few obscure understrappers have ever been put into prison. The number of men sitting at Atlanta and Leavenworth for revolting against the extortions of the government is always ten times as great as the number of government officials condemned for oppressing the taxpayers to their own gain. Thus the combat which goes on is not unlike that between the Anti-Saloon League and the bootleggers. The Anti-Saloon League, it must be manifest, is quite as criminal as the bootleggers; it devotes itself professionally to violating the Bill of Rights; its kept judges have pretty well disposed of all the constitutional guarantees of the citizens. But its control of the government puts it above the law. Its agents, on and off the bench, commit their crimes almost unmolested; only one of them, in fact, has ever got into jail—and that was by a sort of accident.

But public opinion is mainly on the side of the bootleggers. They represent, in the combat, the plain man, eternally oppressed and robbed by his overlords. In their popularity is to be seen the first glimmers of a revolt, not against this or that form of government, but against the tyranny at the bottom of *all* government. Government to-day, is growing too strong to be safe. There are no longer any citizens in the world; there are only subjects. They work day in and day out for their masters; they are bound to die for their masters at call. Out of this working and dying they tend to get less and less. On some bright to-morrow, a geological epoch or two hence, they will come to the end of their endurance, and then such newspapers as survive will have a first-page story well worth its black headlines.

4. Freudian Footnote

That the life of man is a struggle and an agony was remarked by the Brisbanes and Dr. Frank Cranes of the remotest antiquity. The earliest philosophers busied themselves with the fact, and so did the earliest poets. It runs like a *leitmotif* through the literature of the Greeks and the Jews alike. "Vanity of vanities; all is vanity!" "O ye deathward-going tribes of men," chants Sophocles, "what do your lives mean except that they go to nothingness?" But not placidly, not unresistingly, not without horrible groans and gurgles. Man is never honestly the fatalist, nor even the stoic. He fights his fate, often desperately. He is forever entering bold exceptions to the rulings of the bench or gods. This fighting, no doubt, makes for human progress, for it favors the strong and the brave. It also makes for beauty, for lesser men try to escape from a hopeless and intolerable world by creating a more lovely one of their own. Poetry, as everyone knows, is a means to that end—facile, and hence popular. The aim of poetry is to give a high and voluptuous plausibility to what is palpably not true. I offer the Twenty-third Psalm as an example: "The Lord is my shepherd; I shall not want." It is immensely esteemed by the inmates of almshouses, and by gentlemen waiting to be hanged. I have to limit my own reading of it, avoiding soft and yielding moods, for I too, in my way, am a gentleman waiting to be hanged, as you are. If the air were impregnated with poetry, as it is with carbon in Pittsburgh, and alcohol in Hoboken, N.J., and stale incense in Boston, the world would be a more comfortable and caressing place, but the service of the truth would be neglected. The truth is served by prose. The aim of prose is not to conceal the facts, but to display them. It is thus apt to be harsh and painful. All that the philosophers and metaphysicians of the world have accomplished, grinding away in their damp cells since man became cryptococcygeal, is to prove that *Homo sapiens* and *Equus asinus* [the ass] are brothers under the skin. As for the more imaginative *prosateurs*, they have pretty well confined themselves, since the earliest beginnings of their craft, to the lugubrious chronicle of man's struggle and defeat. I know of no first-rate novel that hasn't this theme. In all of them, from *Don Quixote* to *The Brothers Karamazov* and from *Vanity Fair* to *McTeague*," we are made privy to the agonies of a man resisting his destiny, and getting badly beaten.

The struggle is always the same, but in its details it differs in different ages. There was a time, I believe, when it was mainly a combat between the natural instincts of the individual and his yearning to get into Heaven. That was an unhealthy time, for throttling the instincts is almost as deleterious as breathing bad air: it makes for an unpleasant clamminess. The Age of Faith, seen in retrospect, looks somehow pale and puffy: one admires its saints and anchorites without being conscious of any very active desire to shake hands with them and smell them. To-day the yearning to get into Heaven is in abeyance, at least among the vast majority of humankind, and so the ancient struggle takes a new form. In the main, it is a struggle of man with society—a conflict between his desire to be respected and his impulse to follow his own bent. It seems to me that society usually wins. There are, to be sure, free spirits in the world, but their freedom, in the last analysis, is not much greater than that of a canary in a cage. They may leap from perch to perch; they may bathe and guzzle at their will; they may flap their wings and sing. But they are still in the cage, and soon or late it conquers them. What was once a great itch for long flights and the open spaces is gradually converted into a fading memory and nostalgia, sometimes stimulating but more often merely blushful. The free man, made in God's image, is converted into a Freudian case.

Such Freudian cases swarm in modern society; they are hidden in all sorts of unexpected places. Observing a Congressman, one sees only a gross and revolting shape, with dull eyes and prehensile hands. But under that preposterous mask there may be yearnings, and some of them may be of high voltage and laudable delicacy. There are Congressmen, I have no doubt, who regret their lost honor, as women often do in the films. Tossing in their beds on hot, sticky Washington nights, their gizzards devoured by bad liquor, they may lament the ruin that the service of Deimos [god of terror] has brought to their souls. For Congressmen, despite their dishonorable trade, are exactly like the rest of us at bottom, and respond to the same biometric laws. In infancy they go to Sunday-school. Passing through adolescence, they are idealists, and dream of saving the world. Come to young manhood, they suffer the purifying pangs of love. The impulse to seek political preferment, when it arises in them, is not always, not primarily, an impulse to grab something, to victimize and exploit the rest of us. That comes later: even Penrose and Roosevelt started out as altruists and reformers. But the rules of the game run one way, and common honesty and common decency run another. There comes a time when the candidate must surrender either his ideals or his aspirations. If he is in Congress it is a sign that he has preserved the latter.

Democracy produces swarms of such men, in politics and on other planes, and their secret shames and sorrows, I believe, are largely responsible for the generally depressing tone of democratic society. Old Freud, living in a more urbane and civilized world, paid too little heed to that sort of repression. He assumed fatuously that what was repressed was always, or nearly always, something intrinsically discreditable, or, at all events, anti-social—for example, the natural impulse to neck a pretty woman, regardless of her husband's protests. But under democracy that is only half the story. The democrat with yearning to shine before his fellows must not only repress all the common varieties of natural wickedness, he must also repress many of the varieties of natural decency. His impulse to speak his mind freely, to tell the truth as he sees it, to be his own man, comes into early and painful collision with the democratic dogma that such things are not nice—that the most worthy and laudable citizen is that one who is most like all the rest. In youth, as every one knows, this dogma is frequently challenged, and sometimes with great asperity, but the rebellion, taking one case with another, is not of long duration. The campus Nietzsche, at thirty, begins to feel the suction of Rotary; at forty he is a sound Mellon man; at fifty he is fit for Congress.

But his early yearning for freedom and its natural concomitants is still not dead; it is merely imprisoned in the depths of his subconscious. Down there it drags out its weary and intolerable years, protesting silently but relentlessly against its durance. We know, by Dr. Freud's appalling evidence, what the suppression of the common wickednesses can do the individual—how it can shake his reason on its throne, and even give him such things as gastritis, migraine and angina pectoris. Every Sunday-school in the land is full of such works; they recruit the endless brigades of lady policewomen and male wowsers. A vice-crusader is simply an unfortunate who goes about with a brothel in his own cellar; a Prohibitionist is one who has busted rum, but would have been safer drinking it. All this is now a commonplace of knowledge to every American school-girl. The wowsers themselves give the facts a universal dispersion by trying to suppress them. But so far no psychoanalyst has done a tome on the complexes that issue out of moral struggles against common decency, though they are commoner under democracy than the other kind, and infinitely more ferocious. A man who has throttled a bad impulse has at least some consolation in his agonies, but a man who has throttled a good one is in a bad way indeed. Yet this great Republic swarms with such men, and their sufferings are under every eye. We have more of them, perhaps, than all the rest of Christendom, with heathendom thrown in to make it unanimous.

I marvel that no corn-fed Freud or Adler has ever investigated the case of the learned judges among us, and especially those of the Federal rite. Prohibition, I suspect, has filled them with such repressions that even a psychoanalyst, plowing into the matter, would be shocked. Enforcing its savage and anti-social mandates, with fanatics pulling them and blacklegs pushing them, has obviously compelled them to make away with all the pruderies that are natural to men of their class and condition. There may be individuals among them, to be sure, who were born without any pruderies and hence do not suffer, just as there are individuals who were born without any capacity for affection and hence show no trace of the Oedipus complex, but such men must be very rare, even among politicians, even among lawyers. The average judge, I take it, is much like the rest of us. When he is free to do it, he does the decent thing. His natural impulse is to speak the truth as he sees it, to challenge error and imposture, to frown upon fraud. What, now, if his high and solemn duties compel him to treat fraud as if it were divine revelation? What if he must spend his days prospering rogues and oppressing honest men? What if his oath wars horribly with his conscience? No Freud was needed to argue that the effects upon him must be very evil. He cannot perform his work without assassinating his inner integrity. Putting on his black gown, he must simultaneously cram his unconscious with all the sound impulses and natural decencies that make him the noble fellow that he is.

The clinical effects are certainly not occult. One hears constantly of judges coming down with symptoms which, in ordinary men, would be accepted as proofs of inner turmoils, insusceptible to correction by the pharmacopoeia. They break into hysterical tirades from the bench; they speak in unintelligible language; they deliver judgments that upset the laws of logic; they complain of buzzings in the ears, flashes before the eyes, and vague bellyaches. Two Federal judges, of late, have committed suicide. One climbed a high mountain in his motor-car, and then leaped into space: a monstrous act, and no doubt of plain significance to a Freudian adept. The other left a note saying frankly that Prohibition had wrecked him. The faculty has at such disturbances of the psyche by hunting for focal infections and pulling teeth: the whole judiciary tends to become toothless. But it would be easier and cheaper and more effective, I am convinced, to send for a psychoanalyst. The stricken judge would come out of the room cured, and the psychoanalyst would come out with a new outfit of complexes.

I speak of the judges because their sufferings are palpable. But there must be swarms of other victims in this eminent free nation. Every one of us has been under the steam-roller; every one of us, in this way or that, conforms unwillingly, and has the corpse of a good impulse belowstairs. There are probably no exceptions. Psychoanalyze a Methodist bishop, and you'll probably find him stuffed with good impulses, all of them repressed. On blue afternoons, perhaps, there sneaks out of his unconscious a civilized yearning for a decent drink; in the dark watches of the night he remembers a Catholic girl of his youth, and weeps that she was so fair; he may even, passing a public library, feel a sudden, goatish inclination to go in and read a good book. Suppressed, such appetites make him uncomfortable, unhappy, desperate, an enemy to society. Dredged up by some super-Freud, and dissipated in the sunlight, they would leave him an honest and happy man.

5. Bach to Bach!

"Ah, at evening, to be drinking from the glassy pond, to have—oh, better than all marrow bones!—the fresh illusions of lapping up the stars!"

I take the thought from Patou, the forward-looking hound-dog in Rostand's *Chantecler*. Let him stand as a symbol of the whole melancholy company of crib-haltered but aspiring Americans, their hands doomed to go-getting but their hearts leaping into interstellar space. Patou, lifted his hind legs and outfitted with pantaloons, would have made a capital Rotarian. Condemned by destiny to a kennel in a barnyard, he yet had that soaring, humorless Vision which is the essence of Rotary, and the secret, no doubt, of its firm hold upon otherwise unpoetical men. For even in the paradise of Babbitt, Babbitt is vaguely uneasy and unhappy. He needs something more, he finds, than is to be found in bulging order-books, in innumerable caravans of prospects, and in belching chimneys and laden trains. He needs something more than is to be got out of blowing spitballs and playing golf. So he searches for that something in the realms of the fancy, where the husks of things fall and their inner sap is revealed. He reads the dithyrambs of Edgar Albert Guest, Arthur Brisbane, and Dr. Frank Crane. He listens to the exhortations of itinerant rhetoricians, gifted and eloquent men, specialists in what it is all about. He intones "Sweet Adeline," and is not ashamed of the tear that babbles down his nose. Thus Babbitt, too, is tantalized by a Grail; he seeks it up and down the gorgeous corridors of his Statler Hotel, past the cigar-stand and the lair of the hat-check gal, and on to the perfumed catacombs of the lively manicurist and the white-robed chirotonsor. *Non in solo pan vivit homo.* Man cannot live by bread alone. He must hope also. He must dream. He must yearn.

The fact explains the Rotarian and his humble brother, the Kiwanian; more, it strips them of not a little of their superficial obnoxiousness. They are fools, but they are not quite damned. If their quest is carried on in motley, they at least trail after better men. And so do all their brethren of Service, great and small—the Americanizers, the Law Enforcers, the boosters and boomers, and the endless others after their kind. At first glance, one sees in these visionaries only noisy and preposterous fellows, disturbing the peace of their betters. But a closer examination is more favorable to them. They are tortured, in their odd, clumsy fashion, by the same ringing in the ears that maddened Ludwig von Beethoven. They suffer from the same optical delusions, painful and not due to sin, that set the prophets of antiquity to howling: they look at a Harding or a Coolidge and see a Man. What lures them to their bizarre cavortings—and it is surely not to be sniffed at *per se*—is a dim and disturbing mirage of a world more lovely and serene than the one the Lord God has doomed them to live in. What they lack in common, thus diverging from the prophets, is a rational conception of what it ought to be, and might be.

It is somewhat astonishing that 100% Americans should wander so helplessly in this wilderness. For there is a well-paved road across the whole waste, and it issues, at its place of beginning, from the tombs of the Fathers, and their sacred and immemorial dust. Straight as a pistol shot it runs, until at the other end it sweeps up a glittering slope to a shrine upon a high hill. This shrine may be seen on fair days for many leagues, and presents a magnificent spectacle. Its base is confected of the bones of Revolutionary heroes, and out of them rises an heroic effigy of George Washington, in alabaster. Surrounding this effigy, and on a slightly smaller scale, are graven images of Jefferson, Franklin, Nathan Hale, old Sam Adams, John Hancock and Paul Revere, each with a Bible under his arm and the Stars and Stripes fluttering over his shoulder. A bit to the rear, and without the Bible, is a statue of Thomas Paine. Over the whole structure stretch great bands of the tricolor, in silk, satin and other precious fabrics. Red and white stripes run up and down the legs of Washington, and his waistcoat is spattered with stars. The effect is the grandiose one of a Democratic national convention. At night, in the American manner, spotlights play upon the shrine. Hot dogs are on sale nearby, that pilgrims may not hunger, and there is a free park for Fords, with running water and booths for the sale of spare parts. It is the shrine of Liberty!

But where are the pilgrims? One observes the immense parking space and the huge pyramids of hot dogs, and one looks for great hordes of worshipers, fighting their way to the altar-steps. But they are *non est* [non-existent]. Now and then a honeymoon couple wanders in from the rural South or Middle West to gape at the splendors hand in hand, and now and then a school-ma'am arrives with a flock of her pupils, and lectures them solemnly out of a book. More often, perhaps, a foreign visitor is to be seen, with a *couronne* [wreath] of tin bay-leaves under his arm. He deposits the *couronne* at the foot of Washington, crosses himself lugubriously, and retires to the nearest hot dog stand. But where are the Americans? Where are the he-men, heirs to the heroes whose gilded skulls here wait the Judgment Day? Where are the Americanizers? Where are the boosters and boomers? Where are the sturdy Coolidge men? Where are the Rotarians, Kiwanians, Lions? Where are the authors of newspaper editorials? The visionaries of Chautauqua? The keepers of the national idealism? Go search for them, if you don't trust the first report of your eyes! Go search for honest men in Congress! They are simply not present. For among all the visions that now inflame forward-looking and up-and-coming men in this great Republic, there is no sign any more of the one that is older than all the rest, and that is the vision of Liberty. The Fathers saw it, and the devotion they gave to it went far beyond three cheers a week. It survived into Jackson's time, and its glow was renewed in Lincoln's. But now it is no more.

The phenomenon is curious, and deserves far more study by eminent psychologists than it has got. I may undertake that study as an amateur in a work reserved for my senility; at the moment I can only point to the fact. Liberty, to-day, not only lacks its old hot partisans and romantic fanatics in America; it has grown so disreputable that even to mention it, save in terms of a fossilized and hollow rhetoric, becomes a sort of indecorum. I know of but one national organization [ACLU] that advocates it with any genuine heartiness, and that organization, not long ago, was rewarded with a violent denunciation on the floor of the House of Representatives: only one lone Socialist, once in jail himself for the same offense, made bold to defend it. From the chosen elders of the nation, legislative, executive and judicial, one hears only that demanding it is treason. It is the first duty of the free citizen, it appears, to make a willing sacrifice of the Bill of Rights. He must leap to the business gladly, and with no mental reservations. If he pauses, then he is a bolshevik.

I venture to argue that this doctrine is evil, and that renouncing it would yield a sweeter usufruct to the American people than all the varieties of Service that now prevail. Of what use is it for Kiwanis to buy wooden legs for one-legged boys if they must grow up as slaves to the Anti-Saloon

League? What is the net gain to a boomed and boosted town if its people, coincidentally, lose their right to trial by jury and their inviolability of the domicile? Who gives a damn for the Coolidge idealism if its chief agent and executor, even above the Cabinet, is the Board of Temperance, Prohibition and Public Morals of the Methodist Episcopal Church, i.e., a gang of snoutty ecclesiastics, committed unanimously to the doctrines that Christ should have been jailed for the business at Cana, that God sent she-bears to "tare" forty-two little children because they had made fun of Elisha's bald head, and that Jonah swallowed the whale? Imagine an immigrant studying the new science of Americanism, and coming to the eighteen amendments to the Constitution. What will he make of the discovery that only the Eighteenth embodies a categorical imperative—that all the others must yield to it when they conflict with it—that the Fourteenth and Fifteenth are not binding upon the Prohibitionists of the South and that the First, Fourth, Fifth and Sixth are not binding upon Prohibitionists anywhere?

I preach reaction. Bach to Bach? I can't find the word Service in the Constitution, but what is there is sounder and nobler than anything ever heard of where Regular Fellows meet to slap backs and blow spitballs—or, at all events, it was there before January 16, 1920. The Fathers, too, had a Vision. They were, in their way, forward-lookers; they were even go-getters. What they dreamed of and fought for was a civilization based upon a body of simple, equitable and reasonable laws—a code designed to break the chains of lingering medievalism, and set the individual free. The thing they imagined was a commonwealth of free men, all equal before the laws. Some of them had grave doubts about it, and put off making it a reality as long as possible, but in the end the optimists won over the doubters, and they all made the system together. I am myself no partisan of their scheme. It seems to me that there were fundamental defects in it—that some of their primary assumptions were false. But in their intention, at least, there was something exhilarating, and in it there was also something sound. That something was the premise that the first aim of civilization is to augment and safeguard the dignity of man—that it is worth nothing to be citizen of a commonwealth which holds the humblest citizen cheaply and uses him ill.

This is what we have lost, and not all the whooping and yelling of new messiahs can cover the fact. The government, as I have shown, becomes the common enemy of all well-disposed and decent men. It commandeers and wastes their money, it assaults and insults them with outrageous and extravagant laws, and it turns loose upon them a horde of professional blackguards, bent only upon destroying their liberties. The individual, facing this pestilence of tyranny and corruption, finds himself quite helpless. If he goes to the agents of the government itself with his protest, he gets only stupid reviling. If he turns to his fellow victims for support, he is lucky to escape jail. Worse, he is lucky to escape lynching. For the thing has gone so far that the great majority of dull and unimaginative men have begun to take it as a matter of course—almost as the order of nature. The Bill of Rights becomes a mere series of romantic dithyrambs, without solid substance or meaning—say, like the Sermon on the Mount. The school-books of the next generation will omit it. The few fanatics who remember it will keep it on the top shelf, along with the Family Doctor Book, the scientific works of Dr. Marie Scopes, and "Only a Boy."

Against all this I protest, feebly and too late. The land swarms with Men of Vision, all pining for Service. What I propose is that they forget their *brummagem* [cheap, counterfeit] Grails for one week, and concentrate their pep upon a chase that really leads uphill. Let us have a Bill of Rights Week. Let us have a Common Decency Week.

(*Prejudices, Sixth Series*)

THE LAND OF THE FREE

[*In 1925, a year when the First Amendment fully protected all those burning crosses at Methodist revivals/Klan rallies, an Italian immigrant named Carlo Tresca got tossed in the clink for inadvertently running a birth control advertisement in his anarchist newspaper,* Il Martello *(The Hammer). Tresca got a prison sentence of over a year for the advertisement, and the advertiser (another Italian immigrant), got four months. Such a dichotomy in legal procedures, the Klan allowed to run amok while two progressive leftists from papal country got hit right between the eyes, is evidence that the supposed guarantees in the Bill of Rights no more apply to the lives of average Americans than the Magna Carta or Justinian's Code.*

Anyone who doesn't believe this has never had the slightest contact with the legal system or spends too much time watching Fox News. Your constitutional rights go into abeyance any time the cops find those rights inconvenient, and you lose them entirely any time a prosecutor finds it politically expedient to take them and can find a jury dumb enough to convict. And that's almost always. No matter how politically motivated and far fetched the charges, a prosecutor can probably convince a jury to convict you. And once on the wrong side of the law, all you can expect is a few defeated liberals to come by during visiting hours—and then only if your case is high profile.

As an unhappy footnote, agents of Mussolini assassinated Tresca in 1940.]

1

Carlo Tresca is the proprietor of a small Italian paper in New York, by name *Il Martello* [The Hammer]. He runs to Liberal ideas, and when the Fascisti came into power in his native country, and began Ku Kluxing their opponents, he denounced them in his paper, and called upon the Italians in America to repudiate them. His articles were vigorously written, and quickly attracted attention. A great many Italians began to incline toward his views.

That was early in 1923. In the same year certain persons in New York gave a public dinner to honor Judge Elbert H. Gary, chairman of the board of directors of the United States Steel Corporation. Judge Gary, for his services to the Cause of Humanity in America, had been made an honorary member of the Fascisti organization, and one of the guests who came to the dinner to do him honor was Prince Gelesto Caetani, then and now the Italian Ambassador at Washington. Prince Caetani was naturally called upon to make a speech. He made one bitterly denouncing the opponents of Fascismo among the American Italians, and arguing that "a certain Italian paper in New York" ought to be suppressed.

The assembled apostles of Human Liberty knew that he meant *Il Martello*, and applauded him heartily. That there was no law in the United States forbidding a newspaper to criticize a foreign government did not trouble them; they had been through the late war, and knew what could be done. So did the eminent [Henry] Daugherty, and the Postoffice Department. Word was conveyed to Washington, and then back to New York. On July 21 the whole issue of *Il Martello* was held up in the mails. Tresca demanded to know why. The Postoffice Department gave him no answer. He kept on denouncing the Fascisti.

Three weeks later, on August 10, he was suddenly arrested. The charge was that he had printed an article three months before, attacking the Italian monarchy. No such crime, of course, is known to American law, but Tresca was nevertheless arrested. He got out on bail, and kept on denouncing the Fascisti. The charge was allowed to drop. On August 18 the whole issue of *Il Martello* was held up because it contained an account of a raffle; two other Italian papers, containing precisely the same account, went through the mails unmolested. On September 8 it was held up because it contained a two-line advertisement of a book on birth control. On October 27 it was held up because it printed an account of how the Fascisti had forced an Italian woman to swallow an immense dose of castor oil; all the American newspapers printed the same story, but were not molested. On November 10 it was held up because it printed a letter from a reader predicting that Mussolini would come to the same end as Rienzi [Cola di Rienzo, who died while in prison]; other papers had made the same prediction without challenge. On November 24 it was held up for charging Mussolini with misappropriating funds.

2

Meanwhile, Tresca kept on denouncing the Fascisti, and the Italian Ambassador, it may be safely presumed, kept on nursing the conviction that *Il Martello* ought to be suppressed. The war, unfortunately, was over, and so it was not easy to accomplish the business. Holding up the paper day after day, and subjecting it to heavy and arbitrary losses—this was apparently easy, but it was impossible, under the law, to suppress it altogether, and very difficult to get Tresca into jail and keep him there.

Finally, however, juridic science solved the problem. The little two-line advertisement of September, announcing a book in Italian on birth control, showed the way. Experienced witch-hunters from the Department of Justice were rushed to New York, Tresca was indicted for advertising a means of preventing conception, and his trial was called in hot haste. He appeared before Goddard J., in the United States District Court, on November 27. The evidence showed some strange things. Tresca, it appeared, had actually never sent a single copy of the offending issue through the mails. The instant he heard that the Postoffice had held it up he withdrew it, and reprinted a new issue without the two-line advertisement. It appeared, indeed, that other charges were mixed up with the complaint. One was that he had printed an article entitled "Down With the Monarchy." This was plainly not illegal, but the prosecution made much of it. Finally, the assistant district attorney offered to drop the whole case if Tresca would leave the country, i.e., go back to Italy, where the Fascisti could deal with him. He refused, and was convicted. Judge Goddard sentence him to a year and a day at Atlanta.

This was an appallingly heavy sentence—the heaviest ever heard of. In nearly all previous Federal cases the culprit had been simply fined. In none of the State cases had a sentence of more than six months been inflicted, and the average for all of them was less than a month. There was no evidence that Tresca had ever seen the advertisement before it got into his paper. On the contrary, it was shown that the man who brought it in and inserted it was one Vella, the paper's advertising agent. The actual advertiser was one Nieri, an Italian bookseller. He, too, was arrested and convicted. He got four months in jail. But Tresca, who was only constructively guilty, got a year and a day in Atlanta Prison.

And there he sits now, for the Circuit Court of Appeals has upheld his conviction.

3

Such episodes—and they are by no means rare, despite the common superstition that Palmerism has been squeezed out of the Department of Justice and Burlesonism out of the Postoffice—give the student of American history powerfully to think. What becomes of the old notion that the United States is a free country, that it is a refuge for the oppressed of other lands, that here they may voice their grievances and call for help. There was a time when such rebels against tyranny came here as a matter of course, and were received with open arms. The name of [Lajos] Kossuth [Hungarian liberal political leader and orator forced into exile] is even in the school books. But what would happen to a Kossuth today—if the Hungarian Ambassador could convince Judge Gary and company that he ought to be in jail?

Also, what becomes of the old notion that a peaceable man, in this great Republic, should be unmolested—that the *Polizei* should not pursue and harass him day and night, and try by dodge after dodge to get him into their clutches? The Postoffice tackled Tresca at least five times before it finally fetched him. Every one of those times, it must be obvious, he was innocent of any wrongdoing, else he would have been railroaded forthwith. It took six shots to bring him down—and then he was caught on a childish technicality. Every American editor who prints any reference to a book on birth control, even if it be a review denouncing it, is quite as guilty as he was, and perhaps even more guilty. And consider his punishment! The man who offered the book for sale got four months; Tresca, for merely printing two lines about it, got a year and a day!

I attempt no long sermon on the text; it is eloquent enough of itself. The facts, so far as I know, are not disputed by anyone. There was a time when their publication would have caused an uproar; today they go almost unnoticed. The great agencies of Americanism will let Tresca rot in prison before they lift their hands to help him, just as they are letting his fellow Italians, Sacco and Vanzetti, rot in prison. The American Legion, though it still sweats and moans for human liberty, will not protest; on the contrary, it is more likely to pass a resolution urging that the wop be kept behind bars, guilty or not guilty. The Sons of the Revolution will maintain a magnificent silence. Kiwanis and Rotary will not be heard from.

4

So far, indeed, but eight persons in all the United States have gone to Tresca's aid. Four are Italian-American politicians. One is a Liberal pastor. Two are old and battle-scarred libertarians, already marked with the scars of a hundred defeats. The eighth is La Sanger, the birth-control agitator, herself an experienced goat of the New Jurisprudence. No one else will take any interest in the case.

(*The Baltimore Evening Sun*, January 12, 1925)

TWO WASTED LIVES

[*Alexander Berkman and Emma Goldman were two of the leading anarchist writers and activists of the late 19th and early 20th centuries in the United States. As such they were hounded by the authorities, routinely and viciously caricatured in the mainstream press, and ultimately deported back to their native Russia during the post-WWI Red Scare. Their experiences there led to their writing two of the most devastating indictments of the Bolsheviks and Soviet Union, Goldman's* My Disillusionment in Russia *and Berkman's* The Bolshevik Myth.*

Mencken was no anarchist, but he was a dedicated civil libertarian and profoundly anti-Communist. He was also profoundly pessimistic, and couldn't conceive of any type of political and social system that would significantly improve the lot of humanity. So, he rejected Berkman's and Goldman's politics while admiring their ruthlessly honest analysis of the Soviet monstrosity, and he deplored their persecution by the U.S. government.

Unfortunately, Mencken was overly optimistic about the effect of Berkman's and Goldman's books on the American left. A large majority of American leftists rejected their reports out of hand; they simply didn't want to hear them. They clung to their wishful thinking and joined an authoritarian political cult in droves—the so-called Communist Party—that worshipped two of the vilest mass murdering dictators in human history.

Unfortunately, that sort of shameful, degrading behavior is once again rampant in this country. At this writing, Christofascist butt kissers and goose steppers have formed yet another authoritarian political cult and are dead set on reinstalling their vile would-be dictator in power.]

———————————

One commonly hears of such persons as Emma Goldman and Alexander Berkman only as remote and horrendous malefactors, half human and half reptilian. Editorial writers, on dull days, exhume ancient bills of complaint against them and give thanks to God that they are safely be-

yond these Christian shores, and for good. They are denounced by orators
before the American Legion, by suburban pastors and by brave Congressmen. While they were still in our midst one heard only that *Polizei* were
hot on their trail, that the gallant catchpolls of the so-called Department
of Justice were about to trap them, that the hoosegow at Atlanta was being
warmed for them. Since the Buford [ship on which they were deported]
sailed the science of jurisprudence has made immense progress among us.
Had it leaped a step Berkman would have a padlock through his snout,
and La Goldman, I suspect, would have been outfitted with a *ceinture de
patri[moine]* [chastity belt].

All this indignation, unfortunately, conceals something, and that is the
somewhat disconcerting fact that both are extremely intelligent—that once
their aberrant political ideals are set aside they are seen to have very sharp
wits. They think clearly, unsentimentally and even a bit brilliantly. They
write simple, glowing and excellent English. Their feelings, far from being those of yeggmen, cannibals and prohibition enforcement officers, are
those of highly civilized persons. How, then, is their political nonsense to
be explained—their childish belief in the proletariat, their life-long faith
in Utopia? Go ask me something easier! I am no professor of morbid psychology. But I know a very intelligent man, a scientist of national fame,
who believes that drinking a glass of beer is a mortal sin. I know another
man, eminent in public life, who patronizes chiropractors. I know a third,
worth at least $10,000,000, who believes in thought transference. I know a
fourth—

* * *

But it is unnecessary to go on. The fact that a human brain of high amperage, otherwise highly efficient, may have a hole in it is surely not a secret.
All of us, in our several ways, are illogical, irrational, almost insane. It is the
misfortune of Berkman and La Goldman that the form their private folly
takes is very unpopular; that it greatly alarms all the more simpleminded
types of men; that it is the custom in America to combat it, not by laughing
at it, but by yelling for the police. The fact, I believe, has given them undue eminence in the national demonology. They are ranked with Benedict
Arnold, the James brothers, Brigham Young, Sitting Bull and John Wilkes
Booth. What is good in them is completely overlooked.

These reflections are inspired by a reading of Berkman's *The Bolshevik
Myth* (Boni & Liveright), preceded shortly by a reading of Miss Goldman's
My Disillusionment in Russia (Doubleday, Page). Both, it seems to me are

very good books, books of quite unusual distinction—perhaps, indeed, the best books that the Russian debacle has yet produced. There is not the slightest hint of the usual propaganda in them. They were not written either to gild the Bolsheviki as angels or to bedaub them as devils. Both, so to speak, were done against the grain; there is in them a confession of profound error. But they are frank, they are fair and straightforward, and they are written with quite extraordinary skill. I attempt no choice between them. Miss Goldman's volume is perhaps the more moving, for there is something finer in her than in Berkman, but his is surely the more dramatic and devastating.

* * *

Berkman starts with his departure from the United States on the Buford. He was, he says, glad to get away, and I believe him. He had spent more of his years here in prison than in freedom; ahead, at worst, was liberty. He was, of course, an anarchist, and hence an opponent of the Bolsheviki—despite the belief of Federal district attorneys, newspaper editorial writers, members of Congress and other such morons that the two are identical—but he was far more interested in the revolution than in the notions underlying it. Here, at last, the great experiment of his dreams was on. Here, at last, the Chandala had overthrown their masters and were hard at work upon the New Jerusalem.

Berkman stepped upon Russian soil with his heart leaping like that of a Kansas deacon landing at Bimini. The Bolsheviki were instantly polite to him. More intelligent than the rulers of older countries, they had observed the fact that he was a man of parts, and they determined to make use of those parts—perhaps even to win him over by keeping him busy and showing confidence in him. He was received and made much of by the highest dignitaries of the state. He was given important work. He was given authority. He was turned loose.

Alas for the plans of mice and men! His sharp eyes, it quickly appeared, were just a bit too sharp. Day by day they began to penetrate further and further into the Bolshevik sham. They discovered abuses innumerable—graft, injustice, petty tyranny, downright oppression. They found politicians getting rich at the expense of the starving toilers. They found courts run by brutes, and the jails full of innocent men. They found corruption and incompetence everywhere, cynicism and self-seeking in high places, misery almost inconceivable under the surface show. In brief, they found that life in Utopia was ten times as hard, a hundred times as unhappy, a thousand times as savage, as under the hell-hounds of capital—worse even than life in a Pennsylvania mining town; almost as appalling (to a humane man) as life in Los Angeles (to an intelligent man).

* * *

Poor Berkman was staggered. His bald head, I daresay, steamed with clammy sweat. So this was the revolution? This was the end of a lifelong dream, cherished for years and years in dungeons! It would be difficult to imagine any more crushing disillusionment. Nor any more realistic dealing with it. Berkman wasted no time trying to see the better side. He didn't counsel himself to be patient, and wait for a miracle. Instead, he asked for his passport, went to Berlin, got a comfortable pew in a respectable beer house, spit on his hands and wrote *The Bolshevik Myth*. I believe it will do more to blow up that myth than all the pious snuffling of the late Charles Evans Hughes—nay, more than the hottest tears of 10,000 Charles Evans Hugheses.

For Berkman is a transparently honest man. There can be no question of his *bona fides*. Nor of the soundness of his information. Nor of his capacity to weigh it, estimate it, determine its bearings. His book constitutes a criticism that is absolutely shattering. Nothing is left of the Bolshevik balderdash when he has finished with it. He searches out its every weakness; he exposes the dreadful fraudulence of all its principal exponents; he turns it completely inside out. When the Department of State attempted the same job only Babbitts believed it; its own fraudulence was too manifest. But Berkman, I suspect, will convince even the liberals.

Now to my point: It was a great mistake, I am convinced, to let so shrewd, forthright and frank a fellow go, and La Goldman with him. The defect in our system is that it utilizes men badly—that it throttles more talent than it makes any use of. The Bolsheviki seem to be surviving Berkman's devastating onslaught; it may even strengthen them at home, if only by making them more careful. But in the United States, where such criticism is needed quite as sorely as in Russia and where it could be turned to use ten times as well—here the only thing we can think of doing to such a man as Berkman is to lock him up in jail. Because his fulminations alarm a few profiteers, we hunt him as if he were a mad dog—and finally kick him out of the country. And with him goes a shrewder head and a braver spirit than has been seen in public life since the Civil War.

(*Chicago Sunday Tribune*, April 26, 1925)

2

POLITICS

ON GOVERNMENT

[Pretending to channel the thoughts of the Founding Fathers is a classic American pastime, enjoyed by liberals and conservatives alike. In this essay, Mencken shows that he can play the game more effectively than most. Rather than trying to make the case that the Founding Fathers were Christians, or for high or low taxes, or whatever, he simply assumes them to have been intelligent men. Because they were intelligent men, they were cynical about politics and the role of government bureaucracy.

It's almost useless to try to quote Mencken because every sentence is quotable, but the sentence, "If downright revolution is thus incapable of curing the diseases, the ordinary reforms that men believe in sink to the level of bald quackeries," should at least be on an email signature or internet meme somewhere. Social activism is next to useless in a theocratic republic; the America that progressives believe in only exists because of half-a-dozen Supreme Court rulings—and god alone knows how much longer they'll hold given the current makeup of the court.

In sum, this essay is a classic piece of American cynicism which could serve as a rejoinder to Thoreau's On the Duty of Civil Disobedience, *to which Mencken would surely have replied with a resounding "why bother?"]*

1

"Government," said William Godwin in that *Enquiry Concerning Political Justice* which got Shelley two wives and lost him 6,000 pounds a year, "can have no more than two legitimate purposes: the suppression of injustice against individuals within the community, and the common defense against external invasion." The dictum, after a hundred and thirty-one years, remains unimproved and perhaps unimprovable. Today, to be sure, with Darwin behind us, we'd make some change in its terms: what Godwin was trying to say, obviously, was that the central aim of government was to ameliorate the struggle for existence—to cherish and protect the dignity of man in the midst of the brutal strife of *Homo neanderthalensis*. But that change would be simply substituting a cliché of the Nineteenth Century for one of the Eighteenth. All the furious discussion of the subject that has gone on in the intervening time has not changed the basic idea in the slightest. To the plain man of today, as to the most fanatical Liberal or Socialist, government appears primarily as a device for compensating his weakness, a machine for protecting him in rights that he could not make secure with his own arm. Even the Tory holds the same view of it: its essential function, to him, is to safeguard his property against the lascivious desire of those who, if they were not policed, would be tempted to grab it. "Government," said George Washington, "is not reason, it is not eloquence—it is force." Bad government is that which is weak, irresolute and lacking in constabulary enterprise; when one has defined it one has also defined a bad bishop, cavalry captain or policeman. Good government is that which delivers the citizen from the risk of being done out of his life and property too arbitrarily and violently—one that relieves him sufficiently from the barbaric business of guarding them to enable him to engage in gentler, more dignified and more agreeable undertakings, to his own content and profit, and the advantage, it may be, of the commonwealth.

Unfortunately, this function is performed only imperfectly by any of the forms of government now visible in Christendom, and Dr. Johnson was perhaps justified in dismissing them all as but various aspects of the same fraud. The citizen of today, even in the most civilized states, is not only secured but defectively against other citizens who aspire to exploit and injure him—for example, highwaymen, bankers, quack doctors, clergymen, sellers of oil stock and contaminated liquor, and so-called reformers of all sorts,—and against external foes, military, commercial and philosophical; he is also exploited and injured almost without measure by the government itself—in other words, by the very agency which professes to protect him. That agency becomes, indeed, one of the most dangerous and insatiable of the inimical forces present in his everyday environment. He finds it more difficult and costly to survive in the face of it than it is to survive in the face of any other enemy. He may, if he has prudence, guard himself effectively against all the known varieties of private criminals, from stockbrokers to pickpockets and from lawyers to kidnapers, and he may, if he has been burnt enough, learn to guard himself also against the rogues who seek to rob him by the subtler devices of playing upon his sentimentalism and superstitions: charity mongers, idealists, soul-savers, and the tax-gatherer and the policemen, in all their protean and multitudinous guises, than he can escape the ultimate mortician. They beset him constantly, day in and day out, in ever-increasing numbers and in ever more disarming masks and attitudes. They invade his liberty, affront his dignity and greatly incommode his search for happiness, and every year they demand and wrest from him a larger and larger share of his worldly goods. The average American of today works more than a full day in every week to support his government. It already costs him more than his pleasures and almost as much as his vices, and in another half century, no doubt, it will begin to cost as much as his necessities.

These gross extortions and tyrannies, of course, are all practised on the theory that they are not only unavoidable but also laudable—that government oppresses its victims in order to confer upon them the great boons mentioned by Godwin. But that theory, I believe, begins to be quite as dishonest as the chiropractor's pretense that he pummels his patient's spine in order to cure his cancer: the actual object, obviously, is simply to cure his solvency. What keeps such notions in full credit, and safeguards them against destructive analysis, is chiefly the survival into our enlightened age of a concept hatched in the black days of absolutism—the concept, to wit, that government is something that is superior to and quite distinct from all other human institutions—that it is, in its essence, not a mere organization of ordinary men, like the Ku Klux Klan, the United States Steel Corporation or Columbia University, but a transcendental organism composed of aloof and impersonal powers, devoid wholly of self-interest and not to be measured by merely human standards. One hears it spoken of, not uncommonly, as one hears the law of gravitation and the grace of God spoken of—as if its acts had no human motive in them and stood clearly above human fallibility. This concept, I point out not argue, is full of error. The government at Washington is no more impersonal than the cloak and suit business is impersonal. It is operated by precisely the same sort of men, and to almost the same ends. When we say that it has decided to do this or that, that it proposes or aspires to do this or that—usually to the great cost and inconvenience of nine-tenths of us—we simply say that a definite man or group of men has decided to do it; and when we examine this group of men realistically we almost invariably find that it is composed of individuals who are not only not superior to the general, but plainly and depressingly inferior, both in common sense and in common decency— that the act of government we are called upon to ratify and submit to is, in its essence, no more than an act of self-interest by men who, if no mythical authority stood behind them, would have a hard time of it surviving in the struggle for existence.

2

These men, in point of fact, are seldom if ever moved by anything describable as public spirit; there is actually no more public spirit among them than among so many burglars or street-walkers. Their purpose, first, last and all the time, is to promote their private advantages, and to that end, and that end alone, they exercise all the vast powers that are in their hands. Sometimes the thing they want is mere security in their jobs; sometimes they want gaudier and more lucrative jobs; sometimes they are content with their jobs and their pay but yearn for more power. Whatever it is they seek, whether security, greater ease, more money or more power, it has to come out of the common stock, and so it diminishes the shares of all other men. Putting a new job-holder to work decreases the wages of every wage-earner in the land—not enough to be noticed, perhaps, but enough to leave its mark. Giving a job-holder more power takes something away from the liberty of all of us: we are less free than we were in proportion as he has more authority. Theoretically, we get something for what we give up, but actually we usually get absolutely nothing. Suppose two-thirds of the members of the national House of Representatives were dumped into the Washington garbage incinerator tomorrow, what would we lose to offset our gain of their salaries and the salaries of their parasites? It may be plausibly argued, of course, that the House itself is necessary to our happiness and salvation—that we need it as we need trolley conductors, chiropodists and the men who bite off puppies' tails. But even if that be granted—and I, for one, am by no means disposed to grant it—the plain fact remains that all the useful work the House does might be done just as well by fifty men, and that the rest are of no more utility to the commonwealth, in any rational sense, than so many tight-rope walkers or teachers of mah jong.

The Fathers, when they launched the Republic, were under no illusions as to the nature of government. Washington's view of its inner nature I have already quoted; Jefferson it was who said sagely that "that government is best which governs least." The Constitution in its first form, perhaps, was designed chiefly to check the rising pretensions of the lower orders, drunk with the democratic fustian of the Revolutionary era, but when the Bill of

Rights was added to it its guns began to point more especially at the government itself, i.e., at the class of job-holders, ever bent upon oppressing the citizen to the limit of his endurance. It is, perhaps a fact provocative of sour mirth that the Bill of Rights was designed trustfully to prohibit forever two of the favorite crimes of all known governments: the seizure of private property without adequate compensation and the invasion of the citizen's liberty without justifiable cause and due process of law. It is a fact provocative of mirth yet more sour than the execution of these prohibitions was put into the hands of courts, which is to say, into the hands of lawyers, which is to say, into the hands of men specifically educated to discover legal excuses for dishonest, dishonorable, anti-social acts. The actual history of the Constitution, as everyone knows, has been a history of the gradual abandonment of all such impediments to governmental tyranny. Today we live frankly under a government of men, not of laws. What is the Bill of Rights to a Roosevelt, a Wilson, a Palmer, a Dougherty, a Burns? Under such tin-horn Caesars the essential enmity between government and citizen becomes only too plain, and one gets all the proof that is needed of the eternal impossibility of protecting the latter against the former. The government can not only evoke fear in its victims; it can also evoke a sort of superficial reverence. It is thus both an army and a church, and with sharp weapons in both hands it is virtually irresistible. Its personnel, true enough, may be changed, and so may the external forms of the fraud it practises, but the inner nature is immutable.

Politics, as hopeful men practise it in the world, consists mainly of the delusion that a change in form is a change in substance. The American colonists, when they got rid of the Potsdam tyrant [George III], believed fondly that they were getting rid of oppressive taxes forever and setting up complete liberty. They found almost instantly that taxes were higher than ever, and before many years they were writhing under the Alien and Sedition Acts. The French, when they threw off the monarchy at last, looked forward to a Golden Age of peace, plenty and freedom. They are now wracked by war, bankrupted beyond any chance of recovery, and hag-ridden by an apparently unbreakable combination of the most corrupt and cynical politicians ever seen in the world. The experience of the Russians and Germans is even more eloquent. The former have been ruined by their saviors, and in so far as they have any power of reflection left, long for the restoration of the tyranny they once ascribed to the devil. The latter, delivered from the Hohenzollerns, now find the Schmidts and Krauses ten times as expensive and oppressive. Six months after the republic was set up a German cabinet minister, for the first time in the history of the nation, was in flight over the border, his loot under his arm. In the first flush of surprise and indignation the people took to assassinating politicians, but before long they gave it up as hopeless: Schmidt fell but Kraus still lived, and so government kept its vitality and its character. Many Germans, reduced to despair, now advocate a complete abolition of political government; if Stinnes had lived they would have tried to make him dictator of the country. But political government, i.e., government by professional job-holders, would have remained in fact, despite its theoretical abolition, and its nature would have been unchanged.

If downright revolution is thus incapable of curing the disease, the ordinary reforms that men believe in sink to the level of bald quackeries. Consider, for example, the history of so-called Civil Service Reform in the United States. It came in on a wave of intense public indignation against the whole governmental imposture; it represented a violent and romantic effort to substitute an ideal of public service for the familiar harsh reality of public exploitation. For fifty years the American people had sweated and suffered under the spoils system, that lovely legacy of the "reforms" of the Jackson era. By the opening of the eighties they were ready to dispose of it by fair means or foul. The job-holder, once theoretically a freeman discharging a lofty and necessary duty, was seen clearly to be no more than a rat devouring the communal corn; his public position was indistinguishable from that of a child-stealer, a well-poisoner or a Sunday-school superintendent; and that of his brother, the government contractor and purveyor, was even lower. Many men of both classes, including some very important ones, were clapped into jail, and many others had to depart for Canada between days, along with the nightly squad of clerical seducers and absconding bank cashiers. Thereupon seers and prophets arose to lead the people out of the wilderness. A few wild ones proposed, in effect, that government be abolished altogether, but the notion outraged democratic sentiment, and so most of them followed the job-holders into jail; some, in fact, were put to death by more or less due process of law. The majority of soothsayers were less revolutionary; they proposed only that the race of job-holders be reformed by force, that government be purged and denaturized.

This was undertaken by what came to be called Civil Service Reform. The essence of Civil Service Reform was the notion that the job-holder, in return for his high prerogatives and immunities, should be compelled to do an honest day's work he should fit himself for it by hard effort, as a barber fits himself for cutting hair. Led by such men of Vision as E.L. Godkin, Charles J. Bonaparte and Theodore Roosevelt (that, of course, was before Roosevelt deserted the flag and became himself the archetypical job-holder), the reformers proceeded primly toward the dreadful purpose of making the job-holder a mere slave, like a bookkeeper in a wholesale house. His pay and emoluments were cut down and his labors were increased. Once the proudest and most envied citizen of the Republic, free to oppress all other citizens to the limit of their endurance, he became at one stroke a serf groaning in a pen, with a pistol pointed at his head. If, despite the bars and artillery surrounding him, his thrift enabled him to make a show of decent prosperity, he was clapped into prison *ipso facto* [for that very thing], and almost without a trial. A few short years saw his fall from the dizziest heights of ease to the lowest abyss of misery.

This, of course, could not go on, else politics would have tumbled into chaos and government would have lost its basic character; nay its very life. What is more, it did not go on, for human ingenuity, despite the troubles of the time, was still functioning, and presently it found a remedy for the disease—a remedy so perfect, indeed, that the patient did not know he was taking it. That remedy was achieved by the simple process of making two slight changes in the ideal of Civil Service Reform itself. First the word Reform was lopped off, and then the word Civil. There remained then, only Service. This Service saved the day for the job-holder; it gave him a new lease upon his job; it diverted public suspicion from him; it converted him from a criminal into a sort of philanthropist. It remains with us today, the heir and assign of the old spoils system, as the bootlegger is the heir and assign of the saloon-keeper.

3

The chief achievement of Service is that it has shocked reform into the governmental orbit, and so made it official and impeccable—more, highly profitable. The old-time reformer was one who got nothing for his psychic corn-chutes and shin-plasters—who gave them away freely to all comers, seeking only righteousness himself—who often, indeed, took a beating into the bargain. The new reformer, safe in a government job, with a drastic and complex law behind him, is one who is paid in legal tender, unfailingly proffered, for his passionate but usually unintelligible services to humanity—a prophet of the new enlightenment, a priest at a glittering and immense shrine. He is the fellow who enforces the Volstead Act, the Mann Act, all the endless laws for putting down sin. He is the bright evangelist who tours the country teaching mothers how to have babies, spreading the latest inventions in pedagogy, road-making, the export trade, hog-raising and vegetable-canning, waging an eternal war upon illiteracy, hookworm, the white slave trade, patent medicines, the foot and mouth disease, cholera infantum, adultery, rum. He is, quite as often as not, female; he is a lady Ph.D., cocksure, bellicose, very well paid. Male or female, he represents the new governmental tyranny; he is Vision, vice the spoils system, retired. The old-time job-holder, penned in the cage of the Civil Service, is now only a peon, a brother to the ox. He has to work quite as hard as if he labored for Judge Gary or Henry Ford, and he is very much worse paid. The high prerogatives and usufructs of government have slipped out of his hands. They are exercised and enjoyed today by the apostles of Service, a horde growing daily, vastly and irresistibly, in numbers, impudence, power and pay.

Few of the groaning taxpayers of These States, indeed, realize how far this public merchandising of buncombe has displaced the old spoils system, or how much it is costing them every year. During the Civil War an army contractor who went to Washington looking for loot announced frankly what he was after; as a result, he was constantly under suspicion, and was lucky if he got away with as much as $100,000; only a few Vanderbilts and Morgans actually stole more. During the late war he called himself a dollar-a-year-man, put on a major's uniform, took oath to die if need be for the cause of democracy—and went home with million, at least. The job-holder has undergone a similar metamorphosis; maybe apotheosis would be a better aimed word. In the days of the spoils system he was, at least, an amateurish and inept performer. The only reason he ever offered for demanding a place at the public trough was that he deserved it—that he had done his share to elect the ticket. The easy answer to him was that he was an obvious loafer and scoundrel, and deserved nothing. But what answer is to be made to his heir and assign, the evangelist of Service, the prophet of Vision? He doesn't start off with a bad demand for a job; he starts off with a Message. He has discovered the long-sought sure cure for all the sorrows of the world; he has the infallible scheme for putting down injustice, misery, ignorance, suffering, sin; his appeal is not to the rules of a sinister and discreditable game, but to the bursting heart of humanity, the noblest and loftiest sentiments of man. His job is never in the foreground; it is concealed in his Vision. To get at the former one must first dispose of the latter. Well, who is to do it? What true-born American will volunteer for the cynical office? Half are too idiotic and the rest are too cowardly. It takes courage to flaunt and make a mock of Vision—and where is the outrage?

Certainly not in this imperial commonwealth of natural kneebenders and marchers in parades. Nowhere else in Christendom, save only in France, is government more extravagant, nonsensical, unintelligent and corrupt than here, and nowhere else is it so secure. It becomes a sort of crime even to protest against its villainies; all of the late investigations of waste and corruption in Washington were attacked and brought to wreck in the name of duty, decorum, patriotism. The citizen objecting to felony by the agents of the sovereign state, acting in its name, found himself posted as an anarchist? There was, of course, some logic in this imbecility, as there is in everything insane. It was felt that too violent an onslaught upon the disease might do gross damage to the patient, that the attempt to extirpate what was foul and excrescent might imperil what was useful and necessary. Is government, then, useful and necessary? So is a doctor. But suppose the dear fellow claimed the right, every time he was called in to prescribe for a bellyache or a ringing in the ears, to raid the family silver, use the family tooth-brushes, and execute the *droit de seigneur* upon the housemaid? Is it simply a coincidence that the only necessary functionaries who actually perform any necessary comparable brigandage are the lawyers—the very men who, under democracy, chiefly determined the form, policies and acts of the government?

This great pox of civilization, alas, I believe to be incurable, and so I propose no new quackery for its treatment. I am against closing it, and I am against killing it. All I presume to argue is that something would be accomplished by viewing it more realistically—by ceasing to let its necessary and perhaps useful functions blind us to its ever-increasing crimes against the ordinary rights of the free citizen and the common decencies of the world. The fact that it is generally respected—that it possesses effective machinery for propagating and safeguarding that respect—is the main shield of the rogues and vagabonds who use it to exploit the great masses of diligent and credulous men. Whenever you hear anyone bawling for more respect for the laws, whether it be a Coolidge on his imperial throne or an humble county judge in his hedge court, you have before you one who is trying to use them to his private advantage; whenever you hear of new legislation for putting down dissent and rebellion you may be sure that it is promoted by scoundrels. The extortions and oppressions of government will go on so long as such bare fraudulence deceives and disarms the victims—so long as they are ready to swallow the immemorial official theory that protesting against the stealings of the archbishop's secretary's nephew's mistress' illegitimate son is a sin against the Holy Ghost. They will come to an end when the victims begin to differentiate clearly between government as a necessary device for maintaining order in the world and government as a device for maintaining the authority and prosperity of predatory rascals and swindlers. In other words, they will come to an end on the Tuesday following the first Monday of November preceding the Resurrection Morn.

(*Prejudices, Fourth Series*)

In Memoriam W.J.B.

[*William Jennings Bryan, a reliable man of the people at a time when the people's faith could be reliably counted upon, died in 1925 just a few days after disgracing himself during the Scopes Trial in Tennessee. Bryan, God love him, derived some sense of human dignity from the nonsense of the Old Testament and thought the holy spirit would prevail over logic in a court of law. He "won" the case, only on the grounds that a substitute teacher had broken a statute forbidding the teaching of evolution, but the percentage of the American population (probably about 35%) with functioning frontal lobes moved on from Creationism following the trial.*

Insincere eulogies make for the worst form of literature, so thankfully Mencken saw no reason to let Bryan's death remake his opinion of the man's life. Mencken damns Bryan for legitimizing and spreading the evangelical faith, and for making religious belief a "respectable" political platform to run upon. As Mencken writes, "Such is Bryan's legacy to his country. He couldn't be president, but he could at least help magnificently in the solemn business of shutting off the Presidency from every intelligent and self-respecting man." So it has been ever since.]

Has it been duly marked by historians that the late William Jennings Bryan's last secular act on this globe of sin was to catch flies? A curious detail and not without its sardonic overtones. He was the most sedulous fly-catcher in American history, and in many ways the most successful. His quarry, of course, was not *Musca domestica* but *Homo neandertalensis*. For forty years he tracked it with coo and bellow, up and down the rustic backways of the Republic. Wherever the flambeaux of Chautauqua smoked and guttered, and the bilge of Idealism ran in the veins, and Baptist pastors damned the brooks with the heavy laden, and their wives who were full of Peruna [a type of patent medicine] and as fecund as the shad (*alosa sapidissima*)—there the indefatigable Jennings set up his traps and spread his bait. He knew every country town in the South and West, and he could crowd the most remote of them to suffocation by simply winding his horn. The city proletariat, transiently flustered by him in 1896, quickly penetrated his buncombe and would have no more of him; the cockney gallery jeered him at every Democratic national convention for twenty-five years. But out where the grass grows high, and the horned cattle dream away the lazy afternoons, and men still fear the powers and principalities of the air—out there between the corn-cows he held his old puissance to the end. There was no need of beaters to drive in his game. The news that he was coming was enough. For miles the flivver dust would choke the roads. And when he rose at the end of the day to discharge his Message there would be such breathless attention, such a rapt and enchanted ecstasy, such a sweet rustle of amens as the world had not known since Johann fell to Herod's ax.

There was something peculiarly fitting in the fact that his last days were spent in a one-horse Tennessee village, and that death found him there. The man felt at home in such simple and Christian scenes. He liked people who sweated freely, and were not debauched by the refinements of the toilet. Making his progress up and down the Main street of little Dayton, surrounded by gaping primates from the upland valleys of the Cumberland Range, his coat laid aside, his bare arms and hairy chest shining damply, his bald head sprinkled with dust—so accoutred and on display he was obviously happy. He liked getting up early in the morning to the tune of cocks crowing on the dunghill. He liked the heavy, greasy victuals of the farmhouse kitchen. He liked the country sounds and country smells. I believe that this liking was sincere—perhaps the only sincere thing in the man. His nose showed no uneasiness when a hillman in faded overalls and hickory shirt accosted him on the street, and besought him for light upon some mystery of Holy Writ. The simian gabble of the cross-roads was not gabble to him, but wisdom of the occult and superior sort. In the presence of city folks he was palpably uneasy. Their clothes, I suspect, annoyed him, and he was suspicious of their too delicate manners. He knew all the while that they were laughing at him—if not at his baroque theology, then at least at his alpaca pantaloons. But the yokels never laughed at him. To them he was not the huntsman but the prophet, and toward the end, as he gradually forsook mundane politics for more ghostly concerns, they began to elevate him in their hierarchy. When he did he was the peer of Abraham. His old enemy, Wilson, aspiring to the same white and shining robe, came down with a thump. But Bryan made the grade. His place in Tennessee hagiography is secure. If the village barber saved any of his hair, then it is curing gall-stones down there to-day.

But what label will he bear in more urbane regions? One, I fear, of a far less flattering kind. Bryan lived too long, and descended too deeply into the mud, to be taken seriously hereafter by fully literate men, even of the kind who write school-books. There was a scattering of sweet words in his funeral notices, but it was no more than a response to conventional sentimentality. The best verdict the most romantic editorial writer could dredge up, save in the humorless South, was to the general effect that his imbecilities were excused by his earnestness—that under his clowning, as under that of the juggler of Notre Dame, there was the zeal of a steadfast soul. But this was apology, not praise; precisely the same thing might be said of Mary Baker G. Eddy, the late Czar Nicholas, or Czolgosz [assassin of William McKinley]. The truth is that even Bryan's sincerity will probably yield to what is called, in other fields, definitive criticism. Was he sincere when he opposed imperialism in the Philippines, or when he fed it with deserving Democrats in Santo Domingo? Was he sincere when he tried to shove the Prohibitionists under the table, or when he seized their banner and began to lead them with loud whoops? Was he sincere when he bellowed against war, or when he dreamed of himself as a tin-soldier in uniform, with a grave reserved among the generals? Was he sincere when he denounced the late John W. Davis, or when he swallowed Davis? Was he sincere when he fawned over Champ Clark, or when he betrayed Clark? Was he sincere when he pleaded for tolerance in New York, or when he bawled for the faggot and the stake in Tennessee?

This talk of sincerity, I confess, fatigues me. If the fellow was sincere, then so was P.T. Barnum. The word is disgraced and degraded by such uses. He was, in fact, a charlatan, a mountebank, a zany without shame or dignity. His career brought him into contact with the first men of his time; he preferred the company of rustic ignoramuses. It was hard to believe, watching him at Dayton, that he had traveled, that he had been a high officer of state. He seemed only a poor clod like those around him, deluded by a childish theology, full of an almost pathological hatred of all learning, all human dignity, all beauty, all fine and noble things. He was a peasant come home to the barnyard. Imagine a gentleman, and you have imagined everything that he was not. What animated him from end to end of his grotesque career was simply ambition—the ambition of a common man to get his hand upon the collar of his superiors, or, failing that, to get his thumb into their eyes. He was born with a roaring voice, and it had the trick of inflaming half-wits. His whole career was devoted to raising those half-wits against their betters, that he himself might shine. His last battle will be grossly misunderstood if it is thought of as a mere exercise in fanaticism—that is, if Bryan the Fundamentalist Pope is mistaken for one of the bucolic Fundamentalists. There was much more in it than that, as everyone knows who saw him on the field. What moved him, at bottom, was simply hatred of the city men who had laughed at him so long, and brought him at last to so tatterdemalion a state. He lusted for revenge upon them. He yearned to lead the anthropoid rabble against them, to punish them for their execution upon him by attacking the very vitals of their civilization. He went far beyond the bounds of any merely religious frenzy, however inordinate. When he began denouncing the notion that man is a mammal even some of the hinds at Dayton were agape. And when, brought upon Darrow's cruel hook, he writhed and tossed in a very fury of malignancy, bawling against the baldest elements of sense and decency like a man frantic—when he came to that tragic climax of his striving there were snickers among the hinds as well as hosannas.

Upon that hook, in truth, Bryan committed suicide, as a legend as well as in the body. He staggered from the rustic court ready to die, and he staggered from it ready to be forgotten, save as a character in a third-rate farce, witless and in poor taste. It was plain to everyone who knew him, when he came to Dayton, that his great days were behind him—that, for all the old fury of his hatred, he was now definitely an old man, and headed at last for silence. There was a vague, unpleasant manginess about his appearance; he somehow seemed dirty, though a close glance showed him as carefully shaven as an actor, and clad in immaculate linen. All the hair was gone from the dome of his head, and it had begun to fall out, too, behind his ears, in the obscene manner of the late Samuel Gompers. The resonance had departed from his voice; what was once a bugle blast had become reedy and quavering. Who knows that, like Demosthenes, that he had a lisp? In the old days, under the magic of his eloquence, no one noticed it. But when he spoke at Dayton it was always audible.

When I first encountered him, on the sidewalk in front of the office of the rustic lawyers who were his associates in the Scopes case, the trial was yet to begin, and so he was still expansive and amiable. I had printed in the *Nation*, a week or so before, an article arguing that the Tennessee anti-evolution law, whatever its wisdom, was at least constitutional—that the rustics of the State had a clear right to have their progeny taught whatever they chose, and kept secure from whatever knowledge violated their superstitions. The old boy professed to be delighted with the argument, and gave the gaping bystanders to understand that I was a publicist of parts. Not to be outdone, I admired the preposterous country shirt that he wore— sleeveless and with the neck cut very low. We parted in the manner of two ambassadors. But that was the last touch of amiability that I was destined to see in Bryan. The next day the battle joined and his face became hard. By the end of the week he was simply a walking fever. Hour by hour he grew more bitter. What the Christian Scientists call malicious animal magnetism seemed to radiate from him like heat from a stove. From my place in the courtroom, standing upon a table, I looked directly down upon him, sweating horribly and pumping his palm-leaf fan. His eyes fascinated me; I watched them all day long. They were blazing points of hatred. They glittered like occult and sinister gems. Now and then they wandered to me, and I got my share, for my reports of the trial had come back to Dayton, and he had read them. It was like coming under fire.

Then he fought his last fight, thirsting savagely for blood. All sense departed from him. He hit right and left, like a dog with rabies. He descended to demagogy so dreadful that his very associates at the trial table blushed. His one yearning was to keep his yokels heated up—to lead his forlorn mob of imbeciles against the foe. That foe, alas, refused to be alarmed. It insisted upon seeing the whole battle as a comedy. Even Darrow, who knew better, occasionally yielded to the prevailing spirit. One day he lured poor Bryan into the folly I have mentioned: his astounding argument against the notion that man is a mammal. I am glad I heard it, for otherwise I'd never believe in it. There stood the man who had been thrice a candidate for the Presidency of the Republic—there he stood in the glare of the world, uttering stuff that a boy of eight would laugh at! The artful Darrow led him on: he repeated it, ranted for it, bellowed it in his cracked voice. So he was prepared for the final slaughter. He came into life a hero, a Galahad, in bright and shining armor. He was passing out as a mountebank.

The chances are that history will put the peak of democracy in America in his time; it has been on the downward curve among us since the campaign of 1896. He will be remembered perhaps, as its supreme impostor, the *reductio ad absurdum* of its pretension. Bryan came very near being President. In 1896, it is possible, he was actually elected. He lived long enough to make patriots thank the inscrutable gods for Harding, even for Coolidge. Dullness has got into the White House, and the smell of cabbage boiling, but there is at least nothing to compare to the intolerable buffoonery that went on in Tennessee. The President of the United States may be an ass, but he at least doesn't believe that the earth is square, and that witches should be put to death, and that Jonah swallowed the whale. The Golden Text is not painted weekly on the White House wall, and there is no need to keep ambassadors waiting while Pastor Simpson, of Smithville, prays for rain in the Blue Room. We have escaped something—by a narrow margin, but still we have escaped.

That is, so far. The Fundamentalists, once apparently sweeping all before them, now face minorities prepared for battle even in the South—here and there with some assurance of success. But it is too early, it seems to me, to send the firemen home; the fire is still burning on many a far-flung hill, and it may begin to roar again at any moment. The evil that men do lives after them. Bryan, in his malice, started something that it will not be easy to stop. In ten thousand country towns his old heelers, the evangelical pastors, are propagating his gospel, and everywhere the yokels are ready for it. When he disappeared from the big cities, the big cities made the capital error of assuming that he was done for. If they heard of him at all, it was only as a crimp for real-estate speculators—the heroic foe of the unearned increment hauling it in with both hands. He seemed preposterous, and hence harmless. But all the while he was busy among his old lieges, preparing for a *jacquerie* [uprising] that should floor all his enemies at one blow. He did his job competently. He had vast skill at such enterprises. Heave an egg out of a Pullman window, and you will hit a Fundamentalist almost everywhere in the United States to-day. They swarm in the country towns, inflamed by their *shamans*, and with a saint now, to venerate. They are thick in the mean streets behind the gas-works. They are everywhere where learning is too heavy a burden for mortal minds to carry, even the vague, pathetic learning on tap in little red schoolhouses. They march with the Klan, with the Christian Endeavor Society, with the Junior Order of United American Mechanics, with the Epworth League, with all the rococo bands that poor and unhappy folk organize to bring some light of purpose into their lives. They had a thrill, and they are ready for more.

Such is Bryan's legacy to his country. He couldn't be President, but he could at least help magnificently in the solemn business of shutting off the Presidency from every intelligent and self-respecting man. The storm, perhaps, won't last long, as time goes in history. It may help, indeed to break up the democratic delusion, now already showing weakness, and so hasten its own end. But while it lasts it will blow off some roofs.

(*The American Mercury,* October 1925)

THE DRY MILLENNIUM

[*Even more than the Scopes Trial, Mencken's heyday was defined by Prohibition. The 18th Amendment embodied the Puritan absurdities that are central to the American experience.*

The fundamentalists create a secular definition for some sin, then pursue it as a moral evil, then celebrate a law against the sin as a religious victory aligning the U.S. with God's law, then watch as the new law makes the problem they pretend to address worse in ways that could never have been imagined.

All of this had to occur so that the old ladies (of both sexes) heaping their plates at the after-church potluck can feel an air of accomplishment, and the men who promoted and helped pass the laws can express their pieties and then go back to raiding the collection plate and the parishioners' pockets.]

The Holy War

The fact that the enforcement of Prohibition entails a host of oppression and injustices—that it puts a premium upon the lowest sort of spying, affords an easy livelihood to hordes of professional scoundrels, subjects thousands of decent men to the worst sort of blackmail, violates the theoretical sanctity of the domicile, and makes for bitter and relentless enmities,—this fact is now adduced by its ever-hopeful foes as an argument for the abandonment of the whole disgusting crusade. By it they expect to convert even a large minority of the drys, apparently on the theory that the latter got converted emotionally and hastily, and that an appeal to their sense of justice and fair-dealing will debamboozle them.

No hope could be more vain. What all the current optimists overlook is that the illogical and indefensible persecutions certain to occur in increasing number under the Prohibition Amendment constitute the chief cause of its popularity among the sort of men who are in favor of it. The typical Prohibitionist, in other words, is a man full of religious excitement, with the usual sadistic overtones. He delights in persecution for its own sake. He likes to see the other fellow jump and to hear him yell. This thirst is horribly visible in all the salient mad mullahs of the land—that is, in all the genuine leaders of American culture. Such skillful boob-bumpers as Billy Sunday know what that culture is; they know what the crowd wants. Thus they convert the preaching of the alleged Word of God into a rough-and-tumble pursuit of definite sinners—saloon-keepers, prostitutes, Sabbath-breakers, believers in the Darwinian hypothesis, German exegetes, hand-books, poker-players, adulterers, cigarette-smokers, users of profanity. It is the chase that heats up the great mob of Methodists, not the Word. And the fact that the chase is unjust only tickles them the more, for to do injustice with impunity is a sign of power, and power is the thing that the inferior man always craves most violently.

Every time the papers print another account of a Prohibitionist agent murdering a man who resists him, or searching some woman's underwear, or raiding a Vanderbilt yacht, or blackmailing a Legislature, or committing some other inordinate and anti-social act, they simply make a thousand more votes for Prohibition. It is precisely that sort of entertainment that makes Prohibition popular with the boobery. It is precisely because it is unjust, imbecile, arbitrary and tyrannical that they are so hot for it. The incidental violation of even the inferior man's liberty is not sufficient to empty him of delight in the chase. The victims reported in the newspapers are commonly his superiors; he thus gets the immemorial democratic satisfaction out of their discomfiture. Besides, he has no great rage for liberty himself. He is always willing to surrender it at demand. The most popular man under a democracy is not the most democratic man, but the most despotic man. They like him to boss them. Their natural gait is the goose-step.

It was predicted by romantics that the arrival of Prohibition would see the American workingman in revolt against its tyranny, with mills idle and industry paralyzed. Certain boozy labor leaders even went so far as to threaten a general strike. No such strike, of course, materialized. Not a single American workingman uttered a sound. The only protests heard of came from a few barbarous foreigners, and these malcontents were quickly beaten into submission by the *Polizei*. In a week or two all the reserve stocks of beer were exhausted, and every jug of authentic hard liquor was emptied. Since then, save for the ghastly messes that he has brewed behind locked doors, the American workingman has been dry. Worse, he has also been silent. Not a sound has come out of him. . . . But his liver is full of bile? He will get his revenge soon or late at the polls? All moonshine! He will do nothing of the sort. He will actually do what he always does—that is, he will make a virtue of his necessity, and straightaway begin believing that he likes Prohibition, that it is doing him a lot of good, that he wouldn't be without it if he could. This is the habitual process of thought of inferior men, at all times and everywhere. This is the sturdy common sense of the plain people.

(*Prejudices, Second Series*)

JUSTICE UNDER DEMOCRACY

[*At some point, if you were awake, a civics teacher taught you that the American legislative system consists of three branches: a legislative, an executive, and a judicial branch that keep "checks and balances" on each other. In reality, the system is more of a pyramid of influence, with 435 House members at the bottom, 100 senators above them, and nine Supreme Court justices acting as philosopher-kings in an uneasy standoff with the king of the executive branch. Of course, if the judges and president are kings, then the rest of us are subjects.*

Nothing recommends Mencken's critical faculties like "Justice Under Democracy." He understood that Prohibition, a Protestant folly in itself, ultimately revealed the whole democratic conceit to be a sham. If the Congress and federal courts can determine the nature of freedom—and which freedoms we're allowed—that leaves us, American subjects, with no choice. Our freedoms are totally at the whim of judicial and legislative tyrants.]

1

Perhaps the chief victims of Prohibition in the Republic, in the long run, will turn out to be the Federal judges. I do not argue here, of course, that drinking bootleg liquors will kill them bodily; I merely suggest that enforcing the unjust and insane provisions of the Volstead Act will rob them of all their old dignity. A dozen years ago a Federal judge was perhaps the most dignified and respected official yet flourishing under our democracy. The plain people, many years before that, had lost all respect for lawmakers, whether Federal, State or municipal, and save for the President himself, they had very little respect left for the gentlemen of the executive arm, high or low. More, they had begun to view the judiciary of the States very biliously, and showed no sign of surprise when a member of it was taken in judicial adultery. But for the Federal judges they still continued to have a high veneration, and for plain reasons. *Imprimis* [first of all], the Federal judges sat for life, and thus did not have to climb down from their benches at intervals and clamor obscenely for votes. Secondly, the laws that they were told off to enforce, and especially the criminal laws, were few in number, simple in character, and thoroughly in accord with almost universal ideas of right and wrong. No citizen in his right mind had much sympathy for the felons who were shipped to Atlanta each morning by the marshals of the Federal courts—chiefly counterfeiters, fraudulent bankrupts, adulterers of food and drugs, get-rich-quick swindlers, thieving letter-carriers, crooked army officers and so on. Public sentiment was almost unanimously behind the punishment of such rogues, and it rejoiced that that punishment was in the hands of men who carried on the business in an austere and elevated manner, without fear and without favor. It was, in those days, almost unheard of for a petit jury in a Federal court to acquit a prisoner whose guilt was plain; the percentage of convictions in some jurisdictions was beyond ninety per cent. For guilt of the kind then dealt with by those courts met with the reprehension of practically all men not professional criminals themselves—and Federal juries, petit and grand, were picked with some care, as Federal judges themselves were picked.

I describe a Golden Age, now lamentably closed. The Uplift in its various lovely forms has completely changed the character of the work done by a Federal judge. Once the dispenser of varieties of law that only scoundrels questioned, he is now the harassed and ludicrous dispenser of varieties of law that only idiots approve. It was the Espionage Act, I suppose, that brought him to this new and dreadful office, but it is Prohibition—whether of wine-bibbling, or drug-taking, of interstate week-ending, or of what not—that has carried him beyond the bounds of what, to most normal men, is common decency. His typical job today, as a majority of the plain people see it, especially in the big cities, is simply to punish men who have refused or been unable to pay the bribes demanded by Prohibition enforcement officers. In other words, he is now chiefly apprehended by the public, not as a scourge of rascals, but as an agent of rascals and a scourge of peaceable men. He gets a great deal more publicity than he used to get in his palmy days, but it is publicity of a sort that rapidly undermines his dignity. Unfortunately for him, but perhaps very fortunately for what remains of civilized government among us, the plain people have never been able to grasp the difference between law and justice. To them the two things are one—or ought to be. So the fact that the judge is bound by law to enforce all the intolerable provisions of the Volstead Act, including even its implicit provision that men wearing its badges shall get a fair percentage upon every transaction in bootlegging—this fact does not relieve the judge himself of responsibility for the ensuing injustices. All that the vulgar observe is that justice has departed from the courtroom. Once the equal of an archbishop, he is now the equal of a police captain; once respected, he is now distrusted and disliked.

If this were all, of course, it might be possible to dismiss the whole matter on the ground that the public is an ass. That men of the highest worth are not always respected, even when they wear official robes, is a commonplace. But in the present case there is more to it than merely that. Not a few of the Federal judges have begun to show signs that the noisome work that has been forced upon them has begun to achieve its inevitable subjective effects; in other words, not a few begin to attack their sneaking sense of its lack of dignity and good repute by bedizening it with moral indignation. The judicial servant of the Anti-Saloon League thus takes on some of the neo-Christian character of the League's own dervishes and sorcerers. He is not content to send some poor yokel to jail for an artificial crime that, in the view of at least eighty per cent of all even half-civilized Americans, is no crime at all; he must also denounce the culprit from the bench in terms fit for a man accused of arson or mayhem. Here the Freudians, perhaps, may have something to say; the great masses of the innocent and sinful, knowing nothing of Freud, observe only that the learned jurist is silly as well as unjust. There issues from that observation a generally bilious view of the office and his person. He slides slowly down a fatal chute. His day of arctic and envied eminence passes. A few sensitive judges quietly retire from the bench. But the legal mind is usually tougher than that. It can almost always find justifications for doing, as agent of the law, what would be inconceivable privately to a man of honor.

2

The truth is, indeed, that the decline in dignity from which the Federal judges now suffer is not wholly due to the external fact of Prohibition; it is due quite as much to their own growing pliancy and lack of professional self-respect. All that Prohibition does to them is to make brilliantly plain, even to the meanest understanding, their lamentable departure from that high integrity of purpose, that assiduous concern for justice, that jealous watchfulness over the rights of man which simple men, at all times and everywhere, like to find in the judges set over them, and which the simple men of the United States, not so long ago, saw or thought they saw in the learned ornaments of the Federal bench. Before even Volstead emerged from the Christian Endeavor with his preposterous Act, confidence had begun to shake. The country had seen Federal judges who were unmistakably mountebanks; it had seen some who were, to the naked eye, indistinguishable from rascals. It had seen one step down from the highest court in the land to engage in an undignified stumping tour, soliciting the votes of the rabble. It had seen another diligently insinuate himself into the headlines of the yellow press, in competition with Jack Dempsey and Babe Ruth. It had seen others abuse their powers of equity in the frank interest of capital, and deny the commonest justice to poor men in their clutches. And during the war it had grown accustomed to seeing the Federal bench converted into a sort of rival to the rostrum of Liberty Loan orators, with judges hurling pious objurgations at citizens accuse of nothing worse than speaking their minds freely, and all pretense to fair hearings and just punishments abandoned.

Of late the multiplication of such Dogberries has gone on pace as the best of the old-time judges have retired from the bench. These new jurisconsults, rejecting justice openly and altogether, have even begun to reject the Constitution and the law. A judicial process before them is indistinguishable from a bull-fight, with the accused, if he is unpopular enough as the bull. It is their theory, apparently, that the sole function of a judge is to fill the jails. If the accused happens to be guilty or to be reasonably suspected of guilt, well and good. But if, as in the Chicago Socialist trials [the Haymarket Affair], he is obviously innocent, to hell with him anyhow. True enough, a majority of the Federal judges, high and low, still stand clear of such buffooneries. Even in the midst of the worst hysteria of the war there were plenty who refused to be run amok by Palmer, Burleson and company; I need cite only Hand, J., and Rose, J., as admirable examples of a number of judges who preserved their dignity 'mid the rockets' red glare. But the headlines in the newspapers had nothing to say about such judges; their blackest ink was reserved for the other kind. That other kind gradually established a view of the Federal bench that still persists, and that is growing more and more fixed as the farce of Prohibition enforcement unrolls. It is a view which, in brief, holds that the Federal bench is no longer the most exalted and faithful protector of the liberties of the citizen, but the most relentless and inordinate foe of them—that its main purpose is not to dispense justice at all, but to get men into jail, guilty or not guilty, by fair means or foul—that to this end it is willing to lend itself to the execution of any law, however extravagant, and to support that execution with a variety of casuistry that is flatly against every ordinary conception of common sense and common decency. The Espionage Act cases, the labor injunction cases, the deportation cases, and now the Prohibition cases—all of these, impinging in rapid succession upon a people brought up to regard the Bill of Rights as a reality and liberty as precious thing, have bred suspicion of the Federal courts, including the Supreme Court, and, on the heels of that suspicion, a positive and apparently ineradicable distrust. I doubt that the Radical fanatics who dodge about the land have converted any substantial body of Americans to their crazy doctrines; certainly there is not the slightest sign today of the Revolution that they were predicting for last year, and the year before. But when they have denounced the Federal courts and produced the overwhelming evidence, their shots have gone home.

Now and then a judge has argued, defending himself against some manifestation of popular discontent, that he is helpless—that he is the agent, not of justice, but of law. Even in the hey-day of the Espionage Act a few were moved to make that apology from the bench, including, if I remember rightly, the judge who sentenced Debs. The distinction thus set up is one that seems clear to lawyers, but, as I have said, it seldom gets a hospitable hearing from plain men. If the latter believe anything at all it is that law without justice is an evil thing—that such law, indeed, leads inevitably to a contradiction in terms—that the highest duty of the judiciary is not to enforce it pedantically, but to evade it, vitiate it, and, if possible, destroy it. The plain man sees plenty of other sorts of law destroyed by the courts; he can't help wondering why the process is so seldom applied to statues that violate, not merely legal apothegms, but the baldest of common sense. Thus when he beholds a Federal judge fining a man, under a constitutional amendment prohibiting the sale of intoxicating beverages, for selling a beverage that is admittedly not intoxicating, or jailing another man who has got before the bar, as everyone knows, not because he ran a still but because he refused to pay the bribe demanded by the Prohibition enforcement officer, or issuing against a third an injunction whose sole and undisguised purpose is to deprive him, by a legal swindle, of his constitutional right to a trial by jury of his peers—when he observes such monkey-shines going on in the name of the law, is it any wonder that he concludes dismally that the law is an ass, and its agent another? In ordinary life men cannot engage in such lunatic oppression of their fellow-men without paying a penalty for it; even a policeman must be measurably more plausible and discreet. If a judge is bound by his oath to engage in them, then so much the worse for the judge. He can no more hope to be respected than hangman can hope to be respected.

The truth is, of course, that the judges are by no means under the compulsion that is alleged. The injunction clause of the Volstead Act actually has no constitutional mandate behind it; the only constitutional mandate that I can find, bearing upon it at all, is against it. That is to be found in the Fifth and Sixth Amendments. The first of these amendments provides that "no person shall be held to answer for a capital or otherwise infamous crime unless on a presentement or indictment of a grand jury"; the second requires that "in all criminal prosecutions the accused shall enjoy the right to a speedy and public trial by an impartial jury of the State and district wherein the crime shall have been committed." It must be obvious to everyone that the aim of the injunction clause is simply and solely to deprive the accused of these safeguards—to rob him of his clear right to a trial by a jury of his peers. The history of the clause reveals the fact clearly. It was first heard of in Iowa in the early years of the century, and it was invented there, not by Prohibitionists, but by the frantic vice-crusaders who then raged and roared in the hinterland, inflaming the pious with gaudy yearns about white slave traders, seducers armed with hypodermic syringes, and other such phantasms. In Iowa these vice-crusaders specialized in the harassing of the sort of poorer women who keep cheap lodging-houses. When such a woman, by ignorance or inadvertence, admitted a lady no longer a lady to her establishment, they raided her, dragged her to jail, and charged her with keeping a bawdy-house. This was good sport, and the rev. pastors urged it on every Sunday. But after the first uproar, it began to develop defects, and the chief of these defects was that juries refused to convict. Now and then a man of sense and self-respect got upon the panel and spoiled the show. Perhaps he found it impossible to believe the sworn testimony of the vice-crusaders. Perhaps he concluded that the accused, though guilty, had been punished enough by the raid. Whatever his motive, he hung the jury and killed the hunting.

It was then that Christian lawyers came to the rescue of pious and baffled men. They did it by the simple process of throwing the whole responsibility upon the judge. Juries were hard to intimidate; there was always apt to be at least one juror who didn't care a hoot what was said against him from the sacred desk—some hell-cat who positively rejoiced in the indignation of the knock-'em-down-and-drag-'em-out clergy. But judges were tenderer. Some of them were candidates for re-election to the bench; all of them were solicitous about their dignity, and did not care to face ecclesiastical curses, pious whispers, suggestive winks. So the Iowa lawyers amended the law by inventing and inserting the Injunction clause. This clause flatly abolished the right of trial by jury. When the vice-crusaders found a likely victim they simply got a friendly judge to issue an injunction against her, restraining her from using her premises for immoral purposes. Then they watched her closely. The moment they detected a dubious female entering her door they raided her again, dragged her before the same judge—and he jailed her for contempt of court, an offense punishable summarily and without a jury trial. Nine times out of ten, perhaps, a jury would have acquitted her, but the judge was already safely against her.

This scheme gave the vice-crusaders a new lease of life and greatly increased their takings in the Sunday-schools. Naturally enough, the Prohibitionists, who were, in most cases, none other than the vice-crusaders themselves, instantly borrowed it, and so it got into the Prohibition acts of all the dry States. Volstead, as country State's attorney on the Minnesota Stepps, employed it diligently and to vast effect. He put it into the Volstead Act as a matter of course. There it stands today, a dishonest and disgraceful blemish upon American law. Its deliberate aim is to take away from the citizen accused of crime his constitutional right to a jury trial; no imaginable argument in favor of it can dodge the plain fact. When it is invoked, as under the Volstead Act, against a man who has been found guilty of the act, it not only punishes him doubly for that violation; it also punishes him in advance for a second offense that he has admittedly not committed, and deprives him of his constitutional means of defense in case he is subsequently accused. He is, in brief, put absolutely at the mercy of the judge—and the judge is already obviously suspicious of him, and may be a senile sadist or Prohibitionist demagogue to boot. The constitutional provision that a man accused of crime may throw himself upon a jury of plain men like himself, sworn to regard only the evidence actually before them—that if he is able to convince only one of the twelve that he is innocent, or not proved guilty beyond a doubt, he shall go free—this fundamental guarantee of the citizen, this most sacred of all human rights under Anglo-Saxon jurisprudence, is specifically nullified and made a mock of in order to satisfy the frenzy of a minority of fanatics!

That contempt of course should be an offense standing outside the purview of the Fifth and Sixth Amendments—that a judge should have the power to punish summarily all deliberate floutings of his dignity—this my be reasonably argued, though there are many sound considerations against it. But that it should be lawful to convert some other and wholly unrelated offense into contempt of court by a legal fiction, and so get around the Fifth and Sixth Amendments by a swindle—this is surely more than any sensible man would soberly maintain. When it is maintained, it is only by persons who are trying to put men into jail by processes that any average jury would revolt against—mill owners eager to get rid of annoying labor leaders, coal operators bent upon making slaves of their miners, Prohibitionists lusting for the punishment of their opponents. The injunction in strike cases has been a stench for years; it is, indeed, so bad that a large number of Federal judges refuse absolutely to employ it. It is a worse stench in Prohibition cases, for here it is becoming a formidable and favorite weapon, not merely in the hands of property-owners who want to put down strikes, but in the hands of criminal Prohibition agents who seek to wring blackmail from their victims. In brief, it has become a dishonest means of oppression for men who are even more dishonest than it is. Certainly it is idle to talk of respect for the laws when such devices have legislative and judicial sanction. No reasonable man, save he be ignorant of their nature and purpose, can conceivably respect them. If, on the ground that whatever is in the law should be given full faith and credit, he maintains that they should not be resisted, then he maintains that the Bill of Rights is no more than a string of empty phrases, and that any shyster who invents a way to evade and abrogate it is a jurist as dignified as John Marshall.

3

Is a judge bound to lend himself to such gross and dishonest attacks upon the common rights of the citizen? I am no lawyer, but I presume to doubt it. There were judges in 1918 who did not think themselves obliged to sacrifice the Bill of Rights to the Espionage Act, and who resolutely refused to do so, and yet, so far as I know, nothing happened to them; at least one of them, to my knowledge, has been since promoted to a circuit. Why should any judge enforce the injunction clause of the Volstead Act? Its enforcement is surely not an automatic act; it involves deliberation and decision by the judge; he may refuse his injunction without offering any explanation to anyone. What would follow if he arose one day in his high pulpit, and announced simply that his court was purged of all such oblique and dishonest enactments forthwith—that he had resolved to refuse to lend himself to the schemes of blackmailers with badges, or to harass and punish free citizens in violation of their fundamental constitutional rights and their plain dignity as human beings, or, in brief, to engage in any other enterprise as a judge that he would shrink from engaging in as a good citizen and a man of honor? Would the result be impeachment? I should like to meet a Congressman insane enough to move the impeachment of such a judge! Would it be a storm of public indignation? . . . Or would it be a vociferous yell of delight?

It seems to me, indeed, that the first judge who rises to such a rebellion will be the first judge ever to become a popular hero in the Republic—that he will be elevated to the Supreme Court by a sort of acclamation, even if it is necessary to get rid of one of the sitting justices by setting fire to his gown. But even imagining him so elevated, the remaining eight justices will still function, and all of us know what they think of the Bill of Rights. Wouldn't such a rebel judge succumb to the system of which he was a discreet particle? Couldn't the other eight judges nullify and make a mock of his heroic defiance? Could they indeed? Then how? If a judge, high or low, actually called in justice to rescue a citizen from the law, what precisely could the Supreme Court do about it? I know of no appeal by the District Attorney in criminal cases, once the accused has been put in jeopardy; I know only of impeachment for judges who forget the lines of the solemn farce to which they are sworn. But to try to imagine the impeachment of a judge charged with punching a hole in the Volstead Act, and letting in some common justice and common decency!

So far, no such rambunctious and unprecedented judge has been heard of,—none, that is, has objected to the injunction clause in toto and head on—nor do I specifically predict the advent. He may come, but probably he won't. The law is a curse to all of us, but it is a curse of special virulence to lawyers. It becomes for them a sort of discreditable vice, a stealthy and degrading superstition. It robs them of all balance, of all capacity for clear thought, of all imagination. Judges tend to show this decay of the faculties in an exaggerated form; they become mere automata, bound by arbitrary rules, precedents, the accumulated imbecilities of generations of bad logic; to their primary lack of sense as lawyers they add the bombastic manner of bureaucrats. It is then too much to hope for a judge showing any originality or courage; one Holmes in an era of Hardings and Coolidges is probably more than a fair allotment. But while the judges of the District Courts go on driving wild teams of jackasses through the Bill of Rights, and the rev. seniors of the Supreme Court give their approval to the business in solemn form, sometimes but not always with Holmes, J., and Brandeis,

J. dissenting—while all this is going on there are black clouds rolling up from the hinterland, where the Constitution is still taught in the schools and even Methodists are bred to reverence Patrick Henry. The files of Congress already show the way the wind is blowing—constitutional amendments to drag down and denaturize the Supreme Court, simple acts to the same end, other acts providing for the election of Federal judges, yet others even more revolutionary. I know of no such proposal that has any apparent merit. Even the best of them, hamstringing the courts, would only augment the power of a Congress that is ten times worse. But so long as judges pursue fatuously the evil business of converting every citizen into a subject, demagogues will come forward with their dubious remedies, and, soon or late, unless the bench pulls up, some of these demagogues will get themselves heard.

(Prejudices, Fourth Series)

THE POLITICIAN

[*American liberalism is replete with contradictions, probably the worst of which is "oppose the war, but support the troops," which as a tag line is as politically suicidal as it is logically nonsensical. When the left decided to become patriotic, a development that started during FDR's New Deal and calcified during the Second World War, it first flagged and then failed as a movement. This was all made worse by the illusion of progress, which hinged on a few Supreme Court decisions (soon to be, as they were always destined to be, cast aside). Mencken, mercifully, wrote before these developments and was free to express sentiments such as:*

"A professional soldier, regarded realistically, is much worse than a professional politician, for he is a professional murderer and kidnaper, whereas the politician is only a professional sharper and sneakthief. A clergymen, too, begins to shrink and shrivel on analysis; the work he does in the world is basically almost indistinguishable from that of an astrologer, witch-doctor, or fortune-teller."

In the twenty-first century the American military, in a devil's orgy of lies and jingoism, destroyed Iraq by heroically calling in air strikes against a nearly defenseless Iraqi defense force (the equivalent, in every way, of the US military defeating the Wyoming National Guard), which precipitated decades of chaos and slaughter among the peoples of the Middle East. For this, the public had their hearts warmed with beer ads depicting people in airports spontaneously standing and applauding returning soldiers, and online videos of actual returning soldiers surprising elementary school kids at lunch, or receiving a new Ford during halftime of an NFL game.

No one would argue, then or now, that politicians are anything other than what Mencken says they are, but for some reason clergymen and preachers continue to be treated with respect—interviewed they are by somber news reporters after every mass shooting, while offering "thoughts and prayers"—despite millennia of failed predictions and false statements, and cruel, authoritarian pronouncements.]

Half the sorrows the world, I suppose, are caused by making false assumptions. If the truth were only easier to ascertain the remedy for them would consist simply of ascertaining it and accepting it. This business, alas, is usually impossible, but fortunately not always: now and then, by some occult process, half rational and half instinctive, the truth gets itself found out and an ancient false assumption goes overboard. I point, in the field of the social relations, to one which afflicted the human race for millenniums: that one, to wit, which credited the rev. clergy with a mysterious wisdom and awful powers. Obviously, it has ceased to trouble all the superior varieties of men. It may survive in those remote marches where human beings go to bed with the cows, but certainly it has vanished from the cities. Asphalt and the apostolic succession, indeed, seem to be irreconcilable enemies. I can think of no clergyman in any great American city today whose public dignity and influence are much above those of an ordinary Class I Babbitt. It is hard for even the most diligent and passionate of the ancient order to get upon the first pages of the newspapers; he must make a clown-show, discreditable in his fraying cloth, or he must blush unseen. When bishops begin launching thunderheads against heretics, the towns do not tremble; they laugh. When elders denounce sin, sin only grows more popular. Imagine a city man getting a notice from the ordinary of the diocese that he had been excommunicated. It would trouble him far less, I venture, than his morning Katzenjammer hubbub [refers to the comic strip "Katzenjammer Kids"].

The reason for this is not hard to find. All the superior varieties of men—and even the lowest varieties of city workmen are at least superior to peasants—have simply rid themselves of their old belief in devils. Hell no longer affrights and palsies them, and so the magic of those who profess to save them from it no longer impresses them. That profession, I believe, was begun, and its acceptance was therefore a false assumption. Being so, it made men unhappy; getting rid of it has delivered them. They are no longer susceptible to ecclesiastical alarms and extortions; ergo, they sleep and eat better. Think of what life must have been under such princes of damnation as Cotton Mather and Jonathan Edwards, with even bartenders and metaphysicians believing in them! And then compare it to life under Bishop Manning and the Rev. Dr. John Roach Straton, with only a few half-wits believing in them! Or turn to the backwoods of the Republic, where the devil is still feared, and with him his professional exterminators. In the country towns the clergy are still almost as influential as they were in Mather's day, and there, as everyone knows, they remain public nuisances, and civilized life is almost impossible. In such Neolithic regions nothing can go on without their consent, on penalty of anathema and hell-fire; as a result, nothing goes on that is worth recording. It is this survival of sacerdotal authority, I begin to believe, and not hookworm, malaria or the event of April 9, 1865, that is chiefly responsible for the cultural paralysis of the late Confederate States. The South lacks big cities; it is run by country towns—and in every country town there is some Baptist mullah who rules by scaring the peasantry. The false assumption that his pretensions are sound, that he can actually bind and loose, that contumacy to him is variety of cursing God—this false assumption is what makes the yokels so uneasy, so nervous, and hence so unhappy. If they could throw it off they would burn fewer Aframericans and sing more songs. If they could be purged of it they would be purged of the Ku Kluxery too.

The cities got rid of that false assumption half a century ago, and have been making cultural progress ever since. Somewhat later they got rid of its brother, to wit, respect for government, and, in particular, respect for its visible agents, the police. That respect—traditional and hence irrational—had been, for years in increasingly unpleasant collision with a great body of obvious facts. The police, by assumption austere and almost sacrosanct, were gradually discovered to be, in reality, a pack of rogues and but little removed, save by superior impudence and enterprise, from the cut-throats and purse-snatcher they were set to catch. When, a few decades ago, the American people, at least in the big cities, began to accept them frankly for what they were—when the old false assumption of their integrity and public usefulness was quietly abandoned and a new and more accurate assumption of their roguery was adopted in its place—when this change was effected there was a measurable increase, I believe, in the public happiness. It no longer astonished anyone when policemen were taken in evildoing; indignation therefore abated, and with it its pains. If, before that time, the corps of the Prohibition enforcement officers—i.e., a corps of undisguised scoundrels with badges—had been launched upon the populace, there would have been a great roar of wrath, and much anguished gnashing of teeth. People would have felt themselves put upon, injured, insulted. But with the old false assumption about policemen removed from their minds, they met the new onslaught calmly and even smiling. Today no one is indignant over the fact that the extortions of these new *Polizei* increase the cost of potable alcohol. The false assumption that the police are altruistic agents of a benevolent state has been replaced by the sound assumption that they are gentlemen engaged assiduously, like the rest of us, in finding meat and raiment for their families and in laying up funds to buy Liberty Bonds in the next war to end war. This is human progress, for it increases human happiness.

So much for the evidence. The deduction I propose to make from it is simply this: that a like increase would follow if the American people could only rid themselves of another and worse false assumption that still rides them—one that corrupts all their thinking about the great business of politics, and vastly augments their discontent and unhappiness—the assumption, that is, that politicians are divided into two classes, and that one of those classes is made up of good ones. I need not argue, I hope, that this assumption is almost universally held among us. Our whole politics, indeed, is based upon it, and has been based upon it since the earliest days. What is any political campaign save a concerted effort to turn out a set of politicians who are admittedly bad and put in a set who are thought to be better? The former assumption, I believe, is always sound; the latter is just as certainly false. For if experience teaches us anything at all it teaches us this: that a good politician, under democracy, is quite as unthinkable as an honest burglar. His very existence, indeed, is a standing subversion of the public good in every rational sense. He is not one who serves the common weal; he is simply one who preys upon the commonwealth. It is to the interest of all the rest of us to hold down his powers to an irreducible minimum, and to reduce his compensation to nothing; it is to his interest to augment his powers at all hazards, and to make his compensation all the traffic will bear. To argue that these aims are identical is to argue palpable nonsense. The politician, at his ideal best, never even remotely approximated in practice, is a necessary evil; at his worst he is an almost intolerable nuisance.

What I contend is simply that he would be measurably less a nuisance if we got rid of our old false assumption about him, and regarded him in the cold light of fact. At once, I believe, two-thirds of his obnoxiousness would vanish. He would remain a nuisance, but he would cease to be a swindler; the injury of having to pay freight on him would cease to be complicated by the insult of being rooked. It is the insult and not the injury that makes the deeper wounds, and causes the greater permanent damage to the national psyche. All of us have been trained, since infancy, in putting up with necessary evils, plainly recognized as evils. We know, for example, that the young of the human species commonly smell badly; that garbage men, bootblacks and messenger boys commonly smell worse. These facts are not arguable, but they remain tolerable because they are universally assumed—because there is no sense of having been tricked and cozened in their perennial discovery. But to try to imagine how distressing fatherhood would become if prospective fathers were all taught that the human infant radiates an aroma like the rose—if the truth came constantly as a surprise! Each fresh victim of the deception would feel that he had been basely swindled—that his own child was somehow bogus. Not infrequently, I suppose, he would be tempted to make away with it in some quiet manner, and have another— only to be shocked again. That procedure would be idiotic, admittedly, yet it is exactly the one we follow in politicians, insanely assuming that they are better than the set turned out. And at each election we are, they say in the Motherland, done in.

Of late the fraud has become so gross that the plain people begin to show a great restlessness under it. Like animals in a cage, they trot from one corner to another, endlessly seeking a way out. If the Democrats win one year, it is a pretty sure sign that they will lose the next year. State after State becomes doubtful, pivotal, skittish; even the solid South begins to break. In the cities it is still worse. An evil circle is formed. First the poor taxpayers, robbed by the politicians of one great party and then by those of the other, turn to a group of free-lance rogues in the middle ground—nonpartisan candidates, Liberals, reformers or what not: the name is unimportant. Then, flayed and pillaged by these gentry as they never were by the old-time professionals, they go back in despair to the latter, and are flayed and pillaged again. Back to Bach! Back to Tammany! Tammany reigns in New York because the Mitchel outfit was found to be intolerable—in other words, because the reformers were found to be even worse than the professionals. Why should it be? Reformers and professionals are alike politicians in search of jobs; both are trying to bilk the taxpayers. Neither ever has any other motive. If any genuinely honest and altruistic politician had come to the surface in America in my time I'd have heard of him, for I have always frequented newspaper offices, and in a newspaper office the news of such a marvel would cause a dreadful tumult. I can recall no such tumult. The unanimous opinion of all the journalists that I know, excluding a few Liberals who are obviously somewhat balmy—they all believed, for example, that the late war would end war,—is that, since the days of the national Thors and Wotans, no politician who was not out for himself, and for himself alone, has ever drawn the breath of life in the United States.

The gradual disintegration of Liberalism among us, in fact, offers an excellent proof of the truth of my thesis. The Liberals have come to grief by fooling their customers, not merely once too often, but a hundred times too often. Over and over again they have trotted out some new hero, usually from the great open spaces, only to see him taken in the immemorial malpractices within ten days. Their graveyard, indeed, is filled with cracked and upset head-stones, many covered with ribald pencilings. Every time there is a scandal in the grand manner the Liberals lose almost as many general officers as either the Democrats or Republicans. Of late, racked beyond endurance by such catastrophes at home, they have gone abroad for their principal heroes; losing such outstanding paladins as the Hon. Bela Kun, a gentleman who, in any American State, would not only be in the calaboose, but actually in the death-house. [Kun was dictator of the short-lived Hungarian Soviet Republic in the wake of WWI.] But this absurdity is only an offshoot of a deeper one. Their primary error lies in making the false assumption that some politicians are better than others. This error they share with the whole American people.

I propose that it be renounced, and contend that its renunciation would greatly rationalize and improve our politics. I do not argue that there would be any improvement in our politicians; on the contrary, I believe that they would remain substantially as they are today, and perhaps grow even worse. But what I do argue is that recognizing them frankly for what they are would instantly and automatically dissipate the indignation caused by their present abominations, and that the disappearance of this indignation would promote the public contentment and happiness. Under my scheme there would be no more false assumptions and no more false hopes, and hence no more painful surprises, no more bitter resentment of fraud, no more despair. Politicians, in so far as they remained necessary, would be kept at work—but not with any insane notion that they were archangels. Their rascality would be assumed and discounted. Machinery would be gradually developed to limit it and counteract it. In the end, it might be utilized in some publicly profitable manner, as the insensitiveness to filth of garbage men is now utilized. The result, perhaps, would be a world no better than the present one, but it would at least be a world more intelligent.

In all this I sincerely hope that no one will mistake me for one who shares the indignation I have spoken of—that is, for one who believes that politicians can be made good, and cherishes a fond scheme for making them so. I believe nothing of the sort. On the contrary, I am convinced that the art and mystery they practise is essentially and incurably anti-social— that they must remain irreconcilable enemies of the common weal until the end of time. But I maintain that this fact, in itself, is not a bar to their employment. There are, under Christian civilization, many necessary offices that demand the possession of anti-social talents. A professional soldier, regarded realistically, is much worse than a professional politician, for he is professional murderer and kidnaper, whereas the politician is only a professional sharper and sneak-thief. A clergyman, too, begins to shrink and shrivel on analysis; the work he does in the world is basically almost indistinguishable from that of an astrologer, a witch-doctor or a fortune-teller. He pretends falsely that he can get sinners out of hell, and collects money from them on that premise, tacit or express. If he had to go before a jury with that pretension it would probably go hard with him. But we do not send him before a jury; we grant him his hocus-pocus on the ground that it is necessary to his office, and that his office is necessary to civilization, so-called. I pass over the journalist delicately; the time has not come to turn State's evidence. Suffice it to say that he, too, would probably wither under a stiff cross-examination. If he is no murderer, like the soldier, then he is at least a sharper and swindler, like the politician.

What I plead for, if I may borrow a term in disrepute, is simply *Realpolitick*, i.e., realism in politics. I can imagine a political campaign purged of all the current false assumptions and false premises—a campaign to which, on election day, the voters went to the polls clearly informed that the choice between them was not between an angel and a devil, a good man and a bad man, an altruist and a go-getter, but between two frank go-getters, the one, perhaps, excelling at beautiful and nonsensical words and the other at silent and prehensile deeds—the one a chautauqua orator and the other a porch-climber. There would be, in that choice, something candid, free and exhilarating. Buncombe would be adjourned. The voter would make his selection in the full knowledge of all the facts, as he makes his selection between two heads if cabbage, or two evening papers, or two brands of chewing tobacco. Today he chooses his rulers as he buys bootleg whiskey, never knowing precisely what he is getting, only certain that it is not what it pretends to be. The Scotch may turn out to be wood alcohol or it may turn out to be gasoline; in either case it is not Scotch. How much better if it were plainly labelled, for wood alcohol and gasoline have their uses—higher uses, indeed, than Scotch. The danger is that the swindled and poisoned customer, despairing of ever avoiding them when he doesn't want them, may prohibit them even when he does want them, and actually enforce his own prohibition. The danger is that the hopeless voter, forever victimized by his false assumption about politicians, may in the end gather such ferocious indignation that he will abolish them totally and at one insane swoop, and so cause government by the people, for the people and with the people to perish from this earth.

(Prejudices, Fourth Series)

THE DISMAL SCIENCE

[*"The notion that German is a gnarled and unintelligible language arises out of the circumstances that it is so much written by professors."*

A lot of information comes across in this punchy line from "The Dismal Science." German universities, in the 18th century, created the research PhD as a way of formalizing a scientific ranking system that had previously only featured gentlemen "natural philosophers." Up until the coming of the Third Reich, Germany led the world in most forms of science and, to this day, the stereotypical scientist speaks with "ze German accent."

Economics is not quite the homeopathy of the sciences (that would be political science), but it is not far off. Economists, Mencken writes, are not free because their profession upholds the moneyed classes who need economists, much as corporations need lawyers to post facto justify their actions. Economics professors, Mencken implies, conjure up whatever explanation is needed by the wealthy donors to the universities that employ the professors. Those justifications used to be about the necessity of child labor and the need to prevent a living minimum wage. The wealthy are now so rich they have outgrown the need to connect their business activities to any kind of ideology; they can be socially liberal (some are, some aren't) without giving a thought to the working class, and they pay economists to theorize in the way that a patron of music pays to hear the symphony.]

Every man, as the Psalmist says, to his own poison, or poisons, as the case may be. One of mine, following hard after theology, is political economy. What? Political economy, that dismal science? Well, why not? Its dismalness is largely a delusion, due to the fact that its chief ornaments, at least in our own day, are university professors. The professor must be an obscurantist or he is nothing; he has a special and unmatchable talent for dullness; his central aim is not to expose the truth clearly, but to exhibit his profundity, his esotericity—in brief, to stagger sophomores and other professors. The notion that German is a gnarled and unintelligible language arises out of the circumstance that it is so much written by professors. It took a rebel member of the clan, swinging to the antipodes in his unearthly treason, to prove its explicitness, its resiliency, its downright beauty. But Nietzsches are few, and so German remains soggy, and political economy continues to be swathed in dullness. As I say, however, that dullness is only superficial. There is no more engrossing book in the English language than Adam Smith's *The Wealth of Nations*; surely the eighteenth century produced nothing that can be read with greater ease to-day. Nor is there any inherent reason why even the most technical divisions of its subject should have gathered cobwebs with the passing of the years. Taxation, for example, is eternally lively; it concerns nine-tenths of us more directly than either smallpox or golf, and has just as much drama in it; moreover, it has been mellowed and made gay by as many gaudy, preposterous theories. As for foreign exchange, it is almost as romantic as young love, and quite as resistant to formulae. Do the professors make an autopsy of it? Then read the occasional treatises of some professor of it who is not a professor, say, Garet Garrett or John Moody.

Unluckily, Garretts and Moodys are almost as rare as Nietzsches, and so the amateur of such things must be content to wrestle with the professors, seeking violet of human interest beneath the avalanche of their graceless parts of speech. A hard business, I daresay, to one not practiced, and to its hardness there is added the disquiet of a doubt. That doubt does not concern itself with the doctrine preached, at least not directly. There may be in it nothing intrinsically dubious; on the contrary, it may appear as sound as the binomial theorem, as well supported as the dogma of infant damnation. But all the time a troubling question keeps afloat in the air, and that is briefly this: What would happen to the learned professors if they took the other side? In other words, to what extent is political economy, as professors expound and practice it, a free science, in the sense that mathematics and physiology are free sciences? At what place, if any, is speculation pulled up by a rule that beyond lies treason, anarchy and disaster? These questions, I hope I need not add, are not inspired by any heterodoxy in my own black heart. I am, in many fields, a flouter of the accepted, and hence immoral, but the field of economics is not one of them. Here, indeed, I know of no man who is more orthodox than I am. I believe that the present organization of society, as bad as it is, is better than any other that has ever been proposed. I reject all the sure cures in current agitation, from government ownership to the single tax. I am in favor of free competition in all human enterprises, and to the utmost limit. I admire successful scoundrels, and shrink from Socialists as I shrink from Methodists. But all the same, the aforesaid doubt pursues me when I plow through the solemn disproofs and expositions of the learned professors of economics, and that doubt will not down. It is not logical or evidential, but purely psychological. And what it is grounded on is an unshakable belief that no man's opinion is worth a hoot, however well supported and maintained, so long as he is not absolutely free, if the spirit moves him, to support and maintain the exactly contrary opinion. In brief, human reason is a weak and paltry thing so long as it is not wholly free reason. The fact lies in its very nature, and is revealed by its entire history. A man may be perfectly honest in a contention, and he may be astute and persuasive in maintaining it, but the moment the slightest compulsion to maintain it is laid upon him, the moment the slightest external reward goes with his partisanship or the slightest penalty with its abandonment, then there appears a defect in his ratiocination that is more deep-seated than any error in fact and more destructive than any conscious and deliberate bias. He may seek the truth and the truth only, and bring up his highest talents and diligence to the business, but always there is a specter behind his chair, a warning in his ear. Always it is safer and more hygienic for him to think one way than to think another way, and in that bald fact there is excuse enough to hold his whole chain of syllogisms in suspicion. He may be earnest, he may be honest, but he is not free, and if he is not free, he is not anything.

Well, are the reverend professors of economics free? Their colleagues of archaeology may be reasonably called free, and their colleagues of bacteriology, and those of Latin grammar and sidereal astronomy, and those of many another science and mystery, but when one comes to the faculty of political economy, one finds that freedom as plainly conditioned, though perhaps not as openly, as in the faculty of theology. And for a plain reason. Political economy, so to speak, hits the employers of the professors where they live. It deals, not with ideas that affect those employers only occasionally or only indirectly or only as ideas, but with ideas that have an imminent and continuous influence upon their personal welfare and security, and that affect profoundly the very foundations of that social and economic structure upon which their whole existence is based. It is, in brief, the science of the ways and means whereby they have to such estate, and maintain themselves in such estate, that they are able to hire and boss professors. It is the boat in which they sail down perilous waters—and they must needs yell, or be more or less than human, when it is rocked. Now and then that yell duly resounds in the groves of learning. One remembers, for example, the trial, condemnation and execution of Prof. Dr. Scott Nearing at the University of Pennsylvania, a seminary that is highly typical, both in its staff and in its control. Nearing, I have no doubt, was wrong in his notions—honestly, perhaps, but still wrong. In so far as I heard them stated at the time, they seemed to me to be hollow and of no validity. He has since discharged them from the chautauqua stump, and at the usual hinds. They have been chiefly accepted and celebrated by men I regard as asses. But Nearing was not thrown out of the University of Pennsylvania, angrily and ignominiously, because he was honestly wrong, or because his errors made him incompetent to prepare sophomores for their examinations; he was thrown out because his efforts to get at the truth disturbed the security and equanimity of the rich ignoranti who happened to control the university, and because the academic slaves and satellites of these shopmen were restive under his competition for the attention of the student-body. In three words, he was thrown out because he was not safe and sane and orthodox. Had his aberration gone in the other direction, had he defended child labor as ardently as he denounced it and denounced the minimum wage as ardently as he defended it, then he would have been quite as secure in his post, for all his cavorting in the newspapers, as Chancellor Day was at Syracuse.

Now consider the case of the professors of economics, near and far, who have not been thrown out. Who will say that the lesson of the Nearing debacle has been lost upon them? Who will say that the potency of the wealthy men who command our universities—or most of them—has not stuck in their minds? And who will say that, with this sticking remembered, their arguments against Nearing's so-called ideas are as worthy of confidence and respect as they would be if they were quite free to go over to Nearing's side without damage? Who, indeed, will give them full credit, even when they are right, so long as they are hamstrung, nose-ringed and tied up in gilded pens? It seems to me that those considerations are enough to cast a glow of suspicion over the whole of American political economy, at least in so far as it comes from college economists. And, in the main, it has that source, for, barring a few brilliant journalists, all our economists of any repute are professors. Many of them are able men, and most of them are undoubtedly honest men, as honesty goes in the world, but over practically every one of them there stands a board of trustees with its legs in the stock-market and its eyes on the established order, and that board is ever alert for heresy in the science of its being, and has ready means of punishing it, and a hearty enthusiasm for the business. Not every professor, perhaps, may be sent straight to the block, as Nearing was, but there are plenty of pillories and guardhouses on the way, and every last pedagogue must be well aware of it.

Political economy, in so far as it is a science at all, was not pumped up and embellished by any such academic clients and ticket-of-leave men. It was on its legs by inquirers who were not only safe from all dousing in the campus pump, but who were also free from the mental timorousness and conformity which go inevitably with school-teaching—in brief, by men of the world, accustomed to its free air, its hospitality to originality and plain speaking. Adam Smith, true enough, was once a professor, but he threw up his chair to go to Paris, and there he met, not more professors, but all the current enemies of professors—the Nearings and Henry Georges and Karl Marxes of the time. And the book that he wrote was not orthodox, but revolutionary. Consider the others of that bulk and beam: Bentham, Ricardo, Mill and their like. Bentham held no post at the mercy of bankers and tripesellers; he was a man of independent means, a lawyer and politician, and a heretic in general practice. It is impossible to imagine such a man occupying a chair at Harvard or Princeton. He had a hand in too many pies; he was too rebellious and contumacious: he had too little respect for authority, either academic or worldly. Moreover, his mind was too wide for a professor; he could never remain safely in a groove; the whole field of social organization invited his inquiries and experiments. Ricardo? Another man of easy means and great worldly experience—by academic standards, not even educated. To-day, I daresay, such meager diplomas as he could show would not suffice to get him an instructor's berth in a fresh-water seminary in Iowa. As for Mill, he was so well grounded by his father that he knew more, at eighteen, than any of the universities could teach him, and his life thereafter was the exact antithesis of that of a cloistered pedagogue. Moreover, he was a heretic in religion and probably violated the Mann act of those days—an offense almost as heinous, in a college professor of economics, as giving three cheers for Prince Kropotkin.

I might lengthen the list, but humanely refrain. The point is that these early English economists were all perfectly free men, with complete liberty to tell the truth as they saw it, regardless of its orthodoxy or lack of orthodoxy. I do not say that the typical American economist of to-day is not as honest, nor even that he is not as diligent and competent, but I do say that he is not as free—that penalties would come upon him for stating ideas that

Smith or Ricardo or Bentham or Mill, had he so desired, would have been free to state without damage. And in that menace there is an ineradicable criticism of the ideas that he does state, and it lingers even when they are plausible and are accepted. In France and Germany, where the universities and colleges are controlled by the state, the practical effect of such pressure has been frequently demonstrated. In the former country the violent debate over social and economic problems during the quarter century before the war produced a long list of professors cashiered for heterodoxy, headed by the names of Jean Jaures and Gustave Herve. In Germany it needed no Nietzsche to point out the deadening produced by this state control. Germany, in fact, got out of it an entirely new species of economist—the state Socialist who flirted with radicalism with one eye and kept the other fixed upon his chair, his salary and his pension.

The Nearing case and the rebellions of various pedagogues elsewhere show that we in America stand within the shadow of a somewhat similar danger. In economics, as in the other sciences, we are probably producing men who are as good as those on view in any other country. They are not to be surpassed for learning and originality, and there is no reason to believe that they lack honesty and courage. But honesty and courage, as men go in the world, are after all merely relative values. There comes a point at which even the most honest man considers consequences, and even the most courageous looks before he leaps. The difficulty lies in establishing the position of that point. So long as it is in doubt, there will remain, too, the other doubt that I have described. I rise in meeting, I repeat, not as a radical, but as one of the most hunkerous of the orthodox. I can imagine nothing more dubious in fact and wobbly in logic than some of the doctrines that amateur economists, chiefly socialists, have set afloat in this country during the past dozen years. I have even gone to the trouble of writing a book against them; my convictions and instincts are all on the other side. But I should be a great deal more comfortable in those convictions and instincts if I were convinced that the learned professors were really in full and absolute possession of academic freedom—if I could imagine them taking the other tack now and then without damnation to their jobs, their lecture dates, their book sales, and their hides.

(*Prejudices, Third Series*)

3

QUACKERY
& HOAXES

THE FOUNDATIONS OF
QUACKERY

[*When people fall for a conspiracy theory, whether it be about satanic rituals among the elite or vaccines causing autism, all too many swallow it whole. The basic reason for their gullibility is that their critical faculties are all but nonexistent. Anti-vaxxers cannot comprehend that a single shot causes an immune response, and is no more dangerous than a box of chicken tenders. So they bloviate about nonexistent harmful effects, a big pharma/government/media/ scientific conspiracy,* and *an airtight cover up involving the millions upon millions of people comprising all of those entities.*

As Mencken notes, the problem gets worse every year because science progresses as public intelligence regresses.]

No democratic delusion is more fatuous than that which holds that all men are capable of reason, and hence susceptible to conversion by evidence. If religions depended upon evidence for their propagation, then all of them would collapse. It is not only that the great majority of the men they seek to reach are quite incapable of comprehending any evidence, good or bad. They must get at such men through their feelings or resign getting at them altogether.

So in all other regions of the so-called mind. I have often pointed out how politics, under democracy, invariably translates itself from the domain of logical ideas to the domain of mere feelings, usually simple fear—how every great campaign in American history, however decorously it started with a statement of principles, has always ended with a violent pursuit of hobgoblins. The great majority of the half-wits who followed William Jennings Bryan in his three Presidential battles were certainly not attracted to him by his complex and nonsensical economic doctrines; those doctrines, in fact, dealt with such unfamiliar and difficult concepts that not one in ten thousand of the loudest Bryanites could understand them at all. What attracted them was not Bryan's economics but his adroit demonology; an evangelist by divine inspiration, he invented demons that palsied them and took their breath, and so they stormed after him.

The number of men eligible to membership in such mobs is always underestimated. That is to say, the number of men capable of anything properly describable as logical reasoning is always put too high. Worse, the great progress of all the exact sciences in our own time tends to diminish it constantly. There was a time, and it was much less than a century ago, when any man of sound sense and fair education could understand all of the concepts commonly employed in the physical sciences. In medicine, for example, there was nothing beyond the comprehension of the average intelligent layman. But of late that has ceased to be true, to the great damage of the popular respect for knowledge. Only too often, when a physician of today tries to explain to his patient what is the matter with him, he finds it impossible to get the explanation into terms within the patient's understanding. The latter, if he is intelligent enough, will face the fact of his lack of training without rancor, and content himself with whatever parts of the exposition he can grasp. But that sort of intelligence, unluckily, is rather rare in the world; it is confined, indeed, to men of the sort who are said to have the scientific mind, i.e., a very small minority of men. The average man, finding himself getting beyond his depth, instantly concludes that what lies beyond is simply nonsense.

It is this fact which accounts for the great current prosperity of such quackeries as osteopathy, chiropractic and Christian Science. The agents of such quackeries gain their converts by the simple process of reducing the inordinately complex to the absurdly simple. Unless a man is already equipped with a considerable knowledge of chemistry, bacteriology and physiology, no one can ever hope to make him understand what is meant by the term anaphylaxis, but any man, if only he be idiot enough, can grasp the whole theory of chiropractic in twenty minutes. The fact that such imbeciles prosper increasingly in the world, and gain adherents in constantly superior circles—that is, among persons of more and more apparent education and culture—is no more than proof that the physical sciences are becoming increasingly recondite and difficult, and that the relative numbers of persons congenitally incapable of comprehending them is growing year by year.

(*Baltimore Evening Sun*, June 4, 1923)

CHIROPRACTIC

[In the 1920s, thick-handed men, put out of military jobs by international peace and out of hammering work due to the finishing of the major railroads, found that for the price of a mail-order course they could become chiropractors. Mencken found a lot of things absurd, but the chiropractic art alarmed him. Droves of the stiff-necked went to massage artists with meaty forearms in a pseudo-scientific craze not seen since the seances of the 19th century. A séance just left one poorer in mind and pocket, however, whereas a chiropractic session with an "ex-boilermaker" might have left someone in pieces. This is Mencken's funniest piece, if only because we can practically see the cigar dropping out of his mouth at the sight of his countrymen succumbing to a physical pummeling because advertising, and word of mouth from uninformed neighbors, said it was good for them.]

This preposterous quackery flourishes lushly in the back reaches of the Republic, and begins to conquer the less civilized folk of the big cities. As the old-time family doctor dies out in the country towns, with no competent successor willing to take over his dismal business, he is followed by some hearty blacksmith of ice-wagon driver, turned into a chiropractor in six months, often by correspondence. In Los Angeles the Damned there are probably more chiropractors than actual physicians, and they are far more generally esteemed. Proceeding from the Ambassador Hotel to the heart of the town, along Wilshire boulevard, one passes scores of their gaudy signs; there are even many chiropractic "hospitals." The Mormons who pour in from the prairies and deserts, most of them ailing, patronize these "hospitals" copiously and give to the chiropractic pathology the same high respect that they accord to the theology of the town sorcerers. That pathology is grounded upon the doctrine that all human ills are caused by the pressure of misplaced vertebrae upon the nerves which come out of the spinal cord—in other words, that every disease is the result of a pinch. This, plainly enough, is buncombe. The chiropractic therapeutics rest upon the doctrine that the way to get rid of such pinches is to climb upon a table and submit to a heroic pummeling by a retired piano-mover. This, obviously, is buncombe doubly damned.

Both doctrines were launched upon the world by an old quack named Andrew T. Still, the father of osteopathy. For years the osteopaths merchanted them, and made money at the trade. But as they grew opulent they grew ambitious, i.e., they began to study anatomy and physiology. The result was a gradual abandonment of Papa Still's ideas. The high-toned osteopath of today is a sort of eclectic. He tries anything that promises to work, from tonsillectomy to the X-rays. With four years' training behind him, he probably knows more anatomy than the average graduate of the Johns Hopkins Medical School, or at all events, more osteology. Thus enlightened, he seldom has much to say about pinched nerves in the back. But as he abandoned the Still revelation it was seized by the chiropractors, led by another quack, one Palmer. This Palmer grabbed the pinched nerve nonsense and began teaching it to ambitious farm-hands and out-at-elbow Baptist preachers in a few easy lessons. Today the backwoods swarm with chiropractors, and in most States they have been able to exert enough pressure on the rural politicians to get themselves licensed. Any lout with strong hands and arms is perfectly equipped to become a chiropractor. No education beyond the elements is necessary. The takings are often high, and so the profession has attracted thousands of recruits—retired baseball players, work-weary plumbers, truck-drivers, longshoremen, bogus dentists, dubious preachers, cashiered school superintendents. Now and then a quack of some other school—say homeopathy—plunges into it. Hundreds of promising students come from the intellectual ranks of hospital orderlies.

Such quackeries suck in the botched, and help them on to bliss eternal. When these botched fall into the hands of competent medical men they are very likely to be patched up and turned loose upon the world, to beget their kind. But massaged along the backbone to cure their lues [syphilis], they quickly pass into the last stages, and so their pathogenic heritage perishes with them. What is too often forgotten is that nature obviously intends the botched to die, and that every interference with that benign process is full of dangers. That the labors of quacks tend to propagate epidemics and so menace the lives of all of us, as is alleged by their medical opponents—this I doubt. The fact is that most infectious diseases of any seriousness throw out such alarming symptoms and so quickly that no sane chiropractor is likely to monkey with them. Seeing his patient breaking out in pustules, or choking, or falling into a stupor, he takes to the woods at once, and leaves the business to the nearest medical man. His trade is mainly with ambulant patients; they must come to his studio for treatment. Most of them have lingering diseases; they tour all the neighborhood doctors before they reach him. His treatment, being nonsensical, is in accord with the divine plan. It is seldom, perhaps, that he actually kills a patient, but at all events he keeps many a worthy soul from getting well.

The osteopaths, I fear, are finding this new competition serious and unpleasant. As I have said, it was their Hippocrates, the late Dr. Still, who invented all of the thrusts, lunges, yanks, hooks and bounces that the lowly chiropractors now employ with such vast effect, and for years the osteopaths had a monopoly of them. But when they began to grow scientific and ambitious their course of training was lengthened until it took in all sorts of tricks and dodges borrowed from the regular doctors, or resurrection men, including the plucking of tonsils, adenoids and appendices, the use of the stomach-pump, and even some of the legerdemain of psychiatry. They now harry their students furiously, and turn them out ready for anything from growing hair on a bald head to frying a patient with x-rays. All this new striving, of course, quickly brought its inevitable penalties. The osteopathic graduate, having sweated so long, was no longer willing to take a case of delirium tremens for $2, and in consequence he lost patients. Worse, very few aspirants could make the long grade. The essence of osteopathy itself could be grasped by any lively farm-hand or night watchman in a few weeks, but the borrowed magic baffled him. Confronted by the phenomenon of gastrulation, or by the curious behavior of heart muscle, or by any of the current theories of immunity, he commonly took refuge, like his brother of the orthodox faculty, in a gulp of laboratory alcohol, or fled the premises altogether. Thus he was lost to osteopathic science, and the chiropractor took him in; nay, they welcomed him. He was their meat. Borrowing that primitive part of osteopathy which was comprehensible to the meanest understanding, they threw the rest overboard, at the same time denouncing it as a sorcery invented by the Medical Trust. Thus they gathered in the garage mechanics, ash-men and decayed welter-weights, and the land began to fill with their graduates. Now there is a chiropractor at every cross-roads.

I repeat that it eases and soothes me to see them so prosperous, for they counteract the evil work of the so-called science of public hygiene, which now seeks to make imbeciles immortal. If a man, being ill of a pus appendix, resorts to a shaved and fumigated longshoreman to have it disposed of, and submits willingly to a treatment involving balancing him on McBurney's spot and playing on his vertebrae as on a concertina, then I am willing for one, to believe that he is badly wanted in Heaven. And if that same man, having achieved lawfully a lovely babe, hires a blacksmith to cure its diphtheria by pulling its neck, then I do not resist the divine will that there shall be one less radio fan later on. In such matters, I am convinced, the laws of nature are far better guides than the fiats and machinations of medical busybodies. If the latter gentlemen had their way, death, save at the hands of hangmen, policemen and other such legalized assassins, would be abolished altogether, and the present differential in favor of the enlightened would disappear. I can't convince myself that that would work any good to the world. On the contrary, it seems to me that the current coddling of the half-witted should be stopped before it goes too far—if, indeed, it has not gone too far already. To that end nothing operates more cheaply and effectively than the prosperity of quacks. Every time a bottle of cancer oil goes through the mails *Homo americanus* is improved to that extent. And every time a chiropractor spits on his hands and proceeds to treat a gastric ulcer by stretching the backbone the same high end is achieved.

But chiropractic, of course, is not perfect. It has superb potentialities, but only too often they are not converted into concrete cadavers. The hygienists rescue many of its foreordained customers, and, turning them over to agents of the Medical Trust, maintained at the public expense, get them cured. Moreover, chiropractic itself is not certainly fatal: even an Iowan with diabetes may survive its embraces. Yet worse, I have a suspicion that it sometimes actually cures. For all I know (or any orthodox pathologist seems to know) it may be true that certain maladies are caused by the pressure of vagrom vertebrae upon the nerves. And it may be true that a hearty ex-boilermaker, by a vigorous yanking and kneading, may be able to relieve that pressure. What is needed is a scientific inquiry into the matter, under rigid test conditions, by a committee of men learned in the architecture and plumbing of the body, and of a high and incorruptible sagacity. Let a thousand patients be selected, let a gang of selected chiropractors examine their backbones and determine what is the matter with them, and then let these diagnoses be checked up by the exact methods of scientific medicine. Then let the same chiropractors essay to cure the patients whose maladies have been determined. My guess is that the chiropractors' errors in diagnosis will run to at least 95% and that their failures in treatment will push 99%. But I am willing to be convinced.

Where is such a committee to be found? I undertake to nominate it at ten minutes' notice. The land swarms with men competent in anatomy and pathology, and yet not engaged as doctors. There are thousands of hospitals, with endless clinical material. I offer to supply the committee with cigars and music during the test. I offer, further, to supply both the committee and the chiropractors with sound wet goods. I offer, finally, to give a bawdy banquet to the whole Medical Trust at the conclusion of the proceedings.

(from "Dives Into Quackery," *The American Mercury*, December 1924)

EUGENICS

*[Feminist critiques of authors from less enlightened times grate on the nerves,
but it's hard not to fault Mencken for failing to note that Mary Wollstonecraft,
author of the superb* Vindication of the Rights of Women, *gave birth to Mary
Shelley. Mary the first died a few days after giving birth to Mary the second,
and yet Shelley went on to write her own work of genius in* Frankenstein.
*This might be Exhibit A in any discussion about the genetic inheritance of
intelligence, but Mencken seems not to have considered either the mother or
daughter.*

*Yet, is there something to the conceit that genius manifests itself regardless of
environment? That the 19th century forests of southern Illinois and Indiana,
devoid of schools and awash in whiskey, could produce an Abraham Lincoln,
or that the mind of a Friedrich Nietzsche (or an Oppenheimer, or Hawking)
could produce explosions of thought in bodies ravaged by inactivity, chain
smoking, and disease, gives one pause.]*

This great moral cause, like that of criminologists, is much corrupted by
blather. In none of the books of its master minds is there a clear definition
of the superiority they talk about so copiously. At one time they seem to
identify it with high intelligence, at another time with character, i.e., moral
stability, and at yet another time with mere fame, i.e., luck. Was Napoleon
I a superior man, as I am privately inclined to believe, along with many
of the eugenists? Then so was Aaron Burr, if in less measure. Was Paul of
Tarsus? Then so was Brigham Young. Were the Gracchi? Then so were Karl
Marx and William Jennings Bryan.

This matter of superiority, indeed, presents cruel and ineradicable difficulties. If it is made to run with service to the human race, the eugenist
is soon mired, for many men held to be highly useful are obviously second-rate, and leave third-rate progeny behind them, for example, General

Grant. And if it is made to run with intellectual brilliance and originality the troubles that loom up are just as serious, for men of that rare quality are generally felt to be dangerous, and sometimes they undoubtedly are. The case of Friedrich Wilhelm Nietzsche is in point. I suppose that no rational person to-day, not even an uncured Liberty Loan orator or dollar-a-year man, would argue seriously that Nietzsche was inferior. On the contrary, his extraordinary gifts are now unanimously admitted, save perhaps by the rev. clergy. But what of his value to the human race? And what of his eugenic fitness? It is not easy to answer these questions. Nietzsche, in fact, preached a gospel that to most human beings remains unbearable, and it will probably continue unbearable for centuries to come. Its adoption by Dr. Coolidge, by and with the advice and consent of the Senate, would plunge this Republic into dreadful woe. And Nietzsche himself was a chronic invalid who died insane—the sort of wreck who, had he lived into our time, would have been a customer of chiropractors. Worse, he suffered from a malady of a scandalous nature, and of evil effects upon the sufferer's offspring. Was it good or bad luck for the world, eugenically speaking, that he died a bachelor?

But their vagueness about the exact nature of superiority is not the only thing that corrupts the fine fury of the eugenists. Even more dismaying is their gratuitous assumption that all of the socially useful and laudable qualities (whatever they may be) are the exclusive possession of one class of men, and the other classes lack them altogether. This is plainly not true. All that may be truthfully said of such qualities is that they appear rather more frequently in one class than in another. But they are rare in all classes, and the difference in the frequency of their occurrence between this class and that one is not very great, and of little genuine importance. If all the biologists in the United States were hanged to-morrow (as has been proposed by the pastors and newspaper editors of Mississippi) and their children with them, we'd probably still have a sufficiency of biologists in the next generation. There might not be as many as we have to-day, but there would be enough. They would come out of the families of bricklayers and politicians, bootleggers and bond salesmen. Some of them, indeed, might even come out of the families of Mississippi editors and ecclesiastics. For the supply of such men, like the supply of synthetic gin, always tends to run with the demand. Whenever it is short, the demand almost automatically augments it. Every one knows that this is true on the lower levels. Before baseball was invented there were no Ty Cobbs and Babe Ruths; now they appear in an apparently endless series. Before the Wright brothers made their first flight there were no men skilled at aviation; now there are multitudes of highly competent experts. The eugenists forget that the same thing happens also on the higher levels. Whenever the world has stood in absolute need of a genius he has appeared. And though it is true that he has usually come out of the better half of humanity, it is also true that he has sometimes come out of the worse half. Beethoven was the grandson of a cook and the son of a drunkard, and Lincoln's forebears never lifted themselves above the level of village prominenti.

The fact is that the difference between the better sort of human beings and the lower sort, biologically speaking, is very slight. There may be, at the very top, a small class of persons whose blood is decidedly superior and distinguished, and there may be, at the bottom, another class whose blood is almost wholly debased, but both are very small. The folks between are all pretty much alike. The baron has a great deal of peasant blood in him, and the peasant has some blood that is blue. The natural sinfulness of man is enough to make sure of that. No man in this world can ever be quite sure that he is the actual great-great-grandson of the great-great-grandfather whose memory he venerates. Thus, when the relatively superior and distinguished class ceases to be fecund (a phenomenon now visible everywhere in the world), natural selection comes to the rescue by selecting out and promoting individuals from the classes below. These individuals, in the main, are just as sound in blood as any one in the class they enter. Their sound blood has been concealed, perhaps for generations, but it has been there all the time. If Abraham Lincoln's ancestry were known with any certainty, it would probably be found to run back to manifestly able men. There are many more such hidden family-trees in the folk: the eugenists simply overlook them. They are also singularly blind to many familiar biological phenomena—for example, the appearance of mutations or sports. It is not likely that a commonplace family will produce a genius, but nevertheless it is by no means impossible: the thing has probably happened more than once. They forget, too, the influence of environment on human society. Mere environment, to be sure, cannot produce a genius, but it can certainly help him enormously after he is born. If a potential Wagner were born to a Greek bootblack in New York City to-morrow, the chances of his coming to fruition and fame would be at least even. But if he were born to an Arab in the Libyan desert or to a Fundamentalist in Rhea county, Tennessee, the chances are that he would be a total loss. . . .

(from "Dives into Quackery," *The American Mercury*, December 1924)

A NEGLECTED ANNIVERSARY

[*"A Neglected Anniversary"* reads as if it's a simple factual piece, but it's far from it—it's a fabrication from beginning to end. Mencken intended it as an oblique criticism of war propaganda during WWI and how easily people swallowed it, but the piece is so oblique that it's highly doubtful that anyone got the point at the time. In his follow-up piece, "Melancholy Reflections," Mencken stated that there were numerous "obvious" absurdities that should have tipped off readers, but in hindsight many of the absurdities don't seem all that absurd, and even the most blatant come off as oddities, not as obvious falsehoods. It seems that the newspaper editors of Mencken's time didn't question anything about the piece, as not a single paper called out this "obvious" hoax.]

On December 20 there flitted past us, absolutely without public notice, one of the most important profane anniversaries in American history, to wit, the seventy-fifth anniversary of the introduction of the bathtub into These States. Not a plumber fired a salute or hung out a flag. Not a governor proclaimed a day of prayer. Not a newspaper called attention to the day.

True enough, it was not entirely forgotten. Eight or nine months ago one of the younger surgeons connected with the Public Health Service in Washington happened upon the facts while looking into the early history of public hygiene, and at his suggestion a committee was formed to celebrate the anniversary with a banquet. But before the plan was perfected Washington went dry, and so the banquet had to be abandoned. As it was, the day passed wholly unmarked, even in the capital of the nation.

Bathtubs are so common today that it is almost impossible to imagine a world without them. They are familiar to nearly everyone in all incorporated towns; in most of the large cities it is unlawful to build a dwelling house without putting them in; even on the farm they have begun to come into use. And yet the first American bathtub was installed and dedicated so recently as December 20, 1842, and, for all I know to the contrary, it may still be in existence and in use.

Curiously enough, the scene of its setting up was Cincinnati, then a squalid frontier town, and even today surely no leader in culture. But Cincinnati, in those days as in these, contained many enterprising merchants, and one of them was a man named Adam Thompson, a dealer in cotton and grain. Thompson shipped his grain by steamboat down the Ohio and Mississippi to New Orleans, and from there sent it to England in sailing vessels. This trade frequently took him to England, and in that country, during the '30s, he acquired the habit of bathing.

The bathtub was then still a novelty in England. It had been introduced in 1828 by Lord John Russell and its use was yet confined to a small class of enthusiasts. Moreover, the English bathtub, then as now, was a puny and inconvenient contrivance—little more, in fact, than a glorified dishpan—and filling and emptying it required the attendance of a servant. Taking a bath, indeed, was a rather heavy ceremony, and Lord John in 1835 was said to be the only man in England who had yet come to doing it every day.

Thompson, who was of inventive fancy—he later devised the machine that is still used for bagging hams and bacon—conceived the notion that the English bathtub would be much improved if it were made large enough to admit the whole body of an adult man, and if its supply of water, instead of being hauled to the scene by a maid, were admitted by pipes from a central reservoir and run off by the same means. Accordingly, early in 1842 he set about building the first modern bathroom in his Cincinnati home —a large house with Doric pillars, standing near what is now the corner of Monastery and Orleans streets.

There was then, of course, no city water supply, at least in that part of the city, but Thompson had a large well in his garden, and he installed a pump to lift its water to the house. This pump, which was operated by six Negroes, much like an old-time fire engine, was connected by a pipe with a cypress tank in the garret of the house, and here the water was stored until needed. From the tank two other pipes ran to the bathroom. One, carrying cold water, was a direct line. The other, designed to provide warm water, ran down the great chimney of the kitchen, and was coiled inside it like a giant spring.

The tub itself was of new design, and became the grandfather of all the bathtubs of today. Thompson had it made by James Cullness, the leading Cincinnati cabinetmaker of those days, and its material was Nicaragua mahogany. It was nearly seven feet long and fully four feet wide. To make it water-tight, the interior was lined with sheet lead, carefully soldered at the joints. The whole contraption weighed about 1,750 pounds, and the floor of the room in which it was placed had to be reinforced to support it. The exterior was elaborately polished.

In this luxurious tub Thompson took two baths on December 20, 1842—a cold one at 8 a.m. and a warm one some time during the afternoon. The warm water, heated by the kitchen fire, reached a temperature of 105 degrees. On Christmas day, having a party of gentlemen to dinner, he exhibited the new marvel to them and gave an exhibition of its use, and four of them, including a French visitor, Col. Duchanel, risked plunges into it. The next day all Cincinnati—then a town of about 100,000 people—had heard of it, and the local newspapers described it at length and opened their columns to violent discussions of it.

The thing, in fact, became a public matter, and before long there was bitter and double-headed opposition to the new invention, which had been promptly imitated by several other wealthy Cincinnatians. On the one hand it was denounced as an epicurean and obnoxious toy from England, designed to corrupt the democratic simplicity of the Republic, and on the other hand it was attacked by the medical faculty as dangerous to health and a certain inviter of "phthisic, rheumatic fevers, inflammation of the lungs and the whole category of zymotic diseases." (I quote from the *Western Medical Repository* of April 23, 1843.)

The noise of the controversy soon reached other cities, and in more than one place medical opposition reached such strength that it was reflected in legislation. Late in 1843, for example, the Philadelphia Common Council considered an ordinance prohibiting bathing between November 1 and March 15, and it failed of passage by but two votes. During the same year the legislature of Virginia laid a tax of $30 a year on all bathtubs that might be set up, and in Hartford, Providence, Charleston and Wilmington (Del.) special and very heavy water rates were levied upon those who had them. Boston, very early in 1845, made bathing unlawful except upon medical advice, but the ordinance was never enforced and in 1862 it was repealed.

This legislation, I suspect, had some class feeling in it, for the Thompson bathtub was plainly too expensive to be owned by any save the wealthy; indeed, the common price for installing one in New York in 1845 was $500. Thus the low caste politicians of the time made capital by fulminating against it, and there is even some suspicion of political bias in many of the early medical denunciations. But the invention of the common pine bathtub, lined with zinc, in 1847, cut off this line of attack, and thereafter the bathtub made steady progress.

The zinc tub was devised by John F. Simpson, a Brooklyn plumber, and his efforts to protect it by a patent occupied the courts until 1855. But the decisions were steadily against him, and after 1848 all the plumbers of New York were equipped for putting in bathtubs. According to a writer in the Christian Register for July 17, 1857, the first one in New York was opened for traffic on September 12, 1847, and by the beginning of 1850 there were already nearly 1,000 in use in the big town.

After this medical opposition began to collapse, and among other eminent physicians Dr. Oliver Wendell Holmes declared for the bathtub, and vigorously opposed the lingering movement against it in Boston. The American Medical Association held its annual meeting in Boston in 1849, and a poll of the members in attendance showed that nearly 55 per cent of them now regarded bathing as harmless, and that more than 20 per cent advocated it as beneficial. At its meeting in 1850 a resolution was formally passed giving the imprimatur of the faculty to the bathtub. The homeopaths followed with a like resolution in 1853.

But it was the example of President Millard Fillmore that, even more than the grudging medical approval, gave the bathtub recognition and respectability in the United States. While he was still Vice-President, in March, 1850, he visited Cincinnati on a stumping tour, and inspected the original Thompson tub. Thompson himself was now dead, but his bathroom was preserved by the gentlemen who had bought his house from the estate. Fillmore was entertained in this house and, according to Chamberlain, his biographer, took a bath in the tub. Experiencing no ill effects, he became an ardent advocate of the new invention, and on succeeding to the Presidency at Taylor's death, July 9, 1850, he instructed his secretary of war, Gen. Charles M. Conrad, to invite tenders for the construction of a bathtub in the White House.

This action, for a moment, revived the old controversy, and its opponents made much of the fact that there was no bathtub at Mount Vernon, or at Monticello, and that all the Presidents and other magnificoes of the past had got along without any such monarchical luxuries. The elder Bennett, in the New York Herald, charged that Fillmore really aspired to buy and install in the White House a porphyry and alabaster bath that had been used by Louis Philippe at Versailles. But Conrad, disregarding all this clamor, duly called for bids, and the contract was presently awarded to Harper & Gillespie, a firm of Philadelphia engineers, who proposed to furnish a tub of thin cast iron, capable of floating the largest man.

This was installed early in 1851, and remained in service in the White House until the first Cleveland administration, when the present enameled tub was substituted. The example of the President soon broke down all that remained of the old opposition, and by 1860, according to the newspaper advertisements of the time, every hotel in New York had a bathtub, and some had two and even three. In 1862 bathing was introduced into the Army by Gen. McClellan, and in 1870 the first prison bathtub was set up at Moyamensing Prison, in Philadelphia.

So much for the history of the bathtub in America. One is astonished, on looking into it, to find that so little of it has been recorded. The literature, in fact, is almost nil. But perhaps this brief sketch will encourage other inquirers and so lay the foundation for an adequate celebration of the centennial in 1942.

(*New York Evening Mail*, December 28, 1917)

MELANCHOLY REFLECTIONS

[*In a piece titled "Hymn to the Truth," in* Prejudices, Sixth Series, *Mencken dryly states that "Melancholy Reflections" was published "simultaneously in thirty great American newspapers with a combined circulation, according to their own sworn claims, of more than 250,000,000." The wording is "dry" because, according to the Census Bureau, the U.S. population at the time was 117 million. Still, Mencken's exposure of his "bathtub hoax" likely reached tens of millions of readers.*

Yet magazines, newspapers, and even academic researchers continued to cite Mencken's hoax piece as if it were factual. The most amusing example was provided by "the eminent Boston Herald," *which was one of the "great American newspapers" that ran Mencken's exposure of his own hoax. As Mencken put it, "The* Herald, *on that bright May Sunday, printed my article on a leading page of its so-called Editorial Section, under a black and beetling four-column head, and with a two-column cartoon satirically labeled, 'The American Public Will Swallow Anything.' And then, three weeks later, on June 13, in the same Editorial Section, but promoted to page one, the same* Herald *reprinted my ten-year-old fake—soberly and as a piece of news!"*

Nearly a quarter century later, in his Chrestomathy, *Mencken stated that, "Scarcely a month goes by that I do not find the substance of it reprinted, not as foolishness but as fact, and not only in newspapers but in official documents and other works of the highest pretensions."*

Need we—need anyone—ever say anything more about American gullibility and aversion to fact checking? Here, as with so many other things, Mencken has provided the final word.]

On Dec. 28, 1917, I printed in the *New York Evening Mail*, a paper now extinct, an article purporting to give the history of the bathtub. This article, I may say at once, was a tissue of absurdities, all of them deliberate and most of them obvious.

This article, as I say, was planned as a piece of spoofing to relieve the strain of war days, and I confess that I regarded it, when it came out, with considerable satisfaction. It was reprinted by various great organs of the enlightenment, and after a while the usual letters began to reach me from readers. Then, suddenly, my satisfaction turned to consternation. For these readers, it appeared, all took my idle jocosities with complete seriousness. Some of them, of antiquarian tastes, asked for further light on this or that phase of the subject. Others actually offered me corroboration!

But the worst was to come. Pretty soon I began to encounter my preposterous "facts" in the writings of other men. They began to be used by chiropractors and other such quacks as evidence of the stupidity of medical men. They began to be cited by medical men as proof of the progress of public hygiene. They got into learned journals. They were alluded to on the floor of congress. They crossed the ocean, and were discussed solemnly in England and on the continent. Finally, I began to find them in standard works of reference. Today, I believe, they are accepted as gospel everywhere on earth. To question them becomes as hazardous as to question the Norman invasion.

✶ ✶ ✶

And as rare. This is the first time, indeed, that they have ever been questioned, and I confess at once that even I myself, their author, feel a certain hesitancy about doing it. Once more, I suppose, I'll be accused of taking the wrong side for the mere pleasure of standing in opposition. The Cincinnati boomers, who have made much of the boast that the bathtub industry, now running to $200,000,000 a year, was started in their town, will charge me with spreading lies against them. The chiropractors will damn me for blowing up their ammunition. The medical gents, having swallowed my quackery, will now denounce me as a quack for exposing them. And in the end, no doubt, the thing will simmer down to a general feeling that I have once more committed some vague and sinister crime against the United States, and there will be a renewal of the demand that I be deported to Russia.

I recite this history, not because it is singular, but because it is typical. It is out of just such frauds, I believe, that most of the so-called knowledge of humanity flows. What begins as a guess—or, perhaps, not infrequently, as a downright and deliberate lie—ends as a fact and is embalmed in the history books. One recalls the gaudy days of 1914–1918. How much that was then devoured by the newspaper readers of the world was actually true?

Probably not 1 per cent. Ever since the war ended learned and laborious men have been at work examining and exposing its fictions. But every one of these fictions retains full faith and credit today. To question even the most palpably absurd of them, in most parts of the United States, is to invite denunciation as a bolshevik.

So with all other wars. For example, the revolution. For years past American historians have been investigating the orthodox legends. Almost all of them turn out to be blowsy nonsense. Yet they remain in the school history books and every effort to get them out causes a dreadful row, and those who make it are accused of all sorts of treasons and spoils. The truth, indeed, is something that mankind, for some mysterious reason, instinctively dislikes. Every man who tries to tell it is unpopular, and even when, by the sheer strength of his case, he prevails, he is put down as a scoundrel.

* * *

As a practicing journalist for many years, I have often had close contact with history in the making. I can recall no time or place when what actually occurred was afterward generally known and believed. Sometimes a part of the truth got out, but never all. And what actually got out was seldom clearly understood. Consider, for example, the legends that follow every national convention. A thousand newspaper correspondents are on the scene, all of them theoretically competent to see accurately and report honestly, but it is seldom that two of them agree perfectly, and after a month after the convention adjourns the accepted version of what occurred usually differs from the accounts of all of them.

I point to the Republican convention of 1920, which nominated the eminent and lamented Harding. A week after the delegates adjourned the whole country believed that Harding had been put through by Col. George Harvey: Harvey himself admitted it. Then other claimants to the honor arose, and after a year or two it was generally held that the trick had been turned by the distinguished Harry M. Daugherty, by that time a salient light of the Harding cabinet. The story began to acquire corroborative detail. Delegates and correspondents began to remember things that they had not noticed on the spot. What the orthodox tale is today with Daugherty in eclipse, I don't know, but you may be sure that it is full of mysterious intrigue and bold adventure.

What are the facts? The facts are that Harvey had little more to do with the nomination of Harding than I did, and that Daugherty was immensely surprised when good Warren won. The nomination was really due to the intense heat, and to that alone. The delegates, torn by the savage three cornered fight between Lowden, Johnson, and Wood, came to Saturday morning in despair. The temperature in the convention hall was at least 120 degrees. They were eager to get home. When it became apparent that the leaders could not break the deadlock they ran amuck and nominated Harding, as the one aspirant who had no enemies. If any individual managed the business it was not Harvey or Daugherty, but Myron T. Herrick. But so far as I know Herrick's hand in it has never been mentioned.

* * *

I turn to a more pleasant field—that of sport in the grand manner. On July 2, 1921, in the great bowl at Jersey City, the Hon. Jack Dempsey met M. Carpentier, the gallant frog. The sympathy of the crowd was overwhelmingly with M. Carpentier and every time he struck a blow he got a round of applause, even if it didn't land. I had an excellent seat, very near the ring, and saw every move of the two men. From the first moment Dr. Dempsey had it all his own way. He could have knocked out M. Carpentier in the first half of the first round. After that first half he simply waited his chance to do it politely and humanely.

Yet certain great newspapers reported the next morning that M. Carpentier had delivered an appalling wallop in the second round and that Dr. Dempsey had narrowly escaped going out. Others told the truth, but what chance had the truth against that romantic lie? It is believed in to this day by at least 99.99 per cent of all the boxing fans in Christendom. Carpentier himself, when he recovered from his beating, admitted categorically that it was nonsense, but even Carpentier could make no headway against the almost universal human tendency to cherish what is not true. A thousand years hence schoolboys will be taught that the frog had Dempsey going. It may become in time a religious dogma, like the doctrine that Jonah swallowed the whale. Scoffers who doubt it will be damned to hell.

The moral, if any, I leave to psycho-pathologists, if competent ones can be found. All I care to do today is to reiterate, in the most solemn and awful terms, that my history of the bathtub, printed on Dec. 28, 1917, was pure buncombe. If there were any facts in it they got there accidentally and against my design. But today the tale is in the encyclopedias. History, said a great American soothsayer, is bunk.

(*Chicago Tribune*, May 23, 1926)

4

CULTURE

THE GENEALOGY OF ETIQUETTE

[*This first-rate essay offends just about everyone. Mencken's gift for asking un-comfortable questions about both the high-falutin' and the everyday leads him into entertaining territory. Sociology is "monkeyshine" akin to religious drivel. The line, "After all, not many of us care a hoot whether Sir Oliver Lodge and the Indian chief Wok-a-wok-a-mok are happy in heaven, for not many of us have any hope or desire to meet them there," is probably funnier now than it was at the time of the writing. The great gift of modern politically correct cul-ture to literary criticism is that it sees racism, sexism, and homophobia where none was intended, making once-commonplace statements seem shocking.*

Then there is "Why do Americans take off our hats when we meet a flapper on the street, and yet stand covered before a male of the highest eminence?" "Flapper," originally a term for the fringed dresses worn by dancing girls of the jazz clubs, evolved into a catch-all for any woman of supposedly low morals. At first the question seems insulting, but further thought might lead one to the conclusion that Mencken was a proto-feminist. Doffing one's hat to a lady was the polite early 20th Century equivalent of the fairy tale cliche of putting a woman in a castle so she could be rescued. Overextensions of polite behavior, like a refusal to poke fun at any particular group, can be worse than impolite behavior.]

Barring sociology (which is yet, of course, scarcely a science at all, but rather a monkey-shine which happens to pay, like play-acting or theol-ogy), psychology is the youngest of the sciences, and hence chiefly guess-work, empiricism, hocus-pocus, poppycock. On the one hand, there are still enormous gaps in its data, so that the determination of its simplest principles remains difficult, not to say impossible; and on the other hand, the very hollowness and nebulosity of it, particularly around its edges, en-courages a horde of quacks to invade it, sophisticate it and make nonsense of it. Worse, this state of affairs tends to such confusion of effort and direc-tion that the quack and the honest inquirer are often found in the same man. It is, indeed, a commonplace to encounter a professor who spends his days in the laborious accumulation of psychological statistics, sticking pins into babies and platting upon a chart the ebb and flow of their yells, and his nights chasing poltergeists and other such celestial fauna over the hurdles of a spiritualist's atelier, or gazing into a crystal in the privacy of his own chamber. The Binét test and the buncombe of mesmerism are alike the children of what we roughly denominate psychology, and perhaps of equal legitimacy. Even so ingenious and competent an investigator as Prof. Dr. Sigmund Freud, who has told us a lot that is of the first importance about the materials and machinery of thought, has also told us a lot that is trivial and dubious. The essential doctrines of Freudianism, no doubt, come close to the truth, but many of Freud's remoter deductions are far more scandalous than sound, and many of the professed Freudians, both American and European, have grease-paint on their noses and bladders in their hands and are otherwise quite indistinguishable from evangelists and circus clowns.

In this condition of the science it is no wonder that we find it wasting its chief force upon problems that are petty and idle when they are not downright and palpably insoluble, and passing over problems that are of immediate concern to all of us, and that might be quite readily solved, or, at any rate, considerably illuminated by an intelligent study of the data already available. After all, not many of us care a hoot whether Sir Oliver Lodge and the Indian chief Wok-a-wok-a-mok are happy in heaven, for not many of us have any hope or desire to meet them there. Nor are we greatly excited by the discovery that, of twenty-five freshmen who are hit with clubs, 17% will say "Ouch!" and 22% will say "Damn!"; nor by a table showing that 38.2 per centum of all men accused of homicide confess when locked up with the carcasses of their victims, including 23.4 per centum who are innocent; nor by plans and specifications, by Cagliostro out of Lucrezia Borgia, for teaching poor, God-forsaken school children to write before they can read and to multiply before they can add; nor by endless disputes between half-witted pundits as to the precise difference between perception and cognition; nor by even longer feuds, between pundits even crazier, over free will, the subconscious, the endoneurium, the functions of the corpora quadrigemina, and the meaning of dreams in which one is pursued by hyenas, process-servers or grass-widows.

Nay; we do not bubble with rejoicing when such fruits of psychological deep-down-diving and much-mud-upbringing researches are laid before us, for after all they do not offer us any nourishment, there is nothing in them to engage our teeth, they fail to make life more comprehensible, and hence more bearable. What we yearn to know something about is the process whereby the ideas of everyday are engendered in the skulls of those about us, to the end that we may pursue a straighter and a safer course through the muddle that is life. Why do the great majority of Presbyterians (and for that matter, of Baptists, Episcopalians, and Swedenborgians as well) regard it as unlucky to meet a black cat and lucky to find a pin? What are the logical steps behind the theory that it is indecent to eat peas with a knife? By what process does an otherwise sane man arrive at the conclusion that he will go to hell unless he is baptized by total immersion in water? What causes men to be faithful to their wives: habit, fear, poverty, lack of imagination, lack of enterprise, stupidity, religion? What is the psychological basis of commercial morality? What is the true nature of the vague pooling of desires that Rousseau called the social contract? Why does an American regard it as scandalous to wear dress clothes at a funeral, and a Frenchman regards it as equally scandalous not to wear them? Why is it that men trust one another so readily, and women trust one another so seldom? Why are we all so greatly affected by statements that we know are not true?—e.g., in Lincoln's Gettysburg speech, the Declaration of Independence and the CIII Psalm. What is the origin of the so-called double standard of morality? Why are women forbidden to take off their hats in church? What is happiness? Intelligence? Sin? Courage? Virtue? Beauty?

All these are questions of interest and importance to all of us, for their solution would materially improve the accuracy of our outlook upon the world, and with it our mastery of our environment, but the psychologists, busily engaged in chasing their tails, leave them unanswered, and, in most cases, even unasked. The late William James, more acute than the general, saw how precious little was known about the psychological inwardness of religion, and to the illumination of this darkness he addressed himself in his book, "The Varieties of Religious Experience." But life being short and science long, he got little beyond the statement of the problem and the marshaling of the grosser evidence—and even at this business he allowed himself to be constantly interrupted by spooks, hobgoblins, seventh sons and other such characteristic pets of psychologists. In the same way one Gustav le Bon, a Frenchman, undertook a psychological study of the crowd mind—and then blew up. Add the investigations of Freud and his school chiefly into abnormal states of mind, and those of Lombroso [most prominent exponent of phrenology] and his school, chiefly quackish and for the yellow journals, and the idle romancing of such inquirers as Prof.

Dr. Thorstein Veblen, and you have exhausted the list of contributions to what may be called practical and everyday psychology. The rev. professors, I daresay, have been doing some useful plowing and planting. All of their meticulous pin-sticking and measuring and chart-making, in the course of time, will enable their successors to approach the real problems of mind with more assurance than is now possible, and perhaps help to their solution. But in the meantime the public and social utility of psychology remains very small, for it is still unable to differentiate accurately between the true and the false, or to give us any effective protection against the fallacies, superstitions, crazes and hysteria which rage in the world.

In this emergency it is not only permissible but even laudable for the amateur to sniff inquiringly through the psychological pasture, essaying modestly to uproot things that the myopia (or, perhaps more accurately, hypermetropic) professionals have overlooked. The late Friedrich Wilhelm Nietzsche did it often, and the usufructs were many curious and daring guesses, some of them probably close to accuracy, as to the genesis of this, that or the other common delusion of man—i.e., the delusion that the law of the survival of the fittest may be repealed by an act of Congress. Into the same field several very interesting expeditions have been made by Dr. Elsie Clews Parsons, a lady once celebrated by Park Row for her invention of trial marriage—an invention, by the way, in which Nietzsche aforesaid preceded her by at least a dozen years. The records of her researches are to be found in a brief series of books: *The Family, The Old-Fashioned Woman* and *Fear and Conventionality*. Apparently they have wrung relatively little esteem from the learned, for I seldom encounter a reference to them, and Dr. Parsons herself is denied the very modest reward of mention in *Who's Who in America*. Nevertheless, they are extremely instructive books, particularly *Fear and Conventionality*. I know of no other work indeed, which offers a better array of observations upon that powerful complex of assumptions, prejudices, instinctive reactions, racial emotions and unbreakable vices of mind which enters so massively into the daily thinking of all of us. The author does not concern herself, as so many psychologists fall into the habit of doing, with thinking as a purely laboratory phenomenon, a process in vacuum. What she deals with is thinking as it is done by men and women in the real world—thinking that is only half intellectual, the other half being as automatic and unintelligent as swallowing, blinking the eye or falling in love.

The power of the complex that I have mentioned is usually very much underestimated, not only by psychologists, but also by all other persons who pretend to culture. We take pride in the fact that we are thinking animals, and like to believe that our thoughts are free, but the truth is that nine-tenths of them are rigidly conditioned by the babbling that goes on around us from birth, and that the business of considering this babbling objectively, separating the true in it from the false, is an intellectual feat of such stupendous difficulty that very few men are ever able to achieve it. The amazing slanging which went on between the English professors and the German professors in the early days of the late war showed how little even cold and academic men are really moved by the bald truth and how much by hot and unintelligible likes and dislikes. The patriotic hysteria of the war simply allowed these eminent pedagogues to say of one another openly and to loud applause what they would have been ashamed to say in times of greater amenity, and what most of them would have denied stoutly that they believed. Nevertheless, it is probably a fact that before there was a sign of war the average English professor, deep down in his heart, thought that any man who ate sauerkraut, and went to the opera in a sackcoat, and intrigued for the appellation of *Geheimrat* [privy councilor], and preferred German music to English poetry, and venerated Bismarck, and called his wife "mutter," was a scoundrel. He did not say so aloud, and no doubt it would have offended him had you accused him of believing it, but he believed it all the same, and his belief in it gave a muddy, bilious color to his view of German metaphysics, German electro-chemistry, and the German chronology of Babylonian kings. And by the same token the average German professor, far down in the ghostly recesses of his hulk, held that any man who read the London *Times*, and ate salt fish at breakfast, and drank tea of an afternoon, and spoke of Oxford as university, was a *Schafskopf* [blockhead], a *Schuft* [rogue] and possibly even a *Schweinhund* [pig-dog].

Nay, not one of us is a free agent. Not one of us actually thinks for himself, or in any orderly and scientific manner. The pressure of environment, of mass ideas, of the socialized intelligence, improperly so called, is too enormous to be withstood. No American, no matter how sharp his critical sense, can ever get away from the notion that democracy is, in some subtle and mysterious way, more conducive to human progress and more pleasing to a just God than any of the systems of government which stand opposed to it. In the privacy of his study he may observe very clearly that it exalts the facile and specious man above the really competent man, and from this observation he may draw the conclusion that its abandonment would be desirable, but once he emerges from his academic seclusion and resumes the rubbing of noses with his fellow-men, he will begin to be tortured by a sneaking feeling that such ideas are heretical and unmanly, and the next time the band begins to play he will thrill with the best of them— or the worst. The actual phenomenon, in truth, was copiously on display during the war. Having myself the character among my acquaintances of one holding the democratic theory in some doubt, I was often approached by gentlemen who told me, in great confidence, that they had been seized by the same tremors. Among them were journalists employed daily in demanding that democracy be forced upon the whole world, and army officers engaged, at least theoretically, in forcing it. All these men, in reflective moments, struggled with ifs and buts. But every one of them, in his public capacity as a good citizen was then expected to think, and even to a certain inflammatory ranting for what, behind the door, he gravely questioned. . . .

It is the business of Dr. Parsons, in *Fear and Conventionality*, to prod into certain of the ideas which thus pour into every man's mind from the circumambient air, sweeping away, like some huge cataract, the feeble resistance that his own powers of ratiocination can offer. In particular, she devotes herself to an examination of those general ideas which condition the thought and action of man as a social being—those general ideas which govern his everyday attitude toward his fellow-men and his prevailing view of himself. In one direction they lay upon us the bonds of what we call etiquette, i.e., the duty of considering the habits and feelings of those around us—and in another direction they throttle us with what we call morality— i.e., the rules which protect the life and property of those around us. But as Dr. Parsons shows, the boundary between etiquette and morality is very dimly drawn, and it is often impossible to say of a given action whether it is downright immoral or merely a breach of the punctilio. Even when the moral law is plainly running, considerations of mere amenity and politeness may still make themselves felt. Thus, as Dr. Parsons points out, there is even an etiquette of adultery. "The ami de la famille [head of the household] vows not to kiss his mistress in her husband's house"—not in fear, but "as an expression of conjugal consideration," as a sign that he has not forgotten the thoughtfulness expected of a gentleman. And in this delicate field, as might be expected the differences in racial attitudes are almost diametrical. The Englishman, surprising his wife with a lover, sues the rogue for damages and has public opinion behind him, but for an American to do it would be for him to lose caste at once and forever. The plain and only duty of the American is to open upon the fellow with artillery, hitting him if south of the Potomac and missing him if it is above.

I confess to an endless interest in such puzzling niceties, and to much

curiosity as to their origins and meaning. Why do we Americans take off
our hats when we meet a flapper on the street, and yet stand covered before
a male of the highest eminence? A Continental would regard this last as
boorish to the last degree; in greeting any equal or superior, male or female,
actual or merely conventional, he lifts his head-piece. Why does it strike us
as ludicrous to see a man in dress clothes before 6 p.m.? The Continental
puts them on whenever he has a solemn visit to make, whether the hour be
six or noon. Why do we regard it as indecent to tuck the napkin between
the waistcoat buttons—or into the neck!—at meals? The Frenchman does
it without thought of crime. So does the Italian. So does the German. All
three are punctilious men—far more so, indeed, than we are. Why do we
snicker at the man who wears a wedding ring? Most Continentals would
stare askance at the husband who didn't. Why is it bad manners in Europe
and America to ask a stranger his or her age, and a friendly attention in
China? Why do we regard it as absurd to distinguish a woman by her husband's title—e.g., Mrs. Judge Jones, Mrs. Professor Smith? In Teutonic and
Scandinavian Europe the omission of the title would be looked upon as an
affront.

Such fine distinctions, so ardently supported, raise many interesting
questions, but the attempt to answer them quickly gets one bogged. Several
years ago I ventured to lift a sad voice against a custom common in America: that of married men, in speaking of their wives, employing the full
panoply of "Mrs. Brown." It was my contention—supported, I thought, by
logical considerations of the loftiest order—that a husband, in speaking of
his wife to his equals, should say "my wife"—that the more formal mode of
designation should be reserved for inferiors and for strangers of undeter-
mined position. This contention, somewhat to my surprise, was vigorously
combated by various volunteer experts. At first they rested their case upon
the mere authority of custom, forgetting that this custom was by no means
universal. But finally one of them came forward with a more analytical and
cogent defense—the defense, to wit, that "my wife" connoted proprietor-
ship and was thus offensive to a wife's *amour propre* [self-regard]. But what
of "my sister" and "my mother"? Surely it is nowhere the custom for a man,
addressing an equal, to speak of his sister as "Miss Smith." . . . The discussion, however, came to nothing. It was impossible to carry it on logically.
The essence of all such inquiries lies in the discovery that there is a force
within the liver and lights of man that is infinitely more potent than logic.
His reflections, perhaps, may take on intellectually recognizable forms, but
they seldom lead to intellectually recognizable conclusions.

Nevertheless, Dr. Parsons offers something in her book that may conceivably help to a better understanding of them, and that is the doctrine that the strange persistence of these rubber-stamp ideas, often unintelligible and sometimes plainly absurd, is due to fear, and that this fear is the product of a very real danger. The safety of human society lies in the assumption that every individual composing it, in a given situation, will act in a manner hitherto approved as seemly. That is to say, he is expected to react to his environment according to a fixed pattern, not necessarily because that pattern is the best imaginable, but simply because it is determined and understood. If he fails to do so, if he reacts in a novel manner—conducive, perhaps, to his better advantage or to what he thinks is his better advantage—then he disappoints the expectation of those around him, and forces them to meet the new situation he has created by the exercise of independent thought. Such independent thought, to a good many men, is quite impossible, and to the overwhelming majority of men, extremely painful. "To all of us," says Dr. Parsons, "to the animal, to the savage and to the civilized being, few demands are as uncomfortable. . . . disquieting or fearful, as the call to innovate. . . . Adaptations we all of us dislike or hate. We dodge or shirk them as best we may." And the man who compels us to make them against our wills we punish by withdrawing from him that understanding and friendliness which he, in turn, looks for and counts upon. In other words, we set him apart as one who is anti-social and not to be dealt with, and according as his rebellion has been small or great, we call him a boor or a criminal.

The distrust of the unknown, this fear of doing something unusual, is probably at the bottom of many ideas and institutions that are commonly credited to other motives. For example, monogamy. The orthodox explanation of monogamy is that it is a manifestation of the desire to have and to hold property—that the husband defends his solitary right to his wife, even at the cost of his own freedom, because she is the pearl among the chattels. But Dr. Parsons argues, and with a good deal of plausibility, that the real moving force, both in the husband and the wife, may be merely the force of habit, the antipathy to experiment and innovation. It is easier and safer to stick to the one wife than to risk adventures with another wife—and the immense social pressure that I have just described is all on the side of sticking. Moreover, the indulgence of a habit automatically strengthens its bonds. What we have done once or thought once, we are more apt than we were before to do and think again. Or, as the late Prof. William James put it, "the selection of a particular hole to live in, of a particular mate, . . . practically anything, in short, out of a possible multitude . . . carries with it an in-sensibility to other opportunities and occasions—and insensibility which can only be described physiologically as an inhibition of new impulses by the habit of old ones already formed. The possession of homes and wives of our own makes us strangely insensible to the charms of other people. . . . The original impulse which got us homes, wives, . . . seems to exhaust itself in its first achievements and to leave no surplus energy for reacting on new cases." Thus the benedict looks no more on women (at least for a while), and the post-honeymoon bride, as the late David Graham Phillips once told us, neglects the bedizenments which got her a man.

In view of the popular or general character of most of the taboos which put a brake upon personal liberty in thought and action—that is to say, in view of their enforcement by people in the mass, and not by definite spe-cialists in conduct—it is quite natural to find that they are of extra force in democratic societies, for it is the distinguishing mark of democratic soci-eties that they exalt the powers of the majority almost infinitely, and tend to deny the minority any rights whatever. Under a society dominated by a small caste the revolutionist in custom, despite the axiom to the con-trary, has a relatively easy time of it, for the persons whose approval he seeks for his innovation are relatively few in number, and most of them are already habituated to more or less intelligible and independent thinking. But under a democracy he is opposed by a horde so vast that it is a practi-cal impossibility for him, without complex and expensive machinery, to reach and convince all of its members, and even if he could reach them he would find most of them quite incapable of rising out of their accustomed grooves. They cannot understand innovations that are genuinely novel and they don't want to understand them; their one desire is to put them down. Even at this late day, with enlightenment raging through the republic like a pestilence, it would cost the average Southern or Middle Western Con-gressman his seat if he appeared among his constituents in spats, or wear-ing a wrist-watch. And if a Justice of the Supreme Court of the United States, however gigantic his learning and his juridic rectitude, were taken in crim[inal] con[duct] with the wife of a Senator, he would be destroyed instanter. And if, suddenly revolting against the democratic idea, he were to propose, however gingerly, its abandonment, he would be destroyed with the same dispatch.

But how, then, explain the fact that the populace is constantly ravished and set aflame by fresh brigades of moral, political and sociological revo-lutionists—that it is forever playing the eager victim to new mountebanks?

The explanation lies in the simple circumstance that these performers upon the public midriff are always careful to ladle out nothing actually new, and hence nothing incomprehensible, alarming and accursed. What they offer is always the same old panacea with an extra-gaudy label—the tried, tasted and much-loved dose, the colic cure that mother used to make. Superficially, the United States seems to suffer from an endless and astounding neophilism; actually all its thinking is done within the boundaries of a very small group of political, economic and religious ideas, most of them unsound. For example, there is the fundamental idea of democracy—the idea that all political power should remain in the hands of the populace, that its exercise by superior men is intrinsically immoral. Out of this idea spring innumerable notions and crazes that are no more, at bottom, than restatements of it in sentimental terms: rotation in office, direct elections, the initiative and referendum, the recall, the popular primary and so on. Again, there is the primary doctrine that the possession of great wealth is a crime—a doctrine half a religious heritage and half the product of mere mob envy. Out of it have come free silver, trust-busting, government ownership, muck-raking, Populism, Bleaseism, Progressivism, the milder forms of Socialism, the whole gasconade of "reform" politics. Yet again, there is the ineradicable peasant suspicion of the man who is having a better time in the world—a suspicion grounded, like the foregoing, partly upon undisguised envy and partly upon archaic and barbaric religious taboos. Out of it have come all the glittering pearls of the uplift, from Abolition to Prohibition, and from the crusade against horse-racing to the Mann Act. The whole political history of the United States is a history of these three ideas. There has never been an issue before the people that could not be translated into one or another of them. What is more, they also colored the fundamental philosophical (and particularly epistemological) doctrines of the American people, and their moral theory, and even their foreign relations. The late war, very unpopular at the start, was "sold" to them, as the advertising phrase has it, by representing it as a campaign for the salvation of democracy, half religious and half altruistic. So represented to them, they embraced it; represented as the highly obscure and complex thing it actually was, it would have been beyond their comprehension, and hence abhorrent to them.

Outside this circle of their elemental convictions they are quite incapable of rational thought. One is not surprised to hear of Bismarck, a thorough royalist, discussing democracy with calm and fairness, but it would be unimaginable for the American people, or for any other democratic

people, to discuss royalism in the same manner: it would take a cataclysm to bring them to any such violation of their mental habits. When such a cataclysm occurs, they embrace the new ideas that are its fruits with the same adamantine firmness. One year before the French Revolution, disobedience to the king was unthinkable to the average Frenchman; only a few daringly immoral men cherished the notion. But one year after the fall of the Bastille, obedience to the king was equally unthinkable. The Russian Bolsheviki, whose doings have furnished a great deal of immensely interesting material to the student of popular psychology, put the principle into plain words. Once they were in the saddle, they decreed the abolition of the old imperial censorship and announced that speech would be free henceforth—but only so long as it kept within the bounds of the Bolshevist revolution! In other words, any citizen was free to think and speak whatever he pleased—but only so long as it did not violate certain fundamental ideas. This is precisely the sort of freedom that has prevailed in the United States since the first days. It is the only sort of freedom comprehensible to the average man. It accurately reveals his constitutional inability to shake himself free from the illogical and often quite unintelligible prejudices, instincts and mental vices that condition ninety per cent of all his thinking.
. . .

But here I wander into political speculation and no doubt stand in contumacy of some statute of Congress. Dr. Parsons avoids politics in her very interesting book. She confines herself to the purely social relationship, e.g., between man and woman, parent and child, host and guest, master and servant. The facts she offers are vastly interesting, and their discovery and coordination reveal a tremendous industry, but of even greater interest are the facts that lie over the margin of her inquiry. Here is a golden opportunity for other investigators: I often wonder that the field is so little explored. Perhaps the Freudians once they get rid of their sexual obsession, will enter it and chart it. No doubt the inferiority complex described by Prof. Dr. Alfred Adler will one day provide an intelligible explanation of many of the puzzling phenomena of mob thinking. In the work of Prof. Dr. Freud himself there is, perhaps, a clew to the origin and anatomy of Puritanism, that worst of intellectual nephreitises. I live in hope that the Freudians will fall upon the business without much further delay. Why do otherwise sane men believe in spirits? What is the genesis of the American axiom that the fine arts are unmanly? What is the precise machinery of the process called falling in love? Why do people believe newspapers? . . . Let there be light!

(*The Smart Set*, September 1915)

EDUCATION

[*Anthology editors should never write anything as puerile as "this is my favorite piece," but I claim to be no literary genius and, well, "Education" is my favorite Mencken piece—and I've spent decades teaching. Education is a simple process that educational theorists, in hopes of making the profession equal to the study of molecular biology, have tried to complicate into an oft-times expensive theoretical mess.*

Teachers must work in the gap between the simplicity of the profession and the complications of the theories that are supposed to guide it. When students fail, therefore, the theorist can blame the teacher, not the theory. Never mind that no real education can take place without a student's intrinsic interest.

Mencken recognized there were only two ways to create intrinsic educational interest in young people: through rewards and punishments. After criticizing new theories in pedagogy, he writes:

"All this, I need not point out, is in sharp contrast to the old theory of teaching. By that theory mere technic was simplified and subordinated. All that it demanded of the teacher told off to teach, say, geography, was that he master the facts in the geography book and provide himself with a stout rattan. Thus equipped, he was ready for a test of his natural pedagogical genius. First he exposed the facts in the book, then he gilded the with whatever appearance of interest and importance he could conjure up, and then he tested the extent of their transference to the minds of his pupils. Those pupils who had ingested them got apples; those who had failed got fanned with the rattan. Followed the second round, and the same test again, with a second noting of the results. And then the third, and fourth, and the fifth, and so on until the last and least pupil had been stuffed to his subnormal and perhaps moronic brim."

Mencken, like Shakespeare, recommends the rote learning systems that once dominated schools. Such an approach worked and would likely work again if not for the senseless laws that govern the educational system.]

1

Next to the clerk in holy orders, the fellow with the worst job in the world is the schoolmaster. Both are underpaid, both fall steadily in authority and dignity, and both wear out their hearts trying to perform the impossible. How much the world asks of them, and how little they can actually deliver! The clergyman's business is to save the human race from hell: if he saves one-eighth of one per cent, even within the limits of his narrow flock, he does magnificently. The schoolmaster's is to spread the enlightenment, to make the great masses of the plain people intelligent—and intelligence is precisely the thing that the great masses of people are congenitally and eternally incapable of.

Is it any wonder that the poor birchman, facing this labor that would have staggered Sisyphus Aeolusohn, seeks refuge from its essential impossibility in a Chinese maze of empty technic? The ghost of Pestalozzi, once bearing a torch and beckoning toward the heights, now leads down stairways into black and forbidding dungeons. Especially in America, where all that is bombastic and mystical is most esteemed, the art of pedagogics becomes a sort of puerile magic, a thing of preposterous secrets, a grotesque compound of false promises and illogical conclusions. Every year sees a craze for some new solution of the teaching enigma, at once simple and infallible—manual training, playground work, song and doggerel lessons, the Montessori method, the Gary system—an endless series of flamboyant arcanums. The worst extravagances of *privat dozent* [outside lecturer] experimental psychology are gravely seized upon; the uplift pours in its ineffable principles and discoveries; mathematical formulae are worked out for every emergency; there is no sure-cure so idiotic that some superintendent of schools will not swallow it.

A couple of days spent examining the literature of the New Thought in pedagogy are enough to make the judicious weep. Its aim seems to be to reduce the whole teaching process to a sort of automatic reaction, to discover some master formula that will not only take the place of competence and resourcefulness in the teacher but that will also create an artificial receptivity in the child. The merciless application of this formula (which changes every four days) now seems to be the chief end and aim of pedagogy. Teaching becomes a thing to itself, separable from and superior to the thing taught. Its mastery is a special business, a transcendental art and mystery, to be acquired in the laboratory. A teacher well grounded in this mystery, and hence privy to every detail of the new technic (which changes, of course, with the formula), can teach anything to any child, just as a sound dentist can pull any tooth out of any jaw.

All this, I need not point out, is in sharp contrast to the old theory of teaching. By that theory mere technic was simplified and subordinated. All that is demanded of the teacher told off to teach, say, geography, was that he master the facts in the geography book and provide himself with a stout rattan. Thus equipped, he was ready for a test of his natural pedagogical genius. First he exposed the facts in the book, then he gilded them with whatever appearance of interest and importance he could conjure up, and then he tested the extent of their transference to the minds of his pupils. Those pupils who had ingested them got apples; those who had failed got fanned with the rattan. Followed the second round, and the same test again, with a second noting of results. And then the third and fourth, and the fifth, and so on until the last and least pupil had been stuffed to his subnormal and perhaps moronic brim.

I was myself grounded in the underlying delusions of what is called knowledge by this austere process, and despite the eloquence of those who support newer ideas, I lean heavily in favor of it, and regret to hear that it is no more. It was crude, it was rough, and it was often not a little cruel, but it at least had two capital advantages over all the systems that have succeeded it. In the first place, its machinery was simple; even the stupidest child could understand it; it hooked up cause and effect with utmost clarity. And in the second place, it tested the teacher as and how he ought to be tested— that is, for his actual capacity to teach, not for his mere technical virtuosity. There was, in fact, no technic for him to master, and hence none for him to hide behind. He could not conceal a hopeless inability to impart knowledge beneath a correct professional method. That ability to impart knowledge, it seems to me, has very little to do with technical method. It may operate at full function without any technical method at all, and contrariwise, the most elaborate of technical methods, whether out of Switzerland, Italy or Gary, Ind., cannot make it operate when it is not actually present. And what does it consist of? It consists, first, of a natural talent for dealing with children, for getting into their minds, for putting things in a way that they can comprehend. And it consists, secondly, of a deep belief in the interest and importance of the thing taught, a concern about it amounting to a sort of passion. A man who knows a subject thoroughly, a man so soaked in it that he eats it, sleeps it and dreams it—this man can always teach it with success, no matter how little he knows of technical pedagogy. This is because there is enthusiasm in him, and because enthusiasm is almost as contagious as fear or the barber's itch. An enthusiast is willing to go to any trouble to impart the glad news bubbling within him. He thinks that it is important and valuable for to know; given the slightest glow of interest in a pupil to start with, he will fan that glow to a flame. No hollow formalism cripples him and slows him down. He drags his best pupils along as fast as they can go, and he is so full of the thing that he never tires of expounding its elements to the dullest.

This passion, so unordered and yet so potent, explains the capacity for teaching that one frequently observes in scientific men of high attainments in their specialties—for example, Huxley, Ostwald, Karl Ludwig, Virchow, Billroth, Josett, William G. Summer, Halsted and Osler—men who knew nothing whatever about the so-called science of pedagogy, and would have derided its alleged principles if they had heard them stated. It explains, too, the failure of the general run of high-school and college teachers—men who are undoubtedly competent, by the professional standards of pedagogy, but who nevertheless contrive only to make intolerable bores of the things they presume to teach. No intelligent student ever learns much from the average drover of undergraduates; what he actually carries away has come out of his textbooks, or is the fruit of his own reading and inquiry. But when he passes to the graduate school, and comes among men who really understand the subjects they teach, and, what is more, who really love them, his store of knowledge increases rapidly, and in a very short while, if he has any intelligence at all, he learns to think in terms of the thing he is studying.

So far, so good. But an objection still remains, which may be couched in the following terms: that in the average college or high school, and especially in the elementary school, most of the subjects taught are so bald and uninspiring that it is difficult to imagine them arousing the passion I have been describing—in brief, that only an ass could be enthusiastic about them. In witness, think of the four elementals: reading, penmanship, arithmetic and spelling. This objection, at first blush, seems salient and dismaying, but only a brief inspection is needed to show that it is really of very small validity. It is made up of a false assumption and a false inference. The false inference is that there is any sound reason for prohibiting teaching by asses, if only the asses know how to do it, and do it well. The false assumption is that there are no asses in our schools and colleges to-day. The facts stand in almost complete antithesis to these notions. The truth is that the average schoolmaster, on all the lower levels, is and always must be essentially an ass, for how can one imagine an intelligent man engaging in so puerile an avocation? And the truth is that it is precisely his inherent asininity, and not his technical equipment as a pedagogue, that is responsible for whatever modest success he now shows.

I here attempt no heavy jocosity, but mean exactly what I say. Consider, for example, penmanship. A decent handwriting, it must be obvious, is useful to all men, and particularly to the lower orders of men. It is one of the few things capable of acquirement in school that actually helps them to make a living. Well, how is it taught to-day? It is taught, in the main, by schoolmarms so enmeshed in a complex and unintelligible technic that, even supposing them able to write clearly themselves, they find it quite impossible to teach their pupils. Every few years sees a radical overhauling of the whole business. First the vertical hand is to make it easy; then certain curves are the favorite magic; then there is a return to slants and shadings. No department of pedagogy sees a more hideous cavorting of quacks. In none is the natural talent and enthusiasm of the teacher more depressingly crippled. And the result? The result is that our American school children write abominably—that a clerk or stenographer with a simple, legible hand becomes almost as scarce as one with Greek.

Go back, now, to the old days. Penmanship was taught, not mechanically and ineffectively, by unsound and shifting formulae, but by passionate penmen with curly patent-leather hair and far-away eyes—in brief, by the unforgettable professors of our youth, with their flourishes, their heavy down-strokes and their lovely birds-with-letters-in-their-bills. You remember them, of course. Asses all! Pathetic idiots! But they loved penmanship, they believed in the glory and beauty of penmanship, they were fanatics, devotees, almost martyrs of penmanship—and so they got some touch of that passion into their pupils. Not enough, perhaps, to make more flourishers and bird-blazoners, but enough to make sound penmen. Look at your old writing book; observe the excellent legibility, the clear strokes of your "Time is money." Then look at your child's.

Such idiots, despite the rise of "scientific" pedagogy, have not died out in the world. I believe that our schools are full of them, both in pantaloons and in skirts. There are fanatics who love and venerate spelling as a tom-cat loves and venerates catnip. There are grammar maniacs; schoolmarms who would rather parse than eat; specialists in an objective case that doesn't exist in English; strange beings, otherwise sane and even intelligent and comely, who suffer under a split infinitive as you or I would suffer under gastroenteritis. There are geography cranks, able to bound Mesopotamia and Be-luchistan. There are zealots for long division, experts in the multiplication table, lunatic worshipers of the binomial theorem. But the system has them in its grip. It combats their natural enthusiasm diligently and mercilessly. It tries to convert them into mere technicians, clumsy machines. It orders them to teach, not by the process of emotional osmosis which worked in the days gone by, but by formulae that are as baffling to the pupil as they are paralyzing to the teacher. Imagine what would happen to one of them who stepped to the blackboard, seized a piece of chalk, and engrossed a bird that held the class spell-bound—a bird with a thousand flowing feathers, wings bursting with parabolas and epicycloids, and long ribbons stream-ing from its bill! Imagine the fate of one who began "Honesty is the best policy" with an H as florid and—to a child—as beautiful as the initial of a mediaeval manuscript! Such a teacher would be cashiered and handed over to the secular arm; the very enchantment of the assembled infantry would be held as damning proof against him. And yet it is just such teachers that we should try to discover and develop. Pedagogy needs their enthusiasm, their naive belief in their own grotesque talents, their capacity for commu-nicating their childish passion to the childish.

But this would mean exposing the children of the Republic to contact with monomaniacs, half-wits, defectives? Well, what of it? The vast ma-jority of them are already exposed to contact with half-wits in their own homes; they are taught the word of God by half-wits on Sundays; they will grow up into Knights of Pythias, Odd Fellows, Red Men and other such half-wits in the days to come. Moreover, as I have hinted, they are already face to face with half-wits in the actual schools, at least in three cases out of four. The problem before us is not to dispose of this fact, but to utilize it. We cannot hope to fill the schools with persons of high intelligence, for persons of high intelligence simply refuse to spend their lives teaching such banal things as spelling and arithmetic. Among the teachers male we may safely assume that 95 per cent are of low mentality, else they would depart for more appetizing pastures. Even among the teachers female the best are inevitably weeded out by marriage, and only the worst (with a few romantic exceptions) survive. The task before us, as I say, is not to make a vain denial of this cerebral inferiority of the pedagogue, nor to try to com-bat and disguise it by concocting a mass of technical hocus-pocus, but to search out and put to use the value lying concealed in it. For even stupidity, it must be plain, has its uses in the world, and some of them are uses that intelligence cannot meet. One would not tell off a Galileo or a Pasteur to drive an ash-cart or an Ignatius Loyola to be a stock-broker, or a Brahms to lead the orchestra in a Broadway cabaret. By the same token, one would not ask a Herbert Spencer or a Duns Scotus to instruct sucklings. Such men would not only be wasted at the job; they would also be incompetent. The business of dealing with children, in fact, requires a certain childishness of mind. The best teacher, until one comes to adult pupils, is not the one who knows most, but the one who is most capable of reducing knowledge to that simple compound of the obvious and the wonderful which slips easiest into the infantile comprehension. A man of high intelligence, perhaps, may accomplish the thing by a conscious intellectual feat. But it is vastly easier to the man (or woman) whose habits of mind are naturally on the plane of a child's. The best teacher of children, in brief, is one who is essentially childlike.

I go so far with this notion that I view the movement to introduce female bachelors of arts into the primary schools with the utmost alarm. A knowledge of Bergsonism, the Greek aorist, sex hygiene and the dramas of Percy MacKaye is not only no help to the teaching of spelling, it is a positive handicap to the teaching of spelling, for it corrupts and blows up that naive belief in the glory and portentousness of spelling which is at the bottom of all successful teaching of it. If I had my way, indeed, I should expose all candidates for berths in the infant grades to the Binet-Simon test, and reject all those who revealed the mentality of more than fifteen years. Plenty would still pass. Moreover, they would be secure against contamination by the new technic of pedagogy. Its vast wave of pseudo-psychology would curl and break against the hard barrier of their innocent and passionate intellects—as it probably does, in fact, even now. They would know nothing of cognition, perception, the sub-conscious and all the other half-fabulous fowl of the pedagogic aviary. But they would see in reading, writing and arithmetic the gaudy charms of profound and esoteric knowledge, and they would teach these ancient branches, now so abominably in decay, with passionate gusto, and irresistible effectiveness, and a gigantic success.

2

Two great follies corrupt the present pedagogy once it gets beyond the elementals. One is the folly of overestimating the receptivity of the pupil; the other is the folly of overestimating the possible efficiency of the teacher. Both rest upon that tendency to put too high a value upon mere schooling which characterizes democratic and upstart societies—a tendency born of the theory that a young man who has been "educated," who has "gone through college," is in some subtle way more capable of making money than one who hasn't. The nature of the schooling on tap in colleges is but defectively grasped by the adherents of the theory. They view it, I believe, as a sort of extension of the schooling offered in elementary schools—that is, as an indefinite multiplication of training in such obviously valuable and necessary arts as reading, writing and arithmetic. It is, of course, nothing of the sort. If the pupil, as he climbs the educational ladder, is fortunate enough to come into contact with a few Huxleys or Ludwigs, he may acquire a great deal of extremely sound knowledge, and even learn how to think for himself. But in the great majority of cases he is debarred by two things: the limitations of his congenital capacity and the limitations of the teachers he actually encounters. The latter is usually even more brilliantly patent than the former. Very few professional teachers, it seems to me, really know anything worth knowing, even about the subjects they essay to teach. If you doubt it, simply examine their contributions to existing knowledge. Several years ago, while engaged upon my book, "The American Language," I had a good chance to test the matter in one typical department, that of philology. I found a truly appalling condition of affairs. I found that in the whole United States there were not two dozen teachers of English philology—in which class I also include the innumerable teachers of plain grammar—who had ever written ten lines upon the subject worth reading. It was not that they were indolent or illiterate: in truth, they turned out to be enormously diligent. But as I plowed through pyramid after pyramid of their doctrines and speculations, day after day and week after week, I discovered little save a vast laboring of the obvious, with now and then a bold flight into the nonsensical. A few genuinely original philologians revealed themselves—pedagogues capable of observing accurately and reasoning clearly. The rest simply wasted time and paper. Whole sections of the field were unexplored, and some of them appeared to be even unsuspected. The entire life-work of many an industrious professor, boiled down, scarcely made a footnote in my book, itself a very modest work.

This tendency to treat the superior pedagogue too seriously—to view him as, *ipso facto* [by the very fact], a learned man, and one thus capable of conveying learning to others—is supported by the circumstance that he so views himself, and is, in fact, very pretentious and even bombastic. Nearly all discussions of the educational problem, at least in the United States, are carried on by schoolmasters or ex-schoolmasters—for example, college presidents, deans, and other such magnificoes—and so they assume it to be axiomatic that such fellows are genuine bearers of the enlightenment, and hence capable of the transmitting it to others. This is true sometimes, as I have said, but certainly not usually. The average high-school or college pedagogue is not one who has been selected because of his uncommon knowledge; he is simply one who has been stuffed with formal ideas and taught to do a few conventional intellectual tricks. Contact with him, far from being inspiring to any youth of alert mentality, is really quite depressing; his point of view is commonplace and timorous; his best thought is no better than that of any other fourth-rate professional man, say a dentist or an advertisement writer. Thus it is idle to talk of him as if he were a Socrates, an Aristotle, or even a Leschetizky. He is actually much more nearly related to a barber or a lieutenant of marines. A worthy man, industrious and respectable—but don't expect too much of him. To ask him to struggle out of his puddle of safe platitudes and plunge into the whirlpool of surmise and speculation that carries on the fragile shallop of human progress—to do this is as absurd as to ask a neighborhood doctor to undertake major surgery.

In the United States his low intellectual status is kept low, not only by the meager rewards of his trade in a country where money is greatly sought and esteemed, but also by the democratic theory of education—that is, by the theory that mere education can convert a peasant into an intellectual aristocrat, with all of the peculiar superiorities of an aristocrat—in brief, that it is possible to make purses out of sow's ears. The intellectual collapse of the American *Gelehrten* [savants] during the late war—a collapse so nearly unanimous that those who did not share it attained to a sort of immortality overnight—was perhaps largely due to this error. Who were these bawling professors so pathetically poltroonish and idiotic? In an enormous number of cases they were simply peasants in frock coats—oafs from the farms and villages of Iowa, Kansas, Vermont, Alabama, the Dakotas and other such backward states, horribly stuffed with standardized learning in some freshwater university, and then set to teaching. To look for a civilized attitude of mind in such Strassburg geese is to look for honor in a valet; to confuse them with scholars is to confuse the Knights of Pythias with the Knights Hospitaller. In brief, the trouble with them was that they had no sound tradition behind them, that they had not learned to think clearly and decently, that they were not gentlemen. The youth with a better background behind him, passing through an American university, seldom acquires any yearning to linger as a teacher. The air is too thick for him; the rewards are too trivial; the intrigues are too old-maidish and degrading. Thus the chairs, even in the larger universities, tend to be filled more and more by yokels who have got themselves what is called an education only by dint of herculean effort. Exhausted by the cruel process, they are old men at 26 or 28, and so, hugging their Ph.D.'s, they sink into convenient instructorships, and end at 60 as *ordentliche Professoren* [rule-bound professors]. The social status of the American pedagogue helps along the process. Unlike in Europe, where he has a secure and honorable position, he ranks, in the United States, somewhere between a Methodist preacher and a prosperous brickyard owner—certainly clearly below the latter. Thus the youth of civilized upbringings feels that it would be stooping a bit to take up the rattan. But the plow-hand obviously makes a step upward, and is hence eager for the black gown. Thereby a vicious circle is formed. The plow-hand, by entering the ancient guild, drags it down still further, and so makes it increasingly difficult to snare apprentices from superior castes.

A glance at *Who's Who in America* offers a good deal of support for all this theorizing. There was a time when the typical American professor came from a small area in New England—for generations the seat of a high literacy, and even of a certain austere civilization. But to-day he comes from the region of silos, revivals, and saleratus. Behind him there is absolutely no tradition of aristocratic aloofness and urbanity, or even of mere civilized decency. He is a hind by birth, and he carries the smell of the dunghill into the academic grove—and not only the smell, but also some of the dung itself. What one looks for in such men is dullness, superficiality, a great credulity, an incapacity for learning anything save a few fly-blown rudiments, a passionate yielding to all popular crazes, a malignant distrust of genuine superiority, a huge megalomania. These are precisely the things that one finds in the typical American pedagogue of the new dispensation. He is not only a numskull; he is also a boor. In the university president he reaches his heights. Here we have a so-called learned man who spends his time making speeches before chautauquas, chambers of commerce, and Rotary Clubs, and flattering trustees who run both universities and street-railways, and cadging money from such men as Rockefeller and Carnegie.

3

The same educational fallacy which fills the groves of learning with such dunces causes a huge waste of energy and money on lower levels—those, to wit, of the secondary schools. The theory behind the lavish multiplication of such schools is that they outfit the children of the mob with the materials of reasoning, and inculcate in them a habit of indulging in it. I have never been able to discover any evidence in support of that theory. The common people of America—at least the white portion of them—are rather above the world's average in literacy, but there is no sign that they have acquired thereby any capacity for weighing facts or comparing ideas. The school statistics show that the average member of the American Legion can read and write after a fashion, and is able to multiply eight by seven after four trials, but they tell us nothing about his actual intelligence. The returns of the Army itself, indeed, indicate that he is stupid almost beyond belief—that there is at least an even chance that he is a moron. Is such a fellow appreciably superior to the villein of the Middle Ages? Sometimes I am tempted to doubt it. I suspect, for example, that the belief in witchcraft is still almost as widespread among the plain people of the United States, at least outside the large cities, as it was in Europe in the year 1500. In my own state of Maryland all of the negroes and mulattoes believe absolutely in witches, and so do most of the whites. The belief in ghosts penetrates to quite high levels. I know very few native-born Americans, indeed, who reject it without reservation. One constantly comes upon grave defenses of spiritism in some form or other by men theoretically of learning; in the two houses of Congress it would be difficult to muster fifty men willing to denounce the thing publicly. It would not only be politically dangerous for them to do so; it would also go against their consciences.

What is always forgotten is that the capacity for knowledge of the great masses of human blanks is very low—that, no matter how adroitly pedagogy tackles them with its technical sorceries, it remains a practical impossibility to teach them anything beyond reading and writing, and the most elementary arithmetic. Worse, it is impossible to make any appreciable improvement in their congenitally ignoble cases, and so they devote even the paltry learning that they acquire to degrading uses. If the average American reads only the newspapers, as is frequently alleged, it would be bad enough, but the truth is that he reads only the most imbecile parts of the newspapers. Nine-tenths of the matter in a daily paper of the better sort is almost as unintelligible to him as the theory of least squares. The words lie outside of his vocabulary; the ideas are beyond the farthest leap of his intellect. It is, indeed, a sober fact that even an editorial in the New York *Times* is probably incomprehensible to all Americans save a small minority—and not, remember, on the ground that it is too subtle. The same sort of mind that regards Rubinstein's Melody in F as too "classical" to be agreeable is also stumped by the most transparent English.

Like most other professional writers I get a good many letters from my customers. Complaints, naturally, are more numerous than compliments; it is only indignation that can induce the average man to brave the ardors of pen and ink. Well, the complaint that I hear most often is that my English is unintelligible—that it is too full of "hard" words. I can imagine nothing more astounding. My English is actually almost as bald and simple as the English of a college yell. My sentences are short and plainly constructed: I resolutely cultivate the most direct manner of statement; my vocabulary is deliberately composed of the words of everyday. Nevertheless, a great many of my readers in my own country find reading me an uncomfortably severe burden upon their linguistic and intellectual resources. These readers are certainly not below the American average in intelligence; on the contrary, they must be a good deal above the average, for they have at least got to the point where they are willing to put out of the safe harbor of the obvious and respectable, and to brave the seas where more or less novel ideas rage and roar. Think of what the ordinary newspaper reader would make of my compositions! There is, in fact, no need to think; I have tried them on him. His customary response, when, by mountebankish devices I forced him to read—or, at all events, to try to read—, was to demand resolutely that the guilty newspaper cease printing me, and to threaten to bring the matter to the attention of the *Polizei*. I do not exaggerate in the slightest; I tell the literal truth.

It is such idiots that the little red schoolhouse operates upon, in the hope of unearthing an occasional first-rate man. Is that hope ever fulfilled? Despite much testimony to the effect that it is, I am convinced that it really isn't. First-rate men are never begotten by Knights of Pythias; the notion that they sometimes are is due to an optical delusion. When they appear in obscure and ignoble circles it is no more than a proof that only an extremely wise sire knows his own son. Adultery, in brief, is one of nature's devices for keeping the lowest orders of men from sinking to the level of downright simians: sometimes for a few brief years in youth, their wives and daughters are comely—and now and then the baron drinks more than he ought to. But it is foolish to argue that the gigantic machine of popular education is needed to rescue such hybrids from their environment. The truth is that all the education rammed into the average pupil in the average American school could be acquired by the larva of any reasonably intelligent man in no more than six weeks of ordinary application, and that where schools are unknown it actually is so acquired. A bright child, in fact, can learn to read and write without any save the most casual aid a great deal faster than it can learn to read and write in a class-room, where the difficulties of the stupid retard it enormously and it is further burdened by the crazy formulae invented by pedagogues. And once it can read and write, it is just as well equipped to acquire further knowledge as nine-tenths of the teachers it will subsequently encounter in school or college.

4

I know a great many men of great learning—that is, men born with an extraordinary eagerness and capacity to acquire knowledge. One and all, they tell me that they can't recall learning anything of any value in school. All that schoolmasters managed to accomplish with them was to test and determine the amount of knowledge that they had already acquired independently—and not infrequently the determination was made clumsily and inaccurately. In my own nonage I had a great desire to acquire knowledge in certain limited directions, to wit, those of the physical sciences. Before I was ever permitted, by the regulations of the secondary seminary I was penned in, to open a chemistry book I had learned a great deal of chemistry by the simple process of reading the texts and then going through the processes described. When, at last, I was introduced to chemistry officially, I found the teach of it appalling. The one aim of that teaching, in fact, seemed to be to first purge me of what I already knew and then refill me with the same stuff in a formal, doltish, unintelligible form. My experience with physics was even worse. I knew nothing about it when I undertook its study in class, for that was before the days when physics swallowed chemistry. Well, it was taught so abominably that it immediately became incomprehensible to me, and hence extremely distasteful, and to this day I know nothing about it. Worse, it remains unpleasant to me, and so I am shut off from the interesting and useful knowledge that I might otherwise acquire by reading.

One extraordinary teacher I remember who taught me something: a teacher of mathematics. I had a dislike for the science, and knew little about it. Finally, my neglect of it brought me to bay: in transferring from one school to another I found that I was hopelessly short in algebra. What was needed, of course, was not an actual knowledge of algebra, but simply the superficial smattering needed to pass an examination. The teacher that

I mention, observing my distress, generously offered to fill me with that smattering after school hours. He got the whole year's course into me in exactly six lessons of half an hour each. And how? More accurately, why? Simply because he was an algebra fanatic—because he believed that algebra was not only a science of the utmost importance, but also one of the greatest fascination. He was the penmanship professor of years ago, lifted to a higher level. A likable and plausible man, he convinced me in twenty minutes that ignorance of algebra was as calamitous, socially and intellectually, as ignorance of table manners—that acquiring its elements was as necessary as washing behind the ears. So I fell upon the book and gulped it voraciously, greatly to the astonishment of my father, whose earlier mathematical teaching had failed to set me off because it was too pressing—because it bombarded me, not when I was penned in a school and so inclined to make the best of it, but when I had got through a day's schooling, and felt inclined to play. To this day I comprehend the binomial theorem, a very rare accomplishment in an author. For many years, indeed, I was probably the only American newspaper editor who knew what it was.

Two other teachers of that school I remember pleasantly as fellows whose pedagogy profitted me—both, it happens, were drunken and disreputable men. One taught me to chew tobacco, an art that has done more to give me an evil name, perhaps, than my Socinianism. The other introduced me to Shakespeare, Congreve, Wycherly, Marlowe and Sheridan, and so filled me with that taste for coarseness which now offends so many of my customers, lay and clerical. Neither ever came to a dignified position in academic circles. One abandoned pedagogy for the law, became involved in causes of a dubious nature, and finally disappeared into the shades which engulf third-rate attorneys. The other went upon a fearful drunk one Christmastide, got himself shanghaied on the water-front and is supposed to have fallen overboard from a British tramp, bound east for Cardiff. At all events, he has never been heard from since. Two evil fellows, and yet I hold their memories in affection, and believe that they were the best teachers I ever had. For in both there was something a good deal more valuable than mere pedagogical skill and diligence, and even more valuable than correct demeanor, and that was a passionate love of sound literature. This love, given reasonably receptive soil, they knew how to communicate, as a man can nearly always communicate whatever moves him profoundly. Neither ever made the slightest effort to "teach" literature, as the business is carried on by the usual idiot schoolmaster. Both had a vast contempt for the text-books that were official in their school, and used to entertain the

boys by pointing out the nonsense in them. Both were full of derisory objections to the principal heroes of such books in those days: Scott, Irving, Pope, Jane Austen, Dickens, Trollope, Tennyson. But both, discoursing in their disorderly way upon heroes of their own, were magnificently eloquent and persuasive. The boy who could listen to one of them intoning Whitman and stand unmoved was a dull fellow indeed. The boy who could resist the other's enthusiasm for the old essayists was intellectually deaf, dumb and blind.

I often wonder if their expoundings of their passions and prejudices would have been half so charming if they had been wholly respectable men, like their colleagues of the school faculty. It is not likely. A healthy boy is in constant revolt against the sort of men who surround him at school. Their puerile pedantries, their Christian Endeavor respectability, their sedentary pallor, their curious preference for the dull and uninteresting, their general air of so many Y.M.C.A. secretaries—these things infallibly repel the youth who is above milksoppery. In every boys' school the favorite teacher is one who occasionally swears like a cavalryman, or is reputed to keep a jug in his room, or is known to receive a scented note every morning. Boys are good judges of men, as girls are good judges of women. It is not by accident that most of them, at some time or other, long to be cowboys or ice-wagon drivers, and that none of them, not obviously diseased in mind, ever longs to be a Sunday-school superintendent. Put that judgment to a simple test. What would become of a nation in which all of the men were, at heart, Sunday-school superintendents—or Y.M.C.A. secretaries, or pedagogues? Imagine it in conflict with a nation of cowboys and ice-wagon drivers. Which would be the stronger, and which would be the more intelligent, resourceful, enterprising and courageous?

(*Prejudices, Third Series*)

TYPES OF MEN

[*This essay reads like a sketch for a longer piece, or the kind of thing that might have been written in a notebook and then laid on the bedside dresser. The funniest section, on The Believer, should have been enough to put an end to public pronunciations of faith. But it didn't. No matter how many die in mass shootings, there are always thoughts, prayers, church services, and public thanks to the god (who controls all things) responsible for the shootings.*

The fact that Mencken chose to define "Skeptic" with the analogy of a wife who doesn't quite trust her husband speaks to his general view of human nature, particularly when it comes to the below-the-belt nature of men. Wives who trust their husbands too much have a lot in common with those who, from the pew, profess total devotion to a god who answer their prayers at the rate of random chance.]

---

1. The Romantic

There is a variety of man whose eye inevitably exaggerates, whose ear hears more than the band plays, whose imagination inevitably doubles and triples the news brought in by his five senses. He is the enthusiast, the believer, the romantic. He is the sort of fellow who, if he were a bacteriologist, would report the streptococcus pyogenes to be as large as a St. Bernard dog, as intelligent as Socrates, as beautiful as Beauvais Cathedral and as respectable as a Yale professor.

2. The Skeptic

No man ever quite believes in any other man. One may believe in an idea absolutely, but not in a man. In the highest confidence there is always a flavor of doubt—a feeling, half instinctive and half logical, that, after all, the scoundrel may have something up his sleeve. This doubt, it must be obvious, is always more than justified, for no man is worthy of unlimited reliance—his treason, at best only waits for sufficient temptation. The trouble with the world is not that men are too suspicious in this direction, but that they tend to be too confiding—that they still trust themselves too far to other men, even after bitter experience. Women, I believe, are measurably less sentimental, in this as in other things. No married woman ever trusts her husband absolutely, nor does she ever act as if she did trust him. Her utmost confidence is as wary as an American pick-pocket's confidence that the policeman on the beat will stay bought.

3. The Believer

Faith may be defined briefly as an illogical belief in the occurrence of the improbable. Or, psychoanalytically as a wish neurose. There is thus a flavor of the pathological in it; it goes beyond the normal intellectual process and passes into the murky domain of transcendental metaphysics. A man full of faith is simply one who has lost (or never had) the capacity for clear and realistic thought. He is not a mere ass: he is actually ill. Worse, he is incurable, for disappointment, being essentially an objective phenomenon, cannot permanently affect his subjective infirmity. His faith takes on the virulence of a chronic infection. What he usually says, in substance, is this: "Let us trust in God, who has always fooled us in the past."

4. The Worker

All democratic theories, whether Socialistic or bourgeois, necessarily take in some concept of the dignity of labor. If the have-not were deprived this delusion that his sufferings in the sweat-shop are somehow laudable and agreeable to God, there would be little left in his ego save a belly-ache. Nevertheless, a delusion is a delusion, and this is one of the worst. It arises out of confusing the pride of workmanship of the artist with the dogged, painful docility of the machine. The difference is important and enormous. If he got no reward whatever, the artist would go on working just the same; his actual reward, in fact, is often so little that he almost starves. But suppose a garment-worker got nothing for his labor: would he go on working just the same? Can one imagine him submitting voluntarily to hardship and sore want that he might express his soul in 200 more pairs of pantaloons?

5. The Physician

Hygiene is the corruption of medicine by morality. It is impossible to find a hygienist who does not debase his theory of the healthful with a theory of the virtuous. The whole hygienic art, indeed, resolves itself into an ethical exhortation, and, in the sub-department of sex, into a puerile and belated advocacy of asceticism. This brings it, at the end, into diametrical conflict with medicine proper. The aim of medicine is surely not to make men virtuous; it is to safeguard and rescue them from the consequences of their vices. The true physician does not preach repentance; he offers absolution.

6. The Scientist

The value the world sets upon motives is often grossly unjust and inaccurate. Consider, for example, two of them: mere insatiable curiosity and the desire to do good. The latter is put high above the former, and yet it is the former that moves some of the greatest men the human race has yet produced: the scientific investigators. What animates a great pathologist? Is it the desire to cure disease, to save life? Surely not, save perhaps as an after thought. He is too intelligent, deep down in the soul, to see nothing praiseworthy in such a desire. He knows by life-long observation that his discoveries will do quite as much harm as good, that a thousand scoundrels will profit to every honest man, that the folks who most deserve to be saved will probably be the last to be saved. No man of self-respect could devote himself to pathology on such terms. What actually moves him is his unquenchable curiosity—the boundless, almost pathological thirst to penetrate the unknown, to uncover the secret, to find out what has not been found out before. His prototype is not the liberator releasing slaves, the good Samaritan lifting up the fallen, but the dog sniffing tremendously at an infinite series of rat-holes. And yet he is one of the greatest and noblest of men. And yet he stands in the very front rank of the race.

7. The Business Man

It is, after all, a sound instinct which puts business below the professions, and burdens the business man with a social inferiority that he can never quite shake off, even in America. The business man, in fact, acquiesces in this assumption of his inferiority, even when he protests against it. He is the only man who is forever apologizing for his occupation. He is the only one who always seeks to make it appear, when he attains the object of his labors, i.e., the making of a great deal of money, that it was not the object of his labors.

8. The King

Perhaps the most valuable asset that any man can have in this world is a naturally superior air, a talent for sniffishness and reserve. The generality of men are always greatly impressed by it and accept it freely as a proof of genuine merit. One need but disdain them to gain their respect. Their congenital stupidity and timorousness make them turn to any leader who offers, and the sign of leadership that they recognize most readily is that which shows itself in external manner. This is the true explanation of the survival of monarchism, which invariably lives through its perennial deaths. It is the popular theory, at least in America, that monarchism is a curse fastened upon the common people from above—that the monarch saddles it upon them without their consent and against their will. The theory is without support in the facts. Kings are created not by kings, but by the people. They visualize one of the ineradicable needs of all third-rate men, which means of nine men out of ten, and that is the need of something to venerate, to bow down to, to follow and obey.

The king business begins to grow precarious, not when kings reach out for greater powers, but when they begin to resign and renounce their powers. The czars of Russia were quite secure upon the throne so long as they ran Russia like a reformatory, but the moment they began to yield to liberal ideas, i.e., by emancipating the serfs and setting up constitutionalism, their doom was sounded. The people saw this yielding as a sign of weakness; they began to suspect that the czars, after all, were not actually superior to other men. And so they turned to other and antagonistic leaders, all as cock-sure as the czars had once been, and in the course of time they were stimulated to rebellion. These leaders, or, at all events, the two or three most resolute and daring of them, then undertook to run the country in the precise way that it had been run in the palmy days of the monarchy. That is to say, they seized and exerted irresistible power and laid claim to infallible wisdom. History will date their downfall from the day they began to ease their pretensions. Once they confessed, even by implication, that they were merely human, the common people began to turn against them.

9. The Average Man

It is often urged against the so-called scientific Socialists, with their materialistic conception of history, that they overlook certain spiritual qualities that are independent of wage scales and metabolism. These qualities, it is argued, color the aspirations and activities of civilized man quite as much as they are colored by his material condition, and so make it impossible to consider him simply as an economic machine. As examples, the anti-Marxians cite patriotism, pity, the aesthetic sense and the yearning to know God. Unluckily, the examples are ill-chosen. Millions of men are quite devoid of patriotism, pity, and the aesthetic sense, and have no very active desire to know God. Why don't the anti-Marxians cite a spiritual quality that is genuinely universal? There is one readily to hand. I allude to cowardice. It is, in one form or other, visible in every human being; it almost serves to mark off the human race from all the other higher animals. Cowardice, I believe, is at the bottom of the whole caste system, the foundation of every organized society, including the most democratic. In order to escape going to war himself, the peasant was willing to give the warrior certain privileges—and out of those privileges has grown the whole structure of civilization. Go back still further. Property arose out of the fact that a few relatively courageous men were able to accumulate more possessions than whole hordes of cowardly men, and, what is more, to retain them after accumulating them.

10. The Truth-Seeker

The man who boasts that he habitually tells the truth is simply a man who has no respect for it. It is not a thing to be thrown about loosely, like small change; it is something to be cherished and hoarded, and disbursed only when absolutely necessary. The smallest atom of truth represents some man's bitter toil and agony; for every ponderable chunk of it there is a brave truth-seeker's grave upon some lonely ash-dump and a soul roasting in hell.

11. The Pacifist

The normal man's antipathy to his relatives, particularly of the second degree, is explained by psychologists in various tortured and improbable ways. The true explanation, I venture is a good deal simpler. It lies in the plain fact that every man sees in his relatives, and especially in his cousins, a series of grotesque caricatures of himself. They exhibit his qualities in disconcerting augmentation or diminution; they kill him with a disquieting feeling that this, perhaps, is the way he appears to the world and so they wound his *amour propre* [self-love] and give him intense discomfort. To admire his relatives whole-heartedly a man must be lacking in the finer sort of self-respect.

12. The Friend

One of the most mawkish of human delusions is the notion that friendship should be eternal, or, at all events, life-long, and that any act which puts a term to it is somehow discreditable. The fact is that a man of active and resilient mind outwears his friendships just as certainly as he outwears his love affairs, his politics and his epistemology. They become threadbare, shabby, pumped-up, irritating, depressing. They convert themselves from living realities into moribund artificialities, and stand in sinister opposition to freedom, self-respect and truth. It is as corrupting to preserve them after they have grown fly-blown and hollow as it is to keep up the forms of passion after passion itself is a corpse. Every act and attitude that they involve thus becomes an act of hypocrisy, an attitude of dishonesty. . . . A prudent man, remembering that life is short, gives an hour or two, now and then, to a critical examination of his friendships. He weighs them, edits them, tests the metal of them. A few he retains, perhaps with radical changes in their terms. But the majority he expunges from his minutes and tries to forget, as he tries to forget the cold and clammy loves of year before last.

(*Prejudices, Third Series*)

THE CROWD

[*Mencken's style was a gift to American literature, but his greatest contribution
to American ideas was simple: the American people are stupid, vile, mean-
spirited, vulgar, and their default political and social position is fascist. In this
short essay, debunking a sociological theory constructed by academic elitists,
Mencken writes that the theorists were ". . . poisoned by the prevailing delusion
that the lower orders of men are angels. This is nonsense. The lower orders of
men are incurable rascals, either individually or collectively."*

*This is true. A great many of the poor, working or not, wallow in illiteracy
and drug dependency, speak in vulgarities, and abuse the officials during high
school football games. It's simply because the poor tend to rob and shoot only
their peers that the academic class romanticizes them. Attempts to explain
mob behavior through sociological analysis are often attempts to excuse the
subjects of such analysis for their attitudes and actions. (This can lead to serious mistakes if one is ever driving through a bad neighborhood.)*

*But of course idiotic, mob-like behavior isn't the exclusive province of the poor.
It's a characteristic of almost the entire American public. For example, Trump
cultists are better off on average than the other members of their communities.
And yet we still find political and social analysts trying to explain their grotesque demagogue-worship in purely economic terms.*]

Gustave Le Bon [author of *The Crowd: A study of the popular mind*]
and his school, in their discussions of the psychology of crowds, have put
forward the doctrine that the individual man, cheek by jowl with the multitude, drops down an intellectual peg or two, and so tends to show the
mental and emotional reactions of his inferiors. It is thus that they explain
the well-known violence and imbecility of crowds. The crowd, as a crowd,
performs acts that many of its members, as individuals, would never be
guilty of. Its average intelligence is very low; it is inflammatory, vicious, idiotic, almost simian. Crowds, properly worked up by skilled demagogues,
are ready to believe anything, and to do anything.

Le Bon, I daresay, is partly right, but also partly wrong. His theory is probably too flattering to the average numskull. He accounts for the extravagance of crowds on the assumption that the numskull, along with the superior man, is knocked out of his wits by suggestion—that he, too, does things in association that would never think of doing singly. The fact may be accepted, but the reasoning raises a doubt. The numskull runs amuck in a crowd, not because he has been inoculated with new rascality by the mysterious crowd influence, but because his habitual rascality now has its only chance to function safely. In other words, the numskull is vicious, but a poltroon. He refrains from all attempts at lynching a capella, not because it takes suggestion to make him desire to lynch, but because it takes the protection of a crowd to make him brave enough to try it.

What happens when a crowd cuts loose is not quite what Le Bon and his followers describe. The few superior men in it are not straightaway reduced to the level of the underlying stoneheads. On the contrary, they usually keep their heads, and often make efforts to combat the crowd action. But the stoneheads are too many for them; the fence is torn down or the blackamoor is lynched. And why? Not because the stoneheads, normally virtuous, are suddenly criminally insane. Nay, but because they are suddenly conscious of the power lying in their numbers—because they suddenly realize that their natural viciousness and insanity may be safely permitted to function.

In other words, the particular swinishness of a crowd is permanently resident in the majority of its members—in all those members, that is, who are naturally ignorant and vicious—perhaps 95 per cent. All studies of mob psychology are defective in that they underestimate this viciousness. They are poisoned by the prevailing delusion that the lower orders of men are angels. This is nonsense. The lower orders of men are incurable rascals, either individually or collectively. Decency, self-restraint, the sense of justice, courage—these virtues belong only to a small minority of men. This minority never runs amuck. Its most distinguishing character, in truth, is its resistance to all running amuck. The third-rate man, though he may wear the false whiskers of a first-rate man, may always be detected by his inability to keep his head in the face of an appeal to his emotions. A whoop strips off his disguise.

(*A Book of Calumny*)

OPERA

[*Mencken loved music but hated opera. Why? Largely because opera has re-markably little to do with music: it's primarily a means for the upper crust to show off their wealth and compare clothing and companions—all in the guise of a glitzy, melodramatic theatrical performance centered around an absurd story. Mencken held that opera consisted of a kernel of music surrounded by a repulsive husk; he very much preferred the kernel to the husk, and very much preferred symphonic and chamber music to opera.*

In the contemporary United States, both types of music, opera and instrumen-tal, are endangered species, but opera especially so. Americans just won't toler-ate it. It exists only as a comic foil, as a backdrop for Larry the Cable Guy to induce an upper-crust woman to clutch her pearls.

In the present-day U.S., we have "The Grand Ole Opry"—arguably more en-tertaining than actual opera—and Wagner can't be played with a banjo and a jug.]

Opera, to a person genuinely fond of aural beauty, must inevitably ap-pear tawdry and obnoxious, if only because it presents aural beauty in a frame of purely visual gaudiness, with overtones of the grossest sexual provocation. The most successful opera singers of the female sex, at least in America, are not those whom the majority of auditors admire most as singers but those whom the majority of male spectators desire most as mistresses. Opera is chiefly supported in all countries by the same sort of wealthy sentimentalists who also support musical comedy. One finds in the directors' room the traditional stock company of the stage-door alley. Such vermin, of course, pose in the newspapers as devout and almost fa-natical partisans of art; they exhibit themselves at every performance; one hears of their grand doings, through their press agents, almost every day. But one has merely to observe the sort of opera they think is good to get the measure of their actual artistic discrimination.

The genuine music-lover may accept the carnal husk of opera to get at the kernel of actual music within, but that is no sign that he approves the carnal husk or enjoys gnawing through it. Most musicians, indeed, prefer to hear operatic music outside the opera house; that is why one so often hears such things as "The Ride of the Valkyries" in the concert hall. "The Ride of the Valkyries" has a certain intrinsic value as pure music; played by a competent orchestra it may give civilized pleasure. But as it is commonly presented in an opera house, with a posse of flat beldames throwing themselves about the stage, it can only produce the effect of a dose of ipecacuanha. The sort of person who actually delights in such spectacles is the sort of person who delights in plush furniture. Such half-wits are in a majority in every opera house west of the Rhine. They go to the opera, not to hear music, not even to hear bad music, but merely to see a more or less obscene circus. A few, perhaps, have a further purpose: they desire to assist in that circus, to show themselves in the capacity of fashionables, to enchant the yokelry with their splendor. But the majority must be content with the more lowly aim. What they get for the outrageous prices they pay for seats is a chance to feast their eyes upon glittering members of the superior demi-monde, and to abase their groveling souls before magnificoes on their own side of the floodlights. They esteem a performance, not in proportion as true music is on tap, but in proportion to the display of notorious characters on the stage is copious, and the exhibition of wealth in boxes is lavish. A soprano who can gargle her way up to G sharp in alto is more to such simple souls that a whole drove of Johann Sebastian Bachs; her one real rival, in the entire domain of art, is the contralto who has a pension from a grand duke and is expected to be *enceinte* [pregnant or big, heavy] by several profiteers. Heaven visualizes itself as an opera house with forty-eight Carusos, each with forty-eight press agents. . . . On the Continent, where frankness is unashamed, the opera audience often reveals its passion for tone very naively. That is to say, it arises on its hind legs, turns its back upon the stage and gapes at the boxes in charming innocence.

That such ignobles applaud is usually quite as shoddy as they are themselves. To write a successful opera a knowledge of harmony and counterpoint is not enough; one must also be a sort of Barnum. All the first-rate musicians who have triumphed in the opera house have been skilled mountebanks as well. I need cite only Richard Wagner and Richard Strauss. The business, indeed, has almost nothing to do with music. All the actual music one finds in many a popular opera—for example, "Thais"—mounts up to less than one may find in a pair of Gung'l waltzes. It is not this mild flavor of tone that fetches the crowd; it is the tinpot show that goes with it. An opera may have plenty of good music in it and fail, but if it has a good enough show it will succeed.

Such a composer as Wagner, of course, could not write even an opera without getting some music into it. In nearly all of his works, even including "Parsifal," there are magnificent passages, and some of them are very long. Here his natural genius overcame him, and he forgot temporarily what he was about. But those magnificent passages pass unnoticed by the average opera audience. What it esteems in his music dramas is precisely what is cheapest and most mountebankish—for example, the more lascivious parts of "Tristan und Isolde." The sound music it dismisses as tedious. The Wagner it venerates is not the musician, but the showman. That he had a king for a backer and was seduced by Liszt's daughter—these facts, and not the fact of his stupendous talent, are the foundation stones of his fame in the opera house. Greater men, lacking his touch of the quack, have failed where he succeeded—Beethoven, Schubert, Schumann, Brahms, Bach, Haydn, Haendel. Not one of them produced a genuinely successful opera; most of them didn't even try. Imagine Brahms writing for the diamond horseshoe! Or Bach! Or Haydn! Beethoven attempted it, but made a mess of it; "Fidelio" survives to-day chiefly as a set of concert overtures. Schubert wrote more actual music every morning between 10 o'clock and lunch time than the average opera composer produces in 250 years, and yet he always came a cropper in the opera house.

(excerpted from "The Allied Arts," *Prejudices, Second Series*)

Under the Elms

[*The NRA states that the only thing that can stop a bad guy with a gun is a good guy with a gun. They ignore the paradox created by the all-too-common case of a mass shooter who turns the gun on himself. Well, what now? Is he the good guy or the bad guy? Both?*

A similar problem exists in colleges and universities, where administrators take the joyful work of reading, studying, and analyzing, and turn it into a psychological trauma via grades, tests, awards, diplomas, and outrageous costs. Everyone ignores that atrocity until the kids start killing themselves; then the obvious answer (a job and a library card) is ignored in favor of creating a counseling department and increasing administrators' already exorbitant pay.

Mencken's remedy is as sound now as ever. One wishes it were applied more often.]

I see nothing mysterious about these [college student] suicides. The impulse to self-destruction is a natural accompaniment of the educational process. Every intelligent student, at some time or other during his college career decides gloomily that it would be more sensible to die than to go on living. I was myself spared the intellectual humiliations of a college education, but during my late teens, with the enlightening gradually dawning within me, I more than once concluded that death was preferable to life. At that age the sense of humor is in a low state. Later on, by the mysterious workings of God's providence, it usually recovers.

What keeps a reflective and skeptical man alive? In large part, I suspect, it is this sense of humor. But in addition there is curiosity. Human existence is always irrational and often painful, but in the last analysis it remains interesting. One wants to know what is going to happen tomorrow. Will the lady in the mauve frock be more amiable than she is today? Such questions keep human beings alive. If the future were known, every intelligent man would kill himself at once, and the Republic would be peopled wholly by morons. Perhaps we are really moving toward that consummation now.

I hope no one will be upset and alarmed by the fact that various bishops, college presidents, Rotary lecturers and other such damned fools are breaking into print with high-fallutin discussions of the alleged wave of student suicides. Such men, it must be manifest, seldom deal with realities. Their whole lives are devoted to inventing bugaboos, and then laying them. Like the news, they will tire of this bogus wave after a while, and go yelling after some other phantasm. Meanwhile, the world will go staggering on. Their notions are never to be taken seriously. Their one visible function on earth is to stand as living proofs that education is by no means synonymous with intelligence.

What I'd like to see, if it could be arranged, would be a wave of suicides among college presidents. I'd be delighted to supply the pistols, knives, ropes, poisons and other necessary tools. I'd be delighted to load the pistols, hone the knives, and tie the hangman's knots. A college student, leaping uninvited into the arms of God, pleases only himself. But a college president, doing the same thing, would give keen and permanent joy to great multitudes of persons. I drop the idea, and pass on.

(*Trenton Sunday Times*, April 3, 1927)

5

JOURNALISM

THE AMERICAN MAGAZINE

[*While this essay might not be Mencken's most entertaining piece, it is perhaps the piece of greatest historical interest. "The American Magazine" might serve as a preface to the age of the Internet and social media. As Mencken writes, "Considering the noisiness of the American magazines of to-day, it is rather instructive to glance back at the timorous and bloodless quality of their progenitors. All of the early ones, when they were not simply monthly newspapers or almanacs, were depressingly 'literary' in tone..."*

Things had changed by Mencken's day: sensationalism and bra ads were what sold to the masses, not the dry work of sophisticates. For those of us who watched the History Channel chuck documentaries on the French Revolution for "Ice Road Truckers," and who must tolerate the belief that modern-day country and hip hop are legitimate musical genres, this essay aptly describes the great American process of dumbing down the culture, and this always happens no matter how dumb the culture was to begin with.]

It is astonishing, considering the enormous influence of the popular magazine upon American literature, such as it is, that there is but one book in type upon magazine history in the republic. That lone volume is *The Magazine in America*, by Prof. Dr. Algernon Tassin, a learned birchman of the great university of Columbia, and it is so badly written that the interest of the matter is almost concealed—almost, but fortunately not quite. The professor, in fact, puts English to paper with all the traditional dullness of his flatulent order, and, as usual, he is most horribly dull when he is trying most kittenishly to be lively. I spare you examples of his writing; if you know the lady essayists of the United States, and their academic imitators in pantaloons, you know the sort of arch and whimsical jocosity he ladles out. But, as I have hinted, there is something worth attending to in his story, for all the defects of presentation, and so his book is not to be sniffed at. He has, at all events, brought together a great mass of scattered and concealed facts, and arranged them conveniently for whoever deals with them next. The job was plainly a long and laborious one, and rasping to the higher cerebral cortex. The historian had to make his mole-like way through the endless files of old and stupid magazines; he had to read the insipid biographies and autobiographies of dead and forgotten editors, many of them college professors, preachers out of work, pre-historic uplifters and bad poets; he had to sort out the facts from the fancies of such incurable liars as Griswold; he had to hack and blast a path across a virgin wilderness. The thing was worth doing, and, as I say, it has been done with commendable pertinacity.

Considering the noisiness of the American magazine of to-day, it is rather instructive to glance back at the timorous and bloodless quality of their progenitors. All of the early ones, when they were not simply monthly newspapers or almanacs, were depressingly "literary" in tone, and dealt chiefly in stupid poetry, silly essays and artificial fiction. The one great fear of their editors seems to have been that of offending some one; all of the pioneer prospectuses were full of assurances that nothing would be printed which even "the most fastidious" could object to. Literature, in those days,—say from 1830 to 1860—was almost completely cut off from contemporary life. It mirrored, not the struggle for existence, so fierce and dramatic in the new nation, but the pallid reflections of poetasters, self-advertising clergymen, sissified "gentlemen of taste," and other such donkeys. Poe waded into these literati and shook them up a bit, but even after the Civil War the majority of them continued to spin pretty cobwebs. Edmund Clarence Stedman and Donald G. Mitchell were excellent specimens of the clan; its last survivor was the lachrymose William Winter. The "literature" manufactured by these tear-squeezers, though often enough produced in beer cellars, was frankly aimed at the Young Person. Its main purpose was to avoid giving offense; it breathed a heavy and oleaginous piety, a snug niceness, a sickening sweetness. It is as dead to-day as Baalam's ass.

The Atlantic Monthly was set up by men in revolt against this reign of mush, as *Putnam's* had been a few years before, but the business of reform proved to be difficult and hazardous, and it was a long while before a healthier breed of authors could be developed, and a public for them found. "There is not much in the *Atlantic*," wrote Charles Eliot Norton to Lowell in 1874, "that is likely to be read twice save by its writers, and this is what the great public likes. . . . You should hear Godkin express himself in private on this topic." *Harper's Magazine*, in those days, was made up almost wholly of cribbings from England; the *North American Review* had sunk into stodginess and imbecility; *Putnam's* was dead, or dying; the *Atlantic* had yet to discover Mark Twain; it was the era of *Godley's Lady's Book*. The new note, so long awaited, was struck at last by *Scribner's*, now the *Century* (and not to be confused with the *Scribner's* of to-day). It not only threw all the old traditions overboard; it established new traditions almost at once. For the first time a great magazine began to take notice of the daily life of the American people. It started off with a truly remarkable series of articles on the Civil War; it plunged into contemporary politics; it eagerly sought out and encouraged new writers; it began printing decent pictures instead of the old chromos; it forced itself, by the sheer originality and enterprise of its editing, upon the public attention. American literature owes more to the *Century* than to any other magazine, and perhaps American thinking owes almost as much. It was the first "literary" periodical to arrest and interest the really first-class men of the country. It beat the *Atlantic* because it wasn't burdened with *Atlantic's* decaying cargo of Boston Brahmins. It beat all the others because it was infinitely and obviously better. Almost everything that is good in the American magazine of to-day, almost everything that sets it above the English magazine or the Continental magazine, stems from the *Century*.

At the moment, of course, it holds no such clear field; perhaps it has served its function and is ready for a placid old age. The thing that displaced it was the yellow magazine of the *McClure's* type—a variety of magazine which surpassed it in the race for circulation by exaggerating and vulgarizing all its merits. Dr. Tassin seems to think with William Archer, that S.S. McClure was the inventor of this type, but the truth is that its real father was the unknown originator of the Sunday supplement. What McClure—a shrewd literary bagman—did was to apply the sensational methods of the cheap newspaper to a new and cheap magazine. Yellow journalism was rising and he went in on the tide. The satanic Hearst was getting on his legs at the same time, and I daresay that the muck-raking magazines, even in their palmy days, followed him a good deal more than they led him. McClure and the imitators of McClure borrowed his adept thumping of the tom-tom; Munsey and the imitators of Munsey borrowed his mush. *McClure's* and *Everybody's*, even when they had the whole nation by the ears, did little save repeat in solemn, awful tones what Hearst had said before. As for *Munsey's*, at the height of its circulation, it was little more than a Sunday "magazine section" on smooth paper, and with somewhat clearer half-tones than Hearst could print. Nearly all the genuinely original ideas of these Yankee Harmsworths of yesterday turned out badly. John Brisben Walker, with the *Cosmopolitan*, tried to make his magazine a sort of national university, and it went to pot. Ridgway, of *Everybody's*, planned a weekly to be published in a dozen cities simultaneously, and lost a fortune trying to establish it. McClure, facing a situation to be described presently, couldn't manage it, and his magazine got away from him. As for Munsey, there are many wrecks behind him; he is forever experimenting boldly and failing gloriously. Even his claim to have invented the all-fiction magazine is open to caveat; there were probably plenty of such things in substance if not in name, before the *Argosy*. Hearst, the teacher of them all, now openly holds the place that belongs to him. He has galvanized the corpse of the old *Cosmopolitan* into a great success, he has distanced all rivals with *Hearst's*, he has beaten the English on their own ground with *Nash's*, and he has rehabilitated various lesser magazines. More, he has forced the other magazine publishers to imitate him. A glance at *McClure's* to-day offers all the proof that is needed of his influence upon his inferiors.

Dr. Tassin, apparently in fear of making his book too nearly good, halts his chronicle at its most interesting point, for he says nothing of what has gone on since 1900—and very much, indeed, has gone on since 1900. For one thing, the *Saturday Evening Post* has made its unparalleled success, created its new type of American literature for department store buyers and shoe drummers, and bred its school of brisk, business-like, high-speed authors. For another thing, the *Ladies Home Journal*, once supreme in its field, has seen the rise of a swarm of imitators, some of them very prosperous. For a third thing, the moving-picture craze has created an entirely new type of magazine, and it has elbowed many other types from the stands. And for a fifth thing, to make an end, the muck-raking magazine has blown up and is no more.

Why this last? Have all the possible candidates for the rake been raked? Is there no longer any taste for scandal in the popular breast? I have heard endless discussion of these questions and many ingenious answers, but all of them fail to answer. In this emergency I offer one of my own. It is this: that the muck-raking magazine came to grief, not because the public tired of muck-raking, but because the muck-raking that it began with succeeded. That is to say, the villains so long belabored by the Steffenses, the Tarbells and the Phillipines were either driven from the national scene or forced (at least temporarily) into rectitude. Worse, their places in public life were largely taken by nominees whose chemical purity was guaranteed by these same magazines, and so the latter found their occupation gone and their following with it. The great masses of the plain people, eager to swallow denunciation in horse-doctor doses, gagged at the first spoonful of praise. They chortled and read on when Aldrich, Boss Cox, Gas Addicks, John D. Rockefeller and the other bugaboos of the time were belabored every month, but they promptly sickened and went elsewhere when Judge Ben B. Lindsey, Francis J. Heney, Governor Folk and the rest of the bogus saints began to be hymned.

The same phenomenon is constantly witnessed upon the lower level of daily journalism. Let a vociferous "reform" newspaper overthrow the old gang and elect its own candidates, and at once it is in a perilous condition. Its stock in trade is gone. It can no longer give a good show. For what the public wants eternally—at least the American public—is rough work. It delights in vituperation. It revels in scandal. It is always on the side of the man or journal making the charges, no matter how slight the probability that the accused is guilty. The late Roosevelt, perhaps one of the greatest rabble-rousers the world has ever seen, was privy to this fact, and made it the corner-stone of his singularly cynical and effective politics. He was forever calling names, making accusations, unearthing and denouncing demons. Dr. Wilson, a performer of scarcely less talent, has sought to pursue the same plan, with varying fidelity and success. He was a popular hero so long as he confined himself to reviling men and things—the Hell Hounds of Plutocracy, the Socialists, the Kaiser, the Irish, the Senate minority. But the moment he found himself on the side of the defense, he began to wobble, just as Roosevelt before him had begun to wobble when he found himself burdened with the intricate constructive program of the Progressives. Roosevelt shook himself free by deserting the Progressives, but Wilson found it impossible to get rid of the League of Nations, and so, for awhile at least, he presented a quite typical picture of a muck-raker ham-strung by blows from the wrong end of the rake.

That the old appetite for bloody shows is not dead but only sleepeth is well exhibited by the recent revival of the weekly of opinion. Ten years ago the weekly seemed to be absolutely extinct; even the *Nation* survived only as a half-forgotten appendage of the *Evening Post*. Then, of a sudden, the alliance was broken, the *Evening Post* succumbed to Wall Street, the *Nation* started on an independent course—and straightaway made a great success. And why? Simply because it began breaking heads—not the old heads of the *McClure's* era, of course, but nevertheless heads salient enough to make excellent targets. For years it had been moribund; no one read it save a dwindling company of old men; its influence gradually approached nil. But by the elementary device of switching from mild expostulation to violent and effective denunciation it made a new public almost over-night, and is now very widely read, extensively quoted and increasingly heeded. . . . I often wonder that so few publishers of periodicals seem aware of the psychological principle here exposed. It is known to every newspaper publisher of the slightest professional intelligence; all successful newspapers are ceaselessly querulous and bellicose. They never defend any one or anything if they can help it; if the job is forced upon them, they tackle it by denouncing some one or something else. The plan never fails. Turn to the moving-picture trade magazines: the most prosperous of them is given over, in the main, to bitter attacks upon new films. Come back to daily journalism. The New York *Tribune*, a decaying, well nigh rehabilitated itself by attacking Hearst, the cleverest muck-raker of them all. For a moment, apparently dismayed, he attempted a defense of himself—and came near falling into actual disaster. Then, recovering his old form, he began a whole series of counter attacks and cover attacks, and in six months he was safe and sound again. . . .

(*Prejudices, First Series*)

A GANG OF PECKSNIFFS

[*Hating journalists, a rare point of unity among Americans, may be the only thing we collectively do that makes sense. At first it seems paradoxical: Americans cherish the First Amendment, yet despise the journalists who make a living exercising it. The problem is that most Americans don't even have the basic level of awareness necessary to recognize the paradox. We (collectively) just don't have it. Mencken's hatred of media magnates is more nuanced than the average, only because Mencken recognizes that the magnates and their tame journalists defend freedom of speech when they can profit from it.*

As a bonus, in "A Gang of Pecksniffs" Mencken attacks Woodrow Wilson. Occasionally, when the more significant worries in my life give me a moment's peace, I find myself wondering why everyone doesn't hate him. He unnecessarily entangled the country in a European war, was a deadly enemy of free speech, ordered the bashing and jailing of anti-war dissidents, and was without doubt a racist. Among other things, he allowed his cabinet secretaries to segregate their offices, and he screened "Birth of a Nation" in 1915 in the White House—the first film ever shown there; it was such an effective piece of racist propaganda that it spurred the revival of the Klan.

I ask myself why more people don't hate Wilson, and then I remind myself that if Americans remember any Woody at all, it's that other annoying pecker or the bald-headed actor.]

1

On the first page of the eminent *Sunpaper* of last Friday appeared a dispatch from New York reporting that the American Newspaper Publishers' Association, there assembled for its annual convention and booze-guzzle, had passed a solemn resolution protesting that "the liberty of the press has been seriously threatened during the past year," pledging its members to "resist all interference with the right . . . of the press to free expression under the constitutional guarantees," and instructing its Committee on Federal Laws "to exercise its utmost efforts to maintain the liberty of freedom [sic] of the press wherever it may be threatened." On the same page of the Sunpaper, two columns away, appeared a dispatch from Philadelphia reporting that two women had been arrested and jailed for "distributing circulars which petition President Harding to grant amnesty to political prisoners."

Humor? Then the obscene is humorous—as, indeed, most normal Americans seem to hold. As for me, I see nothing to cackle over in the resolution of the publishers. Instead, it should be denounced briefly for what it is: a mass of degraded and disgusting cant. In the history of American journalism during the past half dozen years there is certainly nothing jocose. In all their dealings with the question of free speech the newspapers of the country, and especially the larger and more powerful ones, have been infinitely pusillanimous, groveling, dishonest and indecent. If, as they now pretend so boldly, their editors and proprietors are actually in favor of Article I of the Bill of Rights, then their long acquiescence in its violation proves that they are a herd of poltroons. And if, when it was so grossly violated, they were actually in favor of those who violated it, then their belated resolution proves that they are liars. I see no way to avoid these alternatives. I can imagine no process of reasoning, however subtle and ingenious, whereby persons whose words and acts are so heroically at odds could be converted into honest and honorable men.

2

It is my private impression, born of long familiarity with such fauna, that what brought most of the publishers to the side of the Bill of Rights at last, after all their craven consenting to its invasion, was not any belated enthusiasm for free speech, or, indeed, any intelligent respect for it or understanding of it, but simply and solely a fear that the next violation of Article I would probably cut off some of their revenues. The uplifters are up and doing on all sides, and of late they have uncovered some Great Causes that threaten newspaper profits. For example, there is the matter of race-track information. Practically all American newspapers, however moral they may seem on their editorial pages, print such information on their sporting pages—and it sells a good many papers. Now the uplifters propose a Federal law declaring any paper containing it unmailable. At

once, waking from their long sleep, the publishers begin shedding croco-
dile tears over "the right of the press to free expression under the constitutional guarantee."

It would be difficult to imagine any more gross and obvious pecksniff-
ery. Put beside it, the proceedings of the Anti-Saloon League seem almost
honest. Where were all these publishers when the janissaries of the late
Woodrow were prowling the country clubbing and jailing all citizens who
presumed to question his divinity—when men by the hundred were railroaded to prison for venturing to exercise the constitutional right to free
speech, and other men were harassed and hounded in a dozen other ways,
and publications almost without number were tyrannically barred from
the mails? The answer is simple: they were not only consenting to the business; they were actively promoting it. It was their newspapers—many of
them great and puissant papers—that egged on the Department of Justice,
the Chambers of Commerce, the Americanization Leagues, the American Legion and all other such lawless bands. It was their newspapers that
raised the idiotic alarm about Bolshevism, and brought on the wholesale
jailing and deportation of innocent men. It was their newspapers that distorted and tortured the news to official uses, and debauched the courts,
and connived at crime, and made justice in America a joke. And it was
their newspapers that fawningly approved every time some smaller and
more honorable sheet got into trouble for trying to tell the truth.

3

I am well aware, of course, that there were exceptional journals that
shrunk delicately from much of this swinery—that a few of them came
forward with protests long before the race-track information bill alarmed
the rank and file. I say a few, but at the moment I am sure of but two: the
estimable *Sunpaper* aforesaid and the New York *World*. The World was the
first gag, and then came the Sunpaper. By the time the Palmer buffoonery
about radicals got its height, both were in full revolt, and trying to tell the
truth. But it is not be forgotten that even these very exceptional and almost miraculous gazettes ran a long way behind some of the weeklies and
monthlies—that they were magnificently silent at the times the *Masses* [so-
cialist periodical] was suppressed [in 1917] and the *Nation* was attacked.
In brief, they deserve very little praise for their revolt, for by the time they
came to make it it was quite safe. When they were needed most desperately—when the aid of two such rich and powerful papers would have been

most effective and valuable—they were silent. To have horned in at that time would have been to run grave risks, for Wilson was strutting about in his halo and Palmer and company believed themselves invincible—but it would have been to render a public service of inestimable worth. I believed at that time and I believe now that in a stand-up fight with Wilson they would have won—that public opinion, after the first clash, would have supported them, as it later came to support even the *Masses*. But instead of making the venture they went to the defense of Wilson, and it was not until he was on his knees that they began to gag at his excesses, and, in particular, at his deliberate, cynical and intolerable violations of the Bill of Rights.

Even then they tried ineptly to separate the man from his evil deeds, e.g., to argue that the cad who kept the poor old ass, Debs, in prison was a statesman and a gentleman. Worse, they continued to pussy-foot, even after they had got over that folly. For example, they denounced the crimes against the Constitution perpetrated by the Ku Klux Klan, and were silent about the far more serious crimes perpetrated by the American Legion. But even so, they were a million times more honest and courageous than any other American newspapers. It was at least obvious that something resembling a conscience has begun to gnaw them. The rest of the great American journals continued to display, as usual, the morals and public spirit of so many Prohibition enforcement officers, Congressmen, or street-walkers.

4

These preposterous fakes now begin to snuffle and blubber of the invasion of the Bill of Rights! Hit in the money-bag, they suddenly become fanatical devotees of the Constitution! It is my sincere hope that even Congressmen will have sense enough to penetrate the fraud. To more intelligent and seemly men I offer a ready test of it. Get a copy of any great American journal of Friday, April 28, 1922. See how its news department treated the story from Philadelphia—of the two women dragged to the calaboose by the police for exercising their constitutional right to petition the President for the release of men jailed in violation of their constitutional rights. Then see what the staff Delane has to say about the business on the editorial page—if anything. Don't bother to read his learned discourse on the Genoa mountebankery, the sins of the coal miners, the candidacy of M. Cox. Go straight to his denunciation of this double assault upon the Constitution—if it is there. If you find it, let me know.

(*The Baltimore Sun*, May 2, 1922)

H.L. MENCKEN, BY HIMSELF

[*The primary interest here is in Mencken's charming and disarming descrip-tion of his motives for writing literary criticism. His description of the dunder-headed reactions of* his *critics is also revelatory. It seems that not much has changed since Mencken's time: the lower sorts of men seemingly can't react rationally to writings they disagree with; they seemingly can't debate the mer-its of ideas; rather, they resort to* ad hominem *attack.*]

Ask a professional critic to write about himself and you simply ask him to do what he does every day in the practise of his art and mystery. There is, indeed, no criticism that is not a confidence, and there is no confidence that is not self-revelation. When I denounce a book with mocking and contumely, and fall upon the poor author in the brutal, Asiatic manner of a drunken longshoreman, a Ku Kluxer, or a midshipman at Annapolis, I am only saying, in the trade cant, that the fellow disgusts me—that his ideas and his manner are somehow obnoxious to me, as those of a Methodist, a golf player, or a clog dancer are obnoxious to me—in brief, that I hold my-self to be a great deal better than he is and am eager to say so. And when, on the other hand, I praise a book in high, astounding terms, and speak of its author as if his life and sufferings were of capital importance to the world, then I am merely saying that I detect something in him, of preju-dice, tradition, habit of mind, that is much like something within myself, and that my own life and sufferings are of the utmost importance to me. That is all there ever is in criticism, once it gets beyond cataloguing. No matter how artfully the critic may try to be impersonal and scientific, he is bound to give himself away.

With criticism thus so transparent, so unescapably revelatory, I often marvel that the gentlemen who concern themselves with my own books, often very indignantly, do not penetrate more competently to my essence.

Even for a critic I am excessively garrulous and confidential; nevertheless, it is rare for me to encounter a criticism that hits me where I live and have my being. A great deal of ink is wasted trying to discover and denounce my motive in being a critic at all. I am, by one theory, a German spy told off to flay, terrorize and stampede the Anglo-Saxon. By another I am a secret radical, while professing to adore Coolidge and Genghis Kahn. By a third, I am a fanatical American chauvinist, bent upon defaming and ruining the motherland. All these notions are nonsense; only the first has even the slightest plausibility. The plain truth is—and how could it be plainer?—that I practise criticism for precisely the same reason that every other critic practises it: because I am a vain fellow, and have a great many ideas on all sorts of subjects, and like to put them into words and harass the human race with them. If I could confine this flow of ideas to one subject I'd be a professor and get some respect. If I could reduce it, say, to one idea a year, I'd be a novelist, a dramatist, or a newspaper editorial writer. But being unable to stanch the flux, and having, as I say, a vast and exigent vanity, I am a critic of books, and through books of *Homo sapiens*, and through *Homo sapiens* of God.

So much for the motive. What, now, of the substance? What is the fundamental faith beneath all the spurting and corruscating the ideas that I have just mentioned? What do I primarily and immovably believe in, as a Puritan believes in Hell? I believe in liberty. And when I say liberty I mean the thing in its widest imaginable sense—liberty up to the extreme limits of the feasible and tolerable. I am against forbidding anybody to do anything, or say anything or think anything, so long as it is at all possible to imagine a habitable world in which he would be free to do, say and think it. The burden of proof, as I see it, is always upon the policeman, which is to say upon the lawmaker, the theologian, the right-thinker. He must prove his case doubly, triply, quadruply, and then he must start all over and prove it again. The eye through which I view him is watery and jaundiced. I do not pretend to be "just" to him—any more than a Christian pretends to be just to the Devil. He is the enemy of everything I admire and respect in this world—or everything that makes it various and amusing and charming. He impedes every honest search for the truth. He stands against every sort of good will and common decency. His ideal is that of an animal trainer, an archbishop, a major-general of the Army. I am against him until the last galoot's ashore.

This simple and childlike faith in the freedom and dignity of man—here, perhaps, stated with undue rhetoric—should be obvious, I should think, to

every critic above the mental backwardness of a Federal judge. Nevertheless, very few of them, anatomizing my books, have ever showed any sign
of detecting it. But all the same even the dullest of them has, in his fashion,
sensed it; it colors unconsciously all the diatribes about myself that I have
ever read. It is responsible for the fact that in England, Germany (and, to
the extent that I have ever been heard of at all there, in France and Italy) I
am regarded as a highly typical American—in truth, as almost the archetype of the American. And it is responsible equally for the fact that here at
home I am often denounced as the worst American unhung. The paradox
is only apparent. The explanation of it lies in this: that to most Europeans
the United States is still regarded naively as the land of liberty *par excel-
lence*, whereas to most Americans the thing itself has long since ceased to
have any significance, and to large numbers of them, indeed, it has of late
taken on an extreme obnoxiousness. I know of no civilized country, indeed, in which liberty is less esteemed than it is in the United States today;
certainly there is none in which more persistent efforts are made to limit it
and put it down. I am thus, to Americans, a bad American, but to Europeans, still unaware of the practical effects of the idealism of Wilson and the
saloon-bouncer ethic of Roosevelt I, I seem to be an eloquent spokesman
of the true American tradition. It is a joke, but the joke is not on me.

Liberty, of course, is not for slaves; I do not advocate inflicting it on men
against their conscience. On the contrary, I am strongly in favor of letting
them crawl and grovel all they please—before the Supreme Court of the
United States, Samuel Gompers, J.P. Morgan, Henry Cabot Lodge, the Anti-Saloon League, or whatever other fraud or combination of frauds they
choose to venerate. I am thus unable to make the grade as a Liberal, for
Liberalism always involves freeing human beings against their will—often,
indeed to their obvious damage, as in the cases of Negroes and women.
But all human beings are not congenital slaves, even in America. Here and
there one finds a man or a woman with a great natural passion for liberty—and a hard job getting it. It is, to me at least, a vast pleasure to go to
the rescue of such a victim of the herd, to give him some aid and comfort
in his struggle against the forces that seek to regiment and throttle him. It
is a double pleasure to succor him when the sort of liberty he strives for is
apparently unintelligible and valueless—for example, liberty to address the
conventions of the I.W.W., to read the books of such bad authors as D.H.
Lawrence and Petronius Arbiter, to work twelve hours a day, to rush the
can, to carry red flags in parades, to patronize osteopaths and Christian
Science healers, to belong to the best clubs. Such nonsensical varieties of

liberty are especially sweet to me. I have wrecked my health and dissipated a fortune defending them—never, so far as I know, successfully. Why, then, go on? Ask yourself why a grasshopper goes on jumping.

But what has liberty to do with the art of literary criticism, my principle business in this vale? Nothing—or everything. It seems to me that it is perfectly possible to write profound and valuable literary criticism without entering on the question of freedom at all, either directly or indirectly. Aesthetic judgment may be isolated from all other kinds of judgments, and yet remain interesting and important. But this isolation must be performed by other hands; to me it is as sheer a psychological impossibility as believing that God condemned forty-two little children to death for poking fun at Elisha's bald head. When I encounter a new idea, whether aesthetic, political, theological or epistemological, I ask myself, instantly and automatically, what would happen to its proponent if he should state its exact antithesis. If nothing would happen to him, then I am willing and eager to listen to him. But if he would lose anything valuable by a *volte face* [about face]—if stating his idea is profitable to him, if the act secures his roof, butters his parsnips, gets him a tip—then I hear him with one ear only. He is not a free man. Ergo, he is not a man.

For liberty, when one ascends to the level where ideas swish by and men pursue Truth to grab her by the tail, is the first thing and the last thing. So long as it prevails the show is thrilling and stupendous; the moment it fails the show is a dull and dirty farce.

(*The Nation*, December 5, 1923)

6

LITERATURE

Portrait of an Immortal Soul

[*In the 2006 Robert Town film, Ask the Dust, Colin Farrell played a Depression-era writer with a Mencken obsession. Most viewers probably only watched the movie to see Salma Hayek's ocean-spray nude scene (Mencken would have approved), but those who watched the whole thing might remember a scene where Farrell's character received an encouraging letter from Mencken. And if Mencken showed mercy to anyone, it was to aspiring writers.*

That's what makes "Portrait of an Immortal Soul" a recommendation for Mencken's place in heaven. Mencken writes of how he received a maudlin manuscript, one of those autobiographical pieces of fiction so commonly composed by people who believe they have one book in them, and how he eventually agreed to act as a paid editor for the piece.

"One night, tortured by conscience and by the inquiries and reminders arriving from the author by every post, I took up the sheets and settled down for a depressing hour or two of it. . . . No, I did not read all night. No, it was not a masterpiece. No, it has not made the far-off stranger famous." Yet, Mencken writes, there was something there. He suggested several major changes to the writer which, astonishingly, the author actually made.

With Mencken's help, he eventually landed a book deal for what turned out to be a flop—probably in part because of its atrociously bland title, "One Man," which Mencken had suggested.

No essay better reveals the full character of Mencken than this one.]

One day in Spring, six or eight years ago, I received a letter from a man somewhere beyond the Wabash announcing that he had lately completed a very powerful novel and hinting that my critical judgment upon it would give him great comfort. Such notifications, at that time, reached me far too often to be agreeable, and so I sent him a form-response telling him that I was ill with pleurisy, had just been forbidden by my oculist to use my eyes, and was about to become a father. The aim of this form-response was to shunt all that sort of trade off to other reviewers, but for once it failed. That is to say, the unknown kept on writing to me, and finally offered to pay me an honorarium for my labor. This offer was so unusual that it quite demoralized me, and before I could recover I had received, cashed and dissipated a modest check, and was confronted by an accusing manuscript, perhaps four inches thick, but growing thicker every time I glanced at it.

One night, tortured by my conscience and by the inquiries and reminders arriving from the author by every post, I took up the sheets and settled down for a depressing hour or two of it. . . . No, I did not read all night. No, it was not a masterpiece. No, it has not made the far-off stranger famous. Let me tell the story quite honestly. I am, in fact, far too rapid a reader to waste a whole night on a novel; I had got through this one by midnight and was sound asleep at my usual time. And it was by no means a masterpiece; on the contrary, it was inchoate, clumsy, and, in part, artificial, insincere and preposterous. And to this day the author remains obscure. . . . But underneath all the amateurish writing, the striving for effects that failed to come off, the absurd literary self-consciousness, the recurrent falsity and banality—underneath all these stigmata of a neophyte's book there was yet a capital story, unusual in content, naive in manner and enormously engrossing. What is more, the faults that it showed in execution were, most of them, not ineradicable. On page after page, as I read on, I saw chances to improve it—to get rid of its intermittent bathos, to hasten its action, to eliminate its spells of fine writing, to purge it of its imitations of all the bad novels ever written—in brief, to tighten it, organize it, and, as the painters say, tease it up.

The result was that I spent the next morning writing the author a long letter of advice. It went to him with the manuscript, and for weeks I heard nothing from him. Then the manuscript returned, and I read it again. This time I had a genuine surprise. Not only had the unknown followed my suggestions with much intelligence; in addition, once set up on the right track, he had devised a great many excellent improvements of his own. In its new form, in fact, the thing was a very competent and even dexterous piece of writing, and after re-reading it from the first word to the last with even keener interest than before, I sent it to Mitchell Kennerley, then an active publisher, and asked him to look through it. Kennerley made an offer for it at once, and eight or nine months later it was published with his imprint. The author chose to conceal himself behind the *nom de plume* of Robert Steele; I myself gave the book the title of "One Man." It came from the press—and straightaway died the death. The only favorable review it received was mine in the *Smart Set*. No other reviewer paid any heed to it. No one gabbed about it. No one, so far as I could make out, even read it. The sale was small from the start, and quickly stopped altogether. . . . To this day the fact fills me with wonder. To this day I marvel that so dramatic, so penetrating and so curiously moving a story should have failed so overwhelmingly. . . .

For I have never been able to convince myself that I was wrong about it. On the contrary, I am more certain than ever, re-reading it after half a dozen years, that I was right—that it was and is one of the most honest and absorbing human documents ever printed in America. I have called it, following the author, a novel. It is, in fact, nothing of the sort; it is autobiography. More, it is autobiography unadorned and shameless, autobiography that is as devoid of artistic sophistication as an operation for gall-stones. This so-called Steele is simply too stupid, too ingenuous, too moral to lie. He is the very reverse of an artist; he is a born and incurable Puritan—and in his alleged novel he draws the most faithful and merciless picture of an American Puritan that has ever got upon paper. There is never the slightest effort at amelioration; he never evades the ghastly horror of it; he never tries to palm off himself as a good fellow, a hero. Instead, he simply takes his stand in the center of the platform, where all the spotlights meet, and there calmly strips off his raiment of reticence—first his Sunday plug-hat, then his long-tailed coat, then his boiled shirt, then his shoe and socks, and finally his very B.V.D.'s. The closing scene shows the authentic *mensch-an-sich* [man himself], the eternal blue-nose in the nude, with every wart and pimple glittering and every warped bone and flabby muscle telling its abhorrent tale. There stands the Puritan stripped of every artifice and concealment, like Thackeray's Louis XIV.

Searching my memory, I can drag up no recollection of another such self-opener of secret chambers and skeletonic closets. Set beside this pious babbler, the late Giovanni Jacopo Casanova de Seingalt shrinks to the puny proportions of a mere barroom boaster, a smoking-car Don Juan, an Eighteenth Century stock company leading man or whiskey drummer. So, too, Benvenuto Cellini: a fellow vastly entertaining, true enough, but after all, not so much a psychological historian as a liar, a yellow journalist. One always feels, in reading Benvenuto, that the man who is telling the story is quite distinct from the man about whom it is being told. The fellow, indeed, was too noble an artist to do a mere portrait with fidelity; he could not resist the temptation to repair a cauliflower ear here, to paint out a tell-tale scar there, to shine up the eyes a bit, to straighten the legs down below. But this Steele—or whatever his name may be—never steps out of himself. He is never describing the gaudy one he would like to be, but always the commonplace, the weak, the emotional, the ignorant, the third-rate Christian male that he actually is. He deplores himself, he distrusts himself, he plainly wishes heartily that he was not himself, but he never makes the slightest attempt to disguise and bedizen himself. Such as he is, cheap, mawkish, unaesthetic, conscience-stricken, he depicts himself with fierce and unrelenting honesty.

Superficially, the man that he sets before us seems to be a felonious fellow, for he confesses frankly to a long series of youthful larcenies, to a somewhat banal adventure in forgery (leading to a term in jail), to sundry petty deceits and breaches of trust, and to an almost endless chain of exploits in amour, most of them sordid and unrelieved by anything approaching romance. But the inner truth about him, of course, is that he is really a moralist of the moralists—that his one fundamental and all-embracing virtue is what he himself regards as his viciousness—that he is never genuinely human and likable save in those moments which lead swiftly to his most florid self-accusing. In brief, the history is that of a moral young man, the child of God-fearing parents, and its moral, if it has one, is that a strictly moral upbringing injects poisons into the system that even the most steadfast morality cannot resist. It is, in a way, the old story of the preacher's son turned sot and cut-throat.

Here we see an apparently sound and normal youngster converted into a sneak and rogue by the intolerable pressure of his father's abominable Puritanism. And once a rogue, we see him make himself into a scoundrel by the very force of his horror of his roguery. Every step downward is helped from above. It is not until he resigns himself frankly to the fact of his incurable degradation, and so ceases to struggle against it, that he ever steps out of it.

The external facts of the chronicle are simple enough. The son of a school teacher turned petty lawyer and politician, the hero is brought up under such barbaric rigors that he has already become a fluent and ingenious liar, in sheer self-protection, at the age of five or six. From lying he proceeds quite naturally to stealing: he lifts a few dollars from a neighbor, and then rifles a tin bank, and then takes to filching all sorts of small articles from the store-keepers of the vicinage. His harsh, stupid, Christian father, getting wind of these peccadilloes, has at him in the manner of a mad bull, beating him, screaming at him, half killing him. The boy, for all the indecent cruelty of it, is convinced of the justice of it. He sees himself as one lost; he accepts the fact that he is a disgrace to his family; in the end, he embraces the parental theory that there is something strange and sinister in his soul, that he couldn't be good if he tried. Finally, filled with some vague notion of taking his abhorrent self out of sight, he runs away from home. Brought back in the character of a felon, he runs away again. Soon he is a felon in fact. That is to say, he forges his father's name to a sheaf of checks, and his father allows him to go to prison.

This prison term gives the youngster a chance to think things out for himself, without the constant intrusion of his father's Presbyterian notions of right or wrong. The result is a measurably saner philosophy than that he absorbed at home, but there is still enough left of the old moral obsession to cripple him in all his thinking, and especially in his thinking about himself. His attitude toward women, for example is constantly conditioned by puritanical misgivings and superstitions. He can never view them innocently, joyously, unmorally, as a young fellow of twenty or twenty-one should, but is always oppressed by Sunday-schoolish notions of his duty to them, and to society in general. On the one hand, he is appalled by his ready yielding to those hussies who have at him unofficially, and on the other hand, he is filled with the idea that it would be immoral for him, an ex-convict, to go to the altar with a virgin. The result of these doubts is that he gives a good deal more earnest thought to the woman question than is good for him. The second result is that he proves an easy victim to the discarded mistress of his employer. This worthy working girl craftily snares him and marries him—and then breaks down on their wedding night, unwomaned, so to speak, by the pathetic innocence of the ass, and confesses to a choice roll of her past doings, ending with the news that she is suffering what the vice crusaders mellifluously denominate a "social disease."

Naturally enough, the blow almost kills the poor boy—he is still, in fact, scarcely out of his nonage—and the problems that grow out of the confession engage him for the better part of the next two years. Always he approaches them and wrestles with them morally; always his search is for the way that copy-book maxims approve, not for the way that self-preservation demands. Even when a brilliant chance for revenge presents itself, and he is forced to embrace it by the sheer magnetic pull of it, he does so hesitatingly, doubtingly, ashamedly. His whole attitude to this affair, indeed is that of an Early Christian Father. He hates himself for gathering rosebuds while he may; he hates the woman with a double hatred for strewing them so temptingly in his path. And in the end, like the moral and upright fellow that he is, he sells out the temptress for cash in hand, and salves his conscience by handing over the money to an orphan asylum. This after prayers for divine guidance. A fact! Don't miss the story of it in the book. You will go far before you get another such illuminating glimpse into a pure and righteous mind.

So in episode after episode. One observes a constant oscillation between a pharisaical piety and a hoggish carnality. The praying brother of yesterday is the snuffling penitent and pledge-taker of to-morrow. Finally, he is pulled both ways at once and suffers the greatest of all his tortures. Again, of course, a woman is at the center of it—this time a stenographer. He has no delusions about her virtue—she admits herself, in fact, that it is extinct—but all the same he falls head over heels in love with her, and is filled with an inordinate yearning to marry her and settle down with her. Why not, indeed? She is pretty and a nice girl; she seems to reciprocate his affection; she is naturally eager for the obliterating gold band; she will undoubtedly make him an excellent wife. But he has forgotten his conscience—and it rises up in revenge and floors him. What! Marry a girl with a Past! Take a fancy woman to his bosom! Jealousy quickly comes to the aid of conscience. Will he be able to forget? Contemplating the damsel in the years to come, at breakfast, at dinner, across the domestic hearth, in the cold, blue dawn, will he ever rid his mind of those abhorrent images, those phantasms of men?

Here, at the very end, we come to the most engrossing chapter in this extraordinary book. The duelist of sex, thrust through the gizzard at last, goes off to a lonely hunting camp to wrestle with his intolerable problem. He describes his vacillations faithfully, elaborately, cruelly. On the one side he sets his honest yearning, his desire to have done with light loves, the girl herself. On the other hand he ranges his moral qualms, his sneaking distrusts, the sinister shadows of those nameless ones, his morganatic brothers-in-law. The struggle within his soul is gigantic. He suffers as Prometheus suffered on the rock; his very vitals are devoured. He decides, in the end, that he will marry the girl. She has wasted the shining dowry of her sex; she comes to him spotted and at second-hand; snickers will appear in the polyphony of the wedding music—but he will marry her nevertheless. It will be a marriage unblessed by Holy Writ; it will be a flying in the face of Moses; luck and the archangels will be against it—but he will marry her all the same, Moses or no Moses. And so, with his face made bright by his first genuine revolt against the archaic, barbaric morality that has dragged him down, and his heart pulsing to his first display of authentic, unpolluted charity, generosity and nobility, he takes his departure from us. May the fates favor him with their mercy! May the Lord God strain a point to lift him out of his purgatory at last! He has suffered all the agonies of belief. He has done abominable penance for the Westminster Catechism, and for the moral order of the world, and for all the despairing misery of back-street, black bombazine, Little Bethel goodness. He is Puritanism incarnate, and Puritanism become intolerable. . . .

I daresay any second-hand bookseller will be able to find a copy of the book for you: *One Man*, by Robert Steele. There is some raciness in the detail of it. Perhaps, despite its public failure, it enjoys a measure of pizzicato esteem behind the door. The author, having achieved its colossal self-revelation, became intrigued by the notion that he was a literary man of sorts, and informed me that he was undertaking the story of the girl last-named—the spotted ex-virgin. But he apparently never finished it. No doubt he discovered, before he had gone very far, that the tale was intrinsically beyond him—that his fingers all turned into thumbs when he got beyond his own personal history. Such a writer, once he has told the one big story, is done for.

(Prejudices, First Series)

JACK LONDON

[*If "Portrait of an Immortal Soul" detailed how Mencken dealt with the aspiring, then this eulogy of Jack London (1876–1916) is an example of how he treated the accomplished. Above all, Mencken liked to read well crafted literature, and this is something so difficult to create that a writer who could produce even one or two good novels or stories deserved praise.*

Jack London, Mencken laments, let politics get in the way of his talents, and a few words of historical explanation should be included here, because people with London's politics no longer exist. London was a turn-of-the-century white supremacist who thought that soft living was eroding Anglo-Saxon masculinity. Like Hemingway, London saw the boxing ring as the ultimate arbiter of racial superiority, hence his freakout over the first black heavyweight champion, Jack Johnson. It was London who put out the call for a "Great White Hope" to defeat Johnson. At the same time, London's best fiction reflects his belief that the wild and rugged spaces of America could return men to pioneer-level hardiness.

Racism, rugged individualism, and hyper-masculinity? London must have been a he-man conservative. But no, as Mencken laments, London preached socialism. This was because, in the early twentieth century, "real men" had calluses on their palms and scars on their knuckles. They worked on the docks, in the stockyards, in the mills, and on the farms; and the effete bankers and managers, with their soft clothes and softer bellies, were the practitioners of exploitative capitalism—and the exemplars of political conservatism.

Yet, as Mencken indicates, once London was dead his politics ceased to matter and his writing was all that was left.]

The quasi-science of genealogy, as it is practiced in the United States, is directed almost exclusively toward establishing aristocratic descents for nobodies. That is to say, it records and glorifies decay. Its typical masterpiece is the discovery that the wife of some obscure county judge is the grandchild, infinitely removed, of Mary Queen of Scots, or that the blood of Geoffrey of Monmouth flows in the veins of a Philadelphia stockbroker. How much more profitably its professors might be employed in tracing the lineage of truly salient and distinguished men! For example, the late Jack London. Where did he get his hot artistic passion, his extraordinary skill with words? The man, in truth, was an instinctive artist of a high order, and if ignorance often corrupted his art, it only made the fact of his inborn mastery the more remarkable. No other popular writer of his time did any better writing that you will find in *The Call of the Wild*, or in parts of *John Barleycorn*, or in such short stories as "The Sea Farmer" and "Samuel." Here, indeed, are all the elements of sound fiction: clear thinking, a sense of character, the dramatic instinct, and above all, the adept putting together of words—words charming and slyly significant, words arranged, in a French phrase, for the respiration and the ear. You will never convince me that the aesthetic sensitiveness, so rare, so precious, so distinctively aristocratic, burst into abiogenetic flower on a San Francisco sand-lot. There must have been some intrusion of an alien and superior strain, some pianissimo fillip from above; there was obviously a great deal more to the thing than a routine hatching in low life. Perhaps the explanation is to be sought in a Jewish smear. Jews were not few in California of a generation ago, and one of them, at least, attained to a certain high, if transient, fame with the pen. Moreover, the name London has Jewish smack; the Jews like to call themselves after great cities. I have, indeed, heard this possibility of an Old Testament descent put into an actual rumor. Stranger genealogies are not unknown in seaports. . . .

But London the artist did not live a cappella. There was also London the amateur Great Thinker, and the second often hamstrung the first. That great thinking of his, of course, took color from the sordid misery of his early life; it was, in the main, a jejune Socialism, wholly uncriticised by humor. Some of his propagandist and expository books are almost unbelievably nonsensical, and whenever he allowed any of his so-called ideas to sneak into an imaginative work the intrusion promptly spoiled it. Socialism, in truth, is quite incompatible with art; its cook-tent materialism is fundamentally at war with the first principle of the aesthetic gospel, which is that one daffodil is worth ten shares of Bethlehem Steel. It is not by accident that there has never been a book on Socialism which was also a work of art. Papa Marx's *Das Kapital* at once comes to mind. It is as wholly devoid of graces as *The Origin of Species* or *Science and Health*; one simply cannot conceive a reasonable man reading it without aversion; it is as revolting as a barrel organ. London, preaching Socialism, or quasi-Socialism, or whatever it was that he preached, took over this offensive dullness. The materialistic conception of history was too heavy a load for him to carry. When he would create beautiful books he had to throw it overboard as Wagner threw overboard democracy, the superman and free thought. A sort of temporary Christian created *Parsifal*. A sort of temporary aristocrat created *The Call of the Wild*.

Also in another way London's early absorption of social and economic nostrums damaged him as an artist. It led him into a socialistic exaltation of mere money; it put a touch of avarice into him. Hence his too deadly industry, his relentless thousand words a day, his steady emission of half-done books. The prophet of freedom, he yet sold himself into slavery to the publishers, and paid off with his soul for his ranch, his horses, his trappings of a wealthy cheese-monger. His volumes rolled out almost as fast as those of E. Phillips Oppenheim; he simply could not make them perfect at such a gait. There are books on his list—for example, *The Scarlet Plague* and *The Little Lady of the Big House*—that are little more than garrulous notes for books.

But even in the worst of them one comes upon sudden splashes of brilliant color, stray proofs of the adept penman, half-wistful reminders that London, at bottom, was no fraud. He left enough, I am convinced, to keep him in mind. There was in him a vast delicacy of perception, a high feeling, a sensitiveness to beauty. And there was in him, too, under all his blatancies, a poignant sense of the infinite romance and mystery of human life.

(*Prejudices, First Series*)

JOSEPH CONRAD

[*Probably more than anything, Mencken was a reader, and well-written literature seems to be the one thing that Mencken considered to be beyond satire. Perhaps this was because the act of reading is solitary, and book-writing just does not lend itself to moralistic grandstanding in the way that politics or preaching does. The literary world reveals its absurdity only when the awards are given out (or when critics praise trendy but vacuous work). As Mencken writes, "When one reflects that the Nobel Prize was given up to such third-raters as Benavente, Heidenstam, Gjellerup, and Tagore, with Conrad passed over, one begins to grasp the depth and density of the ignorance prevailing in the world, even among the relatively enlightened."*

In 2021, the Nobel committee assigned the Nobel Prize to Abdulrazak Gurnah, and it's not clear that anyone on the committee had read anything but his name. That the writer turned out to be from Tanzania, one of the more exotic sounding nations on the continent that was the subject of Conrad's most famous work, Heart of Darkness, *turned out to be an unexpected bonus. Readers of literary fiction, a diligent bunch with a high tolerance for exposition, struggled to find Gurnah's works, since he had barely been published outside of the United Kingdom. In the U.S. his books, if available at all, were probably on the shelves next to Benavente, Heidenstam, Gjellerup, and Tagore.*]

Some time ago I put in a blue afternoon re-reading Joseph Conrad's *Youth.* A blue afternoon? What nonsense! The touch of the man is like the touch of Schubert. One approaches him in various and unhappy moods: depressed, dubious, despairing; one leaves him in the clear, yellow sunshine that Nietzsche found in Bizet's music. But here again the phrase is inept. Sunshine suggests the imbecile, barnyard joy of the human kohlrabi—the official optimism of a steadily delighted and increasingly insane Republic. What the enigmatical Pole has to offer is something quite different. If its parallel is to be found in music, it is not in Schubert, but in Beethoven— perhaps even more accurately in Johann Sebastian Bach. It is the joy, not of mere satisfaction, but of understanding—the profound but surely not merry delight which goes with the comprehension of a fundamental fact—above all, of a fact that has been coy and elusive. Certainly the order of the world that Conrad sets forth with such diabolical eloquence and plausibility is no banal moral order, no childish sequence of virtuous causes and edifying effects. Rather, it has an atheistic and even demoniacal smack: to the earnest Bible student it must be more than a little disconcerting. The God he visualizes is no loving papa in a house-coat and carpet-slippers, inculcating the great principles of Christian ethics by applying occasional strokes *a posteriori* [after the fact]. What he sees is something quite different: an extremely ingenious and humorous Improvisatore and Comedian, with a dab of red on His nose and maybe somewhat the worse for drink—a furious and far from amiable banjoist upon the human spine, and rattler of human bones. Kurtz, in *Youth*, makes a capital banjo for that exalted and cynical talent. [This apparently refers to a trilogy of short novels published under the title of one of them, *Youth*, and which contains *Heart of Darkness*; Kurtz is a central figure in *Heart of Darkness*, not *Youth*.] And the music that issues forth—what a superb *Hexentanz* [witch's dance] it is!

One of the curiosities of critical stupidity is the doctrine that Conrad is without humor. No doubt it flows out of a more general error; to wit, the assumption that tragedy is always pathetic, that death itself is inevitably a gloomy business. That error, I suppose, will persist in the world until some extraordinary astute mime conceives the plan of playing *King Lear* as a farce—I mean deliberately. That it is a farce seems to me quite as obvious as the fact that *Romeo and Juliet* is another, this time lamentably coarse. To adopt the contrary theory—to view it as a great moral and spiritual spectacle, capable of purging and uplifting the psyche like marriage to a red-haired widow or a month in the trenches—to toy with such notions is to borrow the critical standards of a party of old ladies weeping over the damnation of the heathen. In point of fact, death, like love, is intrinsically farcical—a solemn kicking of a brick under a plug-hat, and most other human agencies, once they transcend the physical—i.e., the unescapably real—have far more of irony in them than of pathos. Looking back upon them after they have eased one seldom shivers: one smiles—perhaps sourly but nevertheless spontaneously. This, at all events, is the notion that seems to me implicit in every line of Conrad. I give you *Heart of Darkness* as the archetype of his whole work and the keystone of his metaphysical system. Here we have all imaginable human hopes and aspirations reduced to one common denominator of folly and failure, and here we have a play of humor that is infinitely mordant and searching. Turn to pages 136 and 137 of the American edition—the story is in the volume called *Youth*—: the burial of the helmsman. Then to 178–184: Marlowe's last interview with Kurtz's intended. The farce mounts by slow stages to dizzy and breathtaking heights. One hears harsh roars of cosmic laughter, vast splutterings of transcendental mirth, echoing and reechoing down the black corridors of empty space. The curtain descends at last upon a wild dance in a dissecting room. The mutilated dead rise up and jig. . . .

It is curious, re-reading a thrice-familiar story, how often one finds surprises in it. I have been amazed, toward the close of *The End of the Tether*, to discover that the Fair Maid was wrecked, not by the deliberate act of Captain Whalley, but by the machination of the unspeakable Massey. How is one to account for so preposterous an error? Certainly I thought I knew *The End of the Tether* as well as I knew anything in this world—and yet there was that incredible misunderstanding in it, lodged firmly in my mind. Perhaps there is criticism of a sort in my blunder: it may be a fact that the old skipper willed the thing himself—that his willing it is visible in all that goes before—that Conrad, in introducing Massey's puerile infamy at the end, made some sacrifice of inner veracity to the exigencies of what, at bottom, is somewhat too neat and well-made a tale. The story, in fact, belongs to the author's earlier manner; I guess that it was written before *Youth* and surely before *Heart of Darkness*. But for all that, its proportions remain truly colossal. It is one of the most magnificent narratives, long or short, old or new, in the English language, and with *Youth* and *Heart of Darkness* it makes up what is probably the best book of imaginative writing that the English literature of the Twentieth Century can yet show. Conrad learned a great deal after he wrote it, true enough. In *Lord Jim*, in *Victory*, and above all in *A Personal Record*, there are momentary illuminations, blinding flashes of brilliance that he was incapable of in those days of experiment; but no other book of his seems to me to hold so steadily to so high a general level—none other, as a whole, is more satisfying and more marvelous. There is in *Heart of Darkness* a perfection of design which one encounters only rarely and miraculously in prose fiction: it belongs rather to music. I can't imagine taking a single sentence out of that stupendous tale without leaving a visible gap; it is as thoroughly *durch componieri* [throughgoing, of one piece] as a fugue. And I can't imagine adding anything to it, even so little as a word, without doing it damage. As it stands it is austerely and beautifully perfect, just as the slow movement of the Unfinished Symphony is perfect.

I observe of late a tendency to examine the English of Conrad rather biliously. This folly is cultivated chiefly in England, where, I suppose, chauvinistic motives enter into the matter. It is the just boast of great empires that they draw in talents from near and far, exhausting the little nations to augment their own puissance; it is their misfortune that these talents often remain defectively assimilated. Conrad remained the Slav to the end. The people of his tales, whatever he calls them, are always as much Slavs as he is; the language in which he describes them retains a sharp, exotic flavor. But to say that this flavor constitutes a blemish is to say something so preposterous that only schoolmasters and their dupes may be thought of as giving it credit. The truly first-rate writer is not one who uses the language as such dolts demand that it be used; he is the one who reworks it in spite of their prohibitions. It is his distinction that he thinks in a manner different from the thinking of ordinary men; that he is free from that slavery to embalmed ideas which makes them so respectable and so dull. Obviously, he cannot translate his notions into terms of everyday without doing violence to their inner integrity; as well ask Richard Strauss to funnel all his music into the chaste jugs of Prof. Dr. Jadassohn. What Conrad brought into English was a new way of putting words together. His style now amazes and irritates pedants because it does not roll along in the old ruts. Well, it is precisely that rolling along in the old ruts that he tried to avoid—and it was precisely that avoidance which made him what he is. What lies under most of his alleged sins seems to me to be simple enough: he views English logically and analytically, and not through a haze of senseless traditions and arbitrary taboos. No Oxford mincing is in him. If he cannot find his phrase above the salt, he seeks it below. His English, in a word, is innocent. And if, at times, there gets into it a color that is strange and even bizarre, then the fact is something to rejoice over, for a living language is like a man suffering incessantly from small internal hemorrhages, and what it needs above all else is constant transfusions of new blood from other tongues. The day the gates go up, that day it begins to die.

A very great man, this Mr. Conrad. As yet, I believe decidedly under estimated, even by many of his post-mortem advocates. Most of his first acclaimers mistook him for a mere romantic—a talented but somewhat uncouth follower of the Stevenson tradition, with the orthodox cutlass exchanged for the Malay kris. Later on he began to be heard of as a linguistic and vocational marvel; it was astonishing that any man bred to Polish should write English at all, and more astonishing that a country gentleman from the Ukraine should hold a master's certificate in the British merchant marine. Such banal attitudes are now archaic, but I suspect that they have been largely responsible for the slowness with which his fame has spread in the world. At all events, he is vastly less read and esteemed in foreign parts than he ought to be, and very few Continental Europeans have risen to any genuine comprehension of his stature. When one reflects that the Nobel Prize was given to such third-raters as Benavente, Heidenstam, Gjellerup and Tagore, with Conrad passed over, one begins to grasp the depth and density of the ignorance prevailing in the world, even among the relatively enlightened. One *Lord Jim*, as human document and as work of art, is worth all the works produced by all the Benaventes and Gjellerups since the time of Rameses II. It is, indeed, an indecency of criticism to speak of such unlike things in the same breath: as well talk of Brahms in terms of Mendelssohn. Nor is *Lord Jim* a chance masterpiece, an isolated peak. On the contrary, it is but one unit in a long series of extraordinary and almost incomparable works—a series sprung suddenly and overwhelmingly into full dignity with *Almayer's Folly*. I challenge the nobility and gentry of Christendom to point to another Opus 1 as magnificently planned and turned out as *Almayer's Folly*. The more one studies it, the more it seems miraculous. If it is not a work of absolute genius then no work of absolute genius exists on this earth.

(*Prejudices, Fifth Series*)

THE BUGABOO

[*I can always tell when a commentator has actually read Nietzsche, as the man and his philosophy are easy to misunderstand. Leftists tend to dismiss Nietzschean thought by noting his supposed influence on Germany's murderous, antisemitic historical trajectory, ignoring the fact that Nietzsche hated antisemites: at one point he said they should all be shot, and he even refused to attend his own sister's wedding to a notorious antisemite, precisely because of the man's antisemitism. (That sister was his literary executor and was an admirer of Hitler; she was largely responsible for the defamatory myth that Nietzsche was a Nazi progenitor.)*

Unfortunately, that myth is still common, as is misunderstanding of his work, especially the superman concept. Rather than referring to blond-haired, blue-eyed goosesteppers, Nietzsche was referring to self-aware, critically minded individuals who are in control of themselves—*not seeking control over others.*

Mencken was free of such misunderstandings, and was such an admirer of Nietzsche that he not only translated Nietzsche's arguably best book, The Anti-Christ, *into English, but also wrote the first English-language expository work on Nietzsche,* The Philosophy of Friedrich Nietzsche.]

Much of the current blabber against the late Friedrich Wilhelm Nietzsche is grounded upon the doctrine that his capacity for consecutive thought was clearly limited. In support of this doctrine his critics cite the fact that most of his books are no more than strings of apothegms, with the subject changing on every second page. All this, it must be obvious, is fundamentally nonsensical. What deceives the professors is the traditional garrulity and prolixity of philosophers. Because the average philosophical writer, when he essays to expose his ideas, makes such copious drafts upon the parts of speech that the dictionary is almost emptied, these defective observers jump to the conclusion that his intrinsic notions are of corresponding elaborateness. This is not true. I have read Kant, Hegel, Spencer, Spinoza,

Descartes, Leibnitz, Fichte, Locke, Schleiermacher, James and Bergson, not to mention the Greeks and the Romans; the more I read, the more I am convinced that it is not true.

What makes philosophy hard to read is not the complexity of the ideas set forth, but the complexity of the language in which they are concealed. The typical philosopher, having, say, four new notions, drowns them in a sea of words—all borrowed from other philosophers. One must wade through endless chapters of old stuff to get at the minute kernels of the new stuff. . . . This process Nietzsche avoided. He always assumed that his readers knew the books, and that it was unnecessary to rewrite them. Having an idea that seemed to him to be novel and original, he stated it in as few words as possible, and then shut down. Sometimes he got it into a hundred words; sometimes it took a thousand. But he never wrote a word too many; he never pumped up an idea to make it appear bigger than it actually was. . . . The professors are not used to that sort of writing. Nietzsche employed too few words for them—and he had too many ideas.

(*The Smart Set*, January 1920)

FRIEDRICH NIETZSCHE

[This excerpt is from the preface to The Philosophy of Friedrich Nietzsche, *which was published in 1908 and was the first work on Nietzsche to appear in English. Mencken was only 28 at the time, and as part of his research read nearly the entirety of Nietzsche's writings, mostly in the original German. Perhaps the most surprising thing about Mencken's book is how good it is, which in part explains why it's still in print.]*

That Nietzsche has been making progress of late goes without saying. No reader of current literature, nor even of current periodicals, can have failed to notice the increasing pressure of his ideas. When his name was first heard in England and America, toward the end of the nineties, he suffered much by the fact that few of his advocates had been at any pains to understand him. Thus misrepresented, he took on the aspect of an horrific intellectual hobgoblin, half Bakunin and half Byron, a sacrilegious and sinister fellow, the father of all the wilder ribaldries of the day. In brief, like Ibsen before him, he had to bear many a burden that was not his. But in the course of time the truth about him gradually precipitated itself from this cloud of unordered enthusiasm, and his principal ideas began to show themselves clearly. Then the discovery was made that the report of them had been far more appalling than the substance. Some of them, indeed, had already slipped into respectable society in disguise, as the original inspirations of lesser sages, and others, on examination, turned out to be quite harmless, and even comforting. The worst that could be said of most of them was that they stood in somewhat violent opposition to the common platitudes, that they were a bit vociferous in denying this planet to be the best of all possible worlds. Heresy, of course, but falling, fortunately enough, upon ears fast growing attuned to heretical music. The old order now had fewer to defend it than in days gone by. The feeling that it must yield to something better, that contentment must give way to striving and struggle, that any change was better than no change at all—this feeling was abroad in the world. And if the program of change that Nietzsche offered was startling at first hearing, it was at least no more startling than the programs offered by other reformers. Thus he got his day in court at last and thus he won the serious attention of open-minded and reflective folk.

Not, of course, that Nietzsche threatens, today or in the near future, to make a grand conquest of Christendom, as Paul conquered, or the unknown Father of Republics. Far from it, indeed. Filtered through the comic sieve of a Shaw or sentimentalized by a Roosevelt, some of his ideas show a considerable popularity, but in their original state they are not likely to inflame millions. Broadly viewed, they stand in direct opposition to every dream that soothes the slumber of mankind in the mass, and therefore mankind in the mass must needs be suspicious of them, at least for years to come. They are pre-eminently for the man who is not of the mass, for the man whose head is lifted, however little, above the common level. They justify the success of that man, as Christianity justifies the failure of the man below. And so they give no promise of winning the race in general from its old idols, despite the fact that the pull of natural laws and of elemental appetites is on their side. But inasmuch as an idea, to make itself felt in the world, need not convert the many who serve and wait but only the few who rule, it must be manifest that the Nietzschean creed, in the long run, gives promise of exercising a very real influence upon human thought. Reduced to a single phrase, it may be called a counterblast to sentimentality—and it is precisely by breaking down sentimentality, with its fondness for moribund gods, that human progress is made. If Nietzsche had left no other vital message to his time, he would have at least forced and deserved a hearing for his warning that Christianity is a theory for those who distrust and despair of their strength, and not for those who hope and fight on. . . .

Of all modern philosophers Nietzsche is the least dull. He was undoubtedly the greatest German prose writer of his generation, and even when one reads him through the English veil it is impossible to escape the charm and color of his phrases and the pyrotechnic brilliance of this thinking.

(from the Preface to the Third Edition of *The Philosophy of Friedrich Nietzsche*)

AMBROSE BIERCE

[During the Civil War, Ambrose Bierce was shot in the head. That Mencken, who knew Bierce in the intimate way that one old crank knows another, left this detail out of his piece on Bierce speaks to Mencken's thought processes. Who cared if Bierce felt the hot sting of confederate lead? It was the acidic prose and black humor that Mencken valued. He appreciated gallows humor, and no one could tell jokes with his head in the noose like Bierce.

Bierce spent his productive years working on newspapers, writing thousands of pages of work that today hardly anyone would even skim over. He then used his retirement years to compile that work into a dozen untouched, mostly unread volumes—a testament to erroneous self-evaluation. Such erroneous self-regard is so common in writers that, when I read Mencken's piece, I felt envious that Bierce undoubtedly possessed a few devoted and deluded readers who plowed through all twelve volumes of his compilation.

For the rest of us, The Devil's Dictionary *and the Civil War stories suffice.]*

The reputation of Ambrose Bierce, like that of Edgar Saltus, has always had an occult, artificial drug-store flavor. He has been hymned in a passionate, voluptuous, inordinate way by a small band of disciples, and he has been passed over altogether by the great majority of American critics, and no less by the great majority of American readers. Certainly it would be absurd to say that he is generally read, even by the intelligentsia. Most of his books, in fact, are out of print and almost unobtainable, and there is little evidence that his massive Collected Works, printed in twelve volumes between 1909 and 1912, have gone into anything even remotely approaching a wide circulation. I have a suspicion, indeed, that Bierce did a serious disservice to himself when he put those twelve volumes together. Already an old man at the time, he permitted his nostalgia for his lost youth to get the better of his critical faculty, never very powerful at best, and the result was a depressing assemblage of worn-out and fly-blown stuff, much of it quite unreadable. If he had boiled the collection down to four volumes, or even to six, it might have got him somewhere, but as it is, his good work is lost in a morass of bad and indifferent work. I doubt that any one save the Bierce fanatics aforesaid has ever plowed through the whole twelve volumes. They are filled with epigrams against frauds long dead and forgotten, and echoes of old and puerile newspaper controversies, and experiments in fiction that belong to a dark and expired age. But in the midst of all this blather there are some pearls—more accurately, there are two of them. One consists of the series of epigrams called *The Devil's Dictionary*; the other consists of the war stories commonly called "Tales of Soldiers and Civilians." Among the latter are some of the best war stories ever written—things fully worthy to be ranged beside Zola's "L'Attaque du Moulin," Kipling's "The Taking of Lungtungpen," or Ludwig Thoma's "Ein Bayrischer Soldat." And among the former are some of the most gorgeous witticism in the English language.

Bierce, I believe, was the first writer of fiction ever to treat war realistically. He antedated even Zola. It is common to say that he came our of the Civil War with a deep and abiding loathing of slaughter—that he wrote his war stories in disillusion, and as a sort of pacifist. But this is certainly not believed by any one who knew him, as I did in his last years. What he got out of his service in the field was not a sentimental horror of it, but a cynical delight in it. It appeared to him as a sort of magnificent *reductio ad absurdum* of all romance. The world viewed war as something heroic, glorious, idealistic. Very well, he would show how sordid and filthy it was—how stupid and degrading. But to say this is not to say that he disapproved of it. On the contrary, he vastly enjoyed the chance its discussion gave him to set forth dramatically what he was always talking about and gloating over: the infinite imbecility of man. There was nothing of the milk of human kindness in old Ambrose; he did not get the nickname of Bitter Bierce for nothing. What delighted him most in this life was the spectacle of human cowardice and folly. He put man, intellectually, somewhere between the sheep and the horned cattle, and as a hero somewhere below the rats. His war stories, even when they deal with the heroic, do not depict soldiers as heroes; they depict them as bewildered fools, doing things without sense, submitting to torture and outrage without resistance, dying at last like hogs in Chicago, the former literary capital of the United States. So far in this life, indeed, I have encountered no more thorough-going cynic than Bierce was. His disbelief in man went even further than Mark Twain's; he was quite unable to imagine the heroic, in any ordinary sense. Nor, for that matter, the wise. Man to him, was the most stupid and ignoble of animals. But at the same time the most amusing. Out of the spectacle of life about him he got an unflagging and Gargantuan joy. The obscene farce of politics delighted him. He was an almost amorous connoisseur of theology and theologians. He howled with mirth whenever he thought of a professor, a doctor or a husband. His favorites among his contemporaries were such zanies as Bryan, Roosevelt and Hearst.

Another character that marked him, perhaps flowing out of this same cynicism, was his curious taste for the macabre. All of his stories show it. He delighted in hangings, autopsies, dissecting-rooms. Death to him was not something repulsive, but a sort of low comedy—the last act of a squalid and rib-rocking buffoonery. When, grown old and weary, he departed for Mexico, and there—if legend is to believed—marched into the revolution then going on, and had himself shot, there was certainly nothing in the transaction to surprise his acquaintances. The whole thing was typically Biercian. He died happy, one may be sure, if his executioners made a botch of dispatching him—if there was a flash of the grotesque at the end. Once I enjoyed the curious experience of going to a funeral with him. His conversation to and from the crematory was superb—a long series of gruesome but highly amusing witticisms. He had tales to tell of crematories that had caught fire and singed the mourners, of dead bibuli whose mortal remains had exploded, of widows guarding the fires all night to make sure that their dead husbands did not escape. The gentleman whose carcass we were burning had been a literary critic. Bierce suggested that his ashes be molded into bullets and shot at publishers, that they be presented to the library of the New York Lodge of Elks, that they be mailed anonymously to Ella Wheeler Wilcox. Later on, when he heard that they had been buried in Iowa, he exploded in colossal mirth. The last time I saw him he predicted that the Christians out there would dig them up and throw them over the State line. On his own writing desk, he once told me, he kept the ashes of his son. I suggested idly that the ceremonial urn must be a formidable ornament. "Urn hell!" he answered. "I keep them in a cigarbox!"

There is no adequate life of Bierce, and I doubt if any will ever be written. His daughter, with some asperity, has forbidden the publication of his letters, and shows little hospitality to volunteer biographers. One of his disciples, the late George Sterling, wrote about him with great insight and affection, and another, Herman George Scheffauer, has greatly extended his fame abroad, especially in Germany. But Sterling is dead and Scheffauer seems indisposed to do him in the grand manner, and I know of no one else competent to do so. He liked mystification, and there are whole stretches of his long life that are unaccounted for. His end had symmetry in it, too. It is assumed that he was killed in Mexico, but no eyewitness has ever come forward, and so the fact, if it is a fact, remains hanging in the air.

Bierce followed Poe in most of his short stories, but it is only a platitude to say that he wrote much better than Poe. His English was less tight and artificial; he had a far firmer grasp upon character; he was less literary and more observant. Unluckily, his stories seem destined to go the way of Poe's. Their influence upon the modern American short story, at least upon its higher levels, is almost nil. When they are imitated at all, it is by the lowly hacks who manufacture thrillers for the cheap magazines. Even his chief disciples, Sterling and Scheffauer, did not follow him. Sterling became a poet whose glowing romanticism was at the opposite pole to Bierce's cold realism, and Scheffauer, interested passionately in experiment, and strongly influenced by German example, has departed completely from the classicism of the master. Meanwhile it remains astonishing that his wit is so little remembered. In *The Devil's Dictionary* are some of the most devastating epigrams ever written. "Ah, that we could fall into women's arms without falling into their hands"; it is hard to find a match for that in Oscar [Wilde] himself. I recall another: "Opportunity: a favorable occasion for grasping a disappointment." Another: "Once: enough." A third: "Husband: one who having dined is charged with the care of the plate." A fourth: "Our vocabulary is defective: we give the same name to woman's lack of temptation and man's lack of opportunity." A fifth: "Slang is the speech of him who robs the literary garbage cans on their way to the dump."

But I leave the rest to your own exploration—if you can find a copy of *The Devil's Dictionary*. It was never printed in full, save in the ghastly Collected Works that I have mentioned. A part of it, under the title of "The Cynics Word-Book," was first published as a separate volume, but it is long out of print. The other first editions of Bierce are scarce, and begin to command high premiums. Three-fourths of his books were published by obscure publishers, some of them not too reputable. He spent his last quarter of a century in voluntary immolation on a sort of burning ghat, worshiped by his small band of zealots, but almost unnoticed by the rest of the human race. His life was a long sequence of bitter ironies. I believe that he enjoyed it.

(Prejudices, Sixth Series)

THE MAN WITHIN

[*If you raise a child in some fundamentalist, backwater Baptist Church, one that espouses biblical literalism and forces a psychological burka over the heads of preteen girls, one that preaches that Hellfire will roast the feet of "bad" children for the most innocuous of thought crimes, you will mould a person with immutable beliefs.*

If you take that same child, say at the age of 16 or 17, and inundate him with the gifts of logical inquiry, the scientific method, and an understanding of basic biology and statistics, you can turn him into atheist intellectually. But what you'll end up with is a Baptist who doesn't believe in God. The same is true of being an American, and Mencken understood this about Mark Twain.

Twain was outspokenly opposed to America's imperialist adventures, particularly the Philippines invasion, but pulled his punches against religion while he was still alive; his posthumous Letters from the Earth *and* What Is Man?, *though, are blistering.*

Nietzsche didn't pull his punches, and Mencken admired him for it, for foregoing a milquetoast atheism in favor of a raging anti-theism; at the same time he seems to look down on Twain for his reticence. Mencken, an admirer of great fiction, and thus of Huckleberry Finn, *quite possibly stopped himself from accusing Twain of cowardice only because of his admiration for Twain's literary talent.*

But what are we to make of an author like Mark Twain who privately thought like Nietzsche, but publicly wrote like Dave Barry—funny, but fairly innocuous? Was Twain a coward or did he simply have "good sense"? Well, Twain rhymes with Paine, and it's certain that Mark himself recognized what happened to his intellectual predecessor, ol' Thomas, when he blasted religion in The Rights of Man. *Paine's anti-religious stance is still unacceptable to many; some historians omit mention of everything after* Common Sense *when discussing Paine, and worse, some school books refer to Paine as a Quaker.*

Better to light a good cigar, hide your true opinions, throw out a few country aphorisms, and rake in the dough.]

The bitter, of course, goes with the sweet. To be an American is unquestionably, to be the noblest, the grandest, the proudest mammal that ever hoofed the verdure of God's green footstool. Often, in the black abyss of night, the thought that I am one awakes me with a blast of trumpets, and I am thrown into a cold sweat by contemplation of the fact. I shall cherish it on the scaffold; it will console me in Hell. But there is no perfection under Heaven, so even an American has his small blemishes, his scarcely discernible weaknesses, his minute traces of vice and depravity. Mark, alas had them: he was as thoroughly American as a Knight of Pythias, a Wheeling stogie, or Prohibition. One might also exhibit his effigy in a museum as the archetype of *Homo americanus*. And what were these stigmata that betrayed him? In chief, they were two in number, and both lay at the very foundation of his character. On the one hand, there was his immovable moral certainty, his firm belief that he knew what was right from what was wrong, and that all who differed from him were, in some obscure way, men of an inferior and sinister order. And on the other hand, there was his profound intellectual timorousness, his abiding fear of his own ideas, his incurable cowardice in the face of public disapproval. These two characteristics colored his whole thinking; they showed themselves in his every attitude and gesture. They were the visible signs of his limitation as an Emersonian Man Thinking, and they were the bright symbols of his nationality. He was great in every way an American could be great, but when he came to the border of his Americanism he came to the end of his greatness.

The true Mark Twain is only partly on view in his actual books—that is, in his printed books. The real *Mensch* [man] was not the somewhat heavy-handed satirist of *A Tramp Abroad* and *Tom Sawyer*. He was not even the extraordinarily fine and delicate artist of *Joan of Arc* and *Huckleberry Finn*. Nay, he was a different bird altogether—an intensely serious and even lugubrious man, an iconoclast of the most relentless sort, a man not so much amused by the spectacle of life as appalled by it, a pessimist to the last degree. Nothing could be more unsound than the Mark legend—the legend of the lighthearted and kindly old clown. The real Mark was a man haunted to the point of distraction by the endless and meaningless tragedy of existence—a man whose thoughts turned to it constantly, in season and out of season. And to think, with him, was to write; he was, for all his laziness, the most assiduous of scribblers; he piled up notes, sketches of books and articles, even whole books, about it, almost mountain high.

Well, why did these notes, sketches, articles and books get no further? Why do most of them remain unprinted, even to-day? You will find the answer in a prefatory note that Mark appended to *What Is Man?* published privately in 1905. I quote it in full:

> The studies for these papers were begun twenty-five or twenty-seven years ago. The papers were written seven years ago. I have examined them once or twice per year since and found them satisfactory. I have just examined them again, and am still satisfied that they speak the truth. Every thought in them has been thought (and accepted as unassailable truth) by millions upon millions of men—and concealed, kept private. Why did they not speak out? Because they dreaded (and could not bear) the disapproval of the people around them. Why have I not published? The same reason has restrained me, I think. I can find no other.

Imagine a man writing so honest and excellent a book, imagine him examining it and re-examining it and always finding it good—and yet holding off the printing of it for twenty-five years, and then issuing it timorously and behind the door, in an edition of 250 copies, none of them for sale. Even his death did not quench his fear. His executors, taking it over as part of his goods, withheld the book for five years more—and then printed it very discreetly, with the betraying preface omitted. Surely it would be impossible in the literature of any other civilized country since the Middle Ages to find anything to match that long hesitation. Here was a man of the highest dignity in the national letters, and here was a book into which he had put the earnest convictions of his lifetime, a book carefully and deliberately written, a book representing him more accurately any other, both as artist and as man—and yet it had to wait thirty-five years before it saw the light of day. An astounding affair, in conscience—but thoroughly American, Messieurs, thoroughly American. Mark knew his countrymen. He know their intense suspicion of ideas, the blind hatred of heterodoxy, their bitter way of dealing with dissenters. He knew how, their priorities outraged, they would turn upon even the gaudiest hero and roll him in the mud. And knowing, he was afraid. He "dreaded the disapproval of the people around him." But part of that dread, I suspect was peculiarly internal. In brief, Mark himself was also an American, and he shared the national horror of the unorthodox. His own speculations always half appalled him. He was not only afraid to utter what he believed, he was even a bit timorous about believing what he believed.

The weakness takes a good deal from his stature. It leaves him radiating a subtle flavor of the second-rate. With more courage, he would have gone a great deal further, and left a far deeper mark upon the intellectual history of his time. Not, perhaps, intrinsically as an artist. He got as far in that direction as it is possible for a man of his training to go. *Huckleberry Finn* is a truly stupendous piece of work—perhaps the greatest novel ever written in English. And it would be difficult to surpass the sheer artistry of such things as *A Connecticut Yankee, Captain Stormfield, Joan of Arc,* and parts of *A Tramp Abroad.* But there is more to the making of literature than the mere depiction of human beings at their obscene follies; there is also the play of ideas. Mark had ideas that were clear, that were vigorous, and that had an immediate appositeness. True enough, most of them were not quite original. As Prof. Schoenmann, of Harvard, once demonstrated, he got the notion of the *The Mysterious Stranger* from Adolf Wilbrandt's *Der Meister von Palmyra;* much of *What Is Man?* you will find in the forgotten harangues of [Robert] Ingersoll; in other directions he borrowed right and left. But it is only necessary to read either of the books I have just mentioned to see how thoroughly he recast everything he wrote; how brilliantly it came to be marked by the charm of his own personality; how he got his own peculiar and unmatchable eloquence into the merest statement of it. When, entering these regions of his true faith, he yielded to a puerile timidity—when he sacrificed his conscience and his self-respect to the idiotic popularity that so often more than half dishonored him—then he not only did a cruel disservice to his own permanent fame, but inflicted genuine damage upon the national literature. He was greater than all the others because he was more American, but in this one way, at least, he was less than them for the same reason.

Well, there he stands—a bit concealed, a bit fake, but still a colossus. As I have said, I am inclined year by year to rate his achievement higher. In such a work as *Huckleberry Finn* there is something that vastly transcends the merit of all ordinary books. It has a merit that is special and extraordinary; it lifts itself above all hollow standards and criteria; it seems greater every time I read it. The books that gave Mark his first celebrity do not hold up so well. "The Jumping Frog" still wrings snickers, but after all, it is commonplace at bottom; even an Ellis Parker Butler might have conceivably written it. *The Innocents Abroad,* re-read today, is largely tedious. Its humors are artificial; its audacities are stale; its eloquence belongs to the fancy journalism of a past generation. Even *Tom Sawyer* and *A Tramp Abroad* have long stretches of flatness. But in *Huckleberry Finn,* though he didn't know it at the time and never quite realized it, Mark found himself. There, working against the grain, heartily sick of the book before it was done, always putting it off until tomorrow, he hacked out a masterpiece that expands as year chases year. There, if I am not wrong, he produced the greatest work of the imagination that These States have yet seen.

(*The Smart Set*, October 1919)

7

SEX &
MORALITY

THE BLUSHFUL MYSTERY

[*To abstain from sex is to always be thinking about it. One supposes that opposing sex, on grounds of its being a sin, makes the obsession even worse. Mencken's full talent is on display with this passage: "The Puritan, for all his pretensions, is the worst of materialists. Passed through his sordid and unimaginative mind, even the stupendous romance of sex is reduced to a disgusting transaction in physiology. As artist he is thus hopeless; as well expect an auctioneer to qualify for the Sistine Chapel Choir." The writing is not subtle, but the subtext is: sexual prudes are against lovemaking because they are about as good at it as an auctioneer would be in the Sistine choir. In other words, Puritans do it badly, and because of this they see sex as only a debased physical transaction, and because of that they consider it a sin.*

From this, Mencken veers back into familiar territory where he again condemns the fantasies of monogamous marriage. He makes comments about this often enough that one wonders whether he was trying to keep some longing of his own at bay—which he did until he was 50, well after he wrote this essay. Middle-aged married men, like myself, begrudge single men nothing, and see no reason to ridicule their ways of life. Still, one wonders why those who are single by choice never have anything good to say about an institution that, in at least some cases, isn't so bad.]

1. Sex Hygiene

The literature of sex hygiene, once so scanty and so timorous, now piles mountain high. There are at least a dozen formidable series of books of instruction for inquirers of all ages, beginning with *What Every Child of Ten Should Know* and ending with *What a Woman of Forty-five Should Know*, and they all sell amazingly. Scores of diligent authors, some medical, some clerical and some merely shrewdly chautauqual, grow rich at the industry of composing them. One of these amateur Havelock Ellises had the honor, during the last century, of instructing men in the elements of the sacred sciences. He was then the pastor of a fourth-rate church in a decaying neighborhood and I was sent to his Sunday-school in response to some obscure notion that the agony of it would improve me. Presently he disappeared, and for a long while I heard nothing about him. Then he came into sudden prominence as the author of such a series of handbooks and as the chief stockholder, it would seem, in the publishing house printing them. By the time he died, a few years ago, he had been so well rewarded by a just God that he was able to leave funds to establish a missionary college in some remote and heathen land.

This holy man, I believe, was honest, and took his platitudinous compositions quite seriously. Regarding other contributors to the literature it may be said without malice that their altruism is obviously corrupted by a good deal of hocus-pocus. Some of them lecture in the chautauquas, peddling their books before and after charming the yokels. Others, being members of the faculty, seem to carry on medical practice on the side. Yet others are kept in profitable jobs by the salacious old men who finance vice crusaders. So, too, with actual vice crusaders. The books of the latter, like the sex hygiene books, are often sold, not as wisdom, but as pornography. True enough, they are always displayed in the show-window of the small-town Methodist Book Concerns—but you will also find them in the back-rooms of dubious second-hand book-stores, side by side with the familiar scarlet-backed editions of Rabelais, Margaret of Navarre and Balzac's *Droll Tales*. Some time ago, in a book advertisement headed "Snappy Fiction," I found announcements of *My Battles with Vice*, by Virginia Brooks—and *Life of My Heart*, by Victoria Cross. The former was described by the publisher as a record of "personal experiences in the fight against the gray wolves and love pirates of modern society." The book was offered to all comers by mail. One may easily imagine the effects of such an offer.

But even the most serious and honest of the sex hygiene volumes are probably futile, for they are all founded upon a pedagogical error. That is to say, they are all founded upon an attempt to explain a romantic mystery in terms of exact science. Nothing could be more absurd: as well attempt to interpret Beethoven in terms of mathematical physics—as many a famous contrapuntist, indeed, has tried to do. The mystery of sex presents itself to the young, not as a scientific problem to be solved, but as a romantic emotion to be accounted for. The only result of the current endeavor to explain its phenomena by seeking parallels in botany is to make botany obscene.

. . .

2. Art and Sex

One of the favorite notions of the Puritan mullahs who specialize in this moral pornography is that the sex instinct, if suitably repressed may be "sublimated" into the higher sorts of idealism, and especially into aesthetic idealism. That notion is to be found in all their books; upon it they ground the theory that the enforcement of chastity by a huge force of spies, stool pigeons and police would convert the republic into a nation of incomparable uplifters, forward-lookers and artists. All this, of course, is simply pious fudge. If the notion were actually sound, then all the great artists of the world would come from the ranks of the hermetically repressed, i.e., from the ranks of Puritan old maids, male and female. But the truth is, as every one knows, that the great artists of the world are never Puritans, and seldom even ordinarily respectable. No virtuous man—that is, virtuous in the Y.M.C.A. sense—has ever painted a picture worth looking at, or written a symphony worth hearing, or a book worth reading, and it is highly improbable that the thing has ever been done by a virtuous woman. The actual effect of repression, lamentable though it may be, is to destroy idealism altogether. The Puritan, for all his pretensions, is the worst of materialists. Passed through his sordid and unimaginative mind, even the stupendous romance of sex is reduced to a disgusting transaction in physiology. As artist he is thus hopeless; as well expect an auctioneer to qualify for the Sistine Chapel choir. All he ever achieves, taking pen or brush in hand, is a feeble burlesque of his betters, all of whom, by his hog's theology, are doomed to hell.

3. A Loss to Romance

Perhaps the worst thing that this sex hygiene nonsense has accomplished is the thing mourned by Agnes Repplier in *The Repeal of Reticence*. In America, at least, innocence has been killed, and romance has been sadly wounded by the discharge of smutty artillery. The flapper is no longer naive and charming; she goes to the altar of God with a learned and even cynical glitter in her eye. The veriest school-girl of to-day, fed upon Forel, Sylvanus Stall, Reginald Wright Kauffman and the Freud books, knows as much as the midwife of 1885, and spends a good deal more time discharging and disseminating her information. All this, of course, is highly embarrassing to the more romantic and ingenious sort of men, of whom I have the honor to be one. We are constantly in the position of General Mitchener in Shaw's one-acter, *Press Cuttings*, when he begs Mrs. Farrell, the talkative charwoman, to reserve her confidences for her medical adviser. One often wonders, indeed, what women now talk of to doctors. . . .

Please do not misunderstand me here. I do not object to this New Freedom on moral grounds, but on aesthetic grounds. In the relations between the sexes, all beauty is founded upon romance, all romance is founded upon mystery, and all mystery is founded upon ignorance, or, failing that, upon the deliberate denial of the known truth. To be in love is merely to be in a state of perceptual anaesthesia—to mistake an ordinary young man for a Greek god or an ordinary young woman for a goddess. But how can this condition of mind survive the deadly matter-of-factness which sex hygiene and the new science of eugenics impose? How can a woman continue to believe in the honor, courage and loving tenderness of a man after she has learned, perhaps by affidavit, that his hemoglobin count is 117%, that he is free from sugar and albumen, that his blood pressure is 112/79 and that his Wasserman reaction is negative? . . . Moreover, all this new-fangled "frankness" tends to dam up, at least for civilized adults, one of the principal wellsprings of art, to wit, impropriety. What is neither hidden nor forbidden is seldom very charming. If women, continuing their present tendency to its logical goal, end by going stark naked, there will be no more poets and painters, but only dermatologists and photographers. . . .

4. Sex on the Stage

The effort to convert the theater into a forum of solemn sex discussion is another abhorrent by-product of the sex hygiene rumble-bumble. Fortunately, it seems to be failing. A few years ago, crowds flocked to see Brieux's "Les Avariés," but to-day it is forgotten, and its successors are all obscure. The movement originated in Germany with the production of Frank Wedekind's *Fruhlings Erwachen* [Springtime Awakening]. The Germans gaped and twisted in their seats for a season or two, and then abandoned sex as a horror and went back to sex as a comedy. This last is what it actually should be, at least in the theater. The theater is no place for painful speculation; it is a place for diverting representation. Its best and truest sex plays are not such overstrained shockers as *Le Mariage d' Olympe* and *Damaged Goods*, but such penetrating and excellent comedies as *Much Ado About Nothing* and *The Taming of the Shrew*. In *Much Ado* we have an accurate and unforgettable picture of the way in which the normal male of the human species is brought to the altar—that is, by the way of appealing to his hollow vanity, the way of capitalizing his native and ineradicable asininity. And in *The Taming of the Shrew* we have a picture of the way in which the average woman, having so snared him, is purged of her resultant vainglory and bombast, and thus reduced to decent discipline and decorum, that the marriage may go on in solid tranquility.

The whole drama of sex, in real life, as well as on the stage, revolves around these two enterprises. One-half of it consists of pitting the native intelligence of women against the native sentimentality of men, and the other half consists of bringing women into a reasonable order, that their superiority may not be too horribly obvious. To the first division belong the dramas of courtship, and a good many of those of marital conflict. In each case the essential drama is not a tragedy but a comedy—nay, a farce. In each case the essential drama is not between imperishable verities but between mere vanities and pretensions. This is the essence of the comic: the unmasking of fraud, its destruction by worse fraud. Marriage, as we know it in Christendom, though its utility is obvious and its necessity is at least arguable, is just such a series of frauds. It begins with the fraud that the impulse to it is lofty, unearthly and disinterested. It proceeds to the fraud that both parties are equally eager for it and equally benefited by it—which actually happens only when two Mondays come together. And it rests thereafter upon the fraud that what is once agreeable (or tolerable) remains agreeable ever thereafter—that I shall be exactly the same man in 1938 that I am to-day, and that my wife will be the same woman, and intrigued by the merits of the same man. This last assumption is so outrageous that, on purely evidential and logical grounds, not even the most sentimental person would support it. It thus becomes necessary to reinforce it by attaching to it the concept of honor. That is to say, it is held up, not on the ground that it is actually true, but on the ground that a recognition of its truth is part of the bargain made at the altar, and that a repudiation of this bargain would be dishonorable. Here we have honor, which is based upon a sense of the deepest and most inviolable truth, brought in to support something admittedly not true. Here, in other words, we have a situation in comedy, almost exactly parallel to that in which a colored bishop whoops "Onward Christian Soldiers!" like a calliope in order to drown out the crowing of the rooster concealed beneath his chasuble.

In all plays of the sort that are regarded as "strong" and "significant" in Greenwich Village, in the finishing schools and by the newspaper critics, connubial infidelity is the chief theme. Smith, having a wife, Mrs. Smith, betrays her love and trust by running off with Miss Rabinowitz, his stenographer. Or Mrs. Brown, detecting her husband, Mr. Brown, in lamentable proceedings with a neighbor, the grass widow Kraus, forgives him and continues to be true to him in consideration of her children, Fred, Pansy and Little Fern. Both situations produce a great deal of eye-rolling and snuffling among the softies aforesaid. Yet neither contains the slightest touch of tragedy, and neither at bottom is even honest. Both, on the contrary, are based upon an assumption that is unsound and ridiculous—the assumption, to wit, that the position of the injured wife is grounded upon the highest idealism—that the injury she suffers is directed at her lofty and impeccable spirit—that it leaves her standing in an heroic attitude. The fact is that her moving impulse is simply a desire to cut a good figure before the world—in brief, that plain vanity is what animates her.

The public expectation that she will endure and renounce is itself hollow and sentimental, and so much so that it can seldom stand much strain. If, for example, her heroism goes beyond a certain modest point—if she carries it to the extent of complete abnegation and self-sacrifice—her reward is not that she is thought heroic, but that she is thought weak and foolish. And if, by any chance, the external pressure upon her is removed and she is left to go on with her alleged idealism alone—then it is regarded as downright insane for her to continue playing her artificial part.

In frank comedy we see the situation more accurately dealt with and hence more honestly and more instructively. Instead of depicting one party as revolting against the assumption of eternal fidelity melodramatically and the other as facing the revolt heroically and tragically, we have both criticizing it by a good-humored flouting of it—not necessarily by act, but by attitude. This attitude is normal and sensible. It rests upon genuine human traits and tendencies. It is sound, natural, and honest. It gives the comedy of the stage a high validity that the bombastic fustian of the stage can never show, all the sophomores to the contrary notwithstanding.

When I speak of infidelity, of course, I do not mean only the gross infidelity of "strong" sex plays and the divorce courts, but that lighter infidelity which relieves and makes bearable the burdens of theoretical fidelity—in brief, the natural reaction of human nature against an artificial and preposterous assumption. The assumption is that a sexual choice, once made, is irrevocable—more, that all desire to revoke it, even transiently, disappears.

The fact is that no human choice can ever be of the irrevocable character, and that the very existence of such an assumption is a constant provocation to challenge it and rebel against it.

What we have in marriage actually—or in any other such contract—is a constant war between the impulse to give that rebellion objective reality and a social pressure which puts a premium on submission. The rebel, if he strikes out, at once collides with a solid wall, the bricks of which are made up of the social assumption of his docility, and the mortar of which is the frozen sentimentality of his own lost yesterday—his fatuous assumption that what was once agreeable to him would be always agreeable to him. Here we have the very essence of comedy—a situation almost exactly parallel to that of the pompous old gentleman who kicks a plug hat lying on the sidewalk, and stumps his toe against the cobblestone within.

Under the whole of the conventional assumption reposes an assumption even more foolish, to wit, that sexual choice is regulated by some transcendental process, that a mysterious accuracy gets into it, that it is limited by impenetrable powers, that there is for every man one certain woman. This sentimentality not only underlies the theory of marriage, but is also the chief apology for divorce. Nothing could be more ridiculous. The truth is that marriages in Christendom are determined, not by elective affinities, but by the most trivial accidents, and that the issue of those accidents is relatively unimportant. That is to say, a normal man could be happy with any one of at least two dozen women of his acquaintance, and a man specially fitted to accept the false assumptions of marriage could be happy with almost any presentable woman of his race, class and age. He is married to Marie instead of to Gladys because Marie definitely decided to marry him, whereas Gladys vacillated between him and some other. And Marie decided to marry him instead of some other, not because the impulse was irresistibly strong, but simply because the thing seemed more feasible. In such choices, at least among women, there is often not even any self-delusion. They see the facts clearly, and even if, later on, they are swathed in sentimental trappings, the revelation is not entirely obliterated.

Here we have comedy double distilled—a combat of pretensions, on the one side, perhaps risen to self-hallucination, but on the other side more or less uneasily conscious and deliberate. This the true soul of high farce. This is something not to snuffle over but to roar at.

(Prejudices, First Series)

REFLECTIONS ON HUMAN MONOGAMY

[*Marriage is not a sexy relationship. It is, as Mencken deftly points out, essentially the coordination of two revenue streams toward a single piece of property. The union of husband and wife has always made economic sense; early marriage to a working partner is one of the best financial investments anyone can make, but living with someone robs a relationship of the distance and mystery that, in turn, make a relationship interesting.*

What makes this essay on monogamy stand out is that Mencken does not just launch a diatribe against monogamy; he is smart enough (smarter than some modern psychiatrists and sex therapists) to point out that many great men of history remained monogamous because they recognized the hassles and time-waste that come with the alternative.

Men of a certain age, who possess any self-awareness, recognize that almost no one wants to have sex with them (unless they're wealthy or famous). The choice, for most, is between monogamy or nothing. Mencken, a man who would have been ignored by women due to his face and figure, certainly cultivated his writerly talents as a means of attracting women. At the time he wrote this essay he found it convenient to satirize marriage from afar, but he seemed to understand both the apprehension and the appeal. He ultimately succumbed. In 1930, he married a woman with health problems who predictably enough died five years later.]

1. The Eternal Farce

As every attentive patron of the drama is well aware, it is difficult for even the most skillful actors keep Ibsen's *Hedda Gabler* from degenerating to farce in the performance. The reason is certainly not occult. It lies in the plain fact that such transactions as the dramatist here deals with—a neurotic woman's effort to be heavily romantic, her horror when romance is followed by pregnancy, the maneuvers of a satanic and idiotic lover, the cuckolding of a husband wearing whiskers—are intrinsically and incurably farcical. All love affairs, in truth, are farcical—that is, to the spectators. When one hears that some old friend has succumbed to the blandishments of a sweet one, however virtuous and beautiful she may be, one does not gasp and roll one's eyes; one simply laughs. When one hears, a year or two later, that they are quarreling, one laughs again. When one hears that the bride is seeking consolation from the curate of the parish, one laughs a third time. When one hears that the bridegroom, in revenge, is sneaking his stenographer to dinner at an Italian restaurant, one laughs a fourth time. And so on. But when one goes to the theatre, the dramatist often asks one to wear a solemn frown when he displays the same puerile and ludicrous phenomena—that is, while he depicts a fat actress as going crazy when she discovers that her husband, an actor with a face like the abdomen of a ten-pin, has run off to Asbury Park, N.J., with another actress who pronounces all French words in the manner of the Texas Christian University.

The best dramatists, of course, make no such mistake. In Shakespeare love is always depicted as comedy—sometimes light and charming, as in *Twelfth Night*, but usually rough and buffoonish as in *The Taming of the Shrew*. This comic attitude is plainly visible even in such plays as *Hamlet* and *Romeo and Juliet*. In its main outlines, I suppose, *Hamlet* is properly looked upon as a tragedy, but if you believe that the love passages are intended to be tragic then all I ask is that you give a sober reading to the colloquies between Hamlet and Ophelia. They are not only farcical; they are downright obscene; Shakespeare, through the mouth of Hamlet, derides the whole business with almost intolerable ribaldry. As for *Romeo and Juliet*, what is it but a penetrating burlesque upon the love guff that was fashionable in the poet's time? True enough, his head buzzed with such loveliness that he could not write even burlesque without making it beautiful—compare *Much Ado About Nothing* and *Othello*—but nevertheless it is quite absurd to say that he was serious when he wrote this tale of calf-love. Imagine such a man taking seriously spasms and hallucinations of a *Backfisch* [teen girl] of fourteen, and the tinpot heroics of a boy of eighteen! Shakespeare remembered very well the nature of his own amorous fancies at eighteen. It was the year of his seduction by Ann Hathaway, whose brothers later made him marry her, much to his damage and dismay. He wrote the play at forty-five. Tell it to the Marines!

I have a suspicion that even Ibsen, though he seldom permitted himself overt humor, indulged in some quiet spoofing when he wrote *A Doll's House*, *Hedda Gabler*, *The Lady from the Sea* and *Little Eyolf*. The whole last act of *Hedda Gabler* could be converted into burlesque by changing the words; as I have said, it is almost always burlesque as bad actors play it. In the cases of *Ghosts* and *The Master-Builder* there can be no doubt whatever. The former is a piece of buffoonery designed to make fun of the fools who were outraged by *A Doll's House*; the latter is a comic piece founded upon personal experience. At the age of sixty Ibsen amused himself with a flirtation with a girl of sixteen. Following the custom of her sex, she took his casual winks and cheek-pinchings quite seriously, and began hinting to the whole neighborhood that the old boy was hopelessly gone on her, and that he intended to divorce *Fru* [madam] Ibsen and run off with her to Italy. All this gave entertainment to Ibsen, who was a serious man, and he began speculating as to what would happen to a man of his age who actually yielded to the gross provocations of such a wench. The result was *The Master-Builder*. But think of the plot! He makes the master-builder climb a church-steeple, and then jump off! Him regarding such slap-stick farce seriously!

The world has very little sense of humor. It is always wagging its ears solemnly over elaborate jocosities. For 600 years it has gurgled over the *Divine Comedy* of Dante, despite the plain fact that the work is a flaming satire upon the whole Christian hocus-pocus of heaven, purgatory and hell. To have tackled such nonsense head-on, in Dante's time, would have been to flout the hangman; hence the poet clothed his attack in an irony so delicate that the ecclesiastical police were baffled. Why is the poem called a comedy? I have read at least a dozen discussions of the question by modern pedants, all of them labored and unconvincing. The same problem obviously engaged the scholars of the poet's own time. He called the thing simply "comedy"; they added the adjective "divine" in order to ameliorate what seemed to them to be an intolerable ribaldry. Well, here is a "comedy" in which human beings are torn limb from limb, boiled in sulphur, cut up with red-hot knives, and filled with molten lead! Can one imagine a man capable of such a poem regarding such fiendish imbecilities seriously? Certainly not. They appeared just as idiotic to him as they appear to you or me. But the Federal judiciary of the day made it impossible to say so in plain language, so he said so behind a smoke-screen of gaudy poetry. How Dante would have roared if he could have known that six hundred years later an illiterate President of the United States, a good Baptist with money in the bank, married happily to a divorcée—would take the whole thing with utter seriousness, and deliver a nonsensical harangue upon the lessons in it for American Christians!

The case of Wagner's *Parsifal* is still more remarkable. Even Nietzsche was deceived by it. Like the most maudlin German fat woman at Baireuth, he mistook the composer's elaborate and outrageous burlesque of Christianity for a tribute to Christianity, and so denounced him as a jackass and refused to speak to him thereafter. To this day *Parsifal* is given with all the trappings of a religious ceremonial, and pious folks go to hear it who would instantly shut their ears if the band began playing *Tristan und Isolde*. It has become, in fact, a sort of *Way Down East* or *Ben Hur* of musical drama—a bait for luring patrons who are never seen in the opera-house otherwise. But try to imagine such a thumping atheist as Wagner writing a religious opera seriously! And if, by any chance, you succeed in imagining it, then turn to the *Char-Freitag* music, and play it on your victrola. Here is the central scene of the piece, the moment of most austere solemnity—and to it Wagner fits music that is so luscious and fleshly—indeed, so downright lascivious and indecent—that even I, who am almost anaesthetic to such provocations, blush every time I hear it. The Flower Maidens do not raise my blood-pressure a single ohm; I have actually snored through the whole second act of *Tristan*. But when I hear that *Char-Freitag* music all of my Freudian suppressions begin groaning and stretching their legs in the dungeons of my unconscious. And what does *Char-Freitag* mean? Good Friday!

2. Venus at the Domestic Hearth

One inclines to the notion that women—and especially homely women—greatly overestimate the importance of physical beauty in their eternal conspiracy against the liberty of man. It is a powerful lure, to be sure, but it is certainly not the only one that fetches the game, nor even, perhaps, the most effective one. The satisfaction that a man gets out of conquering—which is to say, out of succumbing to—a woman of noticeable pulchritude is chiefly the rather banal one of parading her before other men. He likes to show her off as he likes to show his expensive automobile or his big doorknob factory. It is her apparent costliness that is her principal charm. Her beauty sets up the assumption that she was sought eagerly by other men, some of them wealthy, and that it thus took a lot of money or a lot of skill to obtain the monopoly of her.

But very few men are so idiotic that they are blind to the hollowness of such satisfactions. A husband, after all, spends relatively few hours of his life parading his wife, or even contemplating her beauty. What engages him far more often is the unromantic business of living with her—of listening to her conversation, of trying to fathom and satisfy her whims, of detecting and counteracting her plots against his ego, of facing with her the dull hazards and boredoms of everyday life. In the discharge of this business personal beauty is certainly not necessarily a help; on the contrary, it may be a downright hindrance, if only because it makes for the hollowest and least intelligent of all forms of vanity. Of infinitely more value is a quality that women too often neglect, to wit, the quality of simple amiability. The most steadily charming of all human beings, male or female, is the one who is tolerant, unprovocative, good-humored, kind. A man wants a show only intermittently, but he wants peace and comfort every day. And to get them, if he is sagacious, he is quite willing to sacrifice scenery.

3. The Rat-trap

Much of the discontent with modern marriage centers in the fact that the laws which condition it and safeguard it all assume that its purpose is the founding of a family. This was unquestionably its purpose when those laws were devised, say three thousand years ago, but that purpose, at least among the civilized minority, is now almost forgotten. Very few educated men of today, it seems to me, have any notion of founding a family in mind when they marry. Their vanity takes different forms; moreover, they have rejected the old doctrine that they have any duty in the premises; the *Stammhalter* [first-born male heir] has pretty much disappeared from their visions. Most of them, it is probable, marry without any intelligible purpose whatsoever. Women flatter them, mark them down and lure them to the holy altar: everything else is afterthought. Many an American man finds himself on the brink of marriage without ever having given any sober thought even to so important a matter as the probable charm of his bride-elect as mistress. This explains many connubial calamities.

As things stand, the only legal relief from uncomfortable marriages is afforded by divorce. Every other workable device is frowned upon, and most of them are punished. The chief purpose of legal divorce, of course, is to protect the children of the marriage, i.e., to safeguard the family. But the scheme is clumsy, expensive and cruel. To employ it is to cut off a leg to cure what may be, above all, merely a barked shin—worse, what may be no injury at all. Suppose there are no children? Suppose the marriage is entered upon with the clear understanding that there shall be no children? In the latter case it is obviously insane to surround it with safeguards for the family that will never exist. As well insure a pile of bricks against fire. What is needed is legal recognition of such marriages—recognition that will establish decorum and fair play within their actual limits, but that will not seek to burden them with conditions that look quite outside their limits. Human inertia and sentimentality, of course, will be a long while countenancing any such change. Until quite recently a marriage without children was utterly impossible, save as an act of God, and so the inevitable, by a familiar process, was converted into the creditable. This nonsense survives, despite the disappearance of the excuse for it. It is still believed, by the great majority of beings, that there is something mysteriously laudable about achieving viable offspring. I have searched the sacred and profane scriptures for many years, but have yet to find any logical ground for this notion. To have a child is no more creditable than to have rheumatism—and no more discreditable. Ethically, it is absolutely meaningless. And practically, it is merely a matter of chance.

4. The Love Chase

The notion that man is the aggressor in love is frequently supported by old-fashioned psychologists by pointing to the example of the lower animals. The lion, it appears, stalks the lioness to her shame and undoing; the amorous cock pursues the reluctant and virtuous hen. Granted. But all that this proves, giving the analogy all the value asked for it, is that man is the aggressor as a lover, pure and simple, i.e., as a seducer. Is he also the aggressor as suitor and husband? To ask the question is almost to answer it. ... Well, it is precisely his role as husband that differentiates man from lion and cock. And once he is thus differentiated, all his previous likeness disappears. ... In civilized societies, there is a double stalking: for mistresses and for husbands. The fact that the majority of women retain their virtue to the altar and that the majority of men, soon or late, are married—this offers a capital indication of the relative enthusiasm and pertinacity with which the two varieties of aggression are carried on.

5. Woman as Realpolitiker

Women in general are far too intelligent to have any respect for so-called ideas. One seldom hears of them suffering and dying for any of the bogus Good Truths that men believe in. When a woman is on good terms with her husband she is quite willing to accept his idiotic theorizings on any subject that happens to engage him, whether theological, economic, epistemological or political. When one hears of a Republican man who has a Democratic wife, or vice versa, it is always safe to assume that she has her eye on a handsomer, richer or more docile fellow, and is thinking of calling up a lawyer.

6. Footnote for Suffragettes

The double standard of morality will survive in this world so long as a woman whose husband has been debauched is favored with the sympathetic tears of other women, and a man whose wife has run away with an actor is laughed at by other men.

7. The Helpmate

The notion that a true and loving (and, let us hope, amiable and beautiful) wife inspires a man to high endeavor is largely illusory. Every sane woman knows instinctively, as a matter of fact, that the highest aspirations of her husband are fundamentally inimical to her, and that their realization is apt to cost her her possession of him. What she dreams of is not an infinitely brilliant husband, but an infinitely "solid" one, which is to say, one bound irretrievably by the chains of normalcy. It would delight her to see him go to the White House, for a man in the White House is as relentlessly policed as an archbishop. But it would give her a great deal of disquiet to see him develop into a Goethe or a Wagner.

I have known in my time a good many men of the first talent, as talent is reckoned in America, and most of them have been married. I can't recall one whose wife appeared to view his achievements with perfect ease of mind. In every case the lady was full of a palpable fear—the product of feminine intuition, i.e., of hard realism and common sense—that his rise shook her hold upon him, that he became a worse husband in proportion as he became a better man. In the logic I can discern no flaw. The ideal husband is surely not a man of active and daring mind; he is the man of placid and conforming mind. Here the good business man obviously beats the artist and adventurer. His rewards are all easily translated into domestic comfort and happiness. He is not wobbled by the admiration of other women, none of whom, however much they esteem his virtues as a husband, are under any illusion as to his virtues as a lover. Above all, his mind is not analytical, and hence he is not likely to attempt any anatomising of his marriage—the starting point for the worst sort of domestic infelicity. No man, examining his marriage intelligently, can fail to observe that it is compounded, at least in part, of slavery, and that he is the slave. Happy the woman whose husband is so stupid that he never launches into that coroner's inquest!

8. The Mime

The fundamental objection to actors, stripping the business of all mere sophistry and snobbery, is that they give away the idiotic vanity of the whole male sex. An actor is simply a man who, by word strut, says aloud of *him*self what all normal men think of *them*selves. Thus he exposes, in a highly indiscreet and disconcerting manner, the full force of masculine vanity. But I doubt that he exaggerates it. No healthy male is ever actually modest. No healthy male ever really thinks or talks of anything save himself. His conversation is one endless boast—often covert, but always undiluted. His politics is a mere sneering at what he conceives to be inferiors; his philosophy is simply an exposure of asses; he cannot imagine himself save as superior, dominating, the center of situations. Even his theology is seldom more than a stealthy comparison of himself and God, to the disadvantage of God. . . . The youngest flapper knows all this. Feminine strategy, in the duel of sex, consists almost wholly of an adroit feeding of this vanity. Man makes love by braggadocio. Women make love by listening. . . . Once a woman passes a certain point in intelligence she finds it almost impossible to get a husband: she simply cannot go on listening without snickering.

9. Cavia Cobaya

I find the following in Theodore Dreiser's *Hey-Rub-a-Dub-Dub*:

"Does the average strong, successful man confine himself to one woman? Has he ever?"

The first question sets an insoluble problem. How are we, in such intimate matters, to say what is the average and what is not the average? But the second question is easily answered, and the answer is, He has. Here Dreiser's curious sexual obsession simply leads him into absurdity. His view of the traffic of the sexes remains the naive one of an ex-Baptist nymph in Greenwich Village. Does he argue that Otto von Bismarck was not a "strong, successful man"? If not, then let him remember that Bismarck was a strict monogamist—a man full of sin, but always faithful to his Johanna. Again, there was Thomas Henry Huxley. Again, there was William Ewart Gladstone. Again, there was Robert Edward Lee. Yet again, there were Robert Schumann, Felix Mendelssohn, Johann Sebastian Bach, Ulysses S. Grant, Andrew Jackson, Louis Pasteur, Martin Luther, Helmuth von Moltke, Stonewall Jackson, Lyof Tolstoi, Robert Browning, Henrik Ibsen, William T. Sherman, Carl Schurz, old Sam Adams, . . . I could extend the list to pages. . . . Perhaps I am unfair to Dreiser. His notion of a "strong, successful man" may be, not such a genuinely superior fellow as Bismarck or Bach, but such a mere brigand as Shonts, Yerkes or Jim Fisk. If so, he is still wrong. If so, he still runs aground on John D. Rockefeller.

10. The Survivor

Around every bachelor of more than thirty-five legends tend to congregate, chiefly about the causes of his celibacy. If it is not whispered that he is damaged goods, and hence debarred from marriage by a lofty concept of Service to the unborn, it is told under the breath that he was insanely in love at the age of twenty-six with a beautiful creature who jilted him for an insurance underwriter and so broke his heart beyond repair. Such tales are nearly always moonshine. The reason why the average bachelor of thirty-five remains a bachelor is really very simple. It is, in brief, that no ordinarily attractive and intelligent woman has ever made a serious and undivided effort to marry him.

11. The Veteran's Disaster

The tragedy of experience is that a man no longer believes it when a woman shows all the orthodox signs of having been flustered by him. In youth it give him immense delight to discover that he has made a mash, but when he gets into the middle years the thing merely annoys him. He is irritated that yet another female Cagliostro should try to floor him with the immemorial mumbo-jumbo, and so make a fool of him. The girl he succumbs to is the one who tells him frankly that her heart is buried in France, but that she admires him tremendously and would esteem it a singular honor to be the wife of so meritorious a fellow. This helps to explain, perhaps, why aging men so often succumb to flappers.

12. Moral Indignation

The ill-fame of the Turks in the English-speaking world is not due to their political medievalism, as is usually alleged, but to their practise of polygamy. That practise inevitably excites the erotic imagination of men doomed to monogamy, and particularly of men doomed to monogamy with despotic, prudish and unappetizing wives, which is to say, the normal, typical man of England and the United States. They envy the Turk his larger and more charming joys, and hence hate him. Every time Reuter reports him dragging a fresh herd of dark-eyed, voluptuous Georgian or Armenian women into his seraglio, they hate him the more. The way to arouse a Puritan to his highest pitch of moral indignation is not to burn down an orphan-asylum; the way to do it is to grab a pretty girl around the waist and launch with her into the lascivious measures of *Wiener Walz*. Men always hate most what they envy most.

13. The Man and His Shadow

Every man, whatever his actual qualities, is credited with and judged by certain general qualities that are supposed to appertain to his sex, particularly by women. Thus man the individual is related to Man the species, often to his damage and dismay. Consider my own case. I am by nature one of the most orderly of mortals. I have a place for every article of my personal property, whether a Bible or a cocktail-shaker, an undershirt or an eye-dropper, and I always keep it where it belongs. I never drop cigar-ashes on the floor. I never upset a waste-basket. I am never late for trains. I never run short of collars. I never go out with a purple neck-tie on a blue shirt. I never fail to appear in time for dinner without telephoning or telegraphing. Yet the women who are cursed by God with the care of me maintain and cherish the fiction that I am an extremely careless and even hoggish fellow—that I have to be elaborately nursed, supervised and policed—that the slightest relaxation of vigilance over my everyday conduct would reduce me to a state of helplessness and chaos, with all my clothes mislaid, half my books in the ash-can, my mail unanswered, my face unshaven, and my office not unlike an I.W.W. headquarters after a raid by the *Polizei*. It is their firm theory that, unaided by superior suggestion, I'd wear one shirt six weeks, and a straw hat until Christmas. They never speak of my work-room save in terms of horror, though it is actually the most orderly room in my house. Weekly I am accused of having lost all my socks and handkerchiefs, though they are in my clothes-press all the while. At least once a month formal plans are discussed for reorganizing my whole mode of life, that I may not sink into irremediable carelessness, inefficiency and barbarism.

I note that many other men lie under the same benign espionage and misrepresentation—in fact, nearly all men. But it is my firm belief that very few men are really disorderly. The business of the world is managed by getting order into it, and the feeling for discipline thus engendered is carried over into domestic life. I know of very few men who ever drop ashes on the dining-room rug, or store their collars in their cigar-box, or put on brown socks with their dress-clothes, or forget to turn off the water after they have bathed, or neglect to keep dinner engagements—and most of those few, I am firmly convinced, do it because their women-folk expect it of them, because it would cause astonishment and dismay if they refrained. I myself, more than once, have deliberately hung my hat on an electrolier, or clomped over the parquetry with muddy shoes, or gone out in a snow-storm without an overcoat, or come down to dinner in a ragged collar, or filled my shirt-box with old copies of the Congressional Record, or upset a bottle of green ink, or used Old Dutch Cleanser for shaving, or put olives into Jack Rose cocktails, or gone without a hair-cut for three or four weeks, or dropped an expensive beer *Seidel* [stein] upon the hard concrete of my cellar floor in order to give a certain necessary color to the superstition of my oafishness. If I failed to do such things now and then, I'd become un-popular, and very justly so, for nothing is more obnoxious than a human being who is always challenging and correcting the prevailing view of him. Even now I make no protest; I merely record the facts. On my death-bed, I daresay, I shall carry on the masquerade. That is to say, I shall swallow a clinical thermometer or two, upset my clam-broth over my counterpane, keep an ouija board and a set of dice under my pillow, and maybe, at the end, fall clumsily out of bed.

14. The Balance-Sheet

Marriage, as everyone knows, is chiefly an economic matter. But too often it is assumed that economics concerns only the wife's hats; it also concerns, and perhaps more importantly, the husband's cigars. No man is genuinely happy, married, who has to drink worse gin than he used to drink when he was single.

15. Yearning

Ah, that the eugenists would breed a woman as capable of laughter as the girl of twenty and as adept at knowing when not laugh as the woman of thirty-five!

(*Prejudices, Fourth Series*)

BIRTH CONTROL

[*The politics of the early twentieth century (this piece was written about four decades before the pill) can confound our modern concepts. The fact is, after the 19th Amendment passed, the energy of the suffragette movement shifted to family planning. Birth control, originally, came in the same package of public reforms that got ladies in Methodist pews wagging their fingers at alcohol consumption and pornography.*

The original novel version of Cheaper by the Dozen *was published in 1948. It was a harmless piece of escapism (as were the sitcoms and movies based on it—if you consider glorification of feckless, irresponsible breeding harmless). It depicted a family planning character as a moralizing wag who condemned the semi-fictional Gilbreth family for having too many kids. Mencken, like most people of the time, viewed the birth-control crowd as a sex-control crowd, a perception that would not change until the pill made it possible to officially separate sexual fun from reproductive labor.*

None of this means that Mencken approved of the anti-pornographers either. American history does not lack for male conservative morons—one can gather them up in armfuls on any street corner in Texas—but it is possible that Anthony Comstock (1844-1915) was the most conservative and moronic of them all. Comstock served as the U.S. postal inspector, a job that essentially gave him the role of chief censor. Of him, Mencken writes:

"In 1873, when the late Anthony Comstock began his great Christian work, the American flapper, or, as she was then called the young lady, read Godley's Ladies' Book. *To-day she reads—but if you want to find out what she reads simply take a look at the cheap fiction magazines which rise mountain-high from every news-stand. It is an amusing and at the same time highly instructive commentary upon the effectiveness of moral legislation. The net result of fifty years of Comstockery is complete and ignominious failure. All its gaudy raids and alarms have simply gone for naught."*

Comstock, of course, was an imbecile, and Mencken's real enemy was anyone who sought to impose restrictive Protestant morality on his neighbors, and prohibition, of alcohol or sex, comes from the same Puritan spirit.]

The grotesque failure of the campaign to put down propaganda for birth control in the Republic has a lesson in it for those romantic optimists who believe that in the long run, by some mysterious hook or crook and perhaps with divine help, Prohibition will be enforced. They will not heed that lesson, but it is there nonetheless. Church and state combine to baffle and exterminate the birth controllers. They are threatened with penal servitude and their customers are threatened with hell fire. Yet it must be obvious that they are making progress in the land, for the national birth-rate continues to slide downhill, steadily and rapidly.

Incidentally, it is amusing and instructive to observe that it diminishes with greatest celerity among the educated and highly respectable classes, which is to say, among those who are ordinarily most law-abiding. The same thing is to be noted when one turns to Prohibition. The majority of professional criminals, now as in the old days of sin, are tea-totalers, but when one comes to the good citizens who scorn them and demand incessantly that the *Polizei* butcher them and so have done with them, one comes at once upon a high density of scofflaws. I know many Americans of easy means, some of them greatly respected and even eminent. Not two per cent make any pretense of obeying the Volstead Act. And not two per cent of their wives are innocent of birth control. The reason is not far to seek. Both the Volstead Act and the statute aimed at birth control invade the sanctity of the domestic hearth. They take the roof off a man's house, and invite the world to look in. Obviously, that looking in is unpleasant in proportion as the man himself is dignified. If he is a low fellow, he doesn't care much, for he is used to such snooping by his low neighbors. But if he is one who has a high opinion of himself, and is accustomed to seeing it ratified by others, then he is outraged. And if he has any natural bellicosity in him and resistance seems reasonably safe, he resists with great diligence and vigor.

Here, perhaps, we come upon an explanation of the fact that Prohibition and all other such devices for making men good by force are far less opposed in the country than they are in the cities. The yokel is trained from infancy to suffer espionage. He has scarcely any privacy at all. His neighbors know everything that is to be known about him, including what he eats and what he feeds his quadrupedal colleagues. His religious ideas are matters of public discussion; if he is recusant the village pastor prays for him by name. When his wife begins the sublime biological process of giving him an heir, the news flies around. If he inherits $200 from an uncle in Idaho everyone knows it instantly. If he skins his shin, or buys a new plow, or sees a ghost, or takes a bath it is a public event. Thus living like a gold-fish in a glass globe, he acquires a large tolerance of snoutery, for if he resisted it his neighbors would set him down as an enemy of their happiness, and probably burn his barn. When an official spy or two are added to the volunteer pack he barely notices it. It seems natural and inevitable to him that everyone outside his house should be interested in what goes on inside, and that this interest should be accompanied by definite notions as to what is nice and what is not nice, supported by pressure. So he submits to governmental tyranny as he submits to the village inquisition, and when he hears that city men resist, it only confirms his general feeling that they are scoundrels. They are scoundrels because they have a better time than he has—the sempiternal human reason. The city man is differently trained. He is used to being let alone. Save when he lives in the slums, his neighbors show no interest in him. He would regard it as outrageous for them to have opinions about what goes on within the four walls of his house. If they offered him advice he would invite them to go to hell; if they tried force he would bawl for the police. So he is doubly affronted when the police themselves stalk in. And he resists them with every means at his command, and believes it is his high duty to do so, that liberty may not perish from the earth.

The birth control fanatics profit by this elemental fact. It is their great good fortune that their enemies have tried to put them down, not by refuting their ideas, but by working to shove them into jail. What they argue for, at bottom, remains very dubious, and multitudes of quite honest and intelligent persons are against it. They have by no means proved that a high birth-rate is dangerous, and they have certainly not shown that they know of any sure and safe way to reduce it—that is, any way not already known to every corner druggist. But when an attempt is made to put them down by law, the question whether they are wise falls into the background, and the question whether their rights are invaded comes forward. At once the crowd on their side is immensely reinforced. It now includes not only all the persons who believe in birth control, but also all the persons who believe in free ideas and free speech, and this second group, it quickly appears, is far larger than the first one, and far more formidable. So the birth controllers suddenly find themselves supported by heavy battalions, and that support is sufficient to make them almost invulnerable. Personally, I am inclined to be against them. I believe that the ignorant should be permitted to spawn *ad libitum* [at will], that there may be a steady supply of slaves, and that those of us who are more prudent and sanitary may be relieved of unpleasant work. If the debate were open and fair, I'd oppose the birth controllers with all the subtlest devices of rhetoric, including bogus statistics and billingsgate. But so long as they are denied their plain rights—and, in particular, so long as those rights are denied them by an evil combination of theologians and politicians,—I am for them, and shall remain so until the last galoot's ashore. They have got many more allies on the same terms. And I believe that they are winning.

The law which forbids them to send their brummagem tracts through the mails is obviously disingenuous and oppressive. It is a part of the notorious Post Act, put on the books by Comstock himself, executed by bureaucratic numskulls, and supported by every variety of witch-burner. I know of no intelligent man or woman who is in favor of the principal of such grotesque legislation; even the worst enemies of the birth controllers would not venture to argue that it should be applied generally. The way to dispose of such laws is to flout them and make a mock of them. The theory that they can be got rid of by enforcing them is nonsense. Enforcing them simply inspires the sadists who advocate them to fresh excesses. Worse, it accustoms the people to oppression, and so tends to make them bear it uncomplainingly. Wherever, in the United States, there has been any sincere effort to enforce Prohibition, the anti-evolutionists are already on the warpath, and the Lord's Day Alliance is drumming up recruits. No, the way to deal with such laws is to defy them, and thus make them ridiculous. This is being done in the case of the Volstead Act by millions of patriots, clerical and lay. It is being done in the case of the Comstock Act by a small band, but one full of praiseworthy resolution.

Thus I deliver myself of a whoop for the birth controllers, and pass on to pleasanter concerns. Their specific Great Cause, it seems to me, is full of holes. They draw extremely questionable conclusions from a highly dubious body of so-called facts. But they are profoundly right at bottom. They are right when they argue that anyone who tries to silence them by force is the common enemy of all of us. And they are right when they hold that the best way to get rid of such opposition is to thumb the nose at it.

(from "Four Moral Causes," *Prejudices, Fifth Series*)

RONDO ON AN ANCIENT THEME

[*Regarding women's emancipation and sex, Mencken understood the inherent contradictions well ahead of any second or third wave feminist philosopher. The primary question being: do women want sex or not? Mencken phrases the problem like this:*]

"*Women, plainly enough, are in a far different case. Their emancipation has not yet gone to the length of making them genuinely free. They have rid themselves, very largely, of the absolute need to please men, but they have not yet rid themselves of the impulse to please men. Perhaps they never will: one might easily devise a plausible argument to that effect on biological grounds. But sufficient unto the day is the phenomenon before us: they have to get rid of the old taboo which forbade them to think and talk about sex, and they still labor under the old superstition that sex is a matter of paramount importance.*"

Feminists came to see the sexual liberation era, which was supposed to emancipate women from religious taboos on sexual pleasure, as a scam perpetrated by manipulative men (with their supposedly higher libidos) co-opting feminism to convince women to have more sex. This criticism is not without merit: Hugh Hefner somehow managed to sell his enterprise as at least partially feminist. So, the current feminist movement has circled back around to Puritanism, the problem being that seduction and possibly romance seem to require an asymmetry of power that is no longer considered tolerable.]

It is the economic emancipation of woman, I suppose, that must be blamed for the present wholesale discussion of the sex question, so offensive to the romantic. Eminent authorities have full often described, and with the utmost heat and eloquence, her state before she was delivered from her fetters and turned loose to root or die. Almost her only feasible trade, in those dark days, was that of wife. True enough, she might also become a servant girl, or go to work in a factory, or offer herself upon the streets, but all of those vocations were so revolting that no rational woman followed them if she could help it: she would leave any one of them at a moment's notice at the call of a man, for the call of a man meant promotion for her, economically and socially. The males of the time, knowing what a boon they had to proffer, drove hard bargains. They demanded a long list of high qualities in the woman they summoned to their seraglios, but most of all they demanded what they called virtue. It was not sufficient that a candidate should be anatomically undefiled, she must also be pure in mind. There was, of course, just one way to keep her so pure, and that was by building a high wall around her mind, and hitting her with a club every time she ventured to peer over it. It was as dangerous, in that Christian era, for a woman to show any interest in or knowledge of the great physiological farce of sex as it would be to-day for a presidential candidate to reveal himself in his cups on the hustings. Everyone knew, to be sure, that as a mammal she had sex, and that as a potential wife and mother she probably had some secret interest in its phenomena, but it was felt, perhaps wisely, that even the most academic theorizing had within it the deadly germs of the experimental method, and so she was forbidden to think about the matter at all, and whatever information she acquired at all she had to acquire by a method of bootlegging.

The generation still on its legs has seen the almost total collapse of that naive and constabulary system, and of the economic structure supporting it. Beginning with the eighties of the last century, there rose up a harem rebellion which quickly knocked both to pieces. The women of the Western World not only began to plunge heroically into all of the old professions, hitherto sacred to men; they also began to invent a lot of new professions, many of them unimagined by men. Worse, they began to succeed in them. The working woman of the old days worked only until she could snare a man; any man was better than her work. But the working woman of the new days was under no such pressure; her work made her a living and sometimes more than a living; when a man appeared in her net she took two looks at him, one of them usually very searching, before landing him. The result was an enormous augmentation of her feeling of self-sufficiency, her spirit of independence, her natural inclination to get two sides into the bargaining. The result, secondarily, was a revolt against all the old taboos that had surrounded her, all the childish incapacities and ignorances that had been forced upon her. The result, tertiarily, was a vast running amok in the field that, above all others, had been forbidden to her: that of sexual knowledge and experiment.

We now suffer from the effects of that running amok. It is women, not men, who are doing all the current gabbling about sex, and proposing all the new-fangled modifications of the rules and regulations ordained by God, and they are hard at it very largely, I suppose, because being at it at all is a privilege that is still new to them. The whole order of human females, in other words, is passing through a sort of intellectual adolescence, and it is disturbed as greatly as biological adolescents are by the spouting of the hormones. The attitude of men toward the sex question, it seems to me, has not changed greatly in my time. Barring a few earnest men whose mental processes, here as elsewhere, are essentially womanish, they still view it somewhat jocosely. Taking one with another, they believe that they know all about it that is worth knowing, and so it does not challenge their curiosity, and they do not put in much time discussing it, save mockingly. But among the women, if a bachelor may presume to judge, interest in it is intense. They want to know all that is known about it, all that has been guessed and theorized about it; they bristle with ideas of their own about it. It is hard to find a reflective woman, in these days, who is not harboring some new and startling scheme for curing the evils of monogamous marriage; it is impossible to find any woman who has not given ear to such schemes. Women, not men, read the endless books upon the subject that now rise mountain-high in all the book-stores, and women, not men, discuss and rediscuss the notions in them. An acquaintance of mine, a distinguished critic, owns a copy of one of the most revolutionary of these books, by title *The Art of Love,* that was suppressed on the day of its publication by the alert Comstocks. He tells me that he has already lent it to twenty-six women and that he has more than fifty applications for it on file. Yet he has never read it himself!

As a professional fanatic for free thought and free speech, I can only view all this uproar in the *Frauenzimmer* [women's space, literally women's room] with high satisfaction. It gives me delight to see a taboo violated and that delight is doubled when the taboo is one that is wholly senseless. Sex is more important to women than to men, and so they ought to be free to discuss it as they please, and to hatch and propagate whatever ideas about it occur to them. Moreover, I can see nothing but nonsense in the doctrine that their concerns with such matters damages their charm. So far as I am concerned, a woman who knows precisely what a Graafian follicle is is just as charming as one who doesn't—just as charming, and far less dangerous. Charm in women, indeed, is a variable star, and shows different colors at different times. When their chief mark was ignorance, then the most ignorant was the most charming; now that they begin to think deeply and indignantly there is charm in their singular astuteness. But I am inclined to believe that they have not yet attained to a genuine astuteness in the new field of sex. To the contrary, it seems to me that a fundamental error contaminates their whole dealing with the subject, and that is the error of assuming that sexual questions, whether social, physiological, or pathological, are of vast and even paramount importance to mankind in general—in brief, that sex is really a first-rate matter.

I doubt it. I believe that in this department men show better judgment than women, if only because their information is older and their experience wider. Their tendency is to dismiss the whole thing lightly, to reduce sex to the lowly estate of an afterthought and a recreation, and under that tendency there is a sound instinct. I do not believe that the lives of normal men are much colored or conditioned, either directly or indirectly, by purely sexual considerations. I believe that nine-tenths of them would carry on all the activities which engage them now, and with precisely the same humorless diligence, if there were not a woman in the world. The notion that man would not work if he lacked an audience, and that the audience must be a woman, seems to me to be a hollow sentimentality. Men work because they want to eat, because they want to feel secure, because they long to shine among their fellows, and for no other reason. A man may crave his wife's approbation, or some other woman's approbation, of his social graces, of his taste, of his generosity and courage, of his general dignity in the world, but long before he ever gives thought to such things and long after he has forgotten them he craves the approbation of his fellow men. Above all, he craves the approbation of his fellow craftsmen—the men who understand exactly what he is trying to do, and are expertly competent to judge his doing of it. Can you imagine a surgeon putting the good opinion of his wife above the good opinion of other surgeons? If you can, then you can do something that I cannot.

Here, of course, I do not argue absurdly that the good opinion of his wife is nothing to him. Obviously, it is a lot, for if it does not constitute the principal reward of his work, then it at least constitutes the principal joy of his hours of ease, when his work is done. He wants his wife to respect and admire him; to be able to make her do it is also a talent. But if he is intelligent he must discover very early that her respect and admiration do not necessarily run in direct ratio to his intrinsic worth, that the qualities and acts that please her are not always the qualities and acts that are most satisfactory to the censor within him—in brief, that the relation between man and woman, however intimate they may seem, must always remain a bit casual and superficial—that sex, at bottom, belongs to comedy and the cool of the evening and not to the sober business that goes on in the heat of the day. That sober business, as I have said would still go on if woman were abolished and heirs and assigns were manufactured in rolling-mills. Men would not only work as hard as they do to-day; they would also get almost as much satisfaction out of their work. For of all the men that I know on this earth, ranging from poets to ambassadors and from bishops to statisticians, I know none who labors primarily because he wants to please a woman. They are all hard at it because they want to impress other men and so please themselves.

Women, plainly enough, are in a far different case. Their emancipation has not yet gone to the length of making them genuinely free. They have rid themselves, very largely, of the absolute need to please men, but they have not yet rid themselves of the impulse to please men. Perhaps they never will: one might easily devise a plausible argument to that effect on biological grounds. But sufficient unto the day is the phenomenon before us: they have got rid of the old taboo which forbade them to think and talk about sex, and they still labor under the old superstition that sex is a matter of paramount importance. The result, in my judgment, is an absurd emission of piffle. In every division there is vast and often ludicrous exaggeration. The campaign for birth control takes on the colossal proportions of the war for democracy. The venereal diseases are represented to be as widespread, at least in men, as colds in the head, and as lethal as apoplexy or cancer. Great hordes of viragoes patrol the country, instructing school-girls in the mechanics of reproduction and their mothers in obstetrics. The light-hearted monogamy which produced all of us is denounced as an infamy comparable to cannibalism. Laws are passed regulating the mating of human beings as if they were horned cattle and converting marriage into a sort of coroner's inquest. Over all sounds the battle-cry of quacks and zealots at all times and everywhere: *Veritas liberabit vos!* [The truth will set you free!]

The truth? How much of this new gospel is actually truth? Perhaps two per cent. The rest is idle theorizing, doctrinaire nonsense, mere scandalous rubbish. All that is worth knowing about sex—all, that is, that is solidly established and of sound utility—can be taught to any intelligent boy of sixteen in two hours. Is it taught in the current books, so enormously circulated? I doubt it. Absolutely without exception these books admonish the poor apprentice to renounce sex altogether—to sublimate it, as the favorite phrase is, into a passion for free verse, Rotary or the League of Nations. This admonition is silly, and, I believe, dangerous. It is as much a folly to lock up sex in the hold as it is to put it in command on the bridge. Its proper place is in the social hall. As a substitute for all such nonsense I drop a pearl of wisdom, and pass on. To wit: the strict monogamist never gets into trouble.

(*Prejudices, Fifth Series*)

8

RELIGION

HIGH AND GHOSTLY MATTERS

[*A few moments of critical thought are all that it takes to become an atheist, and in this essay, Mencken spends very little intellectual energy attacking theology. Perhaps he recognized that many great minds have busied themselves correcting the errors of Christian theology, but this has been largely an attempt at social reform. Pushing Christianity out of the social sphere, and out of the minds of children, is no doubt a worthy cause, but readers of Mencken must remember that he was not a social reformer. Nothing in Mencken's writing indicates that he thought humanity could do any better than it was doing; he just produced clean satirical copy by describing the absurdity of the whole social enterprise.*

Instead of giving theology a drubbing, Mencken quickly assumes the reader to be, after perusing a few pages of his retort to Creationism, as much of a disbeliever as he is. Then, by analogy, he shows the theological disbeliever that the concept of romantic love requires just as much faith as a belief in an omnipotent god does. Among men, only the young believe in romantic love, and most will grow out of the idea if given enough time. The fact is, a young man of mild attractiveness and ordinary financial prospects could be hooked up for life with just about any woman of similar characteristics. (Mencken wrote this essay at a time when people frequently married in their late teens or early twenties, and when marriage laws and societal expectations made those unions more permanent. For many of these youngsters, a near-religious belief in romantic partnership was required.)

One can imagine, depending on their nuptial status at the time this essay appeared, that more than a few readers either damned or praised Mencken for having written it.]

1. The Cosmic Secretariat

The argument by design, once the bulwark of Christian apologetics, is so full of holes that it is no wonder that it has had to be abandoned. The more, indeed, the theologian seeks to prove the wisdom and omnipotence of God by His works, the more he is dashed by evidences of divine incompetence and stupidity. The world is not actually well run; it is very badly run, and no Huxley was needed to labor the obvious fact. The human body, very adeptly designed in some details, is cruelly and senselessly bungled in other details, and every reflective first-year medical student must notice a hundred ways to improve it. How are we to reconcile this mixture of fitness and blundering with the concept of a single omnipotent Designer, to whom all problems are equally easy? If He could contrive so efficient and durable a machine as the human hand, then how did He come to make such botches as the tonsils, the gall-bladder, the uterus and the prostate gland? If He could perfect the hip joint and the ear, then why did he boggle the teeth?

Having never encountered a satisfactory—or even a remotely plausible answer to such questions, I have had to go to the trouble of devising one myself. It is, at all events, quite simple, and in strict accord with all the known facts. In brief, it is this: that the theory that the universe is run by a single God must be abandoned, and that in place of it we must set up the theory that it is run by a board of gods, all of equal puissance and authority. Once this concept is grasped all the difficulties that have vexed theologians vanish, and human experience instantly lights up the whole dark scene. We observe in everyday life what happens when authority is divided, and great decisions are reached by consultation and compromise. We know that the effects at times, particularly when one of the consultants runs away with the others, are very good, but we also know that they are usually extremely bad. Such a mixture, precisely, is on display in the cosmos. It presents a series of brilliant successes in the midst of an infinity of failures.

I contend that my theory is the only one ever put forward that completely accounts for the clinical picture. Every other theory, facing such facts as sin, disease and disaster, is forced to admit the supposition that Omnipotence, after all, may not be omnipotent—a plain absurdity. I need toy with no such nonsense. I may assume that every god belonging to the council which rules the universe is infinitely wise and infinitely powerful, and yet not evade the plain fact that most of the acts of that council are ignorant and foolish. In truth, my assumption that a council exists is tantamount to an *a priori* assumption that its acts are ignorant and foolish, for no act of any conceivable council can be otherwise. Is the human hand perfect, or, at all events, practical and praiseworthy? Then I account for it on the ground that it was designed by some single member of the council—that the business was handed over to him by inadvertence or as a result of an irremediable difference of opinion among the others. Had more than one member participated actively in its design it would have been measurably less meritorious than it is, for the sketch offered by the original designer would have been forced to run the gauntlet of criticisms and suggestions from all the other councillors, and human experience teaches us that most of these criticisms and suggestions would have been inferior to the original idea—that many of them, in fact, would have had nothing in them save a petty desire to maul and spoil the original idea.

But do I here accuse the high gods of harboring discreditable human weaknesses? If I do, then my excuse is that it is impossible to imagine them doing the work universally ascribed to them without admitting their possession of such weaknesses. One cannot imagine a god spending weeks and months, and maybe whole geological epochs, laboring over the design of the human kidney without assuming him to have been moved by a powerful impulse to express himself vividly, to marshal and publish his ideas, to win public credit among his fellows—in brief, without assuming him to be egotistic. And one cannot assume to be egotistic without assuming him to prefer the adoption of his own ideas to the adoption of any other god's. I defy anyone to make the contrary assumption without plunging instantly into clouds of mysticism. Ruling it out, one comes inevitably to the conclusion that the inept management of the universe must be ascribed to clashes of egos, i.e., to petty spites and revenges, among the gods, for any one of them alone, since we must assume him to be infinitely wise and powerful, could run it perfectly. We suffer from bad stomachs simply because the god who first proposed making a stomach aroused thereby the ill-nature of those who had not thought of it, and because they proceeded instantly to wreak that ill-nature upon him by improving it, i.e., botching his work. We must reproduce our species in the familiar arduous, uneconomic, embarrassing and almost pathological manner because the god who devised the excellent process prevailing among the protozoa had to be put in his place when he proposed to extend it to Primates.

2. The Nature of Faith

Many years ago, when I was more enterprising intellectually than I am to-day, I proposed the application of Haeckel's celebrated biogenetic law—to wit, that the history of the individual rehearses the history of the species—to the domain of human ideas. So applied, it leads to some superficially startling but probably quite sound conclusions, for example, that an adult poet is simply an individual in a state of arrested development—in brief, a sort of moron. Just as all of us, in utero, pass through a stage in which we are tadpoles, and almost indistinguishable from the tadpoles which afterward become frogs, so all of us pass through a state, in our nonage, when we are poets. A youth of seventeen who is not a poet is simply an ass: his development has been arrested even anterior to the stage of the intellectual tadpole. But a man of fifty who still writes poetry is either an unfortunate who has never developed intellectually, beyond his teens, or a conscious buffoon who pretends to be something that he isn't—something far younger and juicier than he actually is—, just as the late Richard Mansfield, in Schiller's play, pretended, by the use of a falsetto voice and a girlish skip, to be the eighteen-year-old Don Carlos. Something else, of course, may enter into it. The buffoonery may be partly conscious and deliberate, and partly Freudian. Many an aging man keeps on writing poetry simply because it gives him the illusion that he is still young. For the same reason, perhaps, he plays tennis, wears green cravats, and tries to convince himself that he is in love.

It is my conviction that no normal man ever falls in love, within the ordinary meaning of the term, after the age of thirty. He may, at forty, pursue the female of his species with great assiduity, and he may, at fifty, sixty, or even seventy, "woo" and marry a more or less fair one in due form of law, but the impulse that moves him to these follies at such ages is never the complex of illusions and hallucinations that poets describe as love. This complex is quite natural to all males between adolescence and the age of, say, twenty-five, when the kidneys begin to disintegrate. For a youth to reach twenty-one without having fallen in love in an abject and preposterous manner would be for doubts to be raised as to his normalcy. But if he does it after his wisdom teeth are cut, it is no more than a sign that they have been cut in vain—that he is still in his teens, whatever his biological and legal age. Love, so-called, is based upon a view of women that is impossible to any man who has had any experience of them. Such a man may, to the end of his life, enjoy their society vastly, and even respect them and admire them, but, however much he respects and admires them, he nevertheless sees them more or less clearly, and seeing them clearly is fatal to the true romance. Find a man of forty who heaves and moans over a woman in the manner of a poet and you will behold either a man who ceased to develop intellectually at twenty-four or thereabout, or a fraud who has his eye on the lands, tenements and hereditaments of the lady's deceased first husband. Or upon her talents as nurse, cook, amanuensis and audience. This, no doubt, is what George Bernard Shaw meant when he said that every man over forty is a scoundrel.

As I say, my suggestion has not been adopted by psychologists, who, in the main, are a very conservative and unimaginative body of men. If they applied the biogenetic law in the field of religion they might make some interesting observations. Chances are, indeed, that religion belongs exclusively to an extremely early stage of human development, and that its rapid decay in the world since the Reformation is evidence of a very genuine progress. Reduced to its logical essence, every religion now advocated in Christendom is simply the doctrine that there are higher powers, infinitely wise and virtuous, which take an active interest in the sordid everyday affairs of men, and not infrequently intervene in them. This doctrine is not purely romantic and *a priori*; it is based upon what is regarded by its subscribers as objective evidence. But it must be plain that that evidence tends to go to pieces as human knowledge widens—that it appears massive and impressive in direct proportion as the individual impressed is ignorant. A few hundred years ago practically every phenomenon of nature was ascribed to superhuman intervention. The plague, for example, was caused by God's anger. So was war. So was lightning. Today no enlightened man believes anything of the kind. All these phenomena are seen to be but links in an endless chain of amoral causation, and it is known that, given a certain quite intelligible and usually inevitable combination of causes, they will appear infallibly as effects. Thus religion gradually loses its old objective authority, and becomes more and more a mere sentimentality. An enlightened man's view of it is almost indistinguishable from his view of the Spirit of 1776, the Henty books, and the rosewood casket containing his grandmother's false teeth.

Such a man is not "dead" to religion. He was not born with a congenital inaptitude for it. He has simply outgrown it, as he has outgrown poetry, Socialism and love. At adolescence practically all individuals have attacks of attacks of piety, but that is only saying that their powers of perception, at that age, outrun their knowledge. They observe the phenomenon, but cannot account for it. Later on, unless their development is arrested, they gradually emerge from that romantic and spookish fog, just as they emerge from the hallucinations of secular romance. I speak here, of course, of individuals genuinely capable of education—always a small minority. If, as the Army tests of conscripts showed, nearly 50 per cent of American adult males never get beyond the mental development of a twelve-year-old child, then it must be obvious that a much smaller number get beyond the mental development of a youth at the end of his teens. I put that number, at a venture, at 5 per cent. The remaining 95 per cent never quite free themselves from religious superstitions. They may no longer believe it is an act of God every time an individual catches a cold, or sprains his ankle or cuts himself shaving, but they are pretty sure to see some trace of divine intervention in it if he is struck by lightning, or hanged, or afflicted with leprosy or syphilis. That God causes wars has been believed by all the Presidents of the United States, save Grover Cleveland, since Jefferson's time. During the late war the then President actually set aside a day for praying to God to stop what He had started as soon as possible, and on terms favorable to American investments. This was not done, remember, by a voodoo man in the Congo forest, but by a sound Presbyterian, a Ph.D. of Johns Hopkins University, and the best-dressed professor ever seen at Princeton.

I have said that all modern religions are based, at least on their logical side, on this notion that there are higher powers which observe all the doings of man, and constantly take a hand in them. It should be added that a corollary is almost always appended, to the effect that these higher powers also pronounce ethical judgments upon such human acts as happen to be performed without this intervention, and are themselves animated by a lofty and impeccable morality. Most religions, of course, also embrace a concept of higher powers that are not benign, but malignant—that is, they posit the existence of demons as well as of gods. But there are very few in which the demons are regarded as superior to the gods, or even as their full equals. The great majority of creeds, East and West, savage and so-called civilized, put the gods far above the demons, and teach that the gods always wish the good of man, and that man's virtue and happiness run in direct ratio to his obedience to their desires. That is, they are all based upon the doctrine of what is called the goodness of God. This is true pre-eminently of the chief oriental faiths: Buddhism, Brahminism and Confucianism. It is true even of Christianity, despite its luxuriant demonology. No true Christian can believe that God ever deliberately and wantonly injures him, or could conceivably wish him ill. The slings and arrows of God, he believes, are brought down upon him by his own ignorance and contumacy. He believes that if he could be like God he would be perfect.

This doctrine of the goodness of God, it seems to me, is no more, at bottom, than an evidence of arrested intellectual development. It does not fit into what we know of the nature and operations of the cosmos today; it is a survival from a day of universal ignorance. That it is still given credit in the Far East is not surprising, for the intellectual development of the Far East, despite all the nonsense that is talked about Indian and Chinese "philosophy," is really no further advanced than that of Europe was in the time of St. Louis. The most profound Hindoo or Chinese "philosopher" believes, as objective facts, things that would make even a Georgia Fundamentalist snicker, and so his "philosophy" is chiefly worthless, as was that of the Greeks. The Greeks sometimes guessed right, just as the swamis and yogis of Los Angeles sometimes guess right, but in the main their speculations, being based upon false observations, were valueless, and no one would pay any attention to them today if it were not for the advertising they get from theologians, who find them to their taste, and professional "philosophers," who make a living trying to teach them to sophomores. But if the belief in the goodness of God is natural to misinformed orientals, as it was natural to the singularly ignorant Greeks, it is certainly not natural to the enlightened races of the West today, for all their science is simply a great massing of proofs that God, if He exists, is neither good nor bad, but simply indifferent—an infinite Force carrying on the operation of unintelligible processes without the slightest regard, either one way or the other, for the comfort, safety and happiness of man.

Why, then, does this belief survive? Largely, I am convinced, because it is supported by another hoary relic from the adolescence of the race, to wit, the weakness for poetry. The Jews fastened their religion upon the Western world, not because it was more reasonable than the religions of their contemporaries—as a matter of fact, it was vastly less reasonable than many of them—, but because it was far more poetical. The poetry in it was what fetched the decaying Romans, and after them the barbarians of the North; not the so-called Christian evidences. For the Jews were poets of a truly colossal eloquence, and they put their fundamental superstitions into dithyrambs of such compelling loveliness that they disarmed the common sense even of skeptical Romans, and so knocked out all other contemporary religions, many of which were in far closer accord with what was then known of the true operation of the universe. To this day no better poetry has ever been written. It is so powerful in its effects that even men who reject its content in toto are more or less susceptible to it. One hesitates to flout it on purely aesthetic grounds; however dubious it may be in doctrine, it is nevertheless almost perfect in form, and so even the most violent atheist tends to respect it, just as he respects a beautiful but deadly toad-stool. For no man, of course, ever quite gets over poetry. He may seem to have recovered from it, just as he may seem to have recovered from the measles of his school-days, but exact observation teaches us that no such recovery is ever quite perfect; there always remains a scar, weakness and memory.

Now, there is reason for maintaining that the taste for poetry, in the process of human development, marks a stage measurably later than the stage of religion. Savages so little cultured that they know no more of poetry than a cow have elaborate and often very ingenious theologies. If this be true, then it follows that the individual, as he rehearses the life of the species, is apt to carry his taste for poetry further along than he carries his religion—that if his development is arrested at any stage before complete intellectual maturity that arrest is far more likely to leave him with poetical hallucinations than it is to leave him with theological hallucinations. Thus, taking men in the mass, there are many more natural victims of the former than of the latter—and here is where the talent of the ancient Jews does it execution. It holds countless thousands to the faith who are actually against the faith, and the weakness with which it holds them is their weakness for poetry, i.e., for the beautiful but untrue. Put into plain, harsh words most of the articles they are asked to believe would revolt them, but put into sonorous dithyrambs, the same articles fascinate and overwhelm them. It is not the logical substance of the Old Testament that continues to hold the mind of modern man, for that logical substance must often revolt him, even when he is of sub-normal intelligence; it is the sonorous strophes of the ancient bards and prophets. And it is not the epistemology, or the natural history, or the ethical scheme, or the system of jurisprudence of the New Testament that melts his heart and wets his eyes; it is simply the poetical magic of the Sermon on the Mount, the exquisite parables, and the incomparable story of the Child on the Manger.

This persistence of the weakness for poetry, no doubt, explains the great growth of ritualism in an age of skepticism. Almost every day theology gets another blow from science. So badly has it been battered during the past century, indeed, that educated men now give it little more credence than they give to sorcery, its ancient ally. But squeezing out the logical nonsense does no damage to the poetry; on the contrary, it frees, and, in a sense, dignifies the poetry. Paul's chief doctrines, clearly stated, offend the intelligence intolerably, but clothed and concealed by the gorgeous vestments of the mass they separate themselves from logic entirely and take on something of the witchery of beauty. Thus there is a constant movement of Christians, and particularly of newly-intellectual Christians, from the more literal varieties of Christian faith to the more poetical varieties. The normal Babbitt, in the United States, is born a Methodist or a Baptist, but when he begins to lay by money he and his wife tend to go over to the American branch of the Church of England, which is not only more fashionable but also less revolting to the higher cerebral centers. His daughter, when she emerges from the finishing-school, is very High Church; his grand-daughter, if the family keeps its securities, will probably go over to Rome.

In view of all this, I am convinced that the Christian church, as a going concern, is quite safe from danger, despite the rapid growth of agnosticism. The theology it merchants is full of childish and disgusting absurdities; practically all the other religions of civilized and semi-civilized men are more plausible. But all of these religions, including even Modernism, contain the fatal defect that they appeal primarily to the reason. Christianity will survive not only Modernism but also Fundamentalism, a much more difficult business. It will survive because it makes its first and foremost appeal to that moony sense of the poetic which is in all men—to that elemental sentimentality which, in men of arrested mental development, which is to say, in the average men of Christendom, passes for the passion to seek and know beauty.

3. The Devotee

If religion is thus charming to the more enlightened modern Christian only in proportion as it is poetical, i.e., as it is regarded as not literally true, it is charming to the enlightened spectator only when it is formal and hence more or less insincere. A devotee on her knees in some abysmal and mysterious cathedral, the while solemn music sounds, and clouds of incense come down the wing, and priests in luxurious, levantine costumes busy themselves with stately ceremonials in a dead and not too respectable language—this is unquestionably beautiful, particularly if the devotee herself be sightly. But the same devotee aroused to hysterical protestations of faith by the shrieks and contortions of a Methodist dervish in the costume of a Southern member of Congress, her knees trembling with the fear of God, her hands clenched as if to do combat with Beelzebub, her lips discharging hosannas and hallelujahs—this is merely obscene.

4. The Restoration of Beauty

I have said that the poetry which safeguards Christianity from destruction today was borrowed from the ancient Jews, authors of the two Testaments. But there was a long period during which it was overshadowed by purely logical ideas, many of them of a sort that would be called bolshevistic today. The principal Christians of the apostolic age were almost exactly like the modern Calvinists and Wesleyans—men quite without taste or imagination, whoopers and shouters, low vulgarians, cads. So far as is known, their public worship was wholly devoid of the sense of beauty; their sole concern was with the salvation of their so-called souls. Thus they left us nothing worth preserving—not a single church, or liturgy, or even hymn. The objects of art exhumed from the Catacombs are inferior to the drawings and statuettes of Cro-Magnon man. All the moving beauty that adorns the corpse of Christianity today came into being long after the Fathers had perished. The faith was centuries old before Christians began to build cathedrals, and nearly a thousand years old before they learned how to build good ones. It was twelve hundred years old before they invented mariolatry—the prime cause of the appearance of a purely Christian poetry. We think of Christmas as the typical Christian festival, and no doubt it is; none other is so generally kept by Christian sects, or so rich in charm and beauty. Well, Christmas, as we now have it, was almost unknown in Christendom until the Eleventh Century, when the relics of St. Nicholas of Myra, originally the patron of pawnbrokers, were brought from the East to Italy. At this time the Universal Church was already torn by controversies and menaced by schisms, and the shadow of the Reformation was plainly discernible in the West. Religions, in fact, like castles, sunsets and women, never reach their maximum of beauty until they are touched by decay.

5. End-Product

Christendom may be defined briefly as that part of the world in which, if any man stands up in public and solemnly swears that he is a Christian, all his auditors will laugh.

6. Another

At the end of one millennium and nine centuries of Christianity, it remains an unshakable assumption of the law in all Christian countries and of the moral judgment of Christians everywhere that if a man and a woman, entering a room together, close the door behind them, the man will come out sadder and woman wiser.

7. Holy Clerks

Around no class of men do more false assumptions cluster than around the rev. clergy, our lawful commissioners at the throne of Grace. I proceed at once to a crass example: the assumption that clergymen are necessarily religious. Obviously, it is widely cherished, even by clergymen themselves. The most ribald of us, in the presence of a holy clerk, is a bit self-conscious, reticent and awed. I am myself given to criticizing Divine Providence somewhat freely, but in the company of the rector of my parish, even at the *Biertisch* [beer-garden table], I tone down my animadversions to a level of feeble and polite remonstrance. I know the fellow too well, of course, to have any actual belief in his piety. He is, in fact, rather less pious than the average right-thinking Americano, and I doubt gravely that the sorceries he engages in professionally every day awaken in him any emotion more lofty than boredom. I have heard him pray for Coolidge, for the heathen and for rain, but I have never heard him pray for himself. Nevertheless, the public assumption that he is highly devout, though I dispute it, colors all my intercourse with him, and deprives him of hearing some of my most searching and intelligent observations.

All that is needed to expose the hollowness of this ancient delusion is to consider the chain of causes which brings a young man to taking holy orders. Is it, in point of fact, an irresistible religious impulse that sets him to studying exegetics, homiletics and the dog-Greek of the New Testament, and an irresistible religious impulse only, or is it something quite different? I believe that it is something quite different, and that that something may be described briefly as a desire to shine in the world without too much effort. The young theologue, in brief, is commonly an ambitious but somewhat lazy and incompetent fellow, and he studies theology instead of medicine or law because it offers a quicker and easier route to an assured job and public respect. The sacred sciences may be nonsensical bores, but they at least have the vast virtue of short-circuiting, so to speak, the climb up the ladder of security. The young doctor, for a number of years after he graduates, either has to work for nothing or to content himself with the dregs of practise, and the young lawyer, unless he has unusual influence or complete atrophy of the conscience, often teeters on the edge of actual starvation. But the young divine is a safe and distinguished man the moment he is ordained; indeed, his popularity, especially among the faithful who are fair, is often greater at that moment than it ever is afterward. His livelihood is assured instantly. At one stroke, he becomes a person of dignity and importance, eminent in his community, deferred to even by those who question his magic, and vaguely and pleasantly feared by those who credit it.

These facts, you may be sure, are not concealed from ambitious young men of the sort I have mentioned. Such young men have eyes, and even a certain capacity for ratiocination. They observe the nine sons of the police sergeant: one a priest at twenty-five, with a fine house to live in, invitations to all christenings and birthday parties for miles around, and plenty of time to go to the ball-game on Summer afternoons; the others struggling desperately to make their livings as piano-movers, tin-roofers, motormen or bootleggers. They observe the young Methodist dominie in his Ford sedan, flitting about among the women while their husbands labor down in the yards district, a clean collar around his neck, a solid meal of fried chicken in his gizzard, and his name in the local paper every day. They observe the Baptist dervish in his white necktie, raiding saloons, touring the bawdy-houses and raising hell generally, his tabernacle packed every Sunday night, a noble clink of silver in his collection-plates, and a fat purse for him now and then from the Ladies' Aid or the Ku Klux Klan. Only crazy women ever fall in love with young doctors or lawyers, but every young clergyman, if he is so inclined, may have a whole harem, and with infinitely less danger than a struggling lawyer, a bootlegger, or a bank clerk runs every day. Even if he is celibate, the gals bathe him in their smiles; in truth, the more celibate he is, the more attention he gets from them. No wonder his high privileges and immunities propagate the sin of envy? No wonder there are still candidates for the holy shroud, despite the vast growth of atheism among us?

It seems to me that the majority of the young men who are thus sucked into holy orders are not actually pious at all, but rather somewhat excessively realistic—that genuine piety is far more apt to keep a youth out of the pulpit than to take him into it. The true devotee, frequenting the sacred edifice constantly, becomes too familiar with the daily duties of a clergy-man to see any religious satisfaction in them. In the main, they have noth-ing to do with religion at all, but are basically social or commercial. In so far as a clergyman works at all, he works as the general manager of a corporation, and only too often it is in financial difficulties and rent by factions among the stockholders. His specifically religious duties are of a routine and monotonous nature, and must needs depress him mightily, as a surgeon is depressed by the endless snaring of tonsils and excision of appendices. He debases spiritual exaltation by reducing it to a hollow and meaningless formality, as a politician debases patriotism and lady of joy debases love. He becomes, in the end, quite anaesthetic to religion, and even hostile to it. The fact is made distressingly visible by the right rev. the bench of bishops. For a bishop to fall on his knees spontaneously and begin to pray to God would make almost as great a scandal as if he mounted his throne in a bathing-suit. The piety of the ecclesiastic, on such high levels, becomes wholly formal and theoretical. The servant of God has been lifted so near to the saints and become so familiar with the inner workings of the divine machinery that the sense of awe and wonder has oozed out of him. He can no more undergo a genuine religious experience than a veteran scene-shifter can laugh at the wheezes of the First Gravedigger. It is, per-haps, well that this is so. If the higher clergy were actually religious some of their own sermons and pastoral epistles would scare them to death.

(*Prejudices, Fifth Series*)

Protestantism in the Republic

[*Since the 19th century, it's been hard to find a Midwesterner or Southerner whose cognitive development hasn't been arrested, by the age of eleven or twelve, by an unrelenting barrage of idiotic assertions presented as fact, from their parents and the other adults around them.*

In Mencken's time, in most of the country about the only place where a young person would encounter a complete sentence was in the Sunday pew. Maybe this explains his curious reverence for high-church Protestantism and his overestimation of the Bible's literary worth; to his readers who grew up in a house with only one book, that book looked wise, and if they only heard a coherent paragraph spoken in the context of the gospel, then they likely associated its blather with genuine wisdom—and better "Modernism" than Methodism.

Mencken recognized that the real problem with the Midwest and the South was that it was an intellectual and cultural desert that made the public thirst for clean water, if only from the baptismal font. This set up a split in American Christianity, as significant as that in 1517, between the Midwest and South and the more enlightened parts of the country. In urban areas:

"To-day, indeed, even the Methodists who remain Methodists begin to wobble. Tiring of the dreadful din that goes with the orthodox Wesleyan demonology, they talk to ceremonials that grow more and more stately and voluptuous. The sermon ceases to be a cavalry charge, and becomes soft and pizzicato. The choir abandons 'Throw Out the Life-Line' and 'Are Your Ready for the Judgment Day?' and toys with Handel. The rev. pastor throws off the uniform of a bank cashier and puts on a gown."

On the other hand, in the countryside and small towns, this happened:

"All I can detect is a rapid descent to mere barbaric devil-chasing. In all those parts of the Republic where Beelzebub is still as real as Babe Ruth or Dr. Coolidge, and men drink raw fusel oil hot from the still—for example, in the rural sections of the Middle West and everywhere in the South save a few

walled towns—the evangelical sects plunge into an abyss of malignant imbe-
cility, and declare a holy war upon every decency that civilized men cherish."

To those who wonder how one group of Christians blesses same-sex marriages
and another group condemns to hell the person who bakes the cake for the
reception, Mencken provides the answer.]

That Protestantism in this great Christian realm is down with a wasting
disease must be obvious to every amateur of ghostly pathology. The denominational papers are full of alarming reports from the bedside, and all
sorts of projects for the relief of the patient. One authority holds that only
more money is needed to work a cure—that if the Christian exploiters and
usurers of the country would provide a sufficient slush fund, all the vacant
pews would be filled, and the baptismal tanks with them. Another authority argues that the one way to save the churches is to close all other places
of resort and amusement on the Sabbath, from the delicatessen shops to
road-houses, and from movie parlors to jazz palaces. Yet another proposes
a mass attack by prayer, apparently in the hope of provoking a miracle. A
fourth advocates a vast augmentation of so-called institutional effort, i.e.,
the scheme of putting bowling alleys and courting cubicles into church
cellars, and of giving over the rest of every sacred edifice to debates on the
Single Tax, boxing matches, baby shows, mental hygiene clinics, lectures
by converted actors, movie shows, raffles, and opening classes in salesman-
ship, automobile repairing, birth control, interior decoration, and the art
and mystery of the realtor. A fifth, borrowing a leaf from Big Business,
maintains that consolidation and reorganization are what is needed—that
the existence of half a dozen rival churches in every American village profits the devil a great deal more than it profits God. This last scheme seems
to have won a great deal of support among the pious. At least a score of
committees are now trying to draw up plans for possible consolidation and
even the Southern and Northern Methodists, who hate each other violently, have been in peaceful though vain negotiations.

On the merits of these conflicting remedies I attempt no pronounce-
ment, but I have been at some pains to look into the symptoms and nature
of the disease. My report is that it seems to me to be analogous to that
malady which afflicts a star in the heavens when it splits into two halves
and they go slambanging into space in opposite directions. That, in brief,
is what appears to be the matter with Protestantism in the United States
to-day. One half of it is moving with slowly accelerating speed, in the direc-

tion of the Harlot of the Seven Hills: the other is sliding down into voodooism. The former carries the greater part of Protestant money with it;
the latter carries the greater part of Protestant enthusiasm, or, as the word
now is, pep. What remains in the middle may be likened to a torso without
either brains to think with or legs to dance—in other words, something
that begins to be professionally attractive to the mortician, though it still
makes shift to breathe. There is no lack of life on the higher levels, where
the most solvent Methodists and the like are gradually transmogrified into
Episcopalians, and the Episcopalians shin up the ancient bastions of Holy
Church, and there is no lack of life on the lower levels, where the rural
Baptists, by the order of Fundamentalism, the Anti-Saloon League, and the
Ku Klux Klan, rapidly descend to the dogmas and practices of the Congo
jungle. But in the middle there is desiccation and decay. Here is where
Protestantism was once strongest. Here is the region of the plain and godly
Americano, fond of devotion but distrustful of every hint of orgy—the
honest fellow who suffers dutifully on Sunday, pays his share, and hopes
for a few kind words from the pastor when his time comes to die. He stands
to-day on a burning deck. It is no wonder that Sunday automobiling begins
to get him in the clutches. If he is not staggered one day by his pastor's appearance in surplice and stole, he is staggered the day following by a file of
Ku Kluxers marching up the aisle. So he tends to absent himself from pious
exercises, and the news gets about that there is something the matter with
the churches, and the denominational papers bristle with schemes to get
it right, and many up-and-coming pastors, tiring of preaching and parish
work, get excellent jobs as the executive secretaries of these schemes, and
go about the country expounding them to the faithful.

The extent to which Protestantism, in its upper reaches has succumbed
to the harlotries of Rome seems to be but little apprehended by the majority of connoisseurs. I was myself unaware of the whole truth until last
Christmas, when, in the pursuit, of a quite unrelated inquiry, I employed
agents to attend all the services held in the principal Protestant basilicas of
an eminent American city, and to bring in the best reports they could formulate upon what went on in the lesser churches. The substance of these
reports, in so far as they related to churches patronized by the well-to-do
was simple: they revealed a head-long movement to the right, and almost
precipitate flight over the mountain. Six so-called Episcopal churches held
midnight services on Christmas Eve in obvious imitation of Catholic midnight masses, and one of them actually called its service a solemn high
mass. Two invited the nobility and gentry to processions, and a third con-

cealed a procession under the name of a pageant. One offered Gounod's St. Cecilia mass on Christmas morning, and another the Missa Solemnis by the same composer; three others, somewhat more timorous, contented themselves with parts of masses. One, throwing off all pretense and euphemism, summoned the faithful to no less than three Christian masses, naming them by name—two low and one high. All six churches were aglow with candles, and two employed incense.

But that was not the worst. Two Presbyterian churches and one Baptist church, not to mention five Lutheran churches of different synods, had choral services in the dawn of Christmas morning, and the one attended by the only one of my agents who got up early enough—it was in a Presbyterian church—was made gay with candles, and had a palpably Roman smack. Yet worse: a rich and conspicuous Methodist church, patronized by the leading Wesleyan wholesalers and money-lenders of the town, boldly offered a medieval carol service. Medieval? What did that mean? The Middle Ages ended on July 16, 1453, at 12 o'clock meridian [with the printing of Gutenberg's Bible], and the Reformation was not launched by Luther until October 31, 1517, at 10:15 a.m. If medieval, in the sense in which it was here used, does not mean Roman Catholic, then I surely went to school in vain. My agent, born a Methodist, reported that the whole ceremony shocked him excessively. It began with trumpet blasts from the church spire and it concluded with an Ave Maria by a vested choir! Candles were up in glittering ranks behind the chancel rail, and above them glowed a shining electric star. God help us all indeed! What next? Will the rev. pastor, on some near to-morrow, defy the lightnings of Jahweh by appearing in alb and dalmatic? Will he turn his back upon the faithful? Will he put in a telephone-booth for auricular confession? I shudder to think of what old John Wesley would have said about that vested choir and that shining star. Or Bishop Francis Asbury. Or the Rev. Jabez Bunting. Or Robert Strawbridge, that consecrated man.

Here, of course, I do not venture into the contumacy of criticising; I merely marvel. A student of the sacred sciences all my life, I am well learned in the dogmas and ceremonials of the sects, and know what they affect and what they abhor. Does anyone argue that the use of candles in public worship would have had the sanction of the Ur-Wesleyans, or that they would have consented to *Blasmusik* [brass band music] and a vested choir? If so, let the sciolist come forward. Down to fifty years ago, in fact, the Methodists prohibited Christmas services altogether, as Romish and heathen. But now we have ceremonies almost operatic, and the sweet masses of Gounod are just around the corner! As I have said, the Episcopalians—who, in most American cities, are largely ex-Methodists or ex-Presbyterians, or, in New York, ex-Jews—go still further. In three of the churches attended by my agents, Holy Communion was almost indistinguishable from the mass. Two of these churches, according to information placed at my disposal by the police, are very fashionable; to get into one of them is almost as difficult as ordering a suit of clothes from Poole. But the richer the Episcopalian, the more eager he is to forget that he was once baptized by public outcry or total immersion. The Low Church rectors, in the main, struggle with poor congregations, born to the faith but deficient in buying power. As bank accounts increase the fear of the devil diminishes, and there is bred a sense of beauty. This sense of beauty, in its practical effects, is identical with the work of the Paulist Fathers. To-day, indeed, even the Methodists who remain Methodists begin to wobble. Tiring of the dreadful din that goes with the orthodox Wesleyan demonology, they take its ceremonials that grow more and more stately and voluptuous. The sermon ceases to be a cavalry charge, and becomes soft and pizzicato. The choir abandons "Throw Out the Life-Line" and "Are You Ready for the Judgment Day?" and toys with Handel. The rev. pastor throws off the uniform of a bank cashier and puts on a gown. It is an evolution that has, viewed from a tree, a certain merit. The stock of nonsense in the world is sensibly diminished and the stock of beauty augmented. But what would the old-time circuit-riders say of it, imagining them miraculously brought back from hell?

So much for the volatilization that is going on above the diaphragm. What is its progress below? All I can detect is a rapid descent to mere barbaric devil-chasing. In all these parts of the Republic where Beelzebub is still as real as Babe Ruth or Dr. Coolidge, and men drink raw fusel oil hot from the still—for example, in the rural sections of the Middle West and everywhere in the South save a few walled towns—the evangelical sects plunge into an abyss of malignant imbecility, and declare a holy war upon every decency that civilized men cherish. First the Anti-Saloon League, and now the Ku Klux Klan and the various Fundamentalist organizations, have converted them into vast machines for pursuing and butchering unbelievers. They have thrown the New Testament overboard, and gone back to the Old, and particularly the bloodiest parts of it. Their one aim seems to be to break heads, to spread terror, to propagate hatred. Everywhere they have set up enmities that will not die out for generations. Neighbor looks askance at neighbor, the land is filled with spies, every man of the slightest intelligence is suspect. Christianity becomes a sort of psychic cannibalism. Unfortunately, the doings of the rustic gentlemen of God who furnish steam for this movement have been investigated but imperfectly, and in consequence too little is known about them. Even the sources of their power, so far as I know, have not been looked into. My suspicion is that it has increased as the influence of the old-time country-town newspapers has declined. These newspapers, in large areas of the land, once genuinely molded public opinion. They attracted to their service a shrewd and salty class of rustic philosophers, mainly highly alcoholized; they were outspoken in their views and responded only slightly to the prevailing crazes. In the midst of the Bryan uproar, a quarter of a century ago, scores of little weeklies in the South and Middle West kept up a gallant battle for sound money and the Hanna idealism. There were red-hot Democratic papers in Pennsylvania, and others in Ohio; there were Republican sheets in rural Maryland, and even in Virginia. The growth of the big city dailies is what chiefly reduced them to puerility. As communications improved every yokel began following Brisbane, Dr. Frank Crane, and Mutt and Jeff. The rural mail carrier began leaving a 24-page yellow in every second box. The hinds distrusted and detested the politics of these great organs, but enjoyed their imbecilities. The country weekly could not match the latter, and so it began to decline. It is now in a low state everywhere in America. Half of it is boiler-plate and the other half is cross-roads gossip. The editor is no longer the leading thinker of his town; instead, he is commonly a broken and despairing man, cadging for advertisements and hoping for a political job. He used to aspire to the State Senate; now he is content with the post of town bailiff or road surveyor.

His place has been taken by the village pastor. The pastor got into public affairs by the route of Prohibition. The shrewd shysters who developed the Anti-Saloon League made a politician of him, and once he had got a taste of power he was eager for more. It came very quickly. As industry penetrated to the rural regions the new-blown Babbitt began to sense his capacity for safeguarding the established order, so he was given the job: he became a local Billy Sunday. And, simultaneously the old-time politicians, taught a lesson by the Anti-Saloon League, began to defer to him in general, as they had yielded to him particular. He was consulted about candidacies; he had his say about policies. The local school-board soon became his private preserve. The wandering cony-catchers of the tin-pot fraternal orders found him a useful man. He was, by now, a specialist in all forms of public rectitude, from teetotalism to patriotism. He was put up on days of ceremony to sob for the flag, vice the county judge, retired. When the Klan burst upon the peasants all of his new duties synthesized. He was obviously the chief local repository of its sublime principles, theological, social, ethnological and patriotic. In every country town in America to-day, wherever the Klan continues to rowel the hinds, its chief engine is a clerk in holy orders. If the Baptists are strong, their pastor is that engine. Failing Baptists, the heroic work is assumed by the Methodist parson, or the Presbyterian, or the Campbellite. Without these sacerdotal props the Invisible Empire would have faded long ago.

What one mainly notices about these ambassadors of Christ, observing them in the mass, is their vast lack of sound information and sound sense. They constitute, perhaps, the most ignorant class of teachers ever set up to lead a civilized people; they are even more ignorant than the county superintendents of schools. Learning, indeed, is not esteemed in the evangelical denominations, and any literate plow-hand, if the Holy Spirit inflames him, is thought to be fit to preach. Is he commonly sent, as a preliminary, to a training camp, to college? But what a college! You will find one in every mountain valley of the land, with its single building in its bare pasture lot, and its faculty of half-idiot pedagogues and broken-down preachers. One man, in such a college, teaches oratory, ancient history, arithmetic and Old Testament exegesis. The aspirant comes in from the barnyard, and goes back in a year or two to the village. His body of knowledge is that of a street-car motorman or a vaudeville actor. But he has learned the cliches of his craft, and he has got him a long-tailed coat, and so he has made his escape from the harsh labors of his ancestors, and is set up as a fountain of light and learning.

It is from such ignoramuses that the lower half of American Protestantism gets its views of the cosmos. Certainly Fundamentalism should not be hard to understand when its sources are inspected. How can the teacher teach when his own head is empty? Of all that constitutes the sum of human knowledge he is as innocent as an Eskimo. Of the arts he knows absolutely nothing; of the sciences he never so much as heard. No good book ever penetrates to these remote "colleges," nor does any graduate ever take away a desire to read one. He has been warned, indeed, against their blandishments; what is not addressed solely to the paramount business of saving souls is of the devil. So when he hears by chance or the battle of ideas beyond the sky-rim, he quite naturally puts it down to Beelzebub. What comes to him, vaguely and distorted, is unintelligible to him. He is suspicious of it, afraid of it—and he quickly communicates his fears to his dupes. The common man, in many ways, is hard to arouse; it is a terrific job to ram even the most elemental ideas into him. But it is always easy to scare him.

That is the daily business of the evangelical pastors of the Republic. They are specialists in alarms and bugaboos. The rum demon, atheists, Bolsheviki, the Pope, bootleggers, the Jews—all these have served them in turn, and in the demonology of the Ku Klux Klan all have been conveniently brought together. The old stock company of devils has been retired, and with it the old repertoire of private sins. The American peasant of to-day finds it vastly easier to claw into heaven than he used to. Personal holiness has now been handed over to the Holy Rollers and other such survivors from a harsher day. It is sufficient now to hate the Pope, to hate the Jews, to hate the scientists, to hate all foreigners, to hate whatever the cities yield to. These hatreds have been spread in the land by rev. pastors, chiefly Baptists and Methodists. They constitute, with their attendant fears, the basic religion of the American clod-hopper to-day. They are the essence of the new Protestantism, second division, American style.

Their public effects are constantly underestimated until it is too late. I ask no indulgence for calling attention to the case of Prohibition. Fundamentalism, it may be, is sneaking upon the nation in the same disarming way. The cities laugh at the yokels, but meanwhile the politicians take careful notice; such mountebanks as Peay of Tennessee and Blease of South Carolina have already issued their preliminary whoops. As the tide rolls up the pastors will attain to greater and greater consequence. Already, indeed, they swell visibly in power and pretension. The Klan, in its earlier days, kept them discreetly under cover; they labored valiantly in the hold, but only lay go-getters were seen upon the bridge. But now they are everywhere on public display, leading the anthropoid host. The curious thing is that their activity gets little if any attention from the established publicists. Let a lone Red arise to annoy a barroom of Michigan lumber-jacks, and at once the fire-alarm sounds and the full military and naval power of the nation is summoned to put down the outrage. But how many Americans would the Reds convert to their rubbish, even supposing them free to spout it on every street-corner? Probably not enough, all told, to make a day's hunting for a regiment of militia. The American moron's mind simply does not run in that direction; he wants to keep his Ford, even at the cost of losing the Bill of Rights. But the stuff that the Baptist and Methodist dervishes have on tap is very much to his taste; he gulps it eagerly and rubs his tummy. I suggest that it might be well to make a scientific inquiry into the nature of it. The existing agencies of sociological snooting seem to be busy in other directions. There are elaborate surveys of some of the large cities, showing how much it costs to teach a child the principles of Americanism, how often average citizen falls into the hands of the cops, how many detective stories are taken out of the city library daily, and how many children a normal Polish woman has every year. Why not a survey of the rustic areas, where men are he and God still reigns. Why not an attempt to find out just what the Baptist dominies have drilled into the heads of the Tennesseans, Arkansans and Nebraskans? It would be amusing, and it would be instructive. And useful. For it is well, in such matters, to see clearly what is ahead. The United States grows increasingly urban, but its ideas are still hatched in the little towns. What the swineherds credit to-day is whooped to-morrow by their agents and attorneys in Congress, and then comes upon cities suddenly, with all the force of law. Where do the swineherds get it? Mainly from the only publicists and metaphysicians they know: the gentlemen of the sacred faculty. It was not the bawling of the mountebank Bryan, but the sermon of a mountain Bossuet that laid the train of the Scopes case and made a whole State forever ridiculous. I suggest looking more carefully into the notions that such ignoramuses spout.

Meanwhile, what is the effect of all this upon the Protestant who retains some measure of sanity, the moderate and peaceable fellow—him called by William Graham Sumner the Forgotten Man? He is silent while the bombs burst and the stink bombs go off, but what is he thinking? I believe that he is thinking strange and dreadful thoughts—thoughts that would have frozen his own spine a dozen years ago. He is thinking, *imprimis* [first of all], that there must be something in this evolution heresy after all, else Methodist bishops and other such bristling foes to sense would not be so frantically against it. And he is thinking, secondly, that perhaps a civilized man, in the last analysis, would be worse off if Sherman's march were repeated by the Papal Guard. Between these two thoughts American Protestantism is being squeezed, so to speak, to death.

(*Prejudices, Fifth Series*)

SISTER AIMEE

[Americans will watch a hot chick do pretty much anything. An odd but telling piece of evidence for this is provided by the earnings of (yes) drummers. According to one well placed pro, the highest earners are not professionals who've spent a lifetime honing their craft, but bikini-clad women in their twenties who play along with recorded rock tracks on Youtube videos (the only apparent exceptions being a few drummers in the most famous bands).

If the success of the Real Housewives series tells us anything, it's that we especially like to watch hot chicks argue and fight. As much as we like to look at them, and straight women like to look as much or more than guys (undoubtedly checking out the competition), we prefer to watch them do something other than just pose on a beach or strut seductively on a runway—and bouncing around in a bikini while playing drums is a perfect example of this.

In Mencken's day, a man wanting to watch a hot-and-bothered beautiful woman had to have an uplifting reason. And what could be more uplifting than attending a Baptist service? Sister Aimee, the forerunner of today's televangelists, gave her audience a spiritual lap dance, and although Mencken knew the con, he leaves the impression that he planned to tuck in a dollar or two anyway.]

The rev. sister in God [Aimee Semple McPherson], I confess, greatly disappointed me. Arriving in Los Angeles out of the dreadful deserts of Arizona and New Mexico, I naturally made tracks to hear and see the town's most distinguished citizen. Her basilica turned out to be at a great distance from my hotel, far up a high hill and in the midst of a third-rate neighborhood. It was a cool and sunshiny Sunday afternoon, the place was packed, and the whisper had gone around that Aimee was heated up by the effort to jail her, and would give a gaudy show. But all I found myself gaping at, after an hour, was an orthodox Methodist revival, with a few trimmings borrowed from the Baptists and the Holy Rollers—in brief, precisely the sort of thing that goes on in the shabby suburbs and dark back streets of Baltimore, three hundred nights of every year.

Aimee, of course, is richer than most evangelists, and so she has got herself a plant that far surpasses anything ever seen in shabby suburbs. Her temple to the One God is immensely wide—as wide, almost, as the Hippodrome in New York—and probably seats 2,500 customers. There is a full brass band down in front, with a grand piano to one side of it and an organ to the other. From the vast gallery, built like that of a theater, runways run along the side walls to what may be called the proscenium arch, and from their far ends stairways lead down to the platform. As in many other evangelical bull-rings, there are theater seats instead of pews. Some pious texts are emblazoned on the wall behind the platform: I forget what they say. There are no stained glass windows. The architecture, in and out, is of the early *Norddeutscher-Lloyd Rauchzimmer* [plush smoking room] school, with modifications suggested by the filling-stations of the Standard Oil Company of New Jersey. The whole building is very cheaply made. It is large and hideous, but I don't think it cost much. Nothing in Los Angeles appears to have cost much. The town is inconceivably shoddy.

As I say, Aimee has nothing on tap to make my eyes pop, old revival fan that I am. The proceedings began with a solemn march by the brass band, played about as well as the average Salvation Army could have done it, but no better. Then a brother from some remote outpost filed down the aisle at the head of a party of fifty or sixty of the faithful. They sang a hymn, the brother made a short speech, and then he handed Aimee a check for $500 for her Defense Fund. A quartet followed, male, a bit scared, and with Army haircuts. Two little girls then did a duet, to the music of a ukulele played by one of them. Then Aimee prayed. And then she delivered a brief harangue. I could find nothing in it worthy of remark. It was the time-honored evangelical hokum, made a bit more raucous than usual by the loud-speakers strewn all over the hall. A brother who seemed to be a sort of stage manager held the microphone directly under Aimee's nose. When, warmed by her homilectic passion, she turned this way or that, he followed her. It somehow suggested an attentive deck steward, plying his useful art on a rough day. Aimee wore a long white robe, with a very low-cut collar, and over it there was a cape of dark purple. Her thick hair, piled high, turned out to be of mahogany brown. I had heard that it was a flaming red.

The rest of the orgy went on in the usual way. Groups of four, six, eight or twenty got up and sang. A large, pudgy, soapy-looking brother prayed.

Aimee herself led the choir in a hymn with a lively tune and very saucy words, chiefly aimed at her enemies. Two or three times more she launched into brief addresses. But mostly she simply ran the show. While the quartets bawled and the band played she was busy at a telephone behind the altar or hurling orders in a loud stage-whisper at sargeants and corporals on the floor. Obviously, a very managing woman, strongly recalling the madame of a fancy house on a busy Saturday night. A fixed smile stuck to her from first to last.

What brought this commonplace and transparent mountebank to her present high estate, with thousands crowding her tabernacle daily and money flowing in upon her from whole regiments of eager dupes? The answer, it seems to me, is as plain as mud. For years she had been wandering about the West, first as a side-show wriggler, then as a faith healer, and finally as a cow-town evangelist. One day, inspired by God, she decided to try her fortune in Los Angeles. Instantly she was a roaring success. And why? For the plain reason that there were more morons collected in Los Angeles than in any other place on earth—because it was a pasture foreordained for evangelists, and she was the first comer to give it anything low enough for its taste and comprehension.

The osteopaths, chiropractors and other such quacks had long marked and occupied it. It swarmed with swamis, spiritualists, Christian Scientists, crystal-gazers and the allied necromancers. It offered brilliant pickings for real estate speculators, oil-stock brokers, wire-tappers and so on. But the town pastors were not up to its opportunities. They ranged from melancholy High Church Episcopalians, laboriously trying to interest retired Iowa alfalfa kings in ritualism, down to struggling Methodists and Baptists, as earnestly seeking to inflame the wives of the same monarchs with the crimes of the Pope. All this was over the heads of the trade. The Iowans longed for something that they could get their teeth into. They wanted magic and noise. They wanted an excuse to whoop.

Then came Aimee, with the oldest, safest tricks out of the pack of Dr. Billy Sunday, Dr. Gipsy Smith and the rest of the consecrated hell-robbers. To them she added some passes from her circus days. In a month she had Los Angeles sitting up. In six months she had it in an uproar. In a year she was building her rococo temple and her flamboyant Bible College and the half-wits were flocking in from twenty States. Today, if her temple were closed by the police, she could live on her radio business alone. Every word she utters is carried on the air to every forlorn hamlet in those abominable deserts, and every day the mail brings her a flood of money.

The effort to jail her has disingenuousness in it, and the more civilized Angelenos all sympathize with her, and wish her well. Her great success raised up two sets of enemies, both powerful. One was made up of the regular town clergy, who resented her raids upon their customers. The other was composed of the town Babbitts who began to fear that her growing celebrity was making Los Angeles ridiculous. So it was decided to bump her off, and her ill-timed morganatic honeymoon with the bald-headed and wooden-legged Mr. Ormiston offered a good chance. But it must be manifest to any fair observer that there is very little merit in the case against her. What she is charged with, in essence, is perjury, and the chief specification is that, when asked if she had been guilty of unchastity, she said no. I submit that no self-respecting judge in the Maryland Free State, drunk or sober, would entertain such a charge against a woman, and that no Maryland grand jury would indict her. It is unheard of, indeed, in any civilized community for a woman to be tried for perjury uttered in defense of her honor. But in California, as everyone knows, the process of justice is full of unpleasant novelties, and so poor Aimee, after a long obscene hearing, has been held for trial.

The betting odds in the Los Angeles saloons are 50 to 1 that she will either hang the jury or get a clean acquittal. I myself, tarrying in the town, invested some money on the long end, not in avarice, but as a gesture of sympathy for a lady in distress. The local district attorney has the newspapers on his side, and during the progress of Aimee's hearing he filled one of them, in the chivalrous Southern California manner, with denunciations of her. But Aimee herself has the radio, and I believe that the radio will count most in the long run. Twice a day, week in and week out, she caresses the anthropoids of all that dusty, forbidding region with lubricious coos. And twice a day she meets her lieges of Los Angeles face to face, and has at them with her shiny eyes, her mahogany hair, her eloquent hips, and her lascivious voice. It will be a hard job, indeed, to find twelve men and true to send her to the hoosegow. Unless I err grievously, our Heavenly Father is with her.

(Mencken was right about this. The charges against McPherson were dismissed before trial.)

(*Baltimore Evening Sun*, December 13, 1926)

THE HILLS OF ZION

[*Mencken never wrote more effectively than when he acted as Virgil guiding Dante through the Inferno during the Scopes trial. As was the case in the Divine Comedy, the circles of hell burn as hot as a Midwestern sidewalk in summer.*

Mencken guides us through an intellectual hell, full of ingenious tortures contrived by Methodist ministers for the white race. As in the Inferno, the ninth circle freezes, only in this case Beelzebub appears in a conversation with William Jennings Bryan over an ice cold Coca-Cola. If you think that's not so bad, then you've never seen the sign that hangs over the entrance to Dayton, Tennessee: "Abandon all thought ye who enter here."]

It was hot weather when they tried the infidel Scopes at Dayton, but I went down there very willingly, for I had good reports of the sub-Potomac bootleggers and moreover I was eager to see something of evangelical Christianity as a going concern. In the big cities of the Republic, despite the endless efforts of consecrated men, it is laid up with a wasting disease. The very Sunday-school superintendents, taking jazz from the stealthy radio, shake their fire-proof legs; their pupils, moving into adolescence, no longer respond to the proliferating hormones by enlisting for missionary service in Africa, but resort to necking and petting instead. I know of no evangelical church from Oregon to Maine that is not short of money: the graft begins to peter out, like wire-tapping and three-card monte before it. Even in Dayton, though the mob was up to do execution upon Scopes, there was a strong smell of antinomianism. The nine churches of the village were all half empty on Sunday, and weeds choked their yards. Only two or three of the resident pastors managed to sustain themselves by their ghostly science; the rest had to take orders for mail-order pantaloons or work in the adjacent strawberry fields; one, I heard, was a barber. On the courthouse green a score of sweating theologians debated the darker passages of Holy Writ day and night, but I soon found that they were all volunteers, and that the local faithful, while interested in their exegesis as an intellectual exercise, did not permit it to impede the indigenous debaucheries. Exactly twelve minutes after I reached the village I was taken in tow by a Christian man and introduced to the favorite tipple of the Cumberland Range: half corn liquor and half coca-cola. It seemed a dreadful dose to me, spoiled as I was by the bootleg light wines and beers of the Eastern seaboard, but I found that the Dayton illuminati got it down with gusto, rubbing their tummies and rolling their eyes. I include among them the chief local proponents of the Mosaic cosmogony. They were all hot for Genesis, but their faces were far too florid to belong to teetotalers, and when a pretty girl came tripping down the Main street, which was very often, they reached for the places where their neckties should have been with all the amorous enterprise of movie actors. It seemed somehow strange.

An amiable newspaper woman of Chattanooga, familiar with these uplands, presently enlightened me. Dayton, she explained, was simply a great capital like any other great capital. That is to say, it was to Rhea county what Atlanta was to Georgia or Paris is to France. That is to say, it was predominantly epicurean and sinful. A country girl from some remote village of the county, coming into town for her semi-annual bottle of Lydia Pinham's Vegetable Compound, shivered on approaching Robinson's drug-store quite as a country girl from up-State New York might shiver on approaching the Metropolitan Opera House or the Ritz Hotel. In every village lout she saw a potential white-slaver. The hard sidewalks hurt her feet. Temptations of the flesh bristled to all sides of her, luring her to hell. This newspaper woman told me of a session with just such a visitor, holden a few days before. The latter waited outside one of the town hot-dog and coca-cola shops while her husband negotiated with a hardware merchant across the street. The newspaper woman, idling along and observing that the stranger was badly used by the heat, invited her to step into the shop for a glass of coca-cola. The invitation brought forth only a giggle of terror. Coca-cola, it quickly appeared, was prohibited by the country lady's pastor, as a levantine and hell-sent narcotic. He also prohibited coffee and tea— and pies! He had his doubts about white bread and boughten meat. The newspaper woman, interested, inquired about ice-cream. It was, she found, not specifically prohibited, but going into a coca-cola shop to get it would be clearly sinful. So she offered to get a saucer of it, and bring it out to the sidewalk. The visitor vacillated—and came near being lost. But God saved her in the nick of time. When the newspaper woman emerged from the place she was in full flight up the street! Later on her husband, mounted on a mule, overtook her four miles out the mountain pike.

This newspaper woman, whose kindness covered city infidels as well as Alpine Christians, offered to take me back in the hills to a place where the old-time religion was genuinely on tap. The Scopes jury, she explained was composed mainly of its customers, with a few Dayton sophisticates added to leaven the mass. It would thus be instructive to climb the heights and observe the former at their ceremonies. The trip, fortunately, might be made by automobile. There was a road running out of Dayton to Morgantown, in the mountains to the westward, and thence beyond. But foreigners, it appeared would have to approach the sacred grove cautiously, for the upland worshipers were very shy, and at the first sight of a strange face they would adjourn their orgy and slink into the forest. They were not to be feared, for God had long since forbidden them to practice assassination, or even assault, but if they were alarmed a rough trip would go for naught. So, after dreadful bumpings up a long and narrow road, we parked our car in a little woodpath a mile or two beyond the tiny village of Morgantown, and made the rest of the approach on foot, deployed like skirmishers. Far off in a dark, romantic glade a flickering light was visible, and out of the silence came the rumble of exhortation. We could distinguish the figure of the preacher only as a moving mote in the light: it was like looking down the tube of a dark-field microscope. Slowly and cautiously we crossed what seemed to be a pasture, and then we crouched down along the edge of a cornfield, and stealthily edged further and further. The light now grew larger and we could begin to make out what was going on. We went ahead on all fours, like snakes in the grass.

From the great limb of a mighty oak hung a couple of crude torches of the sort that car inspectors thrust under Pullman cars when a train pulls in at night. In the guttering glare was the preacher, and for a while we could see no one else. He was an immensely tall and thin mountaineer in blue jeans, his collarless shirt open at the neck and his hair a tousled mop. As he preached he paced up and down under the smoking flambeaux, and at each turn he thrust his arms into the air and yelled "Glory to God!" We crept nearer in the shadow of the cornfield, and began to hear more of his discourse. He was preaching on the Day of Judgment. The high kings of the earth, he roared, would all fall down and die; only the sanctified would stand up to receive the Lord God of Hosts. One of those kings he mentioned by name, the king of what he called Greece-y. The king of Greece-y,

he said, was doomed to hell. We crawled forward a few more yards and began to see the audience. It was seated on benches ranged round the preacher in a circle. Behind him sat a row of elders, men and women. In front
were the younger folk. We crept on cautiously, and individuals rose out of
the ghastly gloom. A young mother sat suckling her baby, rocking as the
preacher passed up and down. Two scared little girls hugged each other,
their pigtails down their backs. An immensely huge mountain woman, in
a gingham dress, cut in one piece, rolled on her heels at every "Glory to
God!" To one side, and but half visible, was what appeared to be a bed. We
found afterward that half a dozen babies were asleep on it.

The preacher stopped at last, and there arose out of the darkness a woman with her hair pulled back into a tight little knot. She began so quietly
that we couldn't hear what she said, but soon her voice rose resonantly and
we could follow her. She was denouncing the reading of books. Some wandering book agent, it appeared, had come to her cabin and tried to sell her
a specimen of his wares. She refused to touch it. Why, indeed, read a book?
If what was in it was true, then everything in it was already in the Bible.
If it was false, then reading it would imperil her soul. This syllogism from
Caliph Omar complete, she sat down. There followed a hymn, led by a
somewhat fat brother wearing silver-rimmed country spectacles. It droned
on for half a dozen stanzas, and then the first speaker resumed the floor.
He argued that the gift of tongues was real and that education was a snare.
Once his children could read the Bible, he said, they had enough. Beyond
lay only infidelity and damnation. Sin stalked the cities. Dayton itself was
a Sodom. Even Morgantown had begun to forget God. He sat down, and a
female aurochs in gingham got up. She began quietly, but was soon leaping
and roaring, and it was hard to follow her. Under cover of the turmoil we
sneaked a bit closer.

A couple of other discourses followed, and there were two or three
hymns. Suddenly a change of mood began to make itself felt. The last hymn
ran longer than the others, and dropped gradually into a monotonous unintelligible chant. The faithful broke out with exultations. When the singing ended there was a brief palaver that we could not hear, and two of the
men moved a bench into the circle of light directly under the flambeaux.
Then a half-grown girl emerged from the darkness and threw herself upon
it. We noticed with astonishment that she had bobbed hair. "This sister,"
said the leader, "has asked for prayers." We moved a bit closer. We could
now see faces plainly, and hear every word. What followed quickly reached
such heights of barbaric grotesquerie that it was hard to believe it was real.

At a signal all the faithful crowded up to the bench and began to pray—not in unison, but each for himself! At another they all fell on their knees, their arms over the penitent. The leader kneeled facing us, his head alternately thrown back dramatically or buried in his hands. Words spouted from his lips like bullets from a machine-gun—appeals to God to pull the penitent back out of hell, defiances of the demons of the air, a vast impassioned jargon of apocalyptic texts. Suddenly he rose to his feet, threw back his head and began to speak in tongues—blub, blub, blub, gurgle-gurgle-gurgle. His voice rose to a higher register. The climax was a shrill, inarticulate squawk, like that of a man throttled. He fell headlong across the pyramid of suppliants.

A comic scene? Somehow no. The poor half-wits were too horribly in earnest. It was like peeping through a knothole at the writhings of people in pain. From the squirming and jabbering mass a young woman gradually detached herself—a woman not uncomely, with a pathetic homemade cap on her head. Her head jerked back, the veins of her neck swelled, and her fists went to her throat as if she were fighting for breath. She bent backward until she was like half a hoop. Then she suddenly snapped forward. We caught a flash of the whites of her eyes. Presently her whole body began to be convulsed—great throes that began at the shoulders and ended at the hips. She would leap to her feet, thrust her arms in air, and then hurl herself upon the heap. Her praying flattened out into a mere delirious cater-wauling, like that of a Tom cat on a petting party. I describe the thing discreetly, and as a strict behaviorist. The lady's subjective sensations I leave to infidel pathologists, privy to the works of Ellis, Freud and Moll. Whatever they were, they were obviously not painful, for they were accompanied by vast heavings and gurglings of a joyful and even ecstatic nature. And they seemed to be contagious, too, for soon a second penitent, also female, joined the first, and then came a third, and a fourth, and a fifth. The last one had an extraordinary violent attack. She began with mild enough jerks of the head, but in a moment she was bounding all over the place, like a chicken with its head cut off. Every time her head came up a stream of hosannas would issue out of it. Once she collided with a dark, undersized brother, hitherto silent and stolid. Contact with her set him off as if he had been kicked by a mule. He leaped into the air, threw back his head, and began to gargle as if with a mouthful of BB shot. Then he loosed one tremendous, stentorian sentence in the tongues and collapsed.

By this time the performers were quite oblivious to the profane universe and so it was safe to go still closer. We left our hiding and came up to the little circle of light. We slipped into the vacant seats on one of the rickety benches. The heap of mourners was directly before us. They bounced into us as they cavorted. The smell that they radiated, sweating there in that obscene heap, half suffocated us. Not all of them, of course, did the thing in the grand manner. Some merely moaned and rolled their eyes. The female ox in gingham flung her great bulk on the ground and jabbered an unintelligible prayer. One of the men, in the intervals between fits, put on his spectacles and read the Bible. Beside me on the bench sat the young mother and her baby. She suckled it through the whole orgy, obviously fascinated by what was going on, but never venturing to take any hand in it. On the bed just outside the light half a dozen other babies slept peacefully. In the shadows, suddenly appearing and as suddenly going away, were vague figures, whether of believers or of scoffers I do not know. They seemed to come and go in couples. Now and then a couple at the ringside would step out and vanish into the black night. After a while some came back, the males looking somewhat sheepish. There was whispering outside the circle of vision. A couple of Fords lurched up the road, cutting holes in the darkness with their lights. Once some one out of sight loosed a bray of laughter.

All this went on for an hour or so. The original penitent, by this time, was buried three deep beneath the heap. One caught a glimpse, now and then of her yellow bobbed hair, but then she would vanish again. How she breathed down there I don't know; it was hard enough six feet away, with a strong five-cent cigar to help. When the praying brothers would rise up for a bout with the tongues their faces were streaming with perspiration. The fat harridan in gingham sweated like a longshoreman. Her hair got loose and fell down over her face. She fanned herself with her skirt. A powerful old gal she was, plainly equal in her day to a bout with obstetrics and a week's washing. Finally, she fell into a heap, breathing in great, convulsive gasps.

Finally, we got tired of the show and returned to Dayton. It was nearly eleven o'clock—an immensely late hour for those latitudes—but the whole town was still gathered in the courthouse yard, listening to the disputes of the theologians. The Scopes trial had brought them in from all directions. There was a friar wearing a sandwich sign announcing that he was the Bible champion of the world. There was a Seventh Day Adventist arguing that Clarence Darrow was the beast with seven heads and ten horns described in Revelation xiii, and that the end of the world was at hand. There was an evangelist made up like Andy Gump, with the news that atheists in Cincinnati were preparing to descend upon Dayton, hang the eminent Judge

Raulston, and burn the town. There was an ancient who maintained that no Catholic could be a Christian. There was the eloquent Dr. T.T. Martin, of Blue Mountain, Miss., come to town with a truckload of torches and hymn-books to put Darwin in his place. There was a singing brother bellowing apocalyptic hymns. There was William Jennings Bryan, followed everywhere by a gaping crowd. Dayton was having a roaring time. It was better than the circus. But the note of devotion was simply not there; the Daytonians, after listening a while, would slip away to Robinson's drugstore to regale themselves with coca-cola, or to the lobby of the Aqua Hotel, where the learned Raulston sat in state, judicially picking his teeth. The real religion was not present. It began at the bridge over the town creek, where the road takes off for the hills.

(*Prejudices, Fifth Series*)

(There was a very similar piece in the July 13, 1925 *Baltimore Evening Sun*. The long central section, the description of the revival meeting, is identical, but the introductory and concluding sections differ. One suspects that prior to the 1926 publication of *Prejudices, Fifth Series*, Mencken decided that he could do a better job with the introductory and concluding material—and so he did.)

Bibliography

Berkman, Alexander. *The Bolshevik Myth*. Oakland: PM Press, 2017.

Bierce, Ambrose. *The Devil's Dictionary*. Athens, GA: University of Georgia Press, 2002.

Conrad, Joseph. *Heart of Darkness*. New York: Dover, 1990.

Fecher, Charles A. *Mencken: A Study of His Thought*. New York: Knopf, 1978.

Fitzpatrick, Vincent. *H.L. Mencken*. Macon, GA: Mercer University Press, 2004.

Gallagher, Dorothy. *All the Right Enemies: The Life and Murder of Carlo Tresca*. New Brunswick, CT: Rutgers University Press, 1988.

Goldman, Emma. *My Disillusionment in Russia*. New York: Thomas Y. Crowell, 1970.

Hatchett, Louis. *Mencken's Americana*. Macon, GA: Mercer University Press, 2002.

Hobson, Fred. *Mencken: A Life*. New York: Random House, 1994.

Hobson, Fred. *Serpent In Eden: H.L. Mencken and the South*. Baton Rouge: Louisiana State University Press, 1978.

London, Jack. *Call of the Wild*. Readers Library Classics, 2021.

Manchester, William Raymond. *Disturber of the Peace: The Life of H.L. Mencken*. Amherst, MA: University of Massachusetts Press, 1986.

Mencken, Henry Louis. *The Philosophy of Friedrich Nietzsche*. Tucson: See Sharp Press, 2003.

Mencken, Henry Louis. *Happy Days*. Baltimore: Johns Hopkins University Press, 2006.

Mencken, Henry Louis. *Newspaper Days*. Baltimore: Johns Hopkins University Press, 2006.

Mencken, Henry Louis. *Heathen Days*. Baltimore: Johns Hopkins University Press, 2006.

Mencken, Henry Louis. *The American Language: A Preliminary Inquiry into the Development of English in the United States*. New York: Alfred A. Knopf, 1919.

Mencken, Henry Louis. *Prejudices*. Library of America, 2010.

Mencken, Henry Louis. *A Religious Orgy in Tennessee*. New York: Melville House, 2006.

Nietzsche, Friedrich (H.L Mencken tr.). *The Anti-Christ*. Tucson: See Sharp Press, 1998.

Rodgers, Marion Elizabeth. *Mencken: The American Iconoclast: The Life and Times of the Bad Boy of Baltimore*. Oxford, England: Oxford University Press, 2007.

Scruggs, Charles. *The Sage in Harlem: H.L. Mencken and the Black Writers of the 1920s*. Baltimore: Johns Hopkins University Press, 1994.

Teachout, Terry. *The Skeptic: A Life of H.L. Mencken*. New York: Harper Perennial, 2003.

Twain, Mark. *Huckleberry Finn*. New York: Dover, 1994.

Twain, Mark. *What Is Man?* Oxford, England: Oxford University Press, 1996.

INDEX